# Gluten-Free Cooking

## FOR

## DUMMIES®

### 2ND EDITION

**by Danna Korn**

Author of *Living Gluten-Free For Dummies*

**Connie Sarros**

WILEY

John Wiley & Sons, Inc.

**Gluten-Free Cooking For Dummies,® 2nd Edition**

Published by
**John Wiley & Sons, Inc.**
111 River St.
Hoboken, NJ 07030-5774
www.wiley.com

Copyright © 2013 by John Wiley & Sons, Inc., Hoboken, New Jersey

Published by John Wiley & Sons, Inc., Hoboken, New Jersey

Published simultaneously in Canada

For general information on our other products and services, please contact our Customer Care Department within the U.S. at 877-762-2974, outside the U.S. at 317-572-3993, or fax 317-572-4002.

For technical support, please visit www.wiley.com/techsupport.

Wiley publishes in a variety of print and electronic formats and by print-on-demand. Some material included with standard print versions of this book may not be included in e-books or in print-on-demand. If this book refers to media such as a CD or DVD that is not included in the version you purchased, you may download this material at http://booksupport.wiley.com. For more information about Wiley products, visit www.wiley.com.

Library of Congress Control Number: 2012949143

ISBN: 978-1-118-39644-5 (ppk); ISBN 978-1-118-43200-6 (ebk); ISBN 978-1-118-43202-0 (ebk); ISBN 978-1-118-43204-4 (ebk)

Manufactured in the United States of America

10 9 8 7 6 5 4 3

WILEY

# About the Authors

**Danna Korn** is also the author of *Living Gluten-Free For Dummies; Gluten-Free Kids; Wheat-Free, Worry-Free: The Art of Happy, Healthy, Gluten-Free Living;* and *Kids with Celiac Disease: A Family Guide to Raising Happy, Healthy Gluten-Free Children.* Often referred to as "The Gluten-Free Guru" and respected as one of the leading authorities on the gluten-free diet and the medical conditions that benefit from it, she speaks around the world to healthcare professionals, celiacs, parents of celiacs, parents of autistic kids involved in a gluten-free/casein-free dietary intervention program, and others on or considering a gluten-free lifestyle. She has been invited twice to be a presenter at the International Symposium on Celiac Disease, and is frequently featured in the media.

Danna has been researching celiac disease and gluten sensitivity since her son, Tyler, was diagnosed with the condition in 1991. That same year, she founded Raising Our Celiac Kids (ROCK), a support group for families of children on a gluten-free diet. Today, Danna leads more than 100 chapters of ROCK worldwide. She is a partner with General Mills on its gluten-free initiatives and acts as a consultant to retailers, food manufacturers, testing companies, dietitians, nutritionists, and people newly diagnosed with gluten intolerance and celiac disease.

Danna is founder and CEO (Chief Energizing Officer) of Sonic Boom Wellness, a software company that gamifies corporate wellness. Based in Carlsbad, California, Sonic Boom is one of San Diego's fastest-growing companies.

**Connie Sarros** is a pioneer in writing gluten-free cookbooks for celiacs, beginning at a time when few people had even heard of the disease. She has written six cookbooks, a "Newly Diagnosed Survival Kit," and made a DVD that covers all you need to know about gluten-free cooking. She writes weekly menus for people with additional dietary restrictions and distributes two monthly newsletters. Connie is also a staff writer for other celiac newsletters, and she frequently contributes to celiac magazines.

In addition to being a featured speaker at national celiac conferences, Connie travels the country, speaking to celiac and autistic support groups and often meets with dietitians to explain the gluten-free diet.

**Cindy Kleckner,** RD, LD, is a registered and licensed dietitian and culinary nutrition expert who also co-authored *Hypertension Cookbook For Dummies.* She resides in North Texas and has a nutrition consulting practice, working with many quality organizations including the Cooper Clinic, (www.cooper aerobics.com), Mary Kay Corporation, Dallas Cowboy Football Club,

Enterhealth, and Senior Select Home Health Services. She consults with restaurants to establish nutrition benchmarks and teaches nutrition at Collin College Institute for Culinary Arts and Hospitality to inspire culinary professionals to raise the bar in nutrition. She firmly believes good nutrition and good taste can co-exist.

Cindy works individually with clients as a nutrition coach and in groups through her high energy presentations and culinary demonstrations to educate, motivate, inspire, and entertain. As a former media spokesperson for the Texas Dietetic Association, her passion is to translate the science of nutrition into practical solutions for busy people. When not helping others meet their lifestyle goals, Cindy enjoys competitive tennis, travel, fitness, and gourmet cooking. Cindy is married with two sons who are her master taste testers!

# Authors' Acknowledgments

**Danna Korn:** Books are interesting. Authors get all the glory, publishers get all the money, and everyone in between gets forgotten! Well, let it be noted that I haven't forgotten anyone who has made this and my other books possible, starting first and foremost with my family.

After I finished my first book, I swore I'd never do another. And I've made — and broken — that promise five more times. It's with an immense amount of gratitude that I applaud my kids, who understand that they are my highest priorities, even when I have to bury myself in front of a computer for hours on deadline. To Tyler, who is the reason I felt compelled to help others after I found myself treading in the deep end of the gluten-free pool so many years ago — and to Kelsie, a constant source of optimism and inspiration — both of you fill me with so much pride and joy, and your love and support is truly my greatest motivator. To my hot hubby Bryan, not only are you the love of my life, but you encourage me to keep swimming even when I feel like I'm drowning.

Without "real" recipe writers, this book would be little more than zany concoctions that I made up. So thank you, "real" recipe writers, not only for adding substance and validity to this real cookbook, but for your personal touches that helped make this so much more than just a book of recipes.

I'd like to offer a huge thank you to the amazing team at Wiley Publishing, starting with Mike Lewis, acquisitions editor, who got this book rolling and Chad Sievers, my project editor who kept everything on schedule this second time around. Thank you to everyone for bearing with me on yet another *For Dummies* book, and for your attention to detail, keeping me on track, and for putting up with my retuvenantly quirky sense of humor and the overabundance of made-up words.

**Connie Sarros:** In January, 2007, I received a phone call from Danna Korn asking if I would like to create recipes for a new book, *Gluten-Free Cooking For Dummies*. From my heart, I thank Danna for this opportunity and for the confidence she had in me. I would be remiss if I didn't also thank her for her patience and guidance throughout this entire venture. She is absolutely amazing!

I am still awed that John Wiley & Sons chose me to assist Danna with a *For Dummies* book. I am sincerely thankful to the publisher and especially to our editors, Mike Lewis and Chad Sievers, for their help and assistance throughout each phase of the book.

None of my six books would have been written at all if it hadn't been for my father, a celiac, who truly delighted in eating good food. And my dear husband: He has been so patient and understanding as, night after night, he would be my official taste-tester. Some nights we had feasts; other nights my good intentions would end up in the disposal and he would smile as he settled for eggs or a cup of soup. The support of my family has been unwavering.

A less obvious "thanks" is extended to the celiacs in the support groups across the nation. Your feedback and your shared stories gave me the needed encouragement to continue to stretch myself, creating new recipes to respond to your expressed needs. My part in the writing of this book would not have been possible without your confidence and support throughout the years.

## Publisher's Acknowledgments

We're proud of this book; please send us your comments at http://dummies.custhelp.com. For other comments, please contact our Customer Care Department within the U.S. at 877-762-2974, outside the U.S. at 317-572-3993, or fax 317-572-4002.

Some of the people who helped bring this book to market include the following:

*Acquisitions, Editorial, and Vertical Websites*

**Project Editor:** Chad R. Sievers

   *(Previous Edition: Tim Gallan)*

**Acquisitions Editor:** Mike Lewis

**Copy Editor:** Chad R. Sievers

   *(Previous Edition: Vicki Adang)*

**Assistant Editor:** David Lutton

**Editorial Program Coordinator:** Joe Niesen

**Technical Editor and Recipe Tester:**
Emily Nolan

**Nutritional Analysis:** Patty Santinelli

**Editorial Manager:** Carmen Krikorian

**Art Coordinator:** Alicia B. South

**Cover Photos:** ©haoliang/
iStockphoto.com

**Cartoons:** Rich Tennant
(www.the5thwave.com)

*Composition Services*

**Project Coordinator:** Katie Crocker

**Layout and Graphics:** Jennifer Creasey,
Corrie Niehaus, Erin Zeltner

**Proofreaders:** Debbye Butler, John Greenough

**Indexer:** Christine Karpeles

**Photographer:** T.J. Hine Photography, Inc.

**Food Stylist:** Lisa Bishop

---

**Publishing and Editorial for Consumer Dummies**

   **Kathleen Nebenhaus,** Vice President and Executive Publisher

   **Kristin Ferguson-Wagstaffe,** Product Development Director

   **David Palmer,** Associate Publisher

**Publishing for Technology Dummies**

   **Andy Cummings,** Vice President and Publisher

**Composition Services**

   **Debbie Stailey,** Director of Composition Services

# Contents at a Glance

# Recipes at a Glance

# Table of Contents

# Introduction

*W*hen I was asked to write *Gluten-Free Cooking For Dummies,* I panicked. Sure, I know plenty about the gluten-free lifestyle — I've been living (and *loving*) it since 1991, and am proud to frequently be referred to as "The Gluten-Free Guru." I had already written *Living Gluten-Free For Dummies*, so I was familiar with the format of a *For Dummies* book. So why the panic?

Because although I love to cook, I'm a little — ahem — unconventional in my methods. Take measuring, for example. I don't. Oh, and recipes? Nope. I usually can't get past the list of ingredients before going my own way and modifying the recipe to suit my needs.

My ideas for recipes in this book went something like this: "Take a bunch of chicken and sauté it in butter." (Oops — forgot to tell you to cut it and heat the butter — you should have known that.) "Add a dab of whatever spices sound good to you at the moment — maybe a few globs of diced tomatoes and some veggies. When it's done, put it on the gluten-free rice noodles" (that I forgot to tell you to prepare in advance). "Voilà! You have chicken stir-fry on noodles!" That didn't go over too well.

So this book offers you a compromise. I believe in helping people figure out how to make anything gluten-free — without recipes, complicated terms, or ingredients you'll have to fly to Paris to purchase. Chapter 8 shows you how to do that using simple substitutions that you probably already have on hand.

And for those of you Real Cooks who love recipes, we have Real Recipes written by Real Cookbook Author Connie Sarros. Connie specializes in gluten-free cooking, and her recipes are easy to follow and absolutely amazing. She tends to emphasize good nutrition, which also is a passion of mine, and she introduces unique ingredients that are nutritious, delicious, and offer diverse flavors and consistencies. With *Gluten-Free Cooking For Dummies,* Second Edition, we provide additional recipes with Cindy Kleck's help. Cindy has done a great job of simplifying some of the more difficult creations.

Although this book focuses on *cooking* gluten-free, it also touches on medical conditions that benefit from a gluten-free lifestyle, nutritional considerations, and other practical questions and issues that you may face being gluten-free.

This, though, isn't as much about lifestyle as it is about cooking. If you're interested in knowing more about living (and loving) the gluten-free lifestyle, read *Living Gluten-Free For Dummies* (John Wiley & Sons, Inc.).

Written in the easy-to-follow-and-incredibly-comprehensive *For Dummies* style, this book is the reference guide you need to help you create incredible gluten-free delights.

# About This Book

In this second edition of *Gluten-Free Cooking For Dummies,* we've updated it with a new design so you can find one recipe on one page for easy reference. (Don't you hate having to turn the page when you're cooking, and then get the pages all sticky?) We've also replaced some of the more difficult recipes with 20 or so new, easier recipes written by Cindy Kleck. In this updated edition, you can also find a new chapter on meal-planning with our suggestions to make your life a little less hectic.

Readers had asked for a couple of new recipe sections, and we listened. We've added two new recipe chapters — one on quick-and-easy meals and one on ethnic foods.

Like any *For Dummies* book, this book makes it easy to skip around and read whatever floats your boat at the time. But if you're new to gluten-free cooking, I suggest you read the book in order. There are considerations that you'll want to know about for gluten-free cooking that don't relate to regular cooking, such as cross-contamination. To ensure you're making a safe gluten-free meal, make sure you read Chapter 5 before you start cooking.

Chapter 1 provides an overview of the book, so if you read nothing else, you can at least have an intelligent conversation about gluten-free cooking at the next party you attend. And by golly, won't *you* be the life of the party!

For those of you who've been cooking gluten-free for years, you're probably just dying to dig in and try Connie's and Cindy's amazing recipes. I encourage you to do so, but remember that rules have changed and some things that used to be off-limits on the gluten-free diet no longer are. You may want to take a look at Chapter 3 to see if something you've been avoiding is now considered safe.

By the way, I should mention that the recipes in this book have been tested by the publisher's professional recipe tester, so I'm pretty sure they all work as intended.

# Conventions Used in This Book

*For Dummies* books are known for having consistent ground rules and conventions. Some of those used in this book include

- Made-up words are just part of my vocabulary — you'll get used to it, and they're not hard to figure out. For instance, a *glutenivore* is someone who eats gluten; *glutenated* means a product has been contaminated with gluten. *Glutenilicious* is a scrumptious gluten-free meal, and *glutenologism* is a made-up word having to do with gluten!

- When I refer to ingredients throughout this book, you can assume I'm referring to the gluten-free version. Soy sauce, for example — I don't say "gluten-free soy sauce" in the ingredients list. You can assume you should use a gluten-free version (please, do I really need to say that?!?).

- Recipes are designated as vegetarian by using a little tomato icon.

- Nutritional facts accompany all the recipes and are based on the actual ingredients found as the recipes appear in this book. If you make substitutions, the facts may not be valid.

- Speaking of substitutions, feel free to make them. Chapter 8 offers lots of ideas for being creative when creating your concoctions.

- A mixture of gluten-free flours works best when baking. Check out Chapter 9 for a gluten-free flour recipe and advice for storing and using gluten-free flour.

- Milk substitutes can be used in place of milk in most recipes (hence the clever name milk "substitute").

- Unless otherwise noted, all eggs are large.

- Butter and margarine are interchangeable.

- All temperatures are Fahrenheit.

- When a recipe calls for salt and/or pepper, use regular table salt and freshly ground black pepper.

- We use 90 percent lean ground beef when a recipe requires that old standby. It tastes good, has the right amount of fat for our purposes, and isn't hard on the budget.

- All Web addresses appear in `monofont`.

And follow these tips to help ensure your recipes come out tasting scrumptious:

- Read through the recipe from start to finish before you begin cooking. That way, you'll know what tools and pans you need, what ingredients to set on the counter, how the steps progress, and how much time you'll need.

- Preheat ovens and broilers at least 15 minutes before you slide the dish in.

# What You're Not to Read

Well first of all, I'm impressed that you're reading this. This is the *Introduction,* folks! Aren't you just dying to dig into the good stuff?!? Because you're an introduction reader, you're likely to read all the stuff you don't need to read, but if you *want* to skip something, feel free to skip the sidebars. Sidebars are extra bits of information you'll find in shaded boxes throughout the chapters. I think they're sometimes more interesting than the chapters themselves, but you're welcome to skip them if you'd like.

# Foolish Assumptions

When we author types sit down to write a book, we make a bunch of assumptions about our readers — at the same time, you make assumptions about the author. Here are some assumptions I've made about you:

- You're interested in gluten-free cooking (that one was easy).

- You're interested because you've been diagnosed with a condition that requires a gluten-free diet, you're cooking for someone who's been diagnosed with a condition that requires a gluten-free diet, or you're interested in being gluten-free for personal interest or health reasons.

- You're most likely interested in the recipes, but you may also be interested in nutrition, knowing how to make your kitchen as safe as possible for cooking gluten-free foods, and cooking any food gluten-free without the aid of recipes.

- You may have read the many reasons a gluten-free diet is healthier, and you've decided to give it a try.

- You're either a newbie and know very little about the gluten-free diet, or you've been at this for a while and are looking for new ideas. Either way, I have you covered.

No matter why you're cooking gluten-free, you'll find that cooking gluten-free is an art form, and one that sometimes takes a little innovation on your part to figure out what is and isn't allowed on the diet.

Likewise, while I've made assumptions about you, you can make a couple of assumptions about me and what you'll read in this book:

- I'm an expert on the gluten-free diet, and am known to many as "The Gluten-Free Guru." I've been researching the gluten-free lifestyle since 1991, when my son was diagnosed with celiac disease. With absolutely no resources available to me, I set out to learn everything I can — and to help others live and love the lifestyle.

✔ Unlike many authors of gluten-free cookbooks or resource materials, I *do* live the lifestyle. Granted, I didn't go gluten-free back in '91 when my son was diagnosed with celiac disease; I didn't "see the light" until 2002, when I was writing my second book and realized gluten isn't good for anyone. I've been gluten-free ever since.

✔ Connie, author of the recipes in this book, is gluten-free as well. She's the author of several gluten-free cookbooks and is a sought-after speaker, as well.

✔ Although this book is loaded with lots of great information about the medical conditions that benefit from a gluten-free diet, it's not intended to serve as medical advice. See your health-care professional for further guidance if you feel you need it.

# How This Book Is Organized

*Gluten-Free Cooking For Dummies* is easy to navigate. All the parts that should go together do. The book starts out with general information about the gluten-free diet and medical conditions that it benefits; it's an overview of why you might be gluten-free or consider going gluten-free. From there, it gets into preparing to cook, which leads to the recipes. *Gluten-Free Cooking For Dummies* wraps up with the Part of Tens, familiar favorites in all *For Dummies* books. Here's how the four parts break down:

## Part I: Preparing for Your Gluten-Free Cooking Adventures

The eight chapters in this part encompass everything but the recipes. Chapter 1 is a brief overview of the entire book. The next seven chapters discuss what is and isn't gluten-free, nutrition, shopping, setting up your kitchen, and figuring out how to cook anything gluten-free — without recipes.

## Part II: Mouthwatering Main Courses

Part II dives right in, with recipes for main courses served up by Connie. With an emphasis on nutrition and unique ingredients, Connie's recipes are easy to follow, yet absolutely amazing.

## Part III: Dishes to Enjoy Before, After, or Any Time

In this part, you find recipes for appetizers, salads, soups, and snacks. Desserts and baked goods round out this part, with decadent and delicious dishes you'd never guess were gluten-free.

## Part IV: The Part of Tens

Without the Part of Tens, a *For Dummies* book is a *For Dum* — it's not finished. All *For Dummies* books finish with a Part of Tens, which in this book consists of two chapters, each with (get this) *ten* tips or ideas relating to gluten-free cooking. You can find one chapter with suggestions for gluten-free comfort foods and another with ideas for cooking gluten-free with the kids.

# Icons Used in This Book

Like all *For Dummies* books, this book has icons to call out tidbits of information. Here's what the icons mean:

Can you guess what the Tip icon is for? Yep — it's for calling out *tips* that will help you with your gluten-free cooking.

You'll find friendly reminders throughout this book, marked with a Remember icon that looks like this. These are pieces of information that are important enough to have you make note of.

Text flagged with this icon can keep you out of cooking-related or diet-related trouble.

# Where to Go from Here

Where to go from here is completely up to you. Like any *For Dummies* book, you can skip around if you want. You may want to curl up in a snuggly chair and read the first part for background information, or you may want to grab your apron (do people still wear those?) and dive into the recipes!

# Part I

# Preparing for Your Gluten-Free Cooking Adventures

The 5th Wave          By Rich Tennant

"This isn't some sort of fad diet, is it?"

## In this part . . .

Here we give you all the preliminary info you need about gluten-free cooking before you dive in and try the recipes. We cover what is and isn't gluten-free, nutrition, shopping, setting up your kitchen, and figuring out how to cook anything gluten-free even when you don't have recipes.

# Chapter 1

# Gluten-Free: Not Just a Diet, It's a Lifestyle

## In This Chapter

▶ Making long-term choices

▶ Getting the goods on gluten

*1*f you've been eating gluten (technically and in DannaSpeak that would make you a *glutenivore*) for a long time — like, oh, say, most of your life — then giving up foods as you know them like bread, pasta, pizza, cookies, crackers, and, yes, beer may seem like a tough transition at first.

Did I say diet? Because this is really more than that — it's a lifestyle. Sure, it's a diet in the sense that it concerns the things you put in your mouth, but for most people, choosing to be gluten-free is a long-term commitment, and one that affects every aspect of their lives.

Making lifestyle changes requires conscious changes in your outlook on eating. It requires long-term commitments and a great deal of education. Starting with, "What *is* gluten, anyway?!?" This chapter serves as a jumping-off point into the world of gluten-free cooking.

## Defining Gluten in Layman's Terms

You can define gluten in a couple of ways, and interestingly, the definitions actually contradict each other a little bit.

One way to define it is the scientific definition, and it involves life-of-the-party terminology like gliadin, secalin, hordein, and prolamins. This scientific definition further explains that gluten is found in all grains — yep, you heard right. All grains. Rice. Corn. All of 'em. Yet we only eliminate wheat, rye, and barley on the gluten-free diet. Well, that's why there's a layman's definition.

The layman's definition of *gluten* is "a protein found in wheat, rye, and barley."

Although oats don't contain gluten in and of themselves, you avoid them on the gluten-free diet because of cross-contamination issues that may arise during the production process. So something that's gluten-free, by definition, is wheat-free. But it doesn't necessarily hold true the other way around.

## Wheat worries

Gluten-free means wheat-free, but wheat-free doesn't necessarily mean gluten-free. Something can be wheat-free but still contain gluten if it has, for instance, malt, which is usually derived from barley. In that case, the food would be wheat-free but not gluten-free because barley contains gluten.

A lot of confusion is caused by labels claiming to be "wheat-free" when the products are not. Spelt and kamut are two examples. They're definitely not wheat-free (they're actually forms of wheat), yet they're commonly marketed as being wheat-free, or being wheat alternatives. Calling spelt a wheat alternative is like calling me a human alternative. Last time I checked, I was a human, regardless of what some people might think; and spelt is, regardless of what they call it, wheat. And because spelt and kamut are forms of wheat, they are *not* gluten-free, no matter what the package says.

## Common foods that contain gluten

Sometimes when I rattle off the foods that commonly contain gluten, people stare at me as though I've just recited *War and Peace* or something. It's true, the list is long. Our society has become accustomed to eating gobs and gobs of gluten; it's the most prevalent food type by far.

You can find more detail on the foods and ingredients that are okay and those that aren't in Chapter 3. As a general rule, anything with flour (white or wheat) is a no-no when you're avoiding gluten. These are some of the more obvious offenders:

- Bagels
- Baked goods (cookies, cakes, brownies, and so on)
- Beer
- Bread
- Cereal
- Crackers
- Malt
- Pasta
- Pizza
- Pretzels
- Soy sauce

It's important to note that there are not-so-obvious offenders, too, like natural flavorings and licorice. So you'll have to get comfortable reading labels, memorizing ingredients, and calling manufacturers to find out more details about their ingredients. (Again, Chapter 3 can help you.)

Don't be discouraged. Although the list may appear daunting at first, it's important to remember that the list of things you *can* eat on the gluten-free diet is a lot longer than the list of things you can't. Furthermore, for every product in this list, there's a delicious gluten-free substitution available. I talk more about specialty items and where you can find them in Chapter 7.

# Deciding Whether You Should Be Gluten-Free

Many people who go gluten-free do so not because they have any of the conditions listed in this section, but because they're striving for a healthier lifestyle.

Connie and I believe gluten isn't good for anyone (more on that in Chapter 2), especially in the highly refined form that most people know, like bread, bagels, and pasta. Cutting wheat and other gluten-containing grains out of your diet certainly isn't a bad thing and can have significant health benefits if you eat a wholesome, diverse diet. Heck, it can even be the key to maintaining your weight!

Maybe you'll find it compelling to adopt a gluten-free lifestyle when you realize that the gluten-free diet may relieve or even completely alleviate these health problems (and more):

- ✔ Headaches (including migraines)
- ✔ Fatigue
- ✔ Gastrointestinal distress (including gas, bloating, diarrhea, constipation, reflux)
- ✔ Depression and anxiety
- ✔ Joint pain
- ✔ Infertility
- ✔ Autistic behaviors
- ✔ ADD/ADHD behaviors

Wipe that look off your face; I've seen it before. I rattle off all these things that a gluten-free diet can help with, and people give me that incredulous I'm-gonna-make-her-feel-stupid-now-and-catch-her-in-her-exaggeration look, and they challenge me, "Reeeaaally? Allll those things can be helped with a gluten-free diet?" Yeah. Really.

This isn't a diet du jour. I realize that new diets pop up faster than celebrity babies with odd names, and that the diets last about as long as the celebrity marriages do. This is a lifestyle. It's a lifestyle that's perfectly in sync with the way our bodies were designed to eat — and that's why it's so effective in improving our health.

Our bodies weren't designed to eat that junk listed in the "Common foods that contain gluten" section. Bagels? Cereal? Pasta? I don't *think* so! Our bodies can rebel against those foods in ways that can sometimes severely compromise our health, and for many people, the gluten-free diet is the best — sometimes the only — treatment.

Chapter 2 explains more about gluten's effect on the body. For extensive, detailed information about the many medical conditions that benefit from a gluten-free diet, see the companion book to this one, *Living Gluten-Free For Dummies* (John Wiley & Sons, Inc.).

# Doing Gluten-Free Nutritiously

As much as I preach about being gluten-free, I also urge people to eat a healthy diet — and the two don't always go together. I'm tempted to say there's the "right" way and the "wrong" way to do gluten-free, but that would sound a tad opinionated (who, me?!?), so I'll stick to calling them the healthy and unhealthy ways.

The easiest way to do gluten-free is also the unhealthiest. I call it the Simple Substitution method — you stroll through the aisles of your friendly health food store and find product after product with cute little "gluten-free" logos that make it oh-so-easy for you to identify those products as being safe on your gluten-free diet! But being gluten-free doesn't make it healthy. The fact that those products are packaged and labeled generally makes them unhealthy — albeit gluten-free.

The healthiest way to go is to stick to the "If man made it, don't eat it" general rule. That means cutely labeled, processed foods aren't gonna cut it. Don't get me wrong — some very nutritious packaged products are out there. I'm trying to generalize here, and from a bird's-eye view, the healthiest way to be gluten-free is to stick to natural, inherently gluten-free foods.

The healthiest way to eat is to follow the advice: If man made it, don't eat it. It's pretty simple, really. Foods that fall into the "if man made it, don't eat it" allowable selections include lean meat, poultry, fish, seafood, fruits, veggies, nuts, and berries.

One pitfall people fall into when they go gluten-free is that they turn to rice, corn, and potatoes. Those would seem healthy enough, and appear to pass the "if man made it" criterion — but those foods really offer very little in the way of nutritional value, and on top of it, they're high glycemic index foods that may make you pack on the pounds. (If you didn't follow that high glycemic index part, don't worry — we talk about that more in Chapter 4.)

I encourage you to explore unique gluten-free grains-that-aren't-really-grains-but-we-call-them-grains like quinoa, millet, buckwheat, and teff. They're nutritional powerhouses loaded with vitamins, minerals, fiber, and protein — and they offer unique flavors and diverse consistencies. They're a great break from the rice, corn, and potatoes routine and pack a far more powerful nutritional punch. Chapter 3 has a lot more details on these and other gluten-free alternatives.

# Getting Ready to Cook

It's time to get ready to cook! "Getting ready to cook" means more than just donning your favorite apron, especially when you're cooking gluten-free. It usually involves a little planning, some shopping, and preparation to make sure your gluten-free food stays gluten-free. These sections help you get started on the right foot.

The gluten-free lifestyle may be restricted, but it's definitely not *restrictive*.

## Figuring out what to buy and where to buy it

I highly recommend planning your meals in advance. Sometimes gluten-free cooking requires ingredients you might not normally have on hand, and you don't want to get halfway through a recipe to discover you don't happen to have any xanthan gum handy.

I also encourage you to experiment with unique, gluten-free alternatives such as quinoa, millet, buckwheat, teff, sorghum, and wild rice (more on these in Chapter 3). They're loaded with nutrition and offer you the opportunity to think outside your usual menu plan and add new flavors, consistencies, and combinations.

Some of the unusual ingredients you may want to have on hand include xanthan gum, guar gum (when you try it for the first time, don't stray far from the potty because it can cause — ahem — "gastrointestinal distress" in some people), and unique flours like rice, tapioca, potato, and mesquite.

You can buy these specialty items online or at health food or specialty stores, co-ops, or farmers' markets; we talk more about where to find these specialty ingredients in Chapter 7.

Keep in mind that if you do gluten-free the healthiest way possible, you can find all the ingredients you need in a regular grocery store — around the perimeter. You'll just be shopping for lean meats, poultry, fish, seafood, fruits, veggies, nuts, and berries. You'll be happy, healthy, gluten-free, and relieved that you don't have to track down tapioca starch at 10 p.m.

## *Setting up your kitchen*

Thankfully, when you decide to adopt a gluten-free lifestyle, reorganizing and setting up your kitchen is a one-time deal — and you'll pick up some habits that you'll ease into nicely. Oh, and the oven really works in your kitchen!

Setting up your kitchen just means you have to think about *cross-contamination.* Cross-contamination is when you accidentally glutenize your perfectly good gluten-free meal because you toasted your gluten-free bread in a toaster that has gluten-containing crumbs clinging on for dear life.

Crumbs can kill. Not literally, really, but they're killers in a kitchen where gluten-freebies share space with *glutenators* (people who eat gluten). Using separate utensils for cooking, and even having a few separate appliances, is a good idea. Chapter 5 covers everything you need to know about readying your kitchen and pantry for gluten-free cooking.

You don't need completely separate utensils and pots and pans for your gluten-free cooking. Washing thoroughly between preparations is fine for removing gluten left over from cooking.

Wiping away crumbs between dish preparations is crucial, and you'll find that even the order in which you cook things is altered when you're cooking gluten-free. You don't, for instance, want to fry a gluten-free grilled-cheese sandwich in the same pan you just cooked a regular sandwich in unless you thoroughly washed the skillet in between. (The easier solution is to cook the gluten-free sandwich first.) You'll get it; it's not rocket science, but it *is* crucial to keeping your kitchen as safe as it can be.

You may find it helpful to have a separate area in your pantry or kitchen to keep gluten-free products. It makes them easier to find and reduces the chances that someone's going to goof.

# Cooking without Recipes (But You Can Use Them if You Like)

Connie and I believe if you give people a recipe, you feed 'em for a meal. Teach them to make *anything* gluten-free, and you feed 'em for a lifetime. Okay, we kind of borrowed that concept from the Native American saying, "Give a man a fish and you feed him for a meal. *Teach* him to fish and you feed him for a lifetime," but you probably figured that out.

The point is, you *can* make anything gluten-free, and you're not constrained by recipes or the fact that you can't use regular flour or bread crumbs. You only need a little creativity and some basic guidelines for using gluten-free substitutions, which you find in Chapter 7.

If you're a die-hard recipe fan, never fear — we have them here. Real Cookbook Author Connie spent months developing the amazing recipes for this book. Most of them are super-simple to follow but leave your guests with the impression that you spent all day in the kitchen (and being thusly indebted, they're expected to do the dishes).

But I'm not a Real Cookbook Author. I don't "do" recipes. I'm more of a toss-it-in-and-see-how-it-tastes-then-modify-from-there type of cook. It stinks, because I can never make the same dish twice. I don't measure (who has the patience?), I never have all the specified ingredients on hand, nor do I know how to pronounce them or where I'd find them if I looked, and "proofing" to me involves finding typos or errors in my writing (turns out, that's a bread term that means "to rise"). Suffice it to say that I'm no Julia Child, but I don't have to be, and neither do you.

Connie and I believe that the most important element of cooking gluten-free is to be creative and think outside the recipe box. So I hand you a pole and say go forth and fish. May your gluten-free goodies be gastrolicious, and your fish be free of bones.

# Getting Excited about the Gluten-Free Lifestyle

Most people who embark upon a gluten-free lifestyle are doing so because of health issues, and that means they have little or no choice in the matter. When people are forced to make changes in their routine, especially changes that affect what they can and can't eat, they're not always so quick to see the joy in the adjustments.

The truth is, we envision ourselves skipping merrily down a nicely paved road of life, eating what we want when we want. We don't envision ourselves having to dodge cleverly disguised gluten-laden land mines scattered about like worms after a hard rain (worms are gluten-free, in case you were wondering).

So if you're a little less than — ahem — *excited* about being gluten-free, I understand. But prepare yourself to have that frown turned upside down because there are lots of reasons to be excited about the gluten-free lifestyle.

## Gluten-free doesn't mean flavor-free

People who are new to the concept of gluten-free sometimes comment that the diet is boring. When I ask what they're eating, their cuisine routine usually centers around bunny food and rice cakes. Well *duh!* Who wouldn't be bored with that?!? That type of a diet is appalling, not appealing.

I'll tell you right now I *love* food. I love the flavor, the feeling of being full, the nutritional value it provides — most of all, I love to explore new foods I've never tried before, as long as they're gluten-free, of course. There's no way I'd encourage you to endure a diet of blandiose foods that could double as packing materials.

A healthy, gluten-free diet doesn't have to be boring or restrictive. You're not constrained to eating 32 individual portions of fruits and vegetables each day, like a rabbit nibbling nervously on carrots. If you enjoy bland foods, snaps for you. But if you think gluten-free has to be flavor-free, you're in for a pleasant surprise.

Think about it. Spices are gluten-free. Onions, garlic, peppers, and other flavor-enhancing foods are gluten-free. There's really no need to languish over lackluster flavors just because you're enjoying the health benefits of being gluten-free. So slice, dice, and spice it up for a meal that's flavorful, not flavor-free.

## Getting out and about

There's no reason to let the gluten-free lifestyle hold you back from doing anything you want to do. Well, okay, there are some things you can't do — like eat a regular pizza and donuts. But as far as your activities and lifestyle are concerned, it's important to get out and about as you always have.

I realize that for the most part, it's not always as easy as walking into a restaurant and asking for the gluten-free menu (a girl can dream). But eating at restaurants is definitely doable; you just need to master the art of the special order and tune in to contamination concerns. Traveling is a breeze after you're comfortable eating at restaurants *and* when you get a handle on language considerations if you're traveling abroad. Going to social events just requires a little advance planning, and holidays will barely faze you — after you get the hang of getting out and about gluten-free style.

Living your life in a bubble is for helium molecules. The gluten-free lifestyle shouldn't hold you back from doing anything (except eating gluten).

## Raising kids to love the lifestyle

Kids are flexible and resilient. Adopting a new lifestyle like being gluten-free is usually harder for the parents than it is for the child. There are lots of things that are key in raising happy, healthy, gluten-free kids. Some of the highlights include

- Giving them control of their diet from day one
- Always having yummy gluten-free treats on hand
- Reinforcing the benefits of the gluten-free lifestyle
- Always remembering that they're learning from *you* how to feel about their lifestyle

For more inspiration and practical advice, see my book *Kids with Celiac Disease: A Family Guide to Raising Happy, Healthy, Gluten-Free Kids.*

## Setting realistic expectations

Some people call me PollyDanna because they think I have an unrealistically optimistic view of the gluten-free lifestyle. It may be optimistic, but it's not unrealistic.

Set reasonable expectations for what things will be like when you adopt a gluten-free lifestyle, because there *will* be challenges and you need to prepare to handle them well. Friends, family, and loved ones may not understand. They may not accommodate your diet when you hope or expect they will. You may find social events to be overwhelming at first; or you may get confused or frustrated and feel like giving up on the diet. There *will* be challenges — and you *will* overcome them.

## Arming yourself with good information

The good news is that because the gluten-free diet is exploding in popularity, there's lots of information about it. The bad news is there's lots of information about it, and not all of it's accurate. Be leery of what you hear and read, and check the reliability of the source on everything. If you find conflicting information — and I'll warn you now that you will — dig deeper until you find out which source is right.

I cite a few good sources of information in Chapter 3, and I'm sure you'll find more on your own. Just remember to keep a skeptical eye out for the good, the bad, and the completely ludicrous.

# Chapter 2

# So Why Cook Gluten-Free, Anyway?

*I* don't even have to renew my subscription to The Psychic Network to tell you something about you — and I've never even met you before. So what do I know? Well, I know that you're interested in whipping up some gluten-free goodies and you're looking for recipes to steer you in the right direction.

What I *don't* know is *why* you're interested in cooking gluten-free, but I can guess! Maybe you're new to the gluten-free lifestyle and you want to know what you can safely eat and how to turn it into a gluten-free gastronomic delight. Or maybe you've been gluten-free and are looking for some spice in your life and some giddyap in your gluten-free.

Maybe you suspect you have some type of gluten sensitivity, and you're trying the gluten-free diet to see if you feel better; or you're trying the gluten-free diet to help manage your weight (you'll find tons of great information about this in Chapter 4). Or maybe someone you love and cook for (or cook for and love) is going gluten-free and you're doing your best to support, encourage, and nourish your hungry guy or gal.

*Why* you're cooking gluten-free doesn't really matter, because you *are*. And that's awesome. Because the gluten-free diet can be the healthiest diet on the planet (yep, see Chapter 4 for more on that), it may dramatically improve your health, both physical and emotional.

For those of you who really want to dig into the details about the health benefits of a gluten-free diet, you may want to consider buying the companion to this book, *Living Gluten-Free For Dummies*. It contains everything you need to know about the medical conditions, as well as practical and emotional guidelines for living (and *loving*) a gluten-free lifestyle.

For now, we cover the basics so you know why your health may dramatically improve when you go gluten-free. Too good to be true? Read on, my friends, read on.

# Wheat May Not Be Good for Anyone

You've probably been raised to believe that wheat — especially whole wheat — is really good for you. Although wheat does offer some health benefits, the same benefits can easily be found in other foods without the unpleasant side effects that many, if not most, people experience. But here's the bottom line: I believe wheat's not good for anyone, whether you have gluten sensitivity or celiac disease or not. Move over, David Letterman — here's my top-ten list of the problems with wheat.

## 1. Humans don't fully digest wheat

I start with some basic biology. It's a simple fact that the human stomach doesn't fully digest wheat. Cows, sheep, and other ruminant animals do just fine with wheat because they have more than one stomach to complete the digestion process. When the partially digested wheat leaves their stomach, it goes to another stomach where it is further broken down, then to another and another until the process is complete.

Unlike our bovine buddies, we humans have only one stomach. When the wheat leaves our tummies, it's not fully digested. Those undigested portions begin to ferment, and do you know what the byproduct of fermentation is? Gas. Icky, belchable, fart-forming gas. For many people, this accounts for the gas and bloating they feel after they eat wheat, whether they have gluten sensitivity or not.

## 2. Wheat is a pro-inflammatory agent

Recently, lots of books and articles have been written on the subject of *pro-inflammatory foods*. These foods are rapidly converted to sugar, causing a rise in the body's insulin levels (read more about this in number nine on my top-ten list), causing a burst of inflammation at the cellular level. Almost everyone knows that blood sugar rises from eating sweets (cakes, cookies, and candy). But lots of foods not considered sweets have pro-inflammatory effects — foods that have wheat in them, like cereal, pasta, breads, and bagels. These foods can be high in simple starches; when these are broken down, they act the same as sweet foods, raising blood sugar levels, releasing insulin, and causing inflammation. Bear in mind that the inflammation occurs in all people, not just those with wheat or gluten sensitivities.

It turns out that inflammation, once thought to be limited to *"-itis"* conditions like arthritis, may actually be at the root of a number of serious conditions, including heart disease, Alzheimer's, and some types of cancer. And if vanity is the only way to prove a point, consider this: Dr. Nicholas Perricone, renowned author of *The Wrinkle Cure,* considers inflammation to be the "single most powerful cause of the signs of aging."

One great tool for identifying pro-inflammatory foods is the *glycemic index* (remember this term; I'm going to use it again in number nine). The glycemic index measures how fast your blood sugar rises after you eat a food that contains carbohydrates (like pasta, potatoes, and bread). It rates foods on a scale from 0 to 100, where water is 0 and table sugar is 100. The lower the glycemic index rating, the less likely the food is to be pro-inflammatory. Foods made from wheat, especially refined wheat, have a glycemic index in the 50 to 80-plus range, putting them on the high side and classifying them as pro-inflammatory.

# 3. Wheat can cause leaky gut syndrome

So what is leaky gut syndrome? Good question — I'm glad you asked. The simple-and-not-perfectly-correct-but-close-enough answer is that *leaky gut syndrome* is a condition whereby stuff is leaking from your gut into your bloodstream — stuff that shouldn't be there, like toxins (and large molecules like gluten!).

So how does it happen? When people eat wheat, their bodies produce extra amounts of a protein called *zonulin.*

The lining of the small intestine is basically a wall of cells that most materials can't pass through on their own. When important vitamins and minerals are present, zonulin tells the passageways in the intestinal wall to open so those nutrients can pass into the bloodstream. The blood then carries the nutrients to other parts of the body, where they can be used to nourish the body.

But when people eat wheat — not just people with celiac disease, but all people — their zonulin levels rise too high, and the passageways open too much and let things into the bloodstream that shouldn't be there. This increased permeability of the lining of the small intestine, known as leaky gut syndrome, can cause a variety of problems health-wise.

For people with celiac disease, leaky gut syndrome starts the cascade of events that lead to health problems. Gluten is a large molecule that really shouldn't be able to get into the bloodstream, but it does because zonulin levels are too high, and the body allows it in. After it's in the bloodstream, the body sees the gluten molecule as an invader — a toxin — so it launches an attack, and in doing so, it damages the area around the gluten molecule, which includes the lining of the small intestine. The *villi,* which are short hair-like structures that are designed to increase the surface area of the small intestine so it can absorb more nutrients, are damaged in the attack. That's why people with celiac disease who continue to eat gluten often have serious nutritional deficiencies.

For a lot more details on how gluten affects a person who can't tolerate gluten, grab a copy of my book *Living Gluten-Free For Dummies* (John Wiley & Sons, Inc.).

## 4. Refined wheat has little nutritional value

Most of the wheat people eat is *refined*, which means manufacturers take perfectly good wheat — which has some nutritional value, especially in the bran and germ — and they take the good stuff away. You can read "refined" as "little nutritional value" wheat. Sadly, that's the form that most of our wheat-based products use — refined wheat nearly void of nutritional value, making it a high–glycemic index food that just makes you fat and messes with your insulin production.

Did you know that manufacturers actually have to *enrich* refined wheat because they've taken out all the nutrients? And even then, the wheat's not that valuable, nutritionally speaking. Whole wheat provides more nutritional value than non-whole wheat, but it's still wheat, and there are more than just a few reasons that wheat may not be good for anyone.

## 5. Wheat may cause wrinkles

Aha! Now *that* got your attention! Okay, so you can live with the gas, bloating, and leaky gut syndrome, but wrinkles? I think *not!* Well then, put down, that bagel, or buy stock in Botox, because according to some experts, the inflammatory effect of wheat — especially refined wheat — can cause wrinkles (see number two in this top-ten list for more on pro-inflammatory foods).

The most famous of these experts is Dr. Nicholas Perricone, a dermatologist and adjunct professor of medicine at Michigan State University, who maintains that inflammation contributes to accelerated aging and that through diet (and supplements and creams), you can erase scars and wrinkles, increase the production of collagen and elastin, enjoy radiance and glow, and develop a dewy, supple appearance to your skin.

Of course, this wouldn't be relevant unless the "diet" he refers to has something to do with being gluten-free. Although Dr. Perricone doesn't pinpoint gluten as a culprit per se, he does say that the pro-inflammatory response caused by wheat causes the skin to age more quickly, and he maintains that avoiding foods like wheat may help reverse the aging process.

## 6. Wheat may contribute to menopausal symptoms

Menopause, the time in a woman's life between about ages 45 and 55 marking the completion of her childbearing years and the end of her menstrual cycles, is often a time of marked hormonal changes. Depression, anxiety, headaches, leg cramps, varicose veins, irritability, and the famous "hot flashes" that occur are some of the more common symptoms.

But many doctors believe that lifestyle changes can minimize these symptoms, and one of those lifestyle changes is diet. Although there is some debate over wheat's role in these lifestyle changes, many experts, including Christiane Northrup, MD, author of *The Wisdom of Menopause,* believe that eliminating wheat from the diet — especially refined wheat — can help relieve menopausal symptoms.

## 7. Wheat is one of the top-eight allergens

Millions of people are allergic to wheat — so many, in fact, that it has made it onto the top-eight allergen list. Keep in mind that an allergy to wheat is different from celiac disease or other forms of gluten sensitivity — we talk more on that later in this chapter.

Allergic reactions to wheat can include gastrointestinal distress (stomach upset), eczema, hay fever, hives, asthma, and even *anaphylaxis* (a severe, whole-body allergic reaction), which is life-threatening.

Other than the anaphylaxis, these symptoms sound a lot like gluten sensitivity or celiac disease, don't they? That's why sometimes it's hard to tell the difference. That's also why sometimes people get allergy testing and find out they're *not* allergic to wheat — so they're told to go back to a normal diet of pizza, bread, and bagels. Not necessarily good advice, because they could actually have gluten sensitivity or celiac disease. So it's important to be properly tested. (Yep, you guessed it — we talk more about that later in this chapter, too.)

## 8. Wheat can mess up your blood sugar levels

Some foods cause your blood sugar levels to spike, which causes your body to produce insulin. That, in turn, causes your blood sugar to fall dramatically. Basically, your blood sugar levels go from the even keel they should be on, to being the best roller coaster ride in the park. Easy, Evil Knievel. That's not a good thing in this case.

Our bodies are designed to work with stable blood sugar levels. When they're up, then down, and all around, it causes a domino effect of not-so-healthy things to occur. Lots of people talk about *hypoglycemia* — a weak, shaky feeling that usually goes away after eating, especially after eating sweet foods. Although most people don't have "true" hypoglycemia, they may feel hypoglycemic when their blood sugar drops too much. The problem with the idea of "fixing" this feeling with sugary foods is that it just continues this roller coaster of blood sugar levels that are too high, and then too low. One of the most serious conditions that can result from blood sugar whiplash is insulin resistance and diabetes.

## 9. Wheat can make you fat

I'm not talking about the kind of "make you fat" that you deserve if you sit around eating donuts all day. I'm talking about the kind that sneaks up on you when you think you're doing everything right, but those getting-tighter-every-day jeans say otherwise.

It could just be the wheat — especially refined wheat. That's because of what it does to your blood sugar — yeah, you can cheat and look back at number eight if you didn't read it well enough the first time — but again, it's not that complicated. Refined wheat is a high–glycemic index food that causes your blood sugar to spike. That makes your body produce insulin, which, by the way, is often referred to as the "fat-storing hormone."

Yikes. Just when you thought you were being so good by leaving the cream cheese off the bagel — you should probably ditch the bagel altogether.

## 10. Many people have gluten sensitivity or celiac disease and don't know it

I hear things like, "I think I'm allergic to dairy because the cheese on my pizza makes me bloat." Oh, really? What makes you think it's the *cheese?* Because more people have heard of lactose intolerance than gluten intolerance, they figure that must be what's making them feel icky.

*Most* people have no idea that they have a gluten sensitivity or celiac disease, so they usually start pointing to all the wrong culprits: cheese (dairy), tomato sauce (acids), or soy. But they're blaming the wrong foods. These people have no idea that the typical American diet comprised of bagels, pasta, pizza, cakes, cookies, and pretzels could be wreaking havoc on nearly every system in their bodies, so they continue to eat them and wonder why they don't feel good.

So how many people fall into this category? No one knows for sure. We do know that 1 in 100 people has celiac disease — but most don't know it. No one knows how many people have gluten sensitivity, but estimates are that it may be as high as 50 percent, or even 70 percent, of the population. Top that with those who have a wheat allergy, and — here, let me get my calculator out — tons of people + gobs more = an astoundingly high percentage of the population!

# Recognizing Different Types of Gluten-Related Problems

Lots of people — may I dare to say *most* people?!? — have some form of gluten sensitivity (as we assert in number ten of our top-ten list in the previous section). But is it sensitivity, allergy, or celiac disease? Sometimes it's tough to tell. These sections delve deeper into the types of gluten-related issues.

## Allergies to gluten-containing foods

There's really no such thing as an allergy to gluten. If you happen to be allergic to all three gluten-containing grains (wheat, rye, and barley), I guess I could let it slide if you told me you were allergic to gluten — even though you're really allergic to the three grains that fall under the gluten umbrella. But most people misuse the term and say they're allergic to gluten when what they really mean to say is that they have an intolerance or sensitivity to gluten, or they have full-blown celiac disease.

Allergies to gluten-containing foods are just like other food allergies. They're all responses to a food allergen, and the reaction that someone has to those foods varies from person to person and from one food to another.

Allergic symptoms can be respiratory, causing coughing, nasal congestion, sneezing, throat tightness, and even asthma. Acute allergic reactions to food usually start in the mouth, with tingling, itching, a metallic taste, and swelling of the tongue and throat. Sometimes symptoms are farther down the intestinal tract, causing abdominal pain, muscle spasms, vomiting, and diarrhea.

Any severe and acute allergic reaction also has the potential to cause anaphylaxis, or anaphylactic shock. This life-threatening condition affects different organs, and symptoms can include a feeling of agitation, hives, breathing problems, a drop in blood pressure, and fainting. In some cases, an anaphylactic response to an allergen can be fatal unless the person having the allergic reaction receives an epinephrine (adrenaline) injection.

## Distinguishing between gluten sensitivity and celiac disease

*Gluten sensitivity* can mean a lot of different things, and is often misused; it's a very fuzzy term. Basically, it's a sensitivity to gluten — hence the clever term. Often used interchangeably, the terms sensitivity and intolerance mean that your body doesn't react well to a particular food and you should avoid it. Symptoms of gluten sensitivity are usually the same as those of celiac disease, and as with celiac disease, they usually go away on a gluten-free diet.

Unlike gluten sensitivity, *celiac disease* is well-defined. It's a common, yet often misdiagnosed, genetic intolerance to gluten that can develop at any age, in people of any ethnicity. When people with celiac disease eat gluten, their immune systems respond by attacking the gluten molecule, and in so doing, the immune system also attacks the body itself. This is called an *autoimmune response,* and it results in damage to the small intestine, which can cause poor absorption of nutrients.

Although the damage occurs in the gastrointestinal tract (specifically in the small intestine), not all symptoms are gastrointestinal in nature. That's because celiac disease is multisystemic — the symptoms show up in many different ways and can occur in just about every organ of the body. In fact, symptoms are vast and varied, and they sometimes come and go, which makes diagnosis difficult.

Does someone who has gluten sensitivity also have celiac disease? Not necessarily. Or maybe. How's that for ambiguity? I told you it was fuzzy! Let me try to clarify.

### You're told you have gluten sensitivity, but you actually have celiac disease

Some people who are told by a healthcare professional that they have "gluten sensitivity" actually have celiac disease, but their testing was done improperly or was insufficient to yield conclusive results.

Say, for instance, that someone is IgA deficient (*IgA* is a special type of protein that the body produces to fight infections), and many people are. Most of the time it doesn't cause a problem. But it makes testing for celiac disease difficult, because most of the celiac tests are based on starting with a normal level of IgA. If a person doesn't have enough IgA in his body, that would make some of the celiac tests appear to be normal when actually the person's levels should have been elevated (indicating celiac disease) if he weren't IgA deficient. In other words, the person has celiac disease, but because testing was incomplete (the doctors didn't test to determine if he was IgA deficient), the results were interpreted incorrectly.

Another reason you may have celiac disease but be told you have gluten sensitivity is if the *type* of testing you undergo is specific to gluten sensitivity, not celiac disease. For instance, a stool test and a few types of saliva tests check for gluten sensitivity, but if you have celiac disease, they'll be positive. So you would, in fact, have celiac disease — but the only test you're taking in this case is for gluten sensitivity, so that's what you'll be "diagnosed" with.

If you're diagnosed as having gluten sensitivity, you may want to ask if any specific tests were done to test for celiac disease. Some antibody tests are more specific for celiac disease, as well as genetic tests. If those tests weren't performed, you may want to get them done so you have a more definitive diagnosis.

### You don't have celiac disease — YET

Sometimes in the very earliest stages of celiac disease, testing for celiac disease will be negative, but the tests for gluten sensitivity may be positive. In this case, the person has celiac disease, but it's too early to show on tests. If that person continues to eat gluten, the testing will eventually be positive (and damage will be done!).

As far as celiac testing goes, "once tested" doesn't mean "forever tested." In other words, if you're negative today, it doesn't mean you're negative forever. There's no timeline to follow in terms of how often you should have a specific test for celiac disease, but it's important to be aware that it can develop at any time.

### You have gluten sensitivity, not celiac disease

Some people do, in fact, have gluten sensitivity that is not celiac disease. Symptoms are generally the same as those for celiac disease (see the very next section), and, as with the disease, health improves on a gluten-free diet.

# Sorting Out the Symptoms of Gluten Intolerance

Ask most people what the most common symptom of celiac disease or gluten sensitivity is and, if they know anything about either one (and don't look at you and say, "Huh?"), they'll most likely erupt in a loud, unabashed, confident chorus of "diarrhea, diarrhea, diarrhea!"

Yet most people with celiac disease or gluten sensitivity don't have diarrhea. In fact, they don't have any gastrointestinal symptoms at all! And if they do have gastrointestinal symptoms, they're often constipated, or they suffer reflux or gas and bloating.

Gluten sensitivity and celiac disease have hundreds of symptoms. The following sections list some of the more common ones, starting with the symptoms that are gastrointestinal in nature.

## Pinpointing gastrointestinal symptoms

The gastrointestinal symptoms of gluten sensitivity and celiac disease are vast. Although most people think diarrhea is the most common symptom, gastrointestinal symptoms can include constipation, gas, bloating, reflux, and even vomiting.

These are some of the "classic" — though not the most common — symptoms of celiac disease:

- Abdominal pain and distension
- Acid reflux
- Bloating
- Constipation
- Diarrhea
- Gas and flatulence
- Greasy, foul-smelling, floating stools
- Nausea
- Vomiting
- Weight loss or weight gain

# Checking out non-gastrointestinal symptoms

Celiac disease and gluten sensitivity are gastrointestinal conditions because the damage is done to the small intestine. But people more commonly have what are called extraintestinal (outside the intestine) symptoms. These make up an extensive list of more than 250 symptoms, including the following:

- Fatigue and weakness (due to iron-deficiency anemia)
- Vitamin and/or mineral deficiencies
- Headaches (including migraines)
- Joint or bone pain
- Depression, irritability, listlessness, and mood disorders
- "Fuzzy brain" or an inability to concentrate
- Infertility
- Abnormal menstrual cycles
- Dental enamel deficiencies and irregularities
- Seizures
- Ataxia (bad balance)
- Nerve damage (peripheral neuropathy)
- Respiratory problems
- Canker sores (aphthous ulcers)
- Lactose intolerance
- Eczema/psoriasis
- Rosacea (a skin disorder)
- Acne
- Hashimoto's disease, Sjögren's syndrome, lupus erythematosus, and other autoimmune disorders
- Early onset osteoporosis
- Hair loss (alopecia)
- Bruising easily
- Low blood sugar (hypoglycemia)

✔ Muscle cramping

✔ Nosebleeds

✔ Swelling and inflammation

✔ Night blindness

## Watching for symptoms in kids

Kids who have celiac disease tend to have the "classic" gastrointestinal symptoms of diarrhea or constipation. They may also have some of the following symptoms that aren't gastrointestinal in nature:

✔ Inability to concentrate

✔ Irritability

✔ ADD/ADHD or autistic-type behaviors (I go into more detail on these behaviors and their connection to gluten later in this chapter.)

✔ Failure to thrive (In infants and toddlers)

✔ Short stature or delayed growth

✔ Delayed onset of puberty

✔ Weak bones or bone pain

✔ Abdominal pain and distension

✔ Nosebleeds

# Considering Your Options for Testing

With such an overwhelming assortment of symptoms, it's no wonder people are often misdiagnosed before finding out that they have celiac disease or gluten sensitivity. It's also no wonder so many people go undiagnosed.

A *Reader's Digest* article titled "10 Diseases Doctors Miss" cited celiac disease one of the top-ten misdiagnosed diseases. In all fairness to the medical community, it can be tough to diagnose celiac disease when you think of the myriad symptoms. Headaches, fatigue, infertility, depression — if you go to your doctor for any of those things, it's unlikely that he or she is going to say, "Hmm, you're depressed. Let's test you for celiac disease." No, it's far more likely that you'll be given an antidepressant and sent on your way.

Don't despair. Plenty of doctors are extremely knowledgeable about these conditions and who will do proper testing. If yours isn't one of those, keep looking until you find one who is. There are even some tests that you can order yourself without a doctor's intervention.

## Looking into tests

It seems like there should be one single test you can take that would definitively determine whether you have gluten sensitivity, celiac disease, or none of the above. But alas, it's not that simple.

For one thing, there are different types of tests: blood, stool, saliva, and intestinal biopsy. In most cases, one type of test may determine whether you have celiac disease or gluten sensitivity — but most tests don't discern between the two or test for both. In other words, one test looks for gluten sensitivity but not celiac disease; another looks for celiac disease but not gluten sensitivity. And most people only get one (maybe two) of those tests, so they're rarely tested for both conditions.

So which test is best? Sounds like a simple question, but there's no simple answer. The gold standard for testing for celiac disease is a blood test followed by an intestinal biopsy. If both tests are positive, you're deemed to be confirmed as having celiac disease.

What we *can* say for certain — or close to it — is that if you test positive for celiac disease, you have celiac disease. That's because the tests for celiac disease are very specific, highly sensitive, and extremely reliable — especially when they indicate a positive outcome (diagnosis of celiac disease).

However, if the test is negative and your symptoms go away on a gluten-free diet, then you probably have some form of gluten sensitivity.

Unfortunately, there are false negatives and occasional false positives. Some people test negative yet find that they don't feel right when they eat gluten. Perhaps it was a false negative — or maybe gluten just doesn't sit right with you.

Bottom line: If it makes you feel bad, don't eat it!

Sadly, because the protocol for defining and diagnosing gluten sensitivity isn't well established and there's some disagreement about definitions of gluten sensitivity in the medical community, patients are often told to ignore inconclusive or confusing test results and to go back to eating their bagels and pizza. If you aren't sure you can trust your test results, you may want to be tested again at a later time.

For more detailed info on testing and interpreting results, see *Living Gluten-Free For Dummies* (John Wiley & Sons, Inc.), the companion book to this one.

## Going gluten-free without testing

You may be tempted to skip the testing and jump right into a gluten-free diet. If, for instance, you highly suspect you have celiac disease or gluten sensitivity, it makes sense — going gluten-free can help you start healing the minute you start the diet. Most people begin feeling better right away, some take months to improve, but in the long run, you can look forward to improved health — sometimes dramatically improved.

But — and I'm waving a great big caution flag here — if you plan to be tested, don't give up your gluten just yet. You have to be eating gluten for an extended length of time before getting the blood test or the intestinal biopsy.

If you don't eat gluten, or haven't eaten it for long enough, your body may not produce enough antibodies to show up on the tests, and the results *will* come back negative for gluten sensitivity or celiac disease — even if you *do* have the condition.

In other words, the gluten-free diet will "heal" you. Your body will no longer think it has celiac disease or gluten sensitivity. It will stop producing antibodies, and your intestines will heal — so the tests that determine whether you have the conditions will tell you that you don't, even if you do.

After you've gone gluten-free, you can't be properly tested for celiac disease.

No one knows for sure exactly how much gluten you need to eat to be properly tested, but if you eat the equivalent of one or two pieces of gluten-containing bread a day for at least three months, you should have enough gluten in your system to provide a measurable response.

Keep in mind, though, that you may be causing damage to your body by continuing to eat gluten! It's a conundrum, for sure!

If you decide to continue to eat gluten before testing and you have severe symptoms, talk with your doctor to decide whether you should continue to eat gluten.

# Realizing the Consequences of Cheating

If you actually have gluten sensitivity and not celiac disease, you may be able to get away with eating gluten from time to time. Just make sure you remember those pesky false negatives and misdiagnoses, and make *sure* you don't have celiac disease if you're going to indulge.

Some people are told they're gluten sensitive when they really do have celiac disease. If that scenario applies to you and you continue to eat gluten, even if it's just every once in a while, you could do some serious unseen damage, not to mention you may continue to suffer unpleasant symptoms.

On the other hand, if you do have celiac disease and you want to improve your health by following a gluten-free diet, you're going to have to do it 100 percent. A "gluten-free lite" diet won't get rid of your symptoms, and it will continue to damage your body. The next few sections explain why.

Going 100 percent gluten-free is not necessarily easy. You might want to refer to *Living Gluten-Free For Dummies* (John Wiley & Sons, Inc.) for a more detailed manual.

## Compromising your health

If you have gluten sensitivity or celiac disease and you continue to eat gluten, you *are* compromising your health, even if you don't feel any symptoms. Even the tiniest amount of gluten will cause you problems because you're still setting off autoimmune responses and your body is being robbed of important nutrients that it needs to function properly and stay strong.

When you have celiac disease, every bit of gluten you eat affects your intestinal tract adversely and keeps you from making healthy progress. That means you'll need to be extremely careful about reading labels, choosing ingredients, and avoiding contamination while cooking. (See Chapter 5 to find out more about containing contamination risks.)

## Developing associated conditions

Certain conditions are associated with celiac disease. It's usually tough to tell which one developed first, but because awareness of *other* conditions is higher than that of celiac disease, people are usually diagnosed with the other one first.

It's important to understand the association between conditions for a few reasons:

✔ Someone who has one condition is more likely to have the other.

✔ If you don't give up gluten, your chances of developing an associated condition may increase.

 ✔ An associated condition is a red flag that you may also have gluten sensitivity or celiac disease. If you have one of these conditions, you should be tested for gluten sensitivity or celiac disease.

 ✔ If people in your family have an associated condition, you may want to consider urging them to be tested — and being tested yourself.

### Autoimmune diseases

Several autoimmune diseases are associated with celiac disease, including

 ✔ Addison's disease (hypoadrenocorticism)

 ✔ Autoimmune chronic active hepatitis

 ✔ Crohn's disease

 ✔ Insulin-dependent diabetes mellitus (type 1 diabetes)

   About 6 percent of people with type 1 diabetes have celiac disease, but many don't know it. They often find managing blood sugar levels much easier on a gluten-free diet!

 ✔ Myasthenia gravis

 ✔ Raynaud's phenomenon

 ✔ Scleroderma

 ✔ Sjögren's syndrome

 ✔ Systemic lupus erythematosus

 ✔ Thyroid disease (Graves' disease and Hashimoto's disease)

 ✔ Ulcerative colitis

Studies have shown that if you have celiac disease, the earlier in life you go on a gluten-free diet, the lower your risk of developing associated autoimmune diseases. And sometimes symptoms of other autoimmune diseases, like multiple sclerosis, improve on a gluten-free diet.

### Mood disorders

Some of the mood disorders associated with gluten sensitivity and celiac disease include

 ✔ ADD (attention deficit disorder) or ADHD (attention deficit hyperactive disorder)

 ✔ Autism

 ✔ Bipolar disease

 ✔ Depression

### Nutritional deficiencies

Because gluten sensitivity and celiac disease affect the small intestine, nutritional deficiencies usually develop. These can include

- ✔ Specific vitamin and mineral deficiencies
- ✔ Anemia
- ✔ Osteoporosis
- ✔ Osteopenia (low bone mineral density)
- ✔ Osteomalacia (soft bones)

### Neurological conditions

Some neurological conditions are associated with gluten sensitivity and celiac disease, including

- ✔ Epilepsy and cerebral calcifications
- ✔ Brain and spinal cord defects (in newborns born to mothers with celiac disease who are eating gluten)
- ✔ Neurological problems, such as ataxia, neuropathy, tingling, seizures, and optic myopathy

### Other conditions

Several other conditions are commonly associated with celiac disease, including

- ✔ Cancer (such as non-Hodgkin's lymphoma)
- ✔ Down syndrome
- ✔ Internal hemorrhaging
- ✔ Organ disorders (of the gallbladder, liver, spleen, or pancreas)
- ✔ Tooth enamel defects
- ✔ Cystic fibrosis

# Understanding How Gluten Affects Behavior

You're probably not going to get too far in a court of law pleading, "The wheat bread made me do it!" But gluten is sometimes guilty when it comes to affecting behavior and moods.

Gluten can affect your behavior in many ways. Some behavioral manifestations of gluten sensitivity and celiac disease can include

- Inability to concentrate or focus
- Attention deficit disorder (ADD) and attention deficit hyperactive disorder (ADHD) type behaviors
- Autism
- Depression, bipolar disorder, schizophrenia, and mood disorders
- Irritability
- Lack of motivation

## Connecting gluten and autism

Dietary interventions for developmental and behavioral disabilities have been the topic of many heated discussions for decades. One of the most remarkable (in my opinion) things about the gluten-free diet is that it seems to play a role in reversing autistic behaviors — at least in some cases.

Several credible double-blind, placebo-controlled studies are underway at reputable universities to study the relationship between gluten and autism. The results of these studies are eagerly anticipated and will most likely have a dramatic affect on the way pediatricians view the disorder.

For now, I summarize what is known. Gastrointestinal problems seem to be more prevalent in people with autism than in the general public — do they have a higher incidence of celiac disease? No one has studied that. Is there a connection? Maybe. The scientific community believes that there's a genetic basis for autism. But interestingly, there seems to be a nutritional component.

The most popular diet promoted as a "cure" for autism is a gluten-free, casein-free diet (*casein* is the protein found in milk). No one claims that this works in all cases; nor do they say it's truly a cure. But *if* a dietary intervention protocol could actually improve autistic behaviors, wouldn't that be amazing? Some say it can. Just a short time ago, the evidence was largely anecdotal, but now the "Defeat Autism Now!" protocol recommends that every autistic child be placed on a gluten-free, casein-free diet for at least three months.

In some autistic children, gluten and casein are turned into a sort of drug that the brain makes, much like morphine. Essentially, many autistic children are "drugged" on wheat and milk products, as if they were on a morphine drip.

Basically, when people with autism eat gluten and casein, they get a high off of the foods, and they become addicted. This "high" is similar to the one experienced by opiate users, and it may account for some of the typical traits found in autistic kids, such as repetitive movements like head banging and spinning, being withdrawn, and having a fascination with parts of objects (like fixating on one part of a toy rather than the toy itself).

Results on the gluten-free, casein-free diet vary. Some see improvement within a week, some within a year, and others see no improvement at all. Even in those who report behavioral changes, the changes themselves vary. Some people with autism are able to sleep through the night, others become more verbal and interactive, and some are completely "normalized" on the diet.

The gluten-free diet can be *especially* difficult for a person with autism, because these folks tend to develop food preferences, and these usually include gluten-containing foods.

## Delving into depression and other mood disorders

People with celiac disease have a higher incidence of mania, seizures, and other neurological problems. In addition, clinical depression, bipolar disorder, schizophrenia, and a variety of mood disorders can sometimes be associated with or exacerbated by gluten sensitivity and celiac disease. Some journal articles even list these disorders as symptoms of celiac disease, and these conditions sometimes improve on a gluten-free diet.

Schizophrenia has been associated with celiac disease since the 1960s, when it was first noted that restricting gluten and dairy led to improvement in some institutionalized patients. Interestingly, the same opiate-like chemicals found in the urine of autistic people are often found in schizophrenics.

Some investigators have noted that the incidence of schizophrenia is higher in places where wheat is the staple grain than where people normally eat non-gluten-containing grains. In one study done in the highlands of Papua, New Guinea, where little or no grain is consumed, only two people out of 65,000 adults could be identified as chronic schizophrenics. In the coastal area, where wheat is consumed more, the prevalence of schizophrenia was about three times higher.

# Chapter 3

# What's Gluten-Free and What Isn't?

*W*hen you're cooking gluten-free meals, it's crucial to ensure that your ingredients are 100 percent gluten-free. Sounds simple enough, doesn't it? Wheat = gluten; rye = gluten; barley = gluten. So a recipe minus wheat, rye, or barley is gluten-free, right? Um . . . no. Not necessarily.

Unfortunately, figuring out what's gluten-free and what's not isn't so simple. Picture a veggie garden with lots of healthy tomato plants. Well, gluten can be hidden, like those pesky tomato worms in your veggie garden. You can look and look; one day your tomato plants may appear to be free of the disgusting, overgrown amoebas, but when your plants are ruined, you realize you somehow missed spotting the destroyer.

Gluten can be the same way. It can hide in the ingredients you least suspect. And one little bit of it will ruin the entire plant — er, I mean meal!

The gluten-free diet may seem cumbersome at first because the *derivatives* of gluten-containing grains may contain gluten. As if that's not complicated enough, many processed foods — which contain seasonings, additives, and flavorings — can also contain questionable ingredients.

This chapter helps you find your way through the maze of grains, flours, and alternatives that you can safely use in gluten-free cooking. You're about to meet some foods that may be new to you, with exotic names like *quinoa, millet, buckwheat,* and *teff.* And you may have some surprising realizations as you discover that some of these alternatives are far more nutritious than wheat.

To help you ease into what may be unfamiliar territory, I start by separating foods into those that are definite no-nos and those that are definitely okay. Then I explain how to search out hidden gluten. Finally, I introduce you to those incredible gluten-free alternatives.

Keep in mind that the lists of foods that do and don't contain gluten vary, and they're only here to help you get started. You can find up-to-date lists of safe, forbidden, and questionable foods at www.celiac.com.

# Avoiding These Definite No-Nos

Let me get to the point. Here are the grains you need to avoid on a gluten-free diet:

- ✔ **Wheat and almost anything with the word *wheat* in its name:** Okay, we know you're thinking, "She gets her name on a book to tell me I can't eat *wheat!?*" Okay, smarty pants, I realize that staying away from this grain may seem obvious. But it's not that straightforward. Sure, it may be obvious that you'll also need to avoid hydrolyzed wheat protein, wheat starch, wheat germ, and so on, but you may not realize that you need to beware of aliases like flour, bulgur, semolina, spelt, frumento, durum (also spelled duram), kamut, graham, einkorn, farina, couscous, seitan, matzoh, matzah, matzo, and cake flour.

  Wheat grass, like all grasses, is gluten-free.

- ✔ **Wheat starch:** This wheat has had the gluten washed out. In some countries, a special type of wheat starch called Codex Alimentarius wheat starch is allowed on the gluten-free diet — but standards vary from country to country. Codex Alimentarius wheat starch isn't allowed in North America because some people question whether the washing process completely removes all residual gluten.

- ✔ **Barley and its derivatives:** Besides avoiding barley in its pure form, you need to avoid malt and malt flavoring, which are usually derived from malt.

- ✔ **Triticale:** You may never have heard of it. It's a cross between wheat and rye, and was developed to combine the productivity of wheat with the ruggedness of rye.

- ✔ **Rye:** This grain isn't really hidden in any ingredients, so the pure form of rye — usually found in rye bread — is what you need to avoid.

- ✔ **Derivatives of gluten-containing grains:** If you thought you were done with derivatives when you finished your calculus class, you were wrong. You need to avoid derivatives of gluten-containing grains, and the most common one to watch out for is *malt,* which usually comes from barley. Malt, malt flavoring, and malt vinegar are definite no-nos. If malt is derived from another source, such as corn, it will usually say so on the label; for instance, "malt (from corn)." That's not too common, though, so if the source isn't specified, don't eat it.

Here are some foods that *usually* contain gluten. You need to avoid these as well:

- ✔ Beer

  Some great new gluten-free beers are available. Not only are smaller, specialty breweries making them, but even the big boys like Budweiser have come out with a gluten-free beer that you can buy just about anywhere beer is sold.

- ✔ Bread, bread crumbs, biscuits
- ✔ Cereal
- ✔ Cookies, cakes, cupcakes, doughnuts, muffins, pastries, pie crusts, brownies, and other baked goods
- ✔ Cornbread
- ✔ Crackers
- ✔ Croutons
- ✔ Gravies, sauces, and roux
- ✔ Imitation seafood (for example, imitation crab)
- ✔ Licorice
- ✔ Marinades (such as teriyaki)
- ✔ Pasta
- ✔ Pizza crust
- ✔ Pretzels
- ✔ Soy sauce
- ✔ Stuffing

Now, that's not so bad, is it? And I promise you, the list of foods you *can* eat is a lot longer than this one!

# Getting the Green Light: Definitely Okay Foods

Now for the good news! The list of definitely okay foods is impossibly long! There's no way we could list all the okay foods, because most *natural* foods are inherently gluten-free. So in this section, we talk about grains and starchy foods because those are the ones you may question. Some of these things may be strange sounding and new to you, but give 'em a try! You can find more information about each of the foods listed below later in the chapter.

- ✔ Amaranth
- ✔ Arrowroot
- ✔ Buckwheat/groats/kasha
- ✔ Chickpeas
- ✔ Garfava

    Garfava is actually a nutritious blend of garbanzo and fava flours that Authentic Foods developed. Because it's exclusive to that one company, it's not found on many gluten-free food lists, but it has become a popular ingredient in so many cookbooks that we felt compelled to list it here.

- ✔ Job's Tears
- ✔ Mesquite (pinole)
- ✔ Millet
- ✔ Montina (Indian ricegrass)
- ✔ Quinoa (hie)
- ✔ Ragi
- ✔ Rice
- ✔ Sorghum
- ✔ Soy
- ✔ Tapioca (gari, cassava, casaba, manioc, yucca)
- ✔ Taro root
- ✔ Teff

In addition to the grains and starches listed above, plenty of other foods are naturally gluten-free. (**Note:** These refer to plain, unseasoned foods without additives or processed products.)

- ✔ Beans

    Garbanzo beans by any other name are . . . well, they're still garbanzo beans. They can be called besan, cici, chana, or gram — not to be confused with graham, which *does* have gluten.

- ✔ Corn
- ✔ Dairy products

- ✔ Eggs
- ✔ Fish
- ✔ Fruit
- ✔ Legumes
- ✔ Meat
- ✔ Nuts
- ✔ Potatoes
- ✔ Poultry
- ✔ Seafood
- ✔ Vegetables

You can also find specialty products like cookies, cakes, brownies, breads, crackers, pretzels, and other products that have been made with gluten-free ingredients. Chapter 7 helps you figure out where to buy these sorts of goodies.

# Snooping for Hidden Gluten

In the "olden days," the list of questionable foods and ingredients used to be really long. And it was longer than it needed to be, because it included things like vinegar, vanilla, almond extract, and sometimes, foods that were just plain ridiculous to be on the no-no list, like canola oil. For people on a gluten-free diet, staying away from these so-called questionable foods dramatically reduced their cooking and dining choices.

In the last several years, we've come a long way, baby. Thanks to new labeling laws and decades of research, there are far fewer "questionable" ingredients than there used to be. These days, manufacturers have to indicate if a product has wheat in it, and new labeling laws require manufacturers to clearly define the gluten-free status of foods. (For more on reading labels, see the section, "Labeling gluten-free: The law and what it means," later in this chapter.)

These new regulations have opened the pantry door to lots of ingredients that used to be considered off-limits. For example, we now know that regardless of the source, the distillation process eliminates all sources of gluten from vinegar. In other words, even if the vinegar started from wheat (which it usually doesn't), all the gluten is gone after distillation.

Distilled vinegar, cider vinegar, and most vinegars are okay — but malt vinegar is still off limits.

The publication *Gluten-Free Living* and its sister website, www.glutenfree living.com, are excellent sources for sorting out fact from fiction on questionable ingredients.

## Ending the controversy about "questionable" ingredients

The debates will never end. You'll still see ingredients on the no-no list that shouldn't be there — and you'll still see Internet postings from people who swear grapes have gluten in them because they ate a grape and had an upset tummy the next day.

Don't believe everything you read (except in all of my books!). The Internet is loaded with bad information, and even some product guides and printed brochures can't be trusted.

Fortunately, some of the controversy has been put to rest, thanks to new labeling laws and more definitive research. The following ingredients used to be considered questionable, but are now okay on the gluten-free diet:

- Alcohol (distilled)
- Caramel color
- Citric acid
- Dextrin

  Technically, dextrin can be made from wheat, but most companies in the U.S. use corn. Again, because of labeling laws, if it's made from wheat, the ingredients list has to say so.

- Flavoring extracts
- Hydrolyzed plant protein (HPP)
- Hydrolyzed vegetable protein (HVP)

  HVP can be derived from wheat. But because of the new labeling laws, if it *is,* the label has to say that. It would most likely appear on the label as "hydrolyzed wheat protein."

- Maltodextrin

  Maltodextrin confuses people, because of the word *malt* in the name. Dextrin can be made from wheat, but maltodextrin is gluten-free unless it specifically says "wheat maltodextrin" or "maltodextrin (wheat)."

- Modified food starch

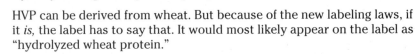

✔ Mono- and diglycerides

✔ Starch (in food)

✔ Vanilla and vanilla extract

✔ Vinegar (except malt vinegar)

✔ Wheat grass

✔ Yeast (except brewer's yeast)

Pharmaceuticals don't have the same labeling requirements that foods have. Some ingredients, like starch, for instance, can contain gluten, and it may not be indicated. For pharmaceuticals that have questionable ingredients listed, you'll need to call the manufacturer (I outline how to do this later in the chapter) or consult a trusted source to know whether it's gluten-free.

Gluten-free guidelines in North America might be different from those in other countries. The gluten-free status of ingredients listed in this book refers to ingredients produced in the U.S. and Canada.

## Knowing which foods to question

Someday, all gluten-free foods will be clearly labeled as such, and there won't be any "questionable" foods. For now, though, you need to question some ingredients before deciding if they're safe for you to eat.

Most of these ingredients rarely contain gluten, but according to the U.S. Food and Drug Administration Code of Federal Regulations (CFR), they *can* contain gluten, which means you need to dig a little deeper to know for sure if they're okay for you to eat. Some of the ingredients you should question include

✔ Brown rice syrup

✔ Fillers

✔ Flavors and natural flavorings

✔ Seasonings and spice blends

✔ Stabilizers

✔ Starch (in pharmaceuticals)

✔ Yeast (it might be brewer's yeast)

Sometimes brewer's yeast is a byproduct of beer. In that case, it's not considered gluten-free. Nutritional supplements that have brewer's yeast in them, though, are sometimes made from sugar, in which case they're okay.

Some foods fall into the questionable category because of contamination issues. For example, oats don't have any gluten, but they're often contaminated in the manufacturing process. We recommend that you avoid them unless you can buy certified contamination-free, gluten-free oats grown in dedicated facilities with no possible risk of cross-contamination. The label will actually say "gluten-free oats." Unfortunately, only a few manufacturers produce gluten-free oats, so they're kind of hard to find, and, frankly, a little pricey. Try your local natural food stores and online sources.

# Getting to Know Gluten-Free Alternatives

Even if you weren't cooking gluten-free, we suggest you give these gluten-free ingredients a go. Not only are they acceptable substitutes for wheat, rye, and barley, but they also offer unique flavors, textures, colors, and characteristics that you don't find in rice, corn, and other flours commonly found in the typical diet. Furthermore, many of them are loaded with nutrition, and they fill you up like a starchy wheat product might.

Lots of people call these grains, but most of them aren't actually grains. They're flowers or fruits. The following sections take a closer look at some of these alternative grains, starches, and cereals. We cover the nutritional values of these foods in Chapter 4.

## Amaranth

A staple of the Aztec culture, this relative of pigweed and cockscomb is loaded with fiber, iron, calcium, other vitamins and minerals, and amino acids, including lysine, which isn't found in most grains. Amaranth is an excellent source of protein (16 percent) and has a pleasant peppery and nutty flavor. The bead-like amaranth seeds should always be cooked before eating. Amaranth can be milled, toasted, popped like popcorn, eaten like hot cereal, or used in soups and granolas. You also can cook its leaves and eat them as greens.

## Arrowroot

You may remember the name *arrowroot* from the baby food aisle. Arrowroot biscuits are one of the first solid foods babies can safely eat (but beware: manufacturers usually add wheat flour to arrowroot biscuits, so they're not gluten-free). With a look and texture similar to cornstarch, arrowroot is an herb thought to soothe the stomach and have antidiarrheal effects (that's music to many people's ears when they have an intolerance to gluten and are used to — ahem — making quick trips to the bathroom). In cooking, arrowroot makes a great substitute for cornstarch and can be used to thicken soups, sauces, and confections.

## Buckwheat/groats/kasha

Boy, this one causes me grief. People think I'm off my rocker when I tell them that buckwheat is gluten-free. Yeah, I know — it has the word *wheat* in its name, but buckwheat isn't even remotely related to wheat. It's a fruit, high in B vitamins, phosphorous, magnesium, iron, copper, manganese, zinc, and all eight essential amino acids (amino acids the body doesn't produce but needs to keep functioning), making it a more complete protein than many other plant sources. It's also a good source of linoleic acid, an essential fatty acid, and is the only grain known to have high levels of ruti, an antioxidant that reportedly improves circulation and prevents LDL cholesterol (the bad kind) from blocking blood vessels.

Also known as *kasha* and *groats,* buckwheat boasts a hearty, earthy flavor. Most of the time it's ground into a gritty, dark flour, and used to make soba noodles, pancakes, or other baked goods. Some people cook it like rice, boiling 1 cup of buckwheat in 2 cups of water.

Although there are pure, gluten-free soba noodles and pancake mixes made from buckwheat, read the labels! Some forms of these products also contain wheat flour.

## Garfava

*Garfava* is the name of a commercial blend of flours made by a company called Authentic Foods. Normally I wouldn't put a specialty item in a list like this, but garfava has become such a common gluten-free flour that it's featured in many cookbooks. This mixture of chickpea (garbanzo beans) and fava bean flours is high in protein, low in fat, and rich in fiber. Its unique nutty taste adds extra flavor to quick breads, muffins, cakes, veggie burgers, and coatings for chicken and fish.

## Job's Tears

Job's Tears is also referred to as coix seed, adlay, or adlai — yeah, like *that* helps at all! Job's Tears is a tall, tropical plant that produces a grain that's gluten-free.

Popular in Asia, Job's Tears is often dried and cooked as a grain like rice or barley, and it has a similar flavor to barley. People in Korea and China use it to make distilled liquors, or as a tea, sometimes by powdering the grain itself and mixing it with hot water; other times, the whole grains are simmered in water and then mixed with sugar. Job's Tears are said to have medicinal properties, helping with gastrointestinal disorders, painful joints, rheumatism, and edema.

Some Asian supermarkets sell Job's Tears as Chinese pearl barley — but it's not. And don't worry, Job's Tears isn't even closely related to barley — if it were, there might be a question about whether it's gluten-free, but there's no question at all.

# Mesquite (pinole)

*Mesquite* — for me, it conjures images of a barbecued, smoky-sweet flavor. But it's also a tree that produces bean pods, which can be dried and ground into flour. It adds a sweet, nutty taste that bears a hint of molasses, and is even used to make jelly, wine, and juice. With soluble fibers that slow the absorption of nutrients and its low glycemic index, mesquite is helpful in controlling blood sugar levels. Its sweet pods and seeds are a good source of fiber, calcium, manganese, iron, zinc, protein, and lysine.

# Millet

Some might say that millet is for the birds — that's because it's the grain found in most bird feeders. But it's good for humans, too! *Millet* is actually a grass — with a small seed that grows in a variety of shapes, sizes, and colors. Packed with vitamins, minerals, and other nutrients, millet is also loaded with fiber, protein, and B-complex vitamins. This easily digested, extremely nutritious seed has been a staple food in Africa and India for thousands of years. In parts of India today, millet flour is combined with sorghum flour to make a common bread called *bhakri*.

Millet is a small, round grain that has a mild, yet nutty flavor, especially if you toast it in a dry skillet for about three minutes. Add millet to soups for extra body, or mix it with brown rice or quinoa to add unique flavors and textures. Millet can be cooked like other grains, using 1 cup of millet to 2½ cups of water. You can use less water for a crunchier flavor or more for a consistency more like mashed potatoes.

# Montina (Indian ricegrass)

Montina is actually a trademarked name by a company called Amazing Grains. Montina is a type of flour made from Indian ricegrass, which was a dietary staple of Native Americans more than 7,000 years ago and today is native to Montana. Loaded with fiber and protein, this bold-flavored grain was a good substitute when maize crops failed or game was in short supply.

Because Montina is a brand name, it comes with a recipe booklet. Because it tastes like wheat and has a hearty texture, it makes a good replacement for regular flour in baking.

# Quinoa (hie)

Pronounced *keen*-wah, ancient Incas considered *quinoa* sacred and referred to it as "the mother of all grains" — but it's actually a fruit. Unlike other grains like wheat or rice, quinoa has a balanced set of essential amino acids and is a complete protein. It's especially high in lysine, an amino acid that most grains lack. Also high in phosphorous, calcium, iron, vitamin E, assorted B vitamins, and fiber, quinoa is exceptionally nutritious. Although quinoa is usually pale yellow, it also comes in pink, orange, red, purple, and black.

Quinoa can be cooked like rice, using 1 cup of the grain to 2 cups of water. You can also throw raw quinoa into soups to thicken and add an interesting texture, or use cooked quinoa under chili or as you would a rice dish. Quinoa flours and pastas are also available, giving you more options for gluten-free variations on gluten-containing favorites.

Quinoa has a coating called *saponin,* which is bitter. But the quinoa we buy has been processed, and the coating has been removed. By the way, that bitter coating may be what makes quinoa such a durable crop. It's likely that the birds and insects that can devastate a crop find the coating too bitter and leave it alone. Attempts to grow quinoa with less of the coating have resulted in crops that are decimated.

# Ragi

Ragi is also referred to as *finger millet* and is grown as a cereal in the arid areas of Africa and Asia. It's especially valuable nutrient-wise, because it has the amino acid methionine, which is lacking in areas where poverty forces people to live on starchy staples like cassava, rice, plantain, or corn meal. Ragi is often ground and cooked into cakes, puddings, or porridge, and is made into a beer-type drink in many parts of Africa.

# Rice

Rice is a common staple in the gluten-free diet because people tend to think of starches as rice, corn, potatoes, and wheat. With wheat off the menu, they turn to rice, corn, and potatoes. Not all rice is created equally, though. White rice has most of the good stuff (germ and bran), nutritionally speaking, removed. Brown rice is a whole grain and far more nutritious than white. By the way, wild rice isn't rice at all! It's the seed of an aquatic grass, grown primarily in Minnesota.

Contrary to what you might guess, glutinous rice doesn't have gluten! Made from high-starch, short-grain rice, glutinous rice thickens sauces and desserts in Asian cooking and is the rice most commonly used in sushi. (Remember, no soy sauce or fake crab in your sushi!)

## Sorghum

Also known as *milo,* this gluten-free insoluble fiber is probably best known for the syrup that comes from one of its varieties. Because sorghum's protein and starch are more slowly digested than that of other cereals, it may be beneficial to diabetics. Sorghum's bland flavor and light color don't change the taste or look of foods when it's used instead of wheat flour.

## Soy

Soy is actually a legume, not a grain. It's commonly used in the gluten-free diet because people know it's gluten-free and it's accessible. Usually, it's mixed with other flours — but beware: It has a strong, distinctive flavor. Either you love it or you don't, and after you've added it, there's no going back.

You can incorporate soy into your diet in plenty of ways. You can use soy milk or yogurt, flour, or tofu, each of which offers a huge variety of cooking options. For soy milk and yogurt, you can simply substitute the soy variety for dairy products. Soy flour can be mixed with other flours and used in baked goods, and tofu can be fried, baked, or grilled.

## Tapioca (gari, cassava, casaba, manioc, yucca)

Think there are enough names for tapioca? Well, *tapioca,* also referred to as *gari, cassava, casaba, manioc,* and *yucca,* is still tapioca. Most people think of tapioca pudding when they think of tapioca. And, unless someone gets really freaky with her recipe, tapioca pudding is gluten-free! But the flour is used in a lot of gluten-free recipes, too. Basically, it doesn't have any flavor, which is a good thing sometimes (see the flavor description for soy!). Because it's flavorless, tapioca flour or starch makes a great thickener for sauces, gravies, soups, stews, puddings, and pies. Tapioca gives a glossy sheen and can tolerate prolonged cooking and freezing. Tapioca is native to South America, so if you visit there, you'll find lots of great tapioca (manioc) breads that are gluten-free!

## Taro root

Most people know *taro* as the ingredient in the Hawaiian dish poi. Also called *kalo,* taro is a starchy tuber vegetable much like a potato, and it's rich in vitamins and minerals. The leaves are a good source of thiamin, riboflavin, iron, phosphorus, and zinc — and also vitamin B6, vitamin C, niacin, potassium, copper, and manganese. They're also a great source of fiber. In its raw form, taro is toxic because it has calcium oxalate, but cooking destroys the toxin, so it's safe for consumption. Like potatoes, taro roots can be fried, baked, roasted, boiled, or steamed.

## Teff (tef)

This nutritional powerhouse is the smallest of the grains that aren't true cereal grains. It's actually a grass with a seed that looks (and cooks) a lot like quinoa and millet, but it's smaller. An important food in Ethiopia, *teff* is used to make a common bread called *injera* (but beware: Most injera has wheat flour, too). Teff packs a protein content of nearly 12 percent and is five times richer in calcium, iron, and potassium than any other grain. Its sweet, nutty flavor makes teff flour a delicious additive to baked goods, or you can cook the whole grain and serve it with sliced fruit or as a breakfast cereal.

# Reading Labels and Getting Answers (Most of the Time)

Reading labels should be so simple — if a product is gluten-free, it should say so, right? Sure. It would list the ingredients, and right there in big, bold letters, it would say, "This product is 100 percent gluten-free, no ifs, ands, or buts." Fortunately, labeling laws are headed that direction, but we're not quite there yet.

The Food Allergen Labeling and Consumer Protection Act of 2004 required clear labeling of all foods that contain any of the top eight allergens — wheat, milk, eggs, fish, shellfish, tree nuts, peanuts, and soybeans. Because of this act, manufacturers must clearly identify wheat and all of its derivatives on food labels. With this act in place, knowing which foods are definitely off-limits because they contain wheat is much easier.

Although wheat and its derivatives are called out on all labels, you still need to watch for other gluten-containing grains (barley, rye, and cross-contaminated oats) and their derivatives, and realize that they can be (but often aren't) hidden in flavorings and additives. And remember that you won't see "gluten-free" on the label — at least not yet — but you don't really need to. (A new law is in the works; you'll find out more about it in the next section.)

Getting the hang of the gluten-free diet means you'll have to memorize ingredients you've never heard of. And yes, even though this is a cookbook and you'll be working with ingredients rather than prepared foods, you'll still have to read the labels on the ingredients you use.

## Labeling gluten-free: The law and what it means

My friend Cynthia Kupper, Executive Director of the Gluten Intolerance Group of North America, has helped me write this section explaining the United States Food and Drug Administration's new guidelines for labeling food products gluten-free. These guidelines are still being finalized at the time of this writing and are a welcome advancement in gluten-free labeling for consumers.

Defining *gluten-free* gives consumers more information and set a standard that manufacturers will have to meet before they can label their products as such. Use of the *gluten-free* label will be voluntary, but the FDA will enforce its requirements on those who choose to use it.

### Defining what a gluten-free label means

*Gluten-free* will most likely be defined as follows:

- ✔ A food can't contain a prohibited grain (wheat, rye, barely, and hybrids of these grains)

  or

- ✔ If a food contains prohibitive grains, it must show that the grain has been altered to remove the protein (generally a chemical process to remove protein and purify the starch or oil)

  and

- ✔ The finished product (as it will be sold) cannot contain more than 20 ppm (parts per million) of gluten. A company can prove this by testing for gluten in its products. Other tests can prove the lack of protein in a food. When there is no protein, there is no gluten.

If a product can meet the above criteria, it can carry the words "gluten-free" on the label.

Twenty parts per million refers to the level of gluten which is known to be very safe for persons with celiac disease. This level is generally set 3 times lower than what research shows is safe, making it virtually impossible to ever consume that amount of gluten daily from products labeled gluten-free. It is a very small amount. An example of 20 ppm is 1 teaspoon of cream in 65 gallons of milk.

*Wheat-free* doesn't necessarily mean gluten-free. Remember that gluten includes wheat, rye, and barley — so something can be wheat-free and still contain malt flavoring derived from barley, for instance.

### Labeled requirements

Labeling a product gluten-free is voluntary. No manufacturer will be required to include the labeling on its products; however, if it does, it must prove the product meets the definition. The law will also include information on the following:

- ✔ If a naturally gluten-free product, such as 100% orange juice, chooses to carry a gluten-free label, it must say that all 100% orange juice is gluten-free.
- ✔ Not all oats can be labeled gluten-free. They must be able to prove that they meet the definition, including containing less than 20 ppm.

## Gluten-free certification

A progressive certification program with an easily recognized logo is making it easier to identify gluten-free foods. The Certified Gluten-Free logo stands for the independent verification of quality, integrity, and purity of products. Products carrying the Certified Gluten-Free logo represent unmatched reliability for meeting strict gluten-free, science-based standards.

Manufacturers requesting this gluten-free certification are inspected by the Gluten-Free Certification Organization (GFCO) (www.gfco.org), the only gluten-free certification program in the world. The GFCO, a program of the Gluten Intolerance Group (GIG), was developed in cooperation with Food Services, Inc., a subsidiary of the Orthodox Union (OU), the world's largest and oldest kosher certification agency. The OU's nearly 500 field representatives, proficient in modern food-production techniques and chemical and biological processes, conduct plant inspections and review products for the GFCO.

Certification is an annual process based on ingredient review, on-site inspection, and product testing. Gluten-free certification is established for each ingredient in the final product, as well as the processing aids. The mark assures that the product contains less than 10 parts per million of gluten and similar proteins from rye and barley.

## Contacting manufacturers

"Hello, does your product contain gluten?"

Don't feel awkward asking that question. Food manufacturers hear it all the time these days. Many manufacturers often voluntarily identify the ingredients in their products in very clear terms. For example, instead of saying "modified *food* starch," they're listing the specific type of starch as "modified *corn* starch." The same is true with vegetable oils. Instead of "hydrolyzed *vegetable* oil," the packaging now shows the specific type of oil, such as "hydrolyzed *corn* oil." And certainly, because of the Food Allergen Labeling and Consumer Protection Act of January 2004, if the ingredient is derived from wheat, it must clearly be identified as such.

However, if you have any doubts, don't hesitate to call the manufacturer.

People sometimes think that if they read labels they don't need to call the manufacturer, but that's not always true. If you find something questionable on a product label, or if you just want to be extra-sure that the product is gluten-free, call a manufacturer and ask. Today's manufacturers understand the gluten-free concept, and they know what you're talking about.

Contacting manufacturers is a lot easier than it used to be. Most packaging includes the manufacturer's toll-free number, or if you're having a hard time locating a manufacturer's contact information, you can always look online. Do a search on your favorite search engine, or try typing in the manufacturer's name followed by ".com" (as in www.fritolay.com).

When in doubt, leave it out. If you're not sure, don't take a chance.

General Mills was one of the first to step up to the plate and provide clear gluten-free labeling. Since then, they have also provided a "one-stop-shop" website with everything a gluten-free person needs. Check out www.glutenfreely.com for a treat!

# Chapter 4

# Making Nutrition Your Mission When You're Cooking Gluten-Free

*In This Chapter*

▶ Eating to fuel, not to fill

▶ Maintaining balanced blood sugar levels

▶ Watching your waistline

*O*kay, I realize this is a cookbook, and you just want to dive into the recipes to start whipping up your soon-to-be-famous gluten-free gastrolicious goodies. But wouldn't you feel better about gorging down the goodies if you knew they were good for you? It's not too tough to eat a healthier diet if you know what's nutritious and what isn't. The problem is, even people who *think* they know often don't.

Nutritious food is more underappreciated than the parent of a teen. But even teenagers appreciate parents more than most people appreciate food for the value it provides. No, I'm not talking about the so-stuffed-you-can't-move feeling you get from pizza and beer. And for those of you who consider yourselves to be health food fanatics because you use skim milk on your frosted flakes, I'm not talking about that, either.

I'm talking about the valuable things food offers — taste, fulfillment, satisfaction, and — oh yeah — *nutrients*.

Food is obviously essential — without it, we'd starve to death. But the *types* of foods we eat have powerful effects on preventing disease; maintaining proper organ function, energy levels, moods, appearance, and athleticism; and even influencing our longevity and how we age. Everything about how we look and feel is directly related to the foods we eat.

You can do the gluten-free diet at least two ways — one is extremely healthy, and the other isn't quite as optimal. Either way, you're cooking gluten-free, which is a good thing, but if you're interested in taking a more nutritious approach to being gluten-free, this chapter's for you.

In this chapter, I take a look at some foods you may have thought were nutritious but aren't — and I explore some foods you may never have heard of that pack a powerful nutritional punch. I offer tips for weight management and energy enhancement, and I give an overview of the optimal diet, which just happens to be entirely gluten-free.

# Feeling Optimal Requires Optimum Nutrition

Sure, you've heard the expression, "you are what you eat." But what does that mean, really? I eat a lot of apples, and I'm not an apple. I think it really should be said that, "your quality of health is dependent upon the quality of food you eat" — but I realize that's not so catchy, and it's tough to grasp.

Few people would argue the fact that you need to eat a nutritious diet — the problem is that most people don't know what that means. And when you're eating gluten-free, you need to be aware of some special considerations when striving for optimal nutrition.

## Fueling versus filling

Lots of people have used the car analogy to explain nutrition. They tell you that to get maximum performance from your vehicle, you have to use high-quality gas — and to get maximum performance from your body, you have to give it high-quality foods. However, we should eat to *fuel,* not to *fill.*

That analogy has a few problems: The first problem is that most people don't know what high-quality foods are. How can you put "good fuel" in your body when you don't really know what good fuel is? The second problem with the car-body analogy is that most people put crummy gas in their cars and their cars run just fine, so they figure they can get away with putting crummy gas in their bodies, and they'll run just fine too — albeit a little gassy from time to time.

What they don't realize is that you can get away with putting crummy gas in an average car — but your bodies aren't your average car. Our bodies are finely tuned, high-performance vehicles. You put crummy gas into a Ferrari, and you're going to find it knocks and pings (gas and bloating), doesn't start as easily (tough time getting out of bed?), doesn't go as fast (lethargic), the engine doesn't burn as cleanly (constipation), it shoots out more exhaust (fartola), and the engine wears out faster (uh-oh — need I say more?).

The last problem with the analogy revolves around individual sensitivities. Imagine now that you *do* know what good fuel is, and that you have pulled into an exclusive gas station that brags of having the highest-quality gasoline from one of the world's best refineries. It should be free of anything that might cause harm to your engine, right? Not necessarily. What if you're driving a diesel-powered car? Just a few minutes running with that "high-quality" gasoline, and your diesel car would be dead. In this case, the gas is good — it's just the wrong fuel type for your car.

## Getting enough nutrients when you're gluten-free

Over the years, many people have claimed that the gluten-free diet is deficient in a variety of nutrients. Their reasoning comes from the fact that flour is generally enriched with vitamins. When we stop eating flour, we're missing that fortification and the supplemental nutrients it provides.

You can probably guess how I feel about that argument. If you follow the "healthy" approach to the gluten-free diet as described in this chapter, you get a nutritionally sound diet.

If you go gluten-free the unhealthy way — simply substituting gluten-free goodies for the breads, bagels, pizzas, pastas, cookies, cakes, and pretzels that you were eating before — then there's some merit to the claim that the gluten-free diet may have some nutritional deficiencies, because you won't have the advantage of the enrichment found in most products made with flour.

If you want more detail on nutrition, and specifically how it relates to the gluten-free diet, check out *Living Gluten-Free For Dummies* (John Wiley & Sons, Inc.). In this book, I just cover the basics — because this is, after all, a *cook*book!

### Fiber

Getting enough fiber in your diet can be an issue in gluten-free diets. Gluten-free flours, such as rice and tapioca, don't offer much fiber and can cause associated problems.

The best source of fiber is fresh fruits and veggies. Broccoli, for instance, provides 25 percent of your daily fiber needs in just 1 cup. Not to mention it has 200 percent of the daily recommended dietary allowances (RDA) for vitamin C, 90 percent of the daily RDA for vitamin A in the form of beta carotene, and lots of niacin, calcium, thiamin, and phosphorus. All this for only 45 calories!

### Other nutrients

People who have gluten sensitivity or celiac disease often become sick and malnourished as a result. They usually have compromised digestion and absorption that may result in nutritional deficiencies, the most common of which are iron, essential fatty acids, vitamins D and K, calcium, magnesium, and folic acid. The good news is that when you go gluten-free, your body heals quickly and regains its ability to absorb nutrients. If you need help, seek the help of a professional to ensure adequate nutrition.

Some people believe that no matter how healthy your diet is, it's still important to take supplements. This reasoning is generally based on the fact that food isn't as nutritious as it used to be. Soils are becoming depleted of important nutrients, so the crops grown in them are less nutrient-dense than they once were. Furthermore, chemicals and genetically modified foods are changing the nutritional composition of even the most wholesome foods. For these reasons, many people believe that supplementation is key to getting all the nutrients you need, especially if you take part in athletic endeavors or exercise heavily.

If you're an athlete and are interested in learning about recommended supplementation, I recommend a book by Dr. Michael Colgan called *Sports Nutrition Guide.*

# Choosing a Healthier Approach to the Gluten-Free Diet

Sometimes people do the math wrong. They know that I believe that gluten-free is the way to be. And they know I have a passion for nutrition. Therefore, they add it up and conclude, erroneously, that gluten-free must be nutritious. But that's not always true. There are two ways to go on the gluten-free diet: one is ultra-healthy, and the other is — well, *not* — and not even close.

## The unhealthy way

For simplicity's sake, and to mess with my editors who like things to go in the order I've referred to them, let's start with the last category — the gluten-free diet that isn't so healthy. This is the version of being gluten-free that could be called the "substitution diet." People continue to eat all the normal foods they ate before — breads, bagels, cookies, cakes, pizza, crackers, and pretzels — but they eat the gluten-free version. Sometimes people who do this actually end up eating *more* junk than they did when they were eating gluten because they use the gluten-free goodies to help them get over their "I'm feeling deprived and restricted" thoughts.

Suffice it to say I'm not a fan of this variety of gluten-free eating. As a matter of fact, it's not just "not healthy," but it's downright *un*healthy. Those foods, with or without gluten, offer very little in the way of nutritional value — they do little more than pack on the pounds and wreak havoc with your blood-sugar levels (which we talk about later in this chapter).

## *The healthy way*

The healthier approach to eating gluten-free is simple: If man made it, don't eat it. In other words, stick to the natural foods that our bodies were designed to eat: lean meats, seafood and fish, fruits, veggies, nuts, and berries. These foods are healthiest for us because our bodies were designed to eat them — it's not surprising to me that they're all naturally gluten-free, as well, because our bodies weren't designed to eat gluten. Sticking to natural, healthy foods is a win-win!

I didn't "invent" this diet — in fact, there's a lot of information about this approach, which is usually referred to as the *Paleolithic diet*. That's because this diet is based on eating the foods that our hunter-gatherer ancestors ate in Paleolithic times (before the Agricultural Revolution). They didn't eat wheat — there wasn't any. They didn't eat grains or dairy — it just didn't exist. Our bodies weren't designed to eat those things, which is why so many people have intolerances to them.

By the way, you can easily see why our Paleolithic ancestors didn't do milk. First, picture them catching a wild boar — what then? It begs the question, "How many cavemen does it take to milk a wild boar?"

You may be thinking that with some scary (and hairy) exceptions, today's humans don't really resemble cavemen, so this line of reasoning about eating what our ancestors ate isn't relevant — but you'd be mistaken. DNA evidence shows that genetically, humans have hardly changed at all in the last 40,000 years.

# *Watching Your Blood Sugar*

Some people figure they don't need to worry about their blood sugar levels because they don't eat sweets. Not true! For one thing, lots of foods that aren't in the sweets category at all can mess with your blood sugar levels. Potatoes, for instance — they're killers when it comes to blood sugar! We talk more about specific foods and how they affect your blood sugar levels later in this section, but first, what does it mean, and why does it matter?

The term *blood sugar* refers to how much glucose is in the blood. *Glucose* is the body's primary source of energy, so it's important stuff. But it has to stay in just the right range — not too high and not too low — or it can cause problems. The body uses hormones called *insulin* and *glucagon* to regulate blood sugar levels, but sometimes the body just can't keep up, often because the foods we're eating cause blood sugar levels to rise too much. Diabetes mellitus is an example of a disease related to the failure of blood sugar regulation.

Blood sugar levels also affect hunger and cravings. Foods that cause your blood sugar to go up quickly (and then come down quickly) cause you to get hungry, even when you shouldn't be. This is only one of the many reasons high glycemic index foods (I explain exactly what those are in the "Understanding the glycemic index of foods" section) result in weight gain.

For more detail on how blood sugar affects hunger and weight gain, check out my book *Living Gluten-Free For Dummies* (John Wiley & Sons, Inc.).

## Moving beyond rice, corn, and potatoes

When adopting a gluten-free lifestyle, people tend to turn to starchy, fill-me-up standbys like rice, corn, and potatoes. People seek these out partly because they *are* starchy foods, a replacement of sorts for the bread, pasta, and bagels we're accustomed to eating when we eat gluten.

So what's the problem with substituting these standbys? They're gluten-free, so they should be fine, right? Well, they're fine from a gluten-free standpoint. But they're pretty much void of nutrients, at least compared to some of the nutritional powerhouses that you *could* be eating.

See, not all carbs are created equal. Fruits and veggies are great. But rice, corn, potatoes, and refined wheat are all high glycemic load foods. High gly-huh? We talk more about what that means in the next section.

For now, all you need to know about high glycemic foods is that they mess with your blood sugar levels, which is especially dangerous for people with diabetes. They also can pack on the pounds almost faster than you can eat them, which is one reason many people who go gluten-free experience weight gain (to find out how to combat the gluten-free gain, check out the "Managing Your Weight When You're Gluten-Free" section later in this chapter).

## Understanding the glycemic index of foods

The *glycemic index* (GI) is a way to measure how much effect a particular food will have on our blood sugar levels. The higher the glycemic index, the more quickly that food is broken down during the digestion process, and the more quickly blood glucose levels will rise. Carbohydrates that break down slowly release glucose into the blood stream more gradually and have a lower glycemic index.

The glycemic index really just concerns foods that are high in carbohydrates. Foods that are high in fat or protein don't have as much of an effect on your blood glucose levels.

The glycemic index is sometimes categorized into three classes: low, medium, and high. Table 4-1 shows GI ranges and some examples:

| Table 4-1 | | Glycemic Index Ranges |
|---|---|---|
| *Classification* | *GI Range* | *Examples* |
| Low GI | 55 or less | Most fruit and vegetables (except potatoes), quinoa, and most other alternative grains |
| Medium GI | 56–69 | Orange juice, some pastas, some brown rices |
| High GI | 70 or more | White bread, baked potato, most white rices, pizza, crackers, bagels, beer |

A food's glycemic index may change depending on how it's prepared and what's eaten with it.

Unfortunately, a food's glycemic index won't be listed on the label. You can find glycemic index tables for specific foods by searching for "glycemic index (food name)" on your favorite search engine. Not all foods are listed, but many are, and it's a great start for understanding which foods cause your blood sugar to soar, and which ones don't.

A great book on the subject of blood sugar and its importance in maintaining overall health is *The New Sugar Busters!* by H. Leighton Steward (Ballantine).

## Relating a gluten-free diet to the glycemic index

Gluten-containing foods like bread, bagels, pizza, pasta, cookies, cakes, and pretzels are super-high on the glycemic index. When you cut those things out of your diet, you're eliminating high GI foods that offer little in the way of nutritional value.

Now keep in mind that if you replace those things with their gluten-free counterparts — like gluten-free bread, bagels, pizza . . . you get the picture — then you're back in the high glycemic ballpark. But if you choose to eat wholesome foods like those described in this chapter as being optimal, you'll be eating gluten-free and healthfully!

People used to think that diabetics should avoid sugar — as in candy bars and table sugar. But some experts now believe that the sugar isn't as important as the effect that the food has on your blood sugar. In other words, instead of simply eliminating sugar, some experts recommend that people with diabetes should stick to a low glycemic index diet. For those people, a gluten-free diet — the kind that includes healthy meats, seafood, fruits, and veggies (but without the yummy gluten-free substitutions for the high glycemic goodies like breads and cookies) — is ideal.

## Choosing healthy starches for that "fill-me-up" feeling

As we've discussed, rice, corn, and potatoes aren't your most nutritious choices, even though they *are* gluten-free. You get lots of calories and little nutrition — that's not a good thing for anyone. But let's face it — there's something to be said for that feeling of contentment you get when you eat starchy foods like that.

So what *can* you eat for that fill-me-up satisfaction when you're cooking gluten-free but you're focused on a healthier diet? Try these foods on for size. They're far more nutritious than rice, corn, and potatoes, and they're low glycemic index foods, too.

- ✔ Amaranth
- ✔ Buckwheat
- ✔ Millet
- ✔ Montina
- ✔ Quinoa
- ✔ Sweet potatoes (or yams)
- ✔ Teff

Sometimes referred to as *alternative grains,* they're not really grains at all. But they're delicious, they provide unique flavors and consistencies, and they're loaded with fiber, vitamins, minerals, and amino acids. In fact, most of them are complete proteins! (Chapter 3 gives you more information about these foods.)

The terms *sweet potato* and *yam* are often used interchangeably, yet the two are very different. It doesn't matter which one you choose, though, because both are gluten-free, loaded with nutrients and antioxidants, and quite low on the glycemic index. There are even new varieties of sweet potatoes that have purple skin and flesh! They contain *anthocyanins,* a powerful antioxidant found in berries.

In staying consistent with the theme of this book, get creative! Try using different vegetables to replace the starchy foods you might ordinarily use. Spaghetti squash is a great alternative for pasta. You can use strips of zucchini or yellow squash instead of lasagna noodles, and you can puree cauliflower instead of using mashed potatoes.

# Managing Your Weight When You're Gluten-Free

Interestingly, the gluten-free diet — when done properly — can not only be your key to better health, but it may also be the key to managing your weight. In fact, it doesn't matter if you weigh too much or too little; if you're not "just right," going gluten-free may be the answer you've been looking for.

## Losing or maintaining weight

For people who need to lose weight, there's no simpler and more effective way to do it than to take the Paleolithic approach we've been talking about in this chapter (see the section, "The healthy way," for more info). Sticking to lean meats, poultry, seafood, fish, fruits, and veggies will help un-stick those unwanted pounds.

When you go gluten-free, you eliminate refined-flour products from your diet — things like bagels, bread, pasta, and of course the sweet baked goods — and that means you're cutting out high glycemic index foods that offer very little in the way of nutrition, but offer more than their fair share of calories. That's why people who go gluten-free the healthy way usually find their weight easier to maintain at healthy levels.

## Dealing with (uh-oh) weight gain

Some people find that they gain weight when they go gluten-free — and it's no wonder! Many of them are busy discovering the wonders of the gluten-free goodie world, including gluten-free brownies, cookies, cakes, pastas, and crackers. Those are foods that may as well be applied directly to the tummy or thighs — because that's where they end up pretty quickly.

These days the gluten-free goodies are delicious — and somewhat irresistible, I suppose. But for some people, eating them is strictly emotional. They tend to get carried away with these foods as a way of compensating for feelings of deprivation or restriction. They believe they're deprived because they can't eat gluten, so they "reward" themselves, or compensate, by eating extras of the goodies that they *can* eat. Before they know it, their jeans look like they belong to the neighbor's kid.

Still others experience weight gain because of the physiological changes that take place when they go gluten-free. This group of people is comprised of those who go gluten-free because they have celiac disease or gluten sensitivity. Most people with celiac disease or gluten-sensitivity don't absorb all of their nutrients, at least until they go 100 percent gluten-free. Lots of these people, while they're still eating gluten and not absorbing nutrients, become accustomed to eating far more calories than they should, because those calories aren't being absorbed, so they maintain their weight in spite of the fact that they eat far too many calories. But it's payback time after they go gluten-free. Their gut begins to heal, and they begin absorbing calories — and before they know it, they've packed on a pound (or 20).

Although I like to think of the gluten-free diet as the best diet on the planet, it's not actually the gluten-free-ness that gets the credit when we're talking about weight management on the gluten-free diet. It's the fact that you're adhering to a high-protein, low glycemic, nutrient-dense diet. And following this healthy diet provides health benefits that extend far beyond being gluten-free.

## Adding some pounds if you're underweight

If you've been underweight, you're likely to find that the gluten-free diet helps you gain enough to be at a healthy weight. I know, it sounds like I'm talking out of both sides of my mouth — how can it help some people *lose* weight, and help others *gain* it?

People who are underweight are often that way because they have gluten sensitivity or celiac disease, and therefore are not absorbing important nutrients, including calories. That is, until they go gluten-free. Then their guts heal, and they begin to absorb those important nutrients again. After they start absorbing the calories they're consuming, they usually gain the weight they need to be at what's considered a healthy weight.

# Chapter 5

# Setting Up Your Kitchen and Pantry

*I* know you're the cooking type and you're eager to get started, and this *is* a cookbook after all, but it's a good idea to take some time to set up your kitchen and pantry, just to make things easier (and safer) on yourself down the road.

If your entire kitchen is already gluten-free, you're excused to skip to another chapter. But if you're going to have a shared kitchen where gluten-ous and gluten-free foods coexist, you'll have to take some important steps to eliminate the risk of *glutenation* (for those of you new to my books, that's DannaSpeak for gluten contamination).

Never fear, though. Although eliminating the risk of glutenation isn't a "simple" modification, it's "simply" a modification. In this chapter, I take you through the steps to ensuring a safe environment for your gluten-free cooking. You discover how to set up a shared kitchen for gluten-eaters as well as non-gluten-eaters, and how to choose appliances that can simplify your life.

## *To Be or Not to Be 100 Percent Gluten-Free*

To clarify, I'm talking about modifying your *kitchen,* not your lifestyle. If you have celiac disease, let me make it clear that I condone a 100 percent gluten-free lifestyle. Even if you don't have celiac disease, I still believe that gluten-free is the way to be — and 100 percent is best of all.

But even if you're 100 percent gluten-free, it doesn't mean your kitchen has to be. So before you lift that ladle, touch that Tupperware, or start pulling the pantry apart, you first need to decide whether it's going to be some or none for you and your food. Will your whole house go gluten-free, or will you be mixing the fixings and cooking both ways?

In many households, when one person needs or wants to go gluten-free, the first inclination is to make the whole house gluten-free. In fact, nearly every cookbook author and expert in this field will tell you that the entire kitchen, pantry, and household should be gluten-free. With serious and sincere respect, I disagree with them, at least for the majority of people. Although going completely gluten-free certainly can make life easier, it's not only unnecessary, but sometimes it's even a bad idea.

Finding an entire family that needs to be gluten-free is pretty rare. More often than not, only one family member needs to stay away from gluten for health reasons. If you have other children or family members who don't need to be gluten-free and you force them to follow the diet anyway, you may create resentment. Yes, even among adults. I've had more than a few e-mails from despairing dads who stop for pizza and beer on the way home from work because they know they're not allowed to indulge in gluten at home.

The next couple of reasons I don't recommend an entirely gluten-free household (unless, of course, all family members need to be on a gluten-free diet) concern kids who are gluten-free.

- **Children need to learn how to make the right choices.** Kids raised in an entirely gluten-free household never have to make a choice — which means they never *learn* to make a choice: Is this food okay to eat? If all the food is gluten-free, that thought process — which really needs to become an unconscious decision later in life — is never required. As the parent of a gluten-free kid, I speak from experience when I say that I believe it's critical for kids to have gluten in the house and know how to make those decisions for themselves.

- **Kids need to learn that the world isn't a gluten-free place.** Children who grow up in an entirely gluten-free household can develop a false sense of reality, and may even assume a sense of entitlement. The child may believe that everyone else should stock his favorite foods, and everyone else should be gluten-free, too. Kids need to know that the rest of the world eats gluten. That doesn't mean people are trying to hurt their feelings or leave them out; it's just the way it is. Isn't it important for children to learn these lessons at home, in a loving and caring environment? I think so!

Unfortunately, I see the opposite decision made all the time. Someone in the family gets diagnosed with a gluten-sensitive medical condition, and the instant reaction is, "We've decided to make our whole family gluten-free!" Sadly, that decision often leads to a negative dynamic and a resentment that even adults can feel.

If you're still convinced that a gluten-free house is the route you're going to take, you can skip the rest of this chapter and go straight to your favorite chapter. On the other hand, if you agree with me that it makes more sense to have gluten in the house and to prepare both glutenous and gluten-free meals, then keep on reading because the rest of this chapter shows you how to simplify the process and make it fun.

# Conquering Contamination Concerns

Oh, good, you're still reading! That means I haven't scared you away and you're ready to get down to business and start thinking about the single most important challenge to maintaining your shared kitchen: containing contamination risks.

I'm not talking contamination of the my-burger-has-e-coli variety (best to avoid that, too) — I'm talking about glutenation. You know — when you have a perfectly good gluten-free meal, and somehow, someway it gets glutenated, and the entire meal is ruined. Kaput. Off limits. Dog food.

It can happen in the most innocent ways. A loving family member sticks a knife laden with gluten crumbs into the mayo jar. You accidentally use the same utensil to toss the gluten-free pasta as you used on the gluten-containing stuff. Or someone stacks the "regular" sandwiches on top of the gluten-free ones. Ugh.

When you keep gluten-containing foods in the house, you run the risk of contamination every time you prepare a meal. Contamination issues are crucial to consider when you're cooking with gluten.

Even if your house is perfectly gluten-free, remember that guests can, unknowingly, contaminate the kitchen. If they bring their own sandwich, for instance, and add it to the stack of gluten-free goodies you've prepared, the entire bunch may be ruined.

When you're sharing a kitchen with gluten, it can contaminate your food in many different ways. Crumbs seem to throw themselves off gluten-containing breads and foods, turning perfectly good gluten-free zones into danger zones in the blink of an eye. If not cleaned well, preparation surfaces, cookware, utensils, and storage containers can all contaminate food as well. Here are some tips for avoiding cross-contamination by some of the most dangerous culprits.

## Keeping crumbs at bay

In a shared kitchen, crumbs are public enemy numero uno. When you're making a sandwich, buttering a piece of toast, or crumbling crackers into your soup, these tiny little crumb-culprits literally fly off the food and soar through the air.

Say you're making a regular sandwich and a gluten-free one. You can't make them both at the same time on the same cutting board. Suppose you've prepared your gluten-free sandwich, and then you set it down on a counter full of gluten-containing crumbs. What do you get? A contaminated sandwich!

From now on, you need to get into the habit of making the gluten-free version first, then making the other, and cleaning the crumbs really well in between. Going on a crumb vendetta is not so crucial if you make the gluten-free sandwich first, but it's certainly a good habit.

## Protecting jars from cross-contamination

Jars are some of the most easily contaminated items in the kitchen. Say you're making a slice of toast with jelly. You dip a knife into your gluten-free jelly, then spread it on your gluten-containing toast. Then you dip the knife back into the jar for more jelly, contaminating the whole jar with those pesky crumbs. Next time you go to make gluten-free toast, those glutenous crumbs are just waiting for you.

### Too many cooks can glutenate a meal

Ah, those wonderful holiday dinners. The house is full of people, fragrant aromas fill the air, and then Helpful Helen manages to contaminate nearly every jar in the kitchen by using the same spoon to dish up gluten-free and glutenous sauces, spreads, and condiments. Cousin Clara puts the croutons in the salad and gives it a thorough toss. Sister Susie surprises you by putting the stuffing inside the turkey. Aunt Ginny mixes the crunchy onion rings into the green bean casserole, and Uncle Sid gets crumbs in the butter after spreading some onto his roll. Last but not least, Aunt Mary spoons gravy over her stuffing, pressing down firmly to make a well, and then sticks the stuffing-crusted spoon back into the gravy boat.

These wonderful, well-meaning relatives had no idea that you planned to serve everything on the side, and that they've completely ruined an entire meal for everyone eating gluten-free.

If you're having dinner guests or visitors who insist on helping in the kitchen, my advice is to tell them how much you appreciate their help, and remember that their intentions are good. Make them feel important by giving them jobs that can't possibly cause contamination, such as setting the table, pouring the drinks, and keeping small children entertained. And definitely don't pass up the opportunity to put them to work on clean-up duty.

People frequently ask, "Can I put the knife back into the jar if I used it to spread something on gluten-free bread?" No, because you'll not only end up with crumbs in the jar, but you won't know whether they were gluten-free or not and you'll end up throwing the whole jar away. I can't tell you how many times I've spent $10 on the 7-gallon size mayonnaise at my local discount shopping warehouse store and had to toss the whole thing in the trash.

Instead of using jars, I recommend getting squeezable containers for your mustard, jelly, mayonnaise, honey, and any other condiments.

## Using utensils in food preparation

I've got a stumper for ya. You're making two types of peanut butter and jelly sandwiches — gluten-free ones and regular ones. How many knives does it take?

Answer: ten. Okay, I'm exaggerating a little, but if you want to guarantee that you won't cause contamination, you can't put the same knife back into the container after the knife has touched the bread. So here's how to make a simple peanut butter sandwich:

Dip a knife into the peanut butter and spread it on the bread. Because it touched the bread, that knife is done. Retire it to the sink. The next knife goes into the jelly, then spreads the jelly onto the bread. Whoops, you didn't get enough jelly. Because that knife also touched the bread, it too must retire to the sink, and you need yet another knife so you can add more jelly.

Wait! I have a better solution! Do a patented maneuver I call the *gob drop!* Instead of using every knife in the house, take a huge gob of your spreadable condiment and drop it onto the bread without letting the knife touch the surface. Flick the knife so it doesn't touch the bread (or use a second knife to scrape the first one off). If you don't get enough the first time, go back for more before the knife touches the bread. A word of caution: After you get the hang of this, you'll find yourself aghast when you see people putting knives back into jars after they've touched food surfaces. Go easy on them; they don't know any better . . . yet!

## Storing food

Some people worry that they can't store gluten-free foods in the same plastic containers that have held glutenous foods. They think that the plastic absorbs the gluten and will contaminate the gluten-free foods. But you can rest easy. Gluten doesn't seep into the pores, and you don't need separate containers as long as you wash everything carefully.

Some gluten-free meals are hard to make. Save time and money by making large batches, and then storing the leftovers in vacuum-sealed bags or plastic containers. Mark them well, and freeze them for later use. Here are a few tips:

- ✔ A permanent marker on aluminum foil works really well.

- ✔ If you have a plastic storage container that you don't want to mark up, use labels instead.

- ✔ You may want to a use color-coded system (red = gluten, green = gluten-free).

- ✔ Sometimes labels fall off or get dislodged. Be sure to put a label inside the container, too.

## Considering cookware

Some people think they need special pots and pans to create their gluten-free meals in because they've heard that gluten can get embedded into Teflon and other cookware surfaces. This opinion is widely circulated on the Internet, but I'm here to tell you that it's nothing more than an urban legend. Gluten does not seep into Teflon or other cookware surfaces. However, scratches and cracks can harbor residue from previous cooking. The key is to thoroughly wash all cookware and utensils. My rule of thumb is that if you'd let your baby lick the pan, it's probably clean enough!

Some people use cast iron pans and "season" them, but don't wash them. If you cook gluten in a cast iron pan and don't wash it with soap and water, don't use that same pan for your gluten-free cooking.

Sometimes after you drain pasta in a colander, a residue remains. I recommend that you have separate colanders for your gluten-free and glutenous foods and mark them with a permanent marker so you'll never get them confused. The same applies to those cute pasta servers with the teeth on the end (do those have a name? I digress . . .). They'll have some residue left that's iffy to remove, so again, I recommend having separate ones.

# Sharing Is Caring When You're Cooking Both Ways

It goes without saying that making separate meals creates extra work for the cook (and because you're reading this book, I'm going to assume that's you!). For instance, if you're having a pasta dinner and you want to make one batch of gluten-free pasta and one regular batch, you're obviously making more work for yourself, but I still think it's the way to go when not everyone in the house has to be gluten-free.

These days, gluten-free pastas and other gluten-free foods are so delicious that it's just as yummy to make the gluten-free version for everyone. Sometimes, however, you'll want to make two versions of a meal, whether it's to save money or for personal preferences.

Having said that, I want to assure you that cooking two versions of a meal can be easier than it sounds. Getting back to that pasta dinner, you may want to make both types of pasta but keep things simple by serving one delicious gluten-free sauce that can go on both.

Sharing is caring when you're cooking both ways, and plenty of foods are available that the whole family can share. Instead of having two varieties of everything, use gluten-free versions of shared foods like sauces, spices, condiments, and salad dressings. Doing so can certainly make your life easier and save you time in the kitchen and the grocery store.

## Planning your menus for easy meal prep

It's 5 p.m., you just got home from work, and you're ready to start making dinner. You were planning to make spaghetti, but you have no gluten-free pasta in the house. Because gluten-free cooking involves special ingredients and preparation processes, you have to plan your cooking in advance and make sure you have all the ingredients on hand.

Gluten-free ingredients aren't always easy to find. For instance, if you're going to make bread and you need xanthan gum, you can't run down to the corner store and get it. And if you don't have it, you're not making bread (unless you cheat and use a mix like I do — oh, *wait* — this is a *cook*book!).

Planning your work and working your plan is essential. Make menus and lists before you head for the store (Chapter 7 has more info on where to find the items you need). Make sure you always have appropriate ingredients on hand. You may have to order some of them online, so give yourself plenty of lead time. If a holiday is coming, plan the meal several weeks in advance in case some of the ingredients are only available on the Internet.

Here's a quick list of basic ingredients to always keep in your pantry:

- All the gluten-free flours.
- Xantham gum.
- Guar gum.

- ✔ A premixed batch of the baking mix you'll find in Chapter 9.

- ✔ Quinoa (a personal favorite — great to toss into soups and other foods).

- ✔ Rice. (As you'll see in Chapter 8, brown rice is best.)

- ✔ Gluten-free bread crumbs. (You can order them online or save them from your own breads.)

- ✔ Gluten-free crackers. (You can crumble them and use them as coatings on foods, fillers in meatloaf, and in soups and salads.)

- ✔ Gluten-free snacks. (Keep them on a level that kids can easily reach. You never want to run out or leave them tempted to snack on something glutenous.)

- ✔ Your favorites. (Order a backup so you don't run out, especially with foods that are hard to get.)

## *Using appliances to make cooking easier*

Just as you don't need separate cookware, you won't need separate appliances for cooking your gluten-free foods — with one exception. I absolutely recommend that you have two toasters, or better yet, two toaster *ovens*.

I know I've mentioned this before, but I really can't say it enough — crumbs literally fly off of bread. No matter how carefully you clean, your toaster will always be home to crumbs that can contaminate your gluten-free foods. I recommend toaster ovens over toasters because thanks to gravity, the crumbs fall down (as opposed to getting stuck on the side of the grates in a regular toaster), and you can wipe them away or put a piece of aluminum foil on the bottom of the oven and easily get rid of them.

Toaster bags are another great invention that no shared kitchen should be without. You just put your bread into the bag, put it into the toaster, and cook as usual. You can even take the bags to restaurants with you and ask the server to toast your bread in them. Use any search engine on the Internet to find toaster bags online.

Here are four appliances that can make gluten-free cooking a whole lot easier:

- ✔ **Bread machine:** Unless you really love the minutiae of baking, a bread machine is a must if you want fresh-baked bread. It makes the job so much easier. You'll find delicious recipes for gluten-free breads in Chapter 11, and some of them can be made in a bread machine. You can also buy mixes made especially for use in bread machines (again, I realize this is a *cook*book and that's somewhat counter to the essence of this book). The smell of fresh-baked bread in a gluten-free home is really awesome. By far, the easiest way to make homemade bread is with a machine.

Gluten-free dough is really heavy compared to regular dough. You need a bread machine with a super-strong motor, or you may catch it on fire or burn it out. (I've done both!)

✔ **Mixer:** You don't need a special mixer, but be sure to clean the beaters and the mixer thoroughly before using this appliance to whip up gluten-free foods because residuals can hang on. Have you ever noticed that film of flour on your kitchen counter after mixing up your cookie dough? That flour floats up as well as down, getting into the underside of your mixer and just waiting to drop into the next thing you make. Clean the mixer thoroughly and shake, bang, or brush it if necessary to dislodge any hidden flour.

✔ **Food processors:** These gadgets are great, but they're really hard to clean. Be especially careful if you're mixing glutenous bread crumbs. You may want to consider a high-end food-processor that comes with multiple mixing bowls. You can use one bowl for gluten-free preparation and the other for everything else.

✔ **Rice cooker:** One tool that can be invaluable is an electric rice cooker. You'll be cooking a lot of rice, and this just makes it easy.

## Changing a few techniques in your two-way kitchen

To successfully share your kitchen, you don't have to change your whole life. You just have to change a few techniques:

✔ I'm a sponge person. I wash them in hot water, keep them super clean, don't use them very long, and never let them stay wet or moldy. If you keep clean sponges handy, you're more apt to wipe up the gluten crumbs that can contaminate a perfectly good gluten-free meal.

✔ If you use hand towels and dish towels to wipe up crumbs and clean countertops, make sure they're always clean.

✔ Use parchment paper or aluminum foil to cover cookie sheets, separate foods, or cover your toaster oven or broiler rack. This is a great way to make sure your gluten-free foods don't get contaminated.

✔ Teach everyone, even the littlest kids, how to do the gob drop (see the "Using utensils in food preparation" section earlier in this chapter for the skinny on this).

✔ Make gluten-free sauces and condiments that everyone can use.

✔ Dedicate a gluten-free area of the pantry.

✔ Make sure all your spices are gluten-free.

✔ When cooking separate meals, make sure the gluten-free version is at least as yummy as the other one.

✔ Cleanliness is next to godliness. Crumbs are a no-no.

✔ When making two varieties of a meal, make the gluten-free version first.

✔ Use brightly colored labels to distinguish gluten-free foods. This is especially helpful when you have baby sitters or other people in the house who may grab the wrong food.

# Chapter 6

# Planning Out Your Gluten-Free Week

## In This Chapter

▶ Planning your week is good technique

▶ Considering great snacks

▶ Celebrating holidays and special occasions with great gluten-free fare

*Y*our tummy is rumbling, and you're staring blankly into the fridge, wondering what you're going to make for dinner. Regardless of the dietary restrictions you and your family may face, coming up with delicious, nutritious snacks and meals day after day can be challenging. Add to that the complexity of ensuring that foods are safely gluten-free, and it can seem a bit overwhelming.

Planning your snacks and meals can not only save you the angst of trying to decide what to make, but it also can save time and help ensure that you have all the ingredients you need on hand, and can even help trim your grocery bill.

Be creative and adventuresome in gluten-free gastronomical adventures. This chapter offers some meal and snack ideas as well as some holiday and special meal suggestions, and, it's meant to be a starting point. You find recipes to go with many of the recommendations in this book's recipes, but feel free to tweak as you see fit, accommodating personal nutritional goals, taste preferences, and other dietary issues. As you tweak, remember that the gluten-free lifestyle can be one of the healthiest on the planet! If nutrition is your mission, try to focus on healthy, non-processed foods.

## Starting the Day with Breakfast

If you aren't convinced of the importance of breakfast, indulge me for a moment as I climb up on my soap box. Breakfast, by definition, means you're "breaking a fast." That's because most of us don't sleep-eat, so by the time morning rolls around, we've usually gone a good 12 to 18 hours without food. Our bodies are literally in a semi-starvation mode. In order to function well, every part of our bodies — brain, muscle, and each and every cell — requires fuel. Semi-starvation doesn't bode well for optimum performance.

I know, you're not hungry in the mornings. Many — maybe even most — people aren't. There's also the argument that "I didn't do anything while I was sleeping; why should I refuel" — but your body *is* doing something while it sleeps, including repairing tissues and forming memories, among other things. Starting the day by fueling up with a nutritious breakfast that will jump-start your mind and body is important.

If you want to read more about optimal nutrition on a gluten-free diet, take a look at Chapter 4. For now, here are some great gluten-free ways to start the day.

### Sunday

Filet and Eggs a la Béarnaise (Chapter 12)

1 cup fresh sliced fruit

A cup of green or black tea

### Monday

1 Egg Burrito (Chapter 10)

1 cup fresh-squeezed orange juice

### Tuesday

1 Raspberry Smoothie (Chapter 10) with 1 tablespoon protein powder

1 cup oatmeal

1 cup skim milk or rice milk

### Wednesday

Farmer's Skillet Eggs (Chapter 11)

1 banana

### Thursday

2 Pumpkin Waffles (Chapter 11)

1 tablespoon almond butter

½ cup frozen berries (thaw in microwave before eating)

### Friday

Make-Ahead Brunch Casserole (Chapter 12)

1 cup grapefruit juice

### Saturday

Look for a local farmers' market over the weekend, and stock up on fresh, local fruit and veggies for the week. Some of these menu suggestions include fresh fruit.

  2 Feather-Light Crepes (Chapter 11)

  2 tablespoons agave syrup

  1 cup sliced fresh fruit

  A cup of black or green tea

# Mapping Light Meals and Snacks

Rather than eating three large meals, eating six times or so throughout the day is better to keep your energy levels up and your metabolism revved. I'm not talking about a four-course meal each time. I mean eating light meals and snacks (heavy emphasis on the word "light"). Try to balance it out; if you have a big lunch, go for a smaller meal in the evening.

Prepare your favorite meals and snacks in advance, and store them in the fridge or freezer for when you're ready. Doing so can keep you from turning to the all-too-convenient-not-usually-so-healthy packaged options.

### Sunday

  Cajun-Stuffed Mushrooms (Chapter 18)

  Sliced fresh tomatoes with balsamic vinegar drizzled on them

  1 cup lemonade

### Monday

  Perky Popcorn (Chapter 21)

  2 stalks of celery with almond butter

  1 cup water with 4 cucumber slices

### Tuesday

  Spinach Mandarin Salad (Chapter 10)

  Cheesy Crisps (Chapter 21)

### Wednesday

  Italian Beef Vegetable Soup (Chapter 13)

  Tortilla chips

### Thursday

Caesar Sandwich (Chapter 10)

1 red bell pepper cut in slices

### Friday

Quinoa-Stuffed Tomatoes (Chapter 17)

Hearty Chicken Broth (Chapter 20)

### Saturday

Marinated Steak Salad (Chapter 19)

Breakfast Biscuit Bread (Chapter 11)

# Going for Heartier Main Meals

Having extolled the virtues of eating six or more small or light meals in the previous section, I readily acknowledge that sometimes it feels good to just "fill 'er up!" When first embarking upon the gluten-free lifestyle, you can feel as those good ol' favorites are off limits, and what was once "comfort food" is now "discomfort food." Take heart, because hearty meals can include many of those meals you thought you'd have to give up, albeit sometimes in a slightly different form. Be sure to save room for the myriad gluten-free goodies that serve as dessert!

If your eyes are bigger than your tummy and you can't finish everything, save the leftovers for snacks or light meals later in the week.

### Sunday

Stuffed Rock Cornish Game Hens (Chapter 15)

Twice-Baked Sweet Potatoes (Chapter 17)

Coconut Lemon Chiffon Pie (Chapter 22)

### Monday

Spinach Lasagna (Chapter 17)

Flatbread Wrap (Chapter 11)

Best-Ever Apple Cobbler (Chapter 22)

### Tuesday

Artichoke Squares (Chapter 18)

Asian Chop Suey (Chapter 13)

Peachy French Toast (Chapter 11) — sliced into inch-wide strips

### Wednesday

Honey Broiled Chicken (Chapter 15)

Stuffed Acorn Squash (Chapter 17)

Trail Mix Bars (Chapter 21)

### Thursday

Best Spare Ribs You'll Ever Eat! (Chapter 16)

Glazed Carrots with Walnuts (Chapter 17)

Better Than S'Mores! (Chapter 22)

### Friday

Salmon with Mustard Dill Sauce (Chapter 14)

Luscious Lentil Salad (Chapter 19)

Sherbet

### Saturday

Beef Pot Roast a la Mushrooms (Chapter 16)

Parmesan Potatoes (Chapter 17)

Banana Chocolate Chip Muffins (Chapter 11)

# Being Festive: Special Occasions and Holidays

Holidays and special occasions are supposed to be joyful times. But because they tend to revolve around celebrations involving food, they can sometimes cause stress and anxiety for those leading a gluten-free lifestyle. Traditional holiday meals are often loaded with gluten. Stuffing, gravy, rolls, and Yorkshire pudding are off-limits in their traditional forms to those who are gluten-free, so the customary Thanksgiving and Christmas dinners just won't do.

The good news is that you can improvise and customize so that the meal can be gluten-free and delicious for everyone to enjoy. Put things into perspective and realize that the celebration is about the occasion or event, *not* the food. If you need a reminder about the many great things about being gluten-free, check out Chapter 1 as well as another book of mine, *Living Gluten-Free For Dummies,* 2nd Edition (John Wiley & Sons, Inc.).

### Thanksgiving feast

Roulade Canape (Chapter 18)

Spicy Chicken Soup (Chapter 20)

Cranberries and Yams (Chapter 17)

Salad with baby greens and olive oil-balsamic dressing

Oven-roasted turkey (following package directions)

Brown or wild rice

Liqueur Cups with Mocha Raspberries (Chapter 22)

### Christmas dinner

Crab Quiche (Chapter 11) — cut into bite-sized pieces and served cold

Roasted Asparagus with Mustard Dressing (Chapter 17)

Prime rib with horseradish on the side

Corn Muffins (Chapter 11)

Chocolate Fleck Cake (Chapter 22)

### Spring and summer BBQs

Flatbread Wrap (Chapter 11)

Potato Salad Nicoise (Chapter 19)

Barbecue Lamb Shanks (Chapter 16)

Assorted grilled veggies with olive-oil drizzled on top

Frosted Fruit Salad (Chapter 19)

### Valentine's Day (gluten-free . . . romantically!)

Crabmeat Dip (Chapter 18)

Strawberries dipped in white chocolate

Parmesan Chicken with Fresh Tomato Salsa (Chapter 15)

Chocolate Raspberry Bars (Chapter 22)

# Chapter 7

# Shopping for the Gluten-Free Stuff You Need

· · · · · · · · · · · · · · · · · · · · · · · · · · · · · · · · · · · · · · · · · · · · · · · · · · · · · · · · · · · · · · · · · · · · · · · · · · · · · · · · · · · · · · · · · · · · · · · · · · ·

### In This Chapter

▶ Hunting for special ingredients

▶ Buying gluten-free affordably

· · · · · · · · · · · · · · · · · · · · · · · · · · · · · · · · · · · · · · · · · · · · · · · · · · · · · · · · · · · · · · · · · · · · · · · · · · · · · · · · · · · · · · · · · · · · · · · · · · ·

*Y*ou may find shopping for gluten-free foods to be a bit of a challenge. I feel your pain. But thankfully, you shouldn't have to endure what I experienced back in the early 1990s when my toddler son was diagnosed with celiac disease. Today not only are foods labeled "gluten-free," or at least "wheat-free," but some stores conveniently stock all the gluten-free items together. It's a whole new world.

In this chapter, I reveal where to find all the ingredients you need for gluten-free cooking, whether you're throwing together a quick gluten-free snack, or creating gluten-free greatness.

If you want a head-start planning and shopping, do yourself a favor and check out www.glutenfreely.com. It has everything you need in one convenient location.

## Coming Up with a Shopping Strategy

The grocery store has all kinds of wonderful foods, even for people who need to live gluten-free. You just have to know what you want to shop for and where you need to shop within the store. The following sections discuss your options in a grocery store.

## Sticking to natural foods

Shopping for your gluten-free creations can be just as easy as shopping for *any* type of cooking. It's even easier if you follow my mantra for optimal nutrition: *If man made it, don't eat it.* Basically I advocate you stick to natural foods as much as possible.

Eating only natural foods makes shopping pretty easy. For the most part, if you avoid packaging, you're set! The best part about this healthy formula for eating is that natural foods are generally gluten-free. Foods like plain meats, poultry, fish, seafood, fruits, and vegetables — they're all gluten-free, and in the long-run, they cost less, too.

From a shopping standpoint, using all-natural ingredients means you get to avoid the middle aisles of the grocery store and only shop the perimeter. That's because the perimeter is where they keep the good stuff like meats (keep 'em lean), fish, poultry, fruits, veggies, nuts, berries . . . you get the picture. If you want to save time and money and eat more nutritiously, stick to the perimeter of the grocery store. The inner aisles of grocery stores are typically loaded with the processed stuff stores want you to buy because their profit margins are higher — foods like cereals, crackers, cookies, chips, breads, and other foods that aren't allowed on the gluten-free diet.

## Buying the occasional manmade item

You'll have to venture into the center aisles of the grocery store to gather basic necessities like spices (most are gluten-free) and household products. You may be lucky enough to have a local grocery store that carries specialty items, like gluten-free pastas or mixes. They'll be in the center aisles, too.

I must confess that I think everyone needs to give in to indulgences from time to time (not gluten-containing ones, though). However, if you must buy man-made foods, read the labels carefully and don't be taken in by the marketing claims on the front of the package.

Words like *wholesome, nutritious,* and *organic* don't mean gluten-free. I have a girlfriend who still can't understand, even after knowing my son for many years, why it's not okay to give him certain products when they say *organic* on the front. Remember, foods can be organic and still contain gluten.

Before you go shopping and start reading labels, make sure you know which ingredients are and are not gluten free. You might want to print out a list such as the one you can find on www.celiac.com. Click on the "Safe Gluten-Free Food List/Unsafe Foods & Ingredients" link.

# Scouting Out the Best Stores

The ingredients you need for your gluten-free goodies can run the gamut from specialty pastas to gluten-free soy sauce to baking mixes, flours, and wacky ingredients like xanthan gum. People have told me they refuse to make gluten-free meals because some of this stuff is just too hard to find. But you're in luck, because I have some ideas! And they won't take a lot of time, cost a small fortune, or require a trek to the far reaches of the continent. This section outlines where you'll have the best luck finding these specialty ingredients.

## Visiting your local grocery stores

These days, you can find many of the ingredients you need for your gluten-free concoctions at regular grocery stores. You may have to search through the specialty aisles or the natural foods section, if the store has one, but give your local grocery store a try before you begin your hunt in other types of stores. If your grocery store *does* carry what you need, you'll save time, money, and the frustration of driving all around town.

Don't forget to check out your nearby "superstore." Although I can't name names, the one that rhymes with "hall cart" is so dedicated to the gluten-free world that it carries more than 1,000 private-label products that are labeled gluten-free. This is a huge signal to the world that gluten-free living is a very big deal.

### Talk to the store manager

One of the first steps to take when embarking on a gluten-free lifestyle is to get to know your grocery store manager. In fact, this person should become your new best friend! Not only can store managers help you find the products you love, but if you bug them enough, they'll start carrying more gluten-free items and maybe even make them easier to find in the store. If you've been mail-ordering these products, you'll be delighted to save on shipping and let the store take care of that. The squeaky wheel definitely gets the grease when it comes to gluten-free shopping.

Your store manager can be one of your best resources for gluten-free foods. Start by asking a few simple questions, such as

- ✔ Does your store have a gluten-free aisle, or do you mix the gluten-free products in with everything else?
- ✔ Would you be willing to start carrying certain products or brands? (This simple request can save you from paying for shipping if you've been ordering online.)

✔ Do you have a list of your gluten-free products and where they can be found? (Many stores also post specialty product lists, including gluten-free, near the main entrance. This list can tell you which products the store carries and where to find them.)

Years ago, one of my favorite gluten-free product lines was very hard to find and available only by mail order. I asked the manager of a natural foods store I frequented to consider carrying the product, and he eagerly said yes. At my local grocery store, where I'd also shopped for many years, I once mentioned that it would be really cool if the store would carry some gluten-free products I wanted. The store manager quickly said, "Just name it and we'll carry it." Today, with gluten-free diets enjoying far more recognition and popularity, I'm sure almost any store would be happy to oblige.

### Get on the web

Another excellent source of information is your store's website. While doing the research for this book, I logged onto the websites of several major grocery chains in various parts of the country. Most offered visitors the ability to search the site, and when I searched for "gluten-free," the sites yielded impressive results. I quickly found all sorts of goodies, ranging from bread, brownie, and pancake mixes to cereals, pizza crusts, tortillas, and seasonings.

## Shopping at specialty stores

Specialty stores include natural food stores, gluten-free stores (yep, they exist!), farmers' markets, kosher stores, and co-ops. You normally pay more to shop at these places, but the convenience and the fact that you probably can pick up everything you need in one spot often makes them worth it. Here's a closer look at the different types of specialty stores and what they have to offer.

✔ **Natural food stores:** Growing in popularity, these stores can be found almost anywhere in the country, and in some areas, they're everywhere you look. Some have end-caps or kiosks that showcase their gluten-free products, and many have developed their own little gluten-free logos that they put on the products or on the shelf tags. Some of these stores are so committed to the gluten-free market that they've even created their own line of gluten-free products.

✔ **Gluten-free stores:** An online search can reveal any stores in your area that are dedicated to gluten-free products. Try using key words like "gluten-free store" and "gluten-free grocery store." I know of several throughout the country.

✔ **Farmers' markets:** These markets are not only full of the "If man made it, don't eat it" products I talk so much about, but they often have alternative grains like quinoa, millet, buckwheat, and others, and many even carry gluten-free breads. You can usually find good prices, and you can even get fresh flowers while you're there.

✔ **Kosher stores:** Kosher stores (or the kosher aisles of your local grocery store) hold an abundance of gluten-free items. Again, try searching online for key words like "kosher stores" and "gluten-free kosher." Now, not all kosher foods are gluten-free, but some are; you still have to read labels. It's important to note that some kosher foods are made differently during Passover; the Passover versions may *not* contain gluten when the non-Passover version does, and vice versa. Again, be sure to read your labels carefully. Any products that contain cake flour or matzo flour also contain gluten because both types of flour have gluten in them.

✔ **Co-ops:** Some parts of the country have co-op stores where buyers band together to take advantage of quantity pricing. An online search for "gluten-free co-op" revealed many different options, including online co-ops with extensive lists of gluten-free products.

Do an online search for "gluten-free coupon" and see what you can find. A lot of gluten-free manufacturers offer discounts on their products with coupons you can print at home and take to any store that carries those products.

## Buying online

Online gluten-free stores abound. To find a specific product or brand, search online for the product you want, either by brand name or product type (such as brownies, cake, and so on). To find an online store, try searching for "gluten-free online shopping" or "gluten-free online store."

One significant advantage with online shopping is that some online stores warehouse their products. That's great news for shoppers because it means lower shipping costs (because all products come from the same source) and faster delivery time. The alternative — ordering products from different manufacturers — can result in higher shipping costs and a bigger investment of your time.

International online shopping can add a whole new dimension to your gluten-free meals. Some international brands are delicious and easily available online. Be careful, though. Some European manufacturers use Codex Alimentarius wheat starch, which is approved as gluten-free in some countries but not in the United States. Always read the ingredient lists carefully.

## Saving Money on Ridiculously Expensive Ingredients

If you're going to buy specialty items, try small quantities first to make sure you like them. After you find items you like, buy in bulk and freeze what you're not going to use right away. If you're ordering by mail, you'll save on both quantity orders and the shipping costs. If you're ordering from a store, don't be afraid to ask for a quantity discount.

Don't be swindled into buying "specialty" items that are already gluten-free. Online and specialty stores sometimes sell high-priced gluten-free condiments and spices, but these things are naturally gluten-free, and there's no need to spend the extra money for a label. You can pick up these types of items in your neighborhood grocery store.

People complain about the high cost of eating gluten-free, but those people usually are eating a lot of the specialty items — breads, crackers, cakes, cookies, brownies, and pretzels. But you don't have to buy specialty items. When you stick with wholesome ingredients like fresh fruits, vegetables, meats, fish, and poultry, you eat healthier and save money. (See the "Sticking to natural foods" section earlier in the chapter for more on this.)

Even if you stick to my "if man made it, don't eat it" philosophy, you'll still need to keep some gluten-free products on hand. And when you need them, you need them badly. One way to save money and always be prepared is to buy in bulk and freeze items. While you're at it, you may as well cook in bulk and freeze the dishes. Ask your store manager if you can get better pricing by ordering larger quantities (such as by the case).

Buying generic is a money-saver, and lots of generic products are gluten-free. Most companies' customer-service representatives can tell you whether the products contain gluten; just call the toll-free number listed on the packaging, or visit the company's website to see if you can find a list of generic gluten-free products. If you can't, the manufacturer can probably send you one. (See Chapter 3 for more information about calling manufacturers to get information on a product's gluten content.)

# Chapter 8

# You Don't Always Need Recipes

...................................................................

## In This Chapter

▶ Making ingredient substitutions

▶ Serving naturally gluten-free foods

▶ Transforming standard recipes into gluten-free masterpieces

▶ Seeing the benefits of mixes

...................................................................

*P*atience isn't my strong suit. So give me a recipe, and the first thing I do is size up the list of ingredients. If there are more than about three things on the list, I'm outta there. It's not that I don't *use* a lot of ingredients — I do. In fact, I probably use far more than what a normal recipe calls for because I tend to get carried away as soon as my creative juices get flowing. But that *list* can be so daunting, and often, I've even never heard of some of the ingredients — seriously, "tragacanth gum powder"?!? And then there's this measuring thing you have to do. Who has all the fancy spoons and cups — and who has the time? A glob, a dopple, and a smidge are fine forms of measurement for me.

I know, people love recipes, and this *is,* after all, a cookbook. You get recipes in the chapters ahead, and better yet, they're created by a real live recipe inventor, so you don't have to worry that I made them up.

But before we start slicing, dicing, mixing, and measuring, I need to point out that you don't always *need* recipes. With a glob, a dopple, and a smidge of creativity, you can turn any meal into a gluten-free favorite. That's right, *any* meal. Gluten-free cooking doesn't have to be complicated. This chapter points you toward convenient mixes, simple substitutes, and fabulous foods that don't require all that mixing, measuring, and sorting of ingredients. And if you have a gluten-filled recipe to start with, this chapter shows you how to alter it and make it work so you can still enjoy all your favorite foods.

# Transforming Any Meal into a Gluten-Free Delight

Transform *any* meal? That's a pretty big promise, but that's exactly what I'm talking about doing. Just because a recipe doesn't say "gluten-free" doesn't mean you can't use it. I'm going to show you how to make some awesome alterations!

I always love it when people tell me they miss their favorite foods. I look at that as a challenge to find a way to make that food available in a gluten-free form. And with the tips in this chapter, you discover that there's nothing you can't make gluten-free and there are no boundaries. At first, it may seem hard to believe. Like many people, you may be thinking that saying hello to a gluten-free lifestyle means saying good-bye to rolls, gravies, lasagnas, and sauces. Well, say hello again because all those foods are back on the menu.

The key to making the transformation is creativity. Forget the ingredients list. Forget the measuring spoons and cups. Whether you're working from a recipe that isn't gluten-free and converting it to a gluten-free goodie, or making it up on the fly, the most important ingredient is creativity. Having good gluten-free substitutions in mind and on hand is important, too.

## Finding fun substitutions

With more and more people adopting wheat-free and gluten-free lifestyles, and with recent improvements in product labeling laws, finding gluten substitutions is easier than ever. Grocery stores and specialty stores offer a wide variety of ingredients. Chapter 7 gives you ideas of where to shop and how to save money on those ingredients, some of which are ridiculously expensive.

As you may already know, a little flexibility goes a long way when you're living a gluten-free lifestyle. Start flexing — here are some savvy substitutions for some of your favorite ingredients:

- ✔ **Flour:** Start with the most obvious and mostly commonly used ingredient. If your recipe calls for flour, consider using cornstarch or a gluten-free flour or mix. I talk more about buying and making your own baking mixes in the "Messing with Mixes" section at the end of this chapter. Experiment with the many new flours available, like bean flours, sorghum, and amaranth. They're nutritious and add flavor, and oh yeah — they're gluten-free!

- ✔ **Breading and coatings:** If a recipe calls for breading, bread crumbs, flour coating, or a similar preparation, consider using a wheat- or gluten-free mix (either homemade or store bought). Bread and muffin mixes work well for coatings on chicken and other fried goodies. Seasoned cornmeal or corn flour (masa) and crushed potato chips (my favorite chips for coatings are barbecue flavor) are also excellent alternatives.

✔ **Thickeners:** Cornstarch, arrowroot flour, and tapioca starch make great substitutes for flour and other thickeners. Dry pudding mix works well for sweet recipes, and bread or baking mixes work well for just about anything.

✔ **Binders:** That's one of those ingredient categories that would make me put away the cookbook, and I personally wouldn't use a recipe if it called for binders. But if you're more culinarily courageous, consider using gelatin, xanthan gum, or guar gum.

✔ **Pie crust:** People think that if something calls for a pie crust — say a quiche or — well, say a *pie* — then it's off limits unless they make a really complicated crust from a really complicated recipe. I say think again! First, consider making the dish *without* the crust. Seriously — a quiche without a crust is still a quiche. And admit it — when you eat a pie, you just eat the crust to be polite, right? The crust is really just a means to get to the gushy stuff inside. Okay, if you really want to make a gluten-free crust without a recipe, crush a couple of handfuls of gluten-free cookies or a sugary gluten-free cereal, add some butter or margarine (a glob or a dopple, whichever you prefer), and press the stuff into a greased pie pan. Then follow the baking instructions for a regular pie. You'll probably just eat the good stuff out of the middle, anyway.

✔ **Bread crumbs:** Many gluten-free breads turn to crumbs when you look at them. And certainly, there are always plenty of crumbs in the bag; just use them as extras for cooking. Or crumble some bread slices and toast or broil the crumbs to make them crunch.

✔ **Croutons:** Cut fresh, gluten-free bread into cubes, deep fry, and then roll in Parmesan cheese and spices. Some people suggest letting the bread get just a tad stale (not moldy) before making croutons this way.

✔ **Granola:** If you can find gluten-free oats, you're set. But if you can't, you can still make granola. Toss together toasted nuts and seeds, and then mix them with gluten-free cereal, honey, vanilla, a tiny bit of oil, and spices or seasonings. How much spices and seasonings? A smidge or so, till it tastes like you like it. Bake at 300 degrees for an hour, stirring every 15 minutes. Add dried fruit that's first been soaked in water for 10 minutes, let cool, and then refrigerate or vacuum seal and freeze.

✔ **Trail mix:** Lots of trail mixes that are available at the stores are already gluten-free, but if you like to make your own, mix some peanuts, raisins, dried fruit, and gluten-free chocolate candies or chips.

Dates and some other dried fruits are often dusted with oat flour. Be sure to check the labels. If they've been dusted with oat flour, the ingredients label will say so.

- **Oatmeal/hot breakfast:** Try corn grits. Prepare them like oatmeal and top with butter, cinnamon, and sugar, or fry them. Hot cereals also are available from the producers of gluten-free flours. Some new amaranth and quinoa hot cereals that are nutritional powerhouses are also available.

- **Buns and flour tortillas:** Substitute lettuce, gluten-free bread, corn tortillas, or rice wraps (found in Asian markets and often used in Thai cooking). If you like *nori* (the seaweed wrap on sushi), you can use it as a wrap with anything stuffed inside.

- **Soy and teriyaki sauce:** Asian markets carry some absolutely amazing Asian sauces that are gluten-free, but you have to read labels carefully (and sometimes that requires a crash course in another language). If you can't find a gluten-free soy sauce, you can substitute Bragg Liquid Aminos. You can find Bragg in the health-food aisle of your grocery store or at a natural-foods retailer. To make your own teriyaki, add equal parts of sugar and wine to your favorite soy sauce substitute.

When in doubt, leave it out. And really, what's the harm in leaving it out, anyway? If your soup recipe calls for a tablespoon or two of flour, try leaving it out and see what you think.

## Putting mindless meals on the menu

Sometimes people get so caught up in "how to do the diet" that they forget how easy cooking can be. I love to experiment and play in the kitchen, but plenty of days I just don't have the time. That's where mindless meals come in. These are easy meals that don't require a recipe. Here are some ideas to get you started.

When starting a gluten-free diet, people often forget they can eat normal, everyday foods like the ones I list here. Just make sure to read the labels and use substitutions for specific ingredients, if needed.

### Breakfast

Most people start their day with a bowl of cereal, bagel, toast, pancakes, or waffles, and those things, unless they're a special gluten-free variety, are definitely not allowed on the gluten-free diet. But that's okay! There are healthier options for starting your day off gluten-free style, and they're quick and easy, too:

- Yogurt or cottage cheese topped with fruit, trail mix, or cereal

- Corn grits with a glob of butter and a little mix of cinnamon and sugar on top

- Eggs, any style, with sausage or bacon

✔ Fruit and cheese

✔ Fruit smoothie (I'd add some extra protein powder myself)

✔ Toast or French toast (made from gluten-free bread, of course)

✔ Quesadillas on a corn tortilla

✔ Leftovers from dinner the night before (my personal favorite)

### Lunch or dinner

No need to scramble for cookbooks and recipes when you're putting together your gluten-free lunch or dinner. You can make plenty of quick and easy meals using easy-to-find ingredients.

✔ Hot dogs or burgers, plain or wrapped in a lettuce "bun" or corn tortilla

✔ Deli meats on a lettuce wrap or corn tortilla, or just plain or rolled up with condiments

✔ Caesar salad with chicken

✔ Roast beef, chicken, or turkey

✔ Premarinated or grilled chicken or turkey (add veggies and you have fajitas!)

✔ Chili

✔ Seafood

✔ Shish kebabs

✔ Frozen tamales

✔ Frozen taquitos

### Side dishes and snacks

Whether you want simple or snazzy, you can prepare endless gluten-free side dishes and snacks without a recipe. The key is to think about what you would eat that has gluten in it, and use the substitution ideas in this book to help you modify the meal. If you're out of ideas, use this list as a starter:

✔ Fruit (fresh or dried)

✔ Vegetables (fresh or cooked)

✔ Quinoa (you can eat it hot or cold — use it as rice or even tabbouleh)

✔ Rice (I recommend brown rice if you're going to eat rice)

✔ Potatoes (sweet potatoes and yams are far more nutritious than other types)

✔ Potato skins (yeah, a little decadent if you goop 'em up with cheese and sour cream, but yummy nonetheless)

- Deviled or hard-boiled eggs
- Tuna
- Nachos or chips
- Cheese squares (you can get all sorts of gluten-free crackers if you want cheese and crackers)
- Cream cheese wrapped in ham or salami
- Rice cakes or popcorn
- Nuts
- Baked beans
- Sloppy Joes (on gluten-free bread, of course)
- Soup (you do have to check labels on commercial brands, but you can find gluten-free soups out there; consider making a super simple version of your own by using a premade stock and tossing in some veggies and gluten-free pasta)
- Celery with peanut butter or cream cheese
- Ice cream (stay away from varieties that contain the cookies, brownies, pretzels, and other gluten-containing treats)

# Converting a Gluten-Filled Recipe into a Gluten-Free Recipe

With gluten-free cooking, thinking outside the recipe box is especially important because you may not be able to find recipes for everything you want to make. You don't have to follow recipes to a T. With a little creativity and a willingness to bend, break, or bury the rules, you can transform any recipe into a gluten-free masterpiece.

In this section, I show you exactly how to transform a recipe, or at least how I do it. For this example, I chose a recipe that's gushing with gluten for dramatic effect. It's called "Fried Broccoli Florets with Soy Curry Sauce." Yikes. The title alone should sound warning bells in your head because "fried" usually means breading, and "soy" is usually followed by the word "sauce." Here's the recipe as it appears online:

# Fried Broccoli Florets with Soy Curry Sauce

This dish can be served as an appetizer or a first course.

**Prep time:** 40 min • **Cook time:** 5 min • **Yield:** 2 servings

| Ingredients | Directions |
|---|---|
| ¼ **cup all-purpose flour** | *1* In a small bowl, whisk together the flour and the beer and let the batter stand for 30 minutes. |
| ¼ **cup plus 1 teaspoon beer** | |
| **1 garlic clove, peeled** | *2* Finely mince the garlic, and on your cutting board, mix in the salt. Mash the garlic and salt together with the blade of a knife until it's a paste. |
| **1 pinch kosher salt** | |
| **1 teaspoon butter** | |
| ¼ **teaspoon curry powder** | *3* In a pan, melt the butter over moderately low heat and cook the curry powder, stirring for 1 minute. |
| ¾ **teaspoon dark brown sugar** | |
| 1½ **teaspoons red wine vinegar** | *4* Stir in the garlic paste, brown sugar, vinegar, lemon juice, and soy sauce, and transfer the sauce to a small dish. |
| **1 teaspoon fresh lemon juice** | |
| ½ **teaspoon soy sauce** | *5* In a deep, heavy skillet, heat 1 inch of oil to 375 degrees. |
| **oil (for deep frying)** | |
| **12 broccoli florets** | |
| | *6* Whisk the beer batter, dip the broccoli florets into it, tossing off the excess batter, and fry them in the oil for 1½ to 2 minutes or until golden. |
| | *7* Transfer the broccoli to paper towels to drain, and serve it while warm with the curry sauce. |

*Per serving: Calories 117; Total fat 2g; Saturated fat 1g; Cholesterol 5mg; Sodium 190mg; Carbohydrate 19g; Fiber 1g; Protein 4g.*

## Converting the ingredients

Okay, so there is all-purpose flour, beer, *more* beer (Why do they do that? Is that one extra teaspoon *really* going to make a difference?!? But I digress . . .), and soy sauce. No go, no go, and no go. *Not* on a gluten-free diet.

So how do I transform this into a gluten-free goodie? Well, first I get rid of the measurements, because this is cooking Danna-style. Table 8-1 shows you what the new ingredients list can look like. (I include the original ingredients list in the left-hand column of the table so you don't have to keep flipping back and forth, only to give up after five or six flips. You're welcome!)

| Table 8-1 | Comparison of Original and Converted Ingredients Lists | |
|---|---|---|
| *Original Ingredient and Measurement* | *My Converted Measurement* | *Gluten-Free Ingredient* |
| ¼ cup all-purpose flour | A fist-full of | Any gluten-free mix you happen to have lying around. All you have is muffin mix, and it's a little sweet? No problem! It might make it even better! |
| ¼ cup beer, plus | A glug of | Gluten-free beer would be the obvious ingredient here, and there are excellent ones on the market now, even available at regular grocery stores. If you don't have access to gluten-free beer, try using chicken broth, ginger ale, or white grape juice. |
| 1 teaspoon beer | Another splash of | Beer substitute (see above). |
| 1 garlic clove, peeled | A bunch of | Garlic. (Personally, I'm a fan of the sliced, diced, and otherwise-ready-to-go variety in a jar.) |

| Original Ingredient and Measurement | My Converted Measurement | Gluten-Free Ingredient |
| --- | --- | --- |
| 1 pinch kosher salt | A pinch of | Kosher salt. (Okay, seriously, does it need to be kosher?) |
| ¼ teaspoon curry powder | A dash or splash of | Curry powder. |
| ¾ teaspoon dark brown sugar | A glob of | Dark brown sugar (or light brown — do you really think it's going to make a difference?). |
| 1½ teaspoons red wine vinegar | A glob of | Red wine vinegar. |
| 1 teaspoon fresh lemon juice | A bunch of squeezes of | Fresh lemon juice. (I like my foods extra lemony, so I upped the amount.) |
| ½ teaspoon soy sauce | A few splashes of | Gluten-free soy sauce. (If you don't like or don't have access to soy sauce, try Bragg Liquid Aminos or an Asian sauce [check the label carefully for gluten].) |
| oil (for deep frying) | Lots of | Oil (for deep frying). |
| 12 broccoli florets | As many as you want | Broccoli florets. |

When you deep-fry glutenous foods, like "regular" breaded items, the oil becomes contaminated with gluten. You can't use that same oil for your gluten-free goodies, or you're defeating the purpose of cooking gluten-free. Always use fresh, non-contaminated oil for frying or deep-frying.

## Interpreting the instructions

Okay, so now it's time for the instruction part of the recipe. In the "real" recipe, the beer and flour have to hang out together for a half-hour or so to do their thing: thicken, bubble, yeastify. Check out Table 8-2 to see how the original steps compare to what I would do.

| Table 8-2 | Formal Instructions versus Danna-Style Instructions |
|---|---|
| *Original Steps* | *My Version of the Steps* |
| 1. In a small bowl, whisk together the flour and the beer and let the batter stand for 30 minutes. | 1. Mix the gluten-free flour mixture and gluten-free beer together and set it aside while you figure out what else you have to do to prepare this dish. |
| 2. Finely mince the garlic, and on your cutting board, mix in the salt. Mash the garlic and salt together with the blade of a knife until it's a paste.<br><br>3. In a pan, melt the butter over moderately low heat and cook the curry powder, stirring for 1 minute.<br><br>4. Stir in the garlic paste, brown sugar, vinegar, lemon juice, and soy sauce, and transfer the sauce to a small dish. | 2. Dump all of the rest of the ingredients *except the broccoli* into a frying pan and heat them up. Swish everything around a little so it's all mixed together. This is going to be your dipping sauce, so when it's finished heating, you can put it into a dipping bowl (if you *have* a dipping bowl, you're far too advanced for these instructions). |
| 5. In a deep, heavy skillet, heat 1 inch of oil to 375 degrees.<br><br>6. Whisk the beer batter, dip the broccoli florets into it, tossing off the excess batter, and fry them in the oil for 1½ to 2 minutes or until golden. | 3. Dunk the broccoli into the flour-and-beer mixture. How you do this without getting the mixture all over your fingers is up to you.<br><br>4. Put the coated broccoli into the hot oil (if I really had to tell you to heat the oil when you knew you were going to *deep-fry* something, skip ahead to the real recipes that call out each step). Deep-fry until it's done. (If I have to tell you when it's done, creative cooking is not for you.) |
| 7. Transfer the broccoli to paper towels to drain, and serve it while warm with the curry sauce. | |

Beer is less acidic than wine, vinegar, or citrus juices, so it tenderizes meats without breaking down the texture as fast. That's why you can use it to tenderize and marinate raw fish, or add it to dishes that call for vinegar. And of course, I don't have to remind you to make sure it's of the gluten-free variety!

Keep in mind that the whole point of this chapter is to be creative and think outside the recipe box. So the example I've given you here is just that — an example. Feel free to modify it however you'd like to suit your fancy.

# Messing with Mixes

Bear with me while I whine for a moment, will you? When I first started "doing gluten-free" in 1991, there weren't any mixes — at least not that I found. Remember, that was before the Internet, before there were any books on the subject, and even before support groups were widely available.

The first gluten-free mixes to hit the streets were basically a little rice flour with a lot of sugar. And hey — I'm the first to admit that a little sugar can go a long way in making up for lost flavor, but they were lacking something. Flavor . . . nutrition . . . the ability to stick together.

We've come a long way, baby. Today you can easily find gluten-free mixes for brownies, cookies, breads, pizza crust, muffins, cakes — you name it. For those who don't want to explore recipes and worry about all the ingredients they involve, mixes are a great alternative.

Even if you're a pro in the kitchen, mixes can be a valuable addition to your pantry shelf. Keep them on hand to use when you're in a hurry or as a ready-made substitute for gluten-containing ingredients. For instance, if your recipe calls for dredging chicken in flour, and you obviously can't use regular white flour, just use a gluten-free bread or muffin mix in its place.

One of my favorite mixes is a blend of several different kinds of flour. You can use flour mixtures like this in recipes that call for regular flour. In Chapter 9, I give you a recipe you can use to make your own flour mixtures, but you can buy them premixed, too. The mixes actually work better than individual flours alone, because each flour adds a cooking characteristic of its own. When you combine different varieties, such as rice, potato, tapioca, quinoa, buckwheat, amaranth, and other flours, they rise better, cook better, and offer more nutritional value than each individual flour alone.

Add some flaxseed to your favorite mix for some extra fiber and omega-3 fatty acids. Omega-3s are important building blocks for our cell membranes, and are essential for good health. Among other things, they play an important role in heart health and in lowering cholesterol.

## Don't let the price tag fool you

Besides the obvious convenience factor, one of the best things about mixes is that although they may *seem* prohibitively expensive, they can actually save you money in the long run.

Personally, I've spent exorbitant sums of money on ingredients for my home-made concoctions (seriously, have you priced xanthan gum?), not to mention hours putting them together, only to end up with inedible bricks of bread, or cookies that crumble when you have the audacity to attempt to remove them from the baking sheet. Sometimes even my dogs couldn't stomach the mixture mishaps.

Mixes today are a sure bet. Not only are they edible (a plus for food products), but they taste great and are often loaded with extra nutrients thanks to the more widespread use of alternative flours such as amaranth, quinoa, and buckwheat. Investing in a sure thing can beat experimentation and save you money in the long run.

## They're easy to find

You can find these incredible mixes in many grocery stores and specialty stores. Even some of the larger grocery stores have gluten-free sections, or they carry these types of products in their health food sections. (Refer to Chapter 7 for more help.)

You can also find a large assortment of mixes and other products online. For a general assortment, search for keywords like "gluten-free products" and "gluten-free mixes." If you know what you're looking for, make your search criteria more specific, like "gluten-free brownie mix" or "gluten-free cookie mix."

# Part II
# Mouthwatering Main Courses

The 5th Wave                    By Rich Tennant

"It's the gluten—free edition."

# In this part . . .

*E*veryone has a busy life. You're rushing around trying to meet work deadlines, taking the kids to their soccer games, completing a volunteer project that you didn't want to do in the first place but didn't know how to say "no" to. So how are you supposed to have time to prepare meals, too? With just a little forethought and planning, you can actually have a balanced, gluten-free meal at home. Honest. Just try a few of the recipes in this part. We provide recipes for the three main meals you eat (or should eat) each day: breakfast, lunch, and dinner.

# Chapter 9

# Gluten-Free Flours: Your Foundation for Great Breads and Pastries

**Recipe in This Chapter**

↻ Gluten-Free Flour Mixture

🌶 🍐 🍆 🥕 ➳

*Y*es, you are a celiac (or you've decided to avoid foods containing gluten). Yes, you must give up all products containing wheat, rye, and barley. And *yes,* you can still enjoy eating *all* your favorite foods. If this sounds contradictory, read on.

This first chapter in the recipe section of this book is devoted to setting your mind at ease by explaining how to use alternative flours successfully. Most people love bread, cakes, pizza, and pasta. Celiacs, especially those who are newly diagnosed, have nightmares of never being able to eat these processed carbohydrates again. None of these foods is traditionally gluten-free — but they can be!

After you understand the basics of baking gluten-free and realize that your food selections aren't limited, you can then peruse the rest of the recipes in this book with peace of mind, knowing that you won't be deprived of your favorite foods.

## Baking Bread without Wheat Flour

If you're living the gluten-free life, you certainly know that you can't go to the store, buy a bag of wheat flour, bring it home, dip your measuring cup into the bag, and begin baking. The properties in wheat are difficult to duplicate, so you need a variety of alternative flours to attain the results you would get from wheat flour. Even then, you're dealing with gluten-free flours that have no, well, no gluten. Gluten gives bread its light, spongy consistency and cakes their airy lift. In a few recipes, you can get away with substituting cornstarch in place of wheat flour, but those instances are rare.

Don't despair. Some viable ways can imitate the texture and taste of wheat flour. When you use the right combination of alternative flours, add some additional flavoring and include something acidic to help the product rise, your cookies, cakes, and pie crusts will taste every bit as good as their wheat counterparts.

Breads are some of the most difficult recipes to convert to gluten-free, and converting them takes a little more understanding. After you've mastered the art of this conversion (I give you some hints in this chapter), you'll have a loaf of bread that is gorgeous to look at, heavenly to smell, and delectable to eat. But it's not quite as simple as that.

The first time you try to convert a wheat yeast bread recipe to gluten-free, you'll most likely end up with a glob that is raw in the center, has a crust that requires a jackhammer to cut through it, and an aftertaste that redefines the word "bitter." If the loaf actually bakes all the way through, then the slices may crumble beyond recognition when you attempt to cut it. Fortunately, you have this book in your hands. It contains excellent bread recipes with all the necessary adjustments, so you don't have to worry about converting your Grandma's homemade bread recipe immediately. Be aware that if you use a different flour mixture with the recipes in this book, you may get different results.

To create a loaf of gluten-free bread that is a masterpiece, the proportion of yeast to salt and sugar has to be correct. Adding an extra egg white to the mix usually results in a lighter texture. Adding a little light flaxseed meal helps the yeast rise. Adding something acidic (usually cider vinegar) also helps with the rising. Additional flavoring is beneficial. Again, the recipes in this book have already had these adjustments made. The finished product may not be as airy as the commercial, non-nutritional, touch-it-and-it-smooshes white bread, but the texture will be light and the taste divine. Some of the ready-made loaves of gluten-free breads that you find at health food stores are edible (that's a generous summation), so seriously consider baking some homemade bread. You deserve to eat a slice of bread that actually tastes great!

# Looking at Alternative Flours

If you tour a health food store, and even some grocery stores, you'll be amazed at the variety of alternative flours available. If you're health-conscious, use three-fourths of the basic gluten-free flour mixture in a recipe, and add up to one-fourth of a different kind of flour so the mixture has more fiber and protein. Experiment with almond flour, light flaxseed meal, light teff, chestnut flour, mesquite flour, or lentil flour.

Where to purchase your flours may be an issue. Alternative flours are readily available at health food stores, and many mainstream grocery stores now have gluten-free sections that offer a large variety of flours.

- **Brown rice flour:** This flour still has the bran layer, so it offers more vitamins, minerals, and fiber than its white counterpart, but the finished product will be slightly darker in color and just a bit nuttier tasting. Even though brown rice flour still has the bran layer, this kind of bran is gluten-free.

- **White rice flour and glutinous white rice flour:** These two aren't inter-changeable. White rice flour is used in the flour mixture for baking. Glutinous white rice flour is *glutinous* (sticky) and is used like cornstarch to thicken gravies. Don't let the name "glutinous" confuse you. *Rice gluten* (which is safe for celiacs) is not the same as *wheat gluten* (which is not safe for celiacs). If you're a newbie, all this flour stuff does make sense after a while.

- **Potato starch flour:** Don't confuse it with potato flour. Potato flour is used as a thickener for gravies; potato starch flour is used as a base for baked goods. The powdery texture helps keep baked foods light in texture and helps with the expansion during baking. It also helps maintain moisture in baked goods.

- **Tapioca (or cassava) flour:** It's a thickening agent that helps prevent breads and cakes from crumbling. It also lightens baked goods while adding a chewiness (perfect for cookies), and it helps gluten-free products to brown. It's very easily digested.

- **Garbanzo bean (chickpea) flour and garfava bean flour:** Both of these flours are slightly yellow in color, and they're excellent sources of protein. Garfava bean flour is a combination of garbanzo beans and fava beans. A little more challenging to locate are **lentil, mung bean,** and **pea flours.** The bean flours add extra nutrition to the mix, and they also help make the product lighter, so it's beneficial to add a *little* bean flour to your flour mixture. Adding too much bean flour may give your product a potent aftertaste and may also cause flatulence (yup — gas).

- **Cornstarch:** Although it has no nutritional value, it is used to lighten the texture of baked goods.

- **Sorghum (or milo) flour:** It offers more nutritional value (protein and fiber) than the rice flours. It's neutral tasting, and it helps keep your baked goods from shrinking.

- **White sweet potato flour:** It's difficult to find, but it adds a delicious flavor to cookies and cakes, and is also higher in fiber than most other flours.

- **Amaranth:** Amaranth is sweeter than most alternative flours with an almost nutty taste. Although the taste is good, the texture tends to be very sticky, so no more than 10 percent of your flour mixture should be amaranth. The advantage to including it is that it's more nutritious than most of the alternative flours. It's high in fiber, iron, and calcium.

- **Soy flour:** This flour is an option, but it tends to leave a distinctive aftertaste, as do **teff** and **buckwheat.** (No, buckwheat does not have wheat in it.)

You'll have a slight glitch if you bake gluten-free products and wheat products in your home (for the celiac and non-celiac members of your family). You'll need to bake the gluten-free baked goods first, and then cover them securely. Flour particles can stay in the air for up to 24 hours, so no matter how careful you are to clean your mixer, baking sheets, and countertops, the gluten-free food may still become contaminated with wheat flour if you bake the wheat product first.

# Baking for Success: A Few Tips

Baking is just as much a science as it is an art. You can't play around with a bread or cake recipe like you can a soup recipe. You have to know what you're doing, which takes practice. Here are some general baking tips that can help as you develop your skills:

- Eggs should be at room temperature when making baked goods. If you forget to take the eggs out of the refrigerator ahead of time, place the eggs (still in their shells) in a bowl of warm water for 5 minutes. Eggs that are cracked or leaking should not be used. Because of the risk of salmonella, none of the recipes in this book contain raw eggs.

- If a recipe calls for softened butter and your butter is still in the refrigerator, cut off the needed amount. Cut that block into 1-tablespoon chunks, set the chunks on a plate, and put the dish in the microwave for 14 seconds to soften.

- If you substitute margarine for butter, only use margarine made with 80 percent fat. Products with a lower fat content may affect the quality and texture of the end product.

- If sifting is called for in a recipe, instead of sifting, you can place all the dry ingredients in a bowl and mix them with a wire whisk or mixer. Or you can place the dry ingredients in the bowl of your food processor and give them a couple of quick pulses.

✔ For baked goods that call for oil, you can replace half of the oil with applesauce to produce a low-fat version of the recipe. You'll need to reduce the baking time just slightly to prevent the product from becoming too dry.

✔ When mayonnaise is called for in a cake recipe, use real mayonnaise (not reduced-calorie, fat-free, or imitation). Anything other than real mayo will break down under the heat of the oven and leave a metallic taste.

✔ When measurements are given, they are level (not heaping) measures. When measuring honey, molasses, or anything sticky, spray the measuring spoon or measuring cup with nonstick cooking spray first so the sticky stuff slides out easily.

# Creating the Gluten-Free Flour Mixture

Setting out all the different alternative flours, the xanthan gum, the cornstarch, and so on can create quite a mess in your kitchen. You'll undoubtedly find flour powder lightly dusting your kitchen counters when you're through with the measuring and sifting.

Precisely because of the mess that occurs when you assemble the flour mixture, we only use one flour mixture throughout this book. Why? Because you can measure and sift once, and then spoon the combined flours into a self-seal plastic bag and freeze it. When you're ready to bake, you don't have to drag out all the different bags of flour — one flour mixture will suffice for all the recipes in this book. Just take the bag out of the freezer, measure the amount you need, and begin baking. It doesn't get much easier than that. It should be noted that in a few of the bread recipes, sorghum flour or flaxseed meal is added to the basic flour mixture to get the right consistency.

When making more than one batch of the flour mixture, measure and sift each batch separately to be certain that the ingredients combine evenly. After one recipe has been sifted into a bowl, stir the mixture with a whisk to guarantee that everything is well blended. Place it in a freezer bag, and then begin mixing up the second batch.

Why should you freeze the flour mixture? The alternative flours don't have the shelf life of wheat flour. By keeping the mixture in the freezer, it will stay fresh for months. After you measure the amount of the gluten-free flour mixture you need for a recipe, let it set out on the kitchen counter for about 15 minutes to reach room temperature before mixing it with other ingredients.

# Gluten-Free Flour Mixture

**Prep time:** 5 min • **Yield:** 5 cups

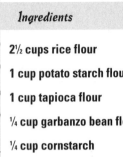

| Ingredients | Directions |
|---|---|
| 2½ cups rice flour | **1** Sift all the ingredients into a large bowl, and then stir them together with a whisk. |
| 1 cup potato starch flour | |
| 1 cup tapioca flour | **2** Spoon the mixture into a self-seal freezer bag and freeze until needed. |
| ¼ cup garbanzo bean flour | |
| ¼ cup cornstarch | |
| 2½ tablespoons xanthan gum | |

*Per ¼ cup: Calories: 138; Total fat: 0g; Saturated fat: 0g; Cholesterol: 0mg; Sodium: 1mg; Carbohydrates: 32g; Fiber: 2g; Sugar: 0g; Protein: 1g.*

## Yes, gum is involved

If you are new to gluten-free baking, you may have panicked when you saw the word *xanthan gum* (pronounced *zan*-thun). It's just a fancy name for a gum (sticky stuff) that will help hold your baked product together. Point of clarification — the *result* of using the gum is sticky, not the gum itself. Xanthan gum is available at most health food stores and even at some mainline grocery stores. It's a cream-colored powder that comes packaged either in a pouch or a jar. Adding just a little of this gum to your flour mixture helps prevent your baked goods from crumbling.

*Guar gum* is sometimes used in place of xanthan gum. It accomplishes the same thing as the xanthan gum (preventing crumbling). Although guar gum is gluten-free, it may cause distress of the lower intestinal tract in some people (that's the politically correct way to say diarrhea). Another alternative to using xanthan gum is to use twice the amount of unflavored gelatin. If the recipe calls for 1 teaspoon of xanthan gum, use 2 teaspoons of unflavored gelatin.

# Chapter 10

# Fast Fixes: Making It Quick & Easy

*1*t's one of those days. You left work later than you intended, the family is famished, and you have no time to be creative. So many mouths to feed and so little time. And when you're gluten-free, you can't just drive through any ol' restaurant or pluck pre-packaged meals mindlessly off the grocery store shelves. You have to think about what you're eating, and research long lists of ingredients you may never have even heard of.

This chapter is loaded with great recipes that are simple to prepare in just minutes. Whether you're trying to stuff a nutritious, delicious meal into their mouths before they leave the house in the morning or fixing quickie meals for the rest of the day, this chapter is filled with fast-and-easy-fare that can fill gluten-free tummies with glee.

# *When Every Minute Counts: Breakfast on the Run*

Breakfast is brain food. Plain and simple, you and your family need a nutritious meal first thing when you wake up in order to get moving in the right direction. Hungry or not, your body needs fuel. After 12 to 18 hours without food, it doesn't have any glycogen. Without glycogen, by the time lunchtime rolls around (or before), you begin to feel fatigued, and most likely lose your ability to concentrate. Check out Chapter 4 for more on glycogen.

Breakfast, as important as it is, doesn't have to be fancy. It should be high in protein and fiber, and low in foods that cause blood-sugar spikes. Here are some easy and quick ways to start your day.

## Separating the wheat from the gaffe: You'll make mistakes!

Because sorting out what's okay and what's not may be more difficult than you may have thought, you *will* make mistakes in the process. That's okay. You'll make mistakes from time to time not because you're lazy, dumb, or subconsciously trying to sabotage your intestines — it's because you're human, and figuring out all of the gluten-free facts can be really tough!

We're not suggesting that you slip and slide your way through the diet, but accidentally ingesting a little glob of gluten is no reason to panic, nor do you need to call 911. Gluten insensitivity isn't like a peanut allergy that can throw you into anaphylactic shock. If you accidentally have a shot of the wrong soy sauce or piece of pizza crust, learn from your mistakes and keep practicing until the diet becomes a way of life.

# Raspberry Smoothie

**Prep time:** 3 min • **Cook time:** None • **Yield:** 4 servings

| Ingredients | Directions |
|---|---|
| 1 cup frozen raspberries | *1* Place all the ingredients in a blender. |
| 12-ounce can frozen lemonade concentrate | *2* Blend on puree for 20 seconds. |
| 2 cups 1 percent low-fat milk | |
| 1 cup frozen vanilla yogurt | *3* Pour the smoothie into 4 glasses. |

*Per serving:* Calories: 354; Total fat: 4g; Saturated fat: 2g; Cholesterol: 6mg; Sodium: 72mg; Carbohydrates: 77g; Fiber: 2g; Sugar: 64g; Protein: 7g.

*Vary It!* For a thicker smoothie, add a banana.

# Smoked Salmon Scramble

**Prep time:** 10 min • **Cook time:** 10 min • **Yield:** 2 servings

| Ingredients | Directions |
|---|---|
| 1 teaspoon tub margarine | *1* Heat skillet for 20 seconds and add margarine over medium-high heat for about 10 seconds. Add eggs to the skillet and begin to scramble them for 15 to 30 seconds until almost set, stirring occasionally, about 1 to 2 minutes. |
| 4 large eggs or 3 large eggs and 2 egg whites, lightly beaten | |
| 1½ ounces thinly sliced smoked salmon, cut into strips | |
| 1 ounce reduced-fat cream cheese, cut into 4 pieces | *2* Sprinkle in salmon and cream cheese over eggs. Cook until eggs are cooked through, about 1 to 2 minutes, but still moist. Season with fresh ground black pepper and sprinkle with fresh chives. |
| Fresh ground pepper | |
| 1 tablespoon fresh chives, chopped | |

*Per serving:* Calories: 202; Total fat: 15g; Saturated fat: 6g; Cholesterol: 383mg; Sodium: 207mg; Carbohydrate: 2g Fiber: 0g; Sugar: 0g; Protein: 14g.

*Tip:* Use any leftover smoked salmon and cream cheese to make a wonderful smoked salmon dip. Add some plain Greek yogurt or sour cream, fresh dill, and a squeeze of lemon. Blend together for some yummy goodness.

# Egg Burrito

**Prep time:** 10 min • **Cook time:** 5 min • **Yield:** 1 serving

| Ingredients | Directions |
|---|---|
| **10-inch gluten-free tortilla** | *1* Preheat the oven to 350 degrees. |
| **2 strips bacon** | *2* Wrap the tortilla in foil and warm it in the oven for 4 minutes. |
| **1 egg** | |
| **2 tablespoons refried beans** | |
| **2 tablespoons shredded cheddar cheese** | *3* Cook the bacon in a large skillet over medium-low heat until it's crisp. Remove the bacon and drain it on a paper towel. Pour out the bacon grease, but don't wipe out the pan. |
| **1 tablespoon salsa** | |
| | *4* Break the egg into the same skillet and scramble it with a fork as it cooks over medium heat. Cook the egg until it's firm but not dry. |
| | *5* In a small saucepan, warm the beans. |
| | *6* Top the tortilla with the beans, bacon, egg, cheese, and salsa. Roll the tortilla into a burrito. |

*Per serving:* Calories: 468; Total fat: 22g; Saturated fat: 8g; Cholesterol: 248mg; Sodium: 1,158mg; Carbohydrates: 42g; Fiber: 4g; Sugar: 3g; Protein: 24g.

*Tip:* Wrap it in wax paper and you transform the burrito into a to-go breakfast sandwich that you can eat in the car on the way to work or school.

*Note:* One can of refried beans makes 10 servings.

# Having Lunch or Dinner in the Fast Lane

Getting out the door in the morning with a good meal in your tummy is tough enough, but making lunch can be even tougher. If you're away from home, you need to plan in advance and make something portable or bring something to prepare at work or on the road. Even if you're home, chances are you're busy, and the idea of making a healthy, gluten-free meal can be overwhelming. Regardless of how you spend your day, finding time to make a midday meal can be a challenge.

Dinners can be daunting, too. After you've hustled and bustled your way through a busy day, taking on the task of preparing a complex gluten-free meal isn't easy, but they don't have to be complex. Take a look at some of the quick-and-easy dinners we have for you here.

## Syrup the saboteur

High fructose corn syrup (HFCS) may be gluten-free, but it can sabotage a weight-loss program faster than a box of old-fashioned gluten-free glazed donuts. Two main hormones signal hunger and appetite to your brain. *Ghrelin* is produced in the stomach, and increases your appetite, while *leptin* is produced by fat cells and tells your body it's full. HFCS, a sugar "substitute" (it actually is a sugar), inhibits leptin secretion so you don't get the "I'm full" message. It also never shuts off ghrelin, so even if you're stuffed, you're still getting an "I'm hungry" memo from your stomach. Beware of HFCS in foods you may not suspect, like ketchup, salad dressings, and lots of low-fat products.

# Caesar Sandwich

**Prep time:** 4 min • **Cook time:** None • **Yield:** 1 serving

| *Ingredients* | *Directions* |
|---|---|
| 2 slices olive oil bread, toasted | *1* Lay the chicken slices on top of 1 slice of toast, and then fold the lettuce leaf on top. Drizzle the dressing on top of the lettuce. |
| 2 slices deli roasted chicken breast | |
| 1 large romaine lettuce leaf | *2* Lay the egg slices on top of the dressing and then sprinkle them with pepper. Top with the second piece of toast. |
| 1 hard-boiled egg, sliced | |
| 2 teaspoons Caesar salad dressing | |
| Dash pepper | |

*Per serving:* Calories: 717; Total fat: 29g; Saturated fat: 7g; Cholesterol: 254mg; Sodium: 1,168mg; Carbohydrates: 88g; Fiber: 4g; Sugar: 17g; Protein: 25g.

*Tip:* If you don't have Caesar salad dressing, use Italian dressing and add 1 teaspoon of grated Parmesan cheese.

*Vary It!* You can make this with deli chicken, but it's even better when it's made with leftover roasted or grilled chicken.

# Italian Grilled Cheese Sandwich

**Prep time:** 5 min • **Cook time:** 4 min • **Yield:** 4 servings

| *Ingredients* | *Directions* |
|---|---|
| 2 tablespoons olive oil | *1* Brush ¼ tablespoon of the oil on one side of two slices of bread. Place them, oiled side down, in a large skillet. |
| 8 thin slices olive oil bread | |
| ¼ cup prepared pesto | |
| 4 slices mozzarella cheese | *2* Spread 1 tablespoon of the pesto on top of each of the two slices of bread in the skillet. Top each with a slice of mozzarella cheese, and then sprinkle 1 tablespoon of minced onion over the two slices, dividing evenly. |
| 2 tablespoons minced onion | |
| 2 red peppers, roasted and cut in half (or use canned, prepared red roasted peppers) | |
| 4 slices provolone cheese | *3* Lay a pepper half on top of the onion. Top each sandwich with a slice of provolone cheese. Lay a slice of ham on top of the provolone. Spread ½ teaspoon of mustard on two slices of bread and place, mustard-side down, on top of the sandwich. Brush ¼ tablespoon of oil on top of the two assembled sandwiches. |
| 4 slices deli ham | |
| 2 teaspoons brown mustard | |
| | *4* Grill the sandwiches over medium-high heat, 2 minutes per side, or until each side is golden. Press lightly with a spatula during cooking so the cheese melts completely. Repeat Steps 1 through 6 to make remaining two sandwiches. Use a griddle if you want to make all four sandwiches at the same time. |

*Per serving:* Calories: 823; Total fat: 39g; Saturated fat: 13g; Cholesterol: 60mg; Sodium: 1,729mg; Carbohydrates: 91g; Fiber: 5g; Sugar: 17g; Protein: 26g.

# Louisiana Shrimp Foil Pouch

**Prep time:** 10 min • **Cook time:** 12 min • **Yield:** 4 servings

| *Ingredients* | *Directions* |
|---|---|
| 2 tablespoons olive oil | *1* Heat gas grill to high. Cut four sheets of aluminum foil about 12 x 15 inches each. Spritz each square with cooking spray. |
| 2 tablespoons catsup | |
| 2 tablespoons Worcestershire sauce | |
| 2 teaspoons soy sauce | *2* In a medium bowl, combine all the sauce ingredients except the shrimp until well blended. Add in the shrimp. |
| 2 teaspoons dry sherry | |
| 1 teaspoon sugar | *3* Divide the shrimp between the four pieces of aluminum. Bring the edges of the foil together. Double-fold the foil at the top. Crimp the edges of the pouch on one side in a tight seal. Pour ¼ of the liquid into the pouch and crimp the remaining edge. |
| 1 teaspoon hot pepper sauce | |
| 1 pound large shrimp, shelled and deveined | |
| | *4* Repeat with the other three pouches. Place the pouches on the preheated grill, close the grill cover, and cook for 5 minutes. Check to be sure the shrimp are done; the shrimp should have changed colors, now orange, indicating that they're thoroughly cooked. When done, open each pouch slightly to allow steam to escape. |

*Per serving:* Calories: 165; Total fat: 8g; Saturated fat: 1g; Cholesterol: 168mg; Sodium: 550mg; Carbohydrate: 5g; Fiber: 0g; Protein: 19g.

*Tip:* Serve with your favorite cooked brown or dirty rice and cooked greens such as Swiss chard or kale.

# Foil-Pouch Chicken Fajitas

**Prep time:** 15 min • **Cook time:** 15 min • **Yield:** 4 servings

| Ingredients | Directions |
|---|---|
| **1 pound boneless, skinless chicken tenders** | **1** Preheat gas grill to high. |
| **1 medium onion, thinly sliced** | **2** Cut four sheets of heavy duty aluminum foil into 12-x-15-inch pieces. Spray nonstick cooking spray in the center on the foil. Evenly distribute onion, bell peppers, and three chicken tenders in each of the four pieces of foil. |
| **1 green bell pepper, cut into strips** | |
| **¼ cup favorite chunky salsa** | |
| **One 1.4-ounce fajita seasoning mix** | **3** Combine the salsa and fajita seasoning mix. Top each packet of chicken tenders with an even amount of the salsa mixture. Bring the opposite ends of the foil together and fold at the top. Crimp the edges of the pouch on the sides in a tight seal. Doing so steam cooks the chicken and preserves the juices inside the packet. Repeat with all four pouches. |
| **8 gluten-free tortillas** | |
| **4 tablespoons shredded Mexican-blend cheese** | |
| **4 tablespoons chopped tomatoes** | |
| **4 to 8 avocado slices** | **4** Place the pouches on the preheated grill and cook for 12 to 15 minutes or until chicken is done. Carefully open each pouch and allow steam to escape. Serve each pouch with two gluten-free tortillas and toppings. |
| **4 tablespoons sour cream** | |

*Per serving:* Calories: 263; Total fat: 11g; Saturated fat: 5g; Cholesterol: 75mg; Sodium: 893mg; Carbohydrate:14g; Fiber: 2g; Sugar: 0g; Protein: 26g.

*Tip:* Foil pouches can also be roasted in an oven preheated to 425 degrees for 15 to 20 minutes. Foil-pouch cooking keeps your food moist and extra juicy! If available, nonstick foil is also an option instead of using the heavy suty aluminum foil sprayed with cooking spray.

*Note:* In place of chicken tenders, use boneless, skinless chicken breasts cut into even strips.

# Grilled Cajun Orange Roughy

**Prep time:** 5 min • **Cook time:** 8 min • **Yield:** 4 servings

| Ingredients | Directions |
|---|---|
| Nonstick cooking spray | **1** Preheat the broiler. |
| Four 5-ounce orange roughy fillets | **2** Using the cooking spray, grease an 8-x-10-inch baking dish. Rinse the fillets, pat them dry, and lay them in a single layer in the baking dish. |
| 2 tablespoons butter, melted | |
| ¼ teaspoon garlic powder | |
| 2 teaspoons paprika | **3** In a small bowl, stir the butter, garlic powder, paprika, cumin, salt, pepper, cayenne pepper, thyme, oregano, and sugar into a paste. |
| ½ teaspoon cumin | |
| ⅛ teaspoon salt | |
| ¼ teaspoon pepper | **4** Spoon ¼ of the mixture on top of each fillet; spread the topping evenly over each piece of fish. |
| ¼ teaspoon cayenne pepper | |
| ¼ teaspoon thyme | **5** Broil the fillets for 7 to 8 minutes or until the fish is baked through. |
| ½ teaspoon oregano | |
| ⅛ teaspoon sugar | |

**Per serving:** *Calories: 164; Total fat: 7g; Saturated fat: 4g; Cholesterol: 100mg; Sodium: 216mg; Carbohydrates: 1g; Fiber: 1g; Sugar: 0g; Protein: 24g.*

**Tip:** Don't overcook the fillets, or the fish may become tough.

# Grilled Lamb Chops with Spiced Peaches

**Prep time:** 15 min  •  **Cook time:** 20 min  •  **Yield:** 4 servings

| Ingredients | Directions |
|---|---|
| ½ **teaspoon ground cumin** | **1** Preheat grill on high heat. |
| ½ **teaspoon dried oregano** | |
| **1 clove garlic, minced** | **2** Combine cumin, oregano, and minced garlic. Gently rub mixture into the lamb chops and set aside. |
| **8 rib lamb chops, about ¾-inch thick, visible fat trimmed** | |
| **1 pound fresh or frozen peaches, peeled, pitted, and sliced** | **3** In a small bowl, toss peaches with lemon juice, peach preserves, and cardamom. Let stand for at least 10 minutes to allow flavors to blend. |
| ½ **tablespoon lemon juice** | **4** Reduce heat to medium-high. Place lamb chops on preheated grill or grill pan and sear for about 2 minutes. Flip over and cook for another 3 minutes for medium-rare and 3½ minutes for medium. Serve two lamps chops per serving along with the spiced peaches. Garnish with oregano sprigs. |
| **2 tablespoons peach preserves, melted** | |
| ¼ **teaspoon ground cardamom** | |
| **Oregano sprigs** | |

*Per serving:* *Calories: 599; Total fat: 36g; Saturated fat: 16g; Cholesterol: 179mg; Sodium: 144mg; Carbohydrate: 18g Fiber: 2g; Protein: 46g.*

*Tip:* Instead of the frozen peach mixture, you can grill fresh peach halves sprinkled with cardamom to serve with the lamb chops.

*Note:* Use a meat thermometer to check for doneness: 145 degrees for medium rare, 160 degrees for medium well, and 170 degrees for well done.

# Serving up Speedy Salads and Snacks

Appetizers and salads are like jewelry. They're not the centerpiece of the meal (or outfit, as the case may be), but when done right, they make a great impression and bring the entire meal — or outfit — together. Lots of times people forego these "extras" because they can be a hassle to make, but we have some great ideas for simple yet elegant dishes that can show off your centerpiece meal.

Snacks are dangerous territory. Grabbing a bag of junk food loaded with empty calories is a lot easier, but then you suffer the guilt later. Well, you can put the bags away, because we have some delicious snack ideas that you can make in a matter of minutes.

# Spinach Mandarin Salad

**Prep time:** 8 min  •  **Cook time:** 6 min  •  **Yield:** 4 servings

| *Ingredients* | *Directions* |
|---|---|
| ¼ **cup pine nuts** | *1* Preheat the oven to 400 degrees. |
| **Nonstick spray** | |
| **2 tablespoons orange juice** | *2* Place pine nuts in a small skillet that has been sprayed with nonstick spray. On medium-high heat, toast the nuts, stirring frequently, until they're lightly browned. Remove the pan from the stove and cool. |
| **1½ tablespoons balsamic vinegar** | |
| **2 tablespoons olive oil** | |
| ⅛ **teaspoon salt** | *3* In a small bowl, whisk together the orange juice, balsamic vinegar, oil, salt, pepper, honey, and mustard. |
| ⅛ **teaspoon pepper** | |
| **2 teaspoons honey** | |
| ½ **teaspoon brown mustard** | *4* In a large bowl, toss together the spinach and dressing until evenly coated. |
| **4 cups fresh baby spinach leaves** | |
| ¼ **red onion, sliced thin** | *5* Add the onion, oranges, and pine nuts and toss till evenly distributed. |
| **15-ounce can mandarin oranges, drained** | |

**Per serving:** *Calories: 199; Total fat: 13g; Saturated fat: 1g; Cholesterol: 0mg; Sodium: 114mg; Carbohydrates: 19g; Fiber: 2g; Sugar: 17g; Protein: 2g.*

**Tip:** When you toast the pine nuts, watch them carefully. After they start to brown, they can burn quickly.

# Mix-and-Match Salads

**Prep time:** 10 min • **Cook time:** none • **Yield:** 2 to 3 servings

| *Ingredients* | *Directions* |
|---|---|
| **4 cups any combination of salad greens:** romaine, red or green leaf lettuce, baby spinach, mesclun, arugula, radicchio | *1* Choose your favorite salad greens. Add a variety of chopped vegetables and protein and toss with a few additional flavorful ingredients. Toss with dressing or a simple oil and vinegar when ready to serve. |
| **2 cups combination of vegetables:** cucumber, tomatoes, carrots, bell peppers, broccoli florets, celery, marinated artichokes, onions | |
| **6 ounces combination of proteins:** garbanzo beans, black beans, cheese, hard-cooked egg, lean poultry or meat, or seafood | |
| **Flavor add-ins:** olives, capers, toasted nuts, dried fruit | |
| **1 to 2 tablespoons favorite salad dressing** | |

**Per serving:** *Calories: 238; Total fat: 11g; Saturated fat: 2g; Cholesterol :76mg; Sodium: 167mg; Carbohydrate: 9g; Fiber: 4g; Protein: 27g.*

**Tip:** Buy the ready-to-eat dark green salad mixes and chopped vegetables for a real timesaver.

**Note:** Salads are a quick-and-easy way to clean out the fridge of all the week's leftovers. Out of lettuce? No problem! Any combination of vegetables works. They provide a great source of nutrients and fiber. Balance out your meal using protein for increased energy value. Go easy on the dressing; use just enough for flavor!

# Macho Nachos

**Prep time:** 5 min • **Cook time:** 5 min • **Yield:** 10 servings

| Ingredients | Directions |
|---|---|
| 40 gluten-free tortilla chips | *1* Preheat the oven to 400 degrees. |
| 9-ounce can bean dip | *2* Lay the tortilla chips in a single layer on 2 nonstick baking sheets. (You don't need to grease the baking sheets.) |
| 1¼ cups shredded Colby cheese | *3* Spread each chip with bean dip (approximately 1 scant tablespoon per chip). |
| ¼ cup shredded Monterey Jack cheese | *4* Sprinkle the cheese over the chips. |
| 1 cup salsa | *5* Bake the chips at 400 degrees for 7 to 10 minutes, or until the cheese has melted. |
| | *6* Put the salsa in a bowl and serve it as a dip for the nachos. |

*Per serving: Calories: 142; Total fat: 8g; Saturated fat: 0g; Cholesterol: 18mg; Sodium: 441mg; Carbohydrates: 10g; Fiber: 1g; Sugar: 0g; Protein: 6g.*

# Doing Desserts Quickly

Sometimes dessert is the best part of the meal, but what do you do when you don't have time to make anything, even from a box? Fear not . . . you can have your gluten-free cake and eat it, too.

This section features quick-and-easy gluten-free sweet treats that can satisfy your sweet tooth in a matter of minutes.

## Desserts can be guilt-free and gluten-free

You've surely heard the expression: "Life's short — eat dessert first!" That's not bad advice if you realize that dessert doesn't by definition have to be bad for you. Most people picture dessert as a sugary, ooey-gooey concoction loaded with fat and calories. But dessert doesn't have to be decadent, and it can even be good for you.

When gluten-free began to emerge as a popular lifestyle in the early 1990s, manufacturers seemed to all be thinking: "Aha! We can make gluten-free goodies taste good by using gobs of sugar and butter!" And so they did. And yes, things tasted good, but really, *must* people rely on such crutches to make food taste good? I think not.

Using fruits and even sweet veggies is a great way to create nutritious desserts that the entire family will love. Because fruits and veggies aren't packaged, you don't need to worry that they'll contain gluten, so get creative. If you must resort to the tried-and-true "make-it-a-dessert-by-adding-sugar" philosophy, feel free. Fruit dipped in chocolate is tasty and can be turned into an adventure with chocolate waterfalls and fondues. Sliced fruit and sweet veggies like jicama (technically jicama is a root) are great with a little yogurt or powdered sugar on top.

If you have kids, using healthy foods like fruit as dessert is especially important. Kids today have become conditioned to like sweeter and sweeter things (think candy and chocolate), so sweet fruits don't taste as good to them. Referring to fruit and naturally sweet foods as dessert is a great way to send the message that naturally sweet is a yummy treat!

# Nutty Fruit Bark

**Prep time:** 10 min • **Cook time:** 10 min • **Yield:** 60 servings

| Ingredients | Directions |
|---|---|
| **12 ounces bittersweet chocolate, finely chopped** | *1* Place chocolate in a microwave-safe glass bowl and microwave on medium power (50 percent) to avoid scorching. Heat in 30-second to 1-minute intervals just until chocolate is almost melted. Stir until smooth (the chocolate will continue to melt). |
| ½ **cup almonds, toasted and coarsley chopped** | |
| ½ **cup walnuts, toasted and coarsley chopped** | *2* Stir in almonds, walnuts, cherries, blueberries, and cinnamon until completely coated. Spread the mixture over parchment paper or baking mat to ¼-inch thickness. |
| ½ **cup dried cherries** | |
| ½ **cup dried blueberries** | |
| **Dash ground cinnamon** | *3* Refrigerate until chocolate is firm, about 30 minutes. Break the bark into 30 pieces. |

*Per serving:* *Calories: 49; Total fat: 4g; Saturated fat: 1g; Cholesterol: 0mg; Sodium: 0mg; Carbohydrate: 5g; Fiber 1g; Protein: 1g.*

*Tip:* You can store bark in an airtight container in refrigerator for up to a month.

*Tip:* To toast almonds and walnuts, bake in preheated oven at 350 degrees for 5 to 8 minutes or until golden and fragrant. Watch closely to avoid burning the nuts.

*Note:* Estimating the exact amount of time to melt the chocolate is difficult because it depends on your oven's wattage. A rough estimate is approximately 3 minutes at 30-second to 1-minute intervals.

*Note:* Some chocolate bars are gluten-free and others have no gluten ingredients but might be processed near foods that contain gluten. Check manufacturer labels and websites for specifics brands.

# Grilled Bananas Foster Boats

**Prep time:** 10 min  •  **Cook time:** 10 min  •  **Yield:** 4 servings

| Ingredients | Directions |
|---|---|
| 6 small unpeeled bananas | *1* Preheat grill or oven to 350 degrees. |
| 4 tablespoons nuts and dried fruit trail mix | *2* Place each banana on a 12-inch square of heavy-duty aluminum foil; crimp and shape foil around the bananas so they stand upright forming a gondola. Slice each banana lengthwise about ½-inch deep leaving ½-inch uncut at both ends. Gently pull each banana peel open, forming a pocket. The foil crimped around the banana allows it to stand upright. |
| ⅓ cup miniature marshmallows | |
| 2 tablespoons banana liqueur | |
| 1 tablespoon dark rum | |
| ½ teaspoon ground cinnamon | *3* Mix together the banana liqueur, dark rum, and cinnamon. |
| | *4* Fill the banana pockets with trail mix and marshmallows and drizzle banana boats with the rum mixture. Grill or bake for 4 to 5 minutes or until marshmallows are melted and golden. |

*Per serving: Calories: 199; Total fat: 4g; Saturated fat: 1g; Cholesterol: 0mg; Sodium: 25mg; Carbohydrate: 43g; Fiber: 4g; Protein: 3g.*

*Tip:* Some trail mixes contain dates that have been rolled in oat flour. Oat flour can be contaminated with gluten, so carefully read the label or call the manufacturer to be sure.

*Note:* Bananas are one of the healthiest, most affordable, natural power foods. This version of a simple adult dessert is perfect for outdoor entertaining or at the campfire.

*Vary It!* You can omit the dried fruit and nuts or serve this yummy dessert with a scoop of your favorite frozen yogurt or ice cream.

# Caramel Milkshakes

**Prep time:** 3 min • **Cook time:** None • **Yield:** 2 servings

| Ingredients | Directions |
|---|---|
| 3 cups frozen vanilla yogurt | **1** Place all the ingredients in a blender. |
| ¾ cup milk | |
| ¼ teaspoon vanilla | **2** Puree, with the lid on, for 20 seconds, or until smooth. Pour into 2 glasses. |
| 1 teaspoon cinnamon | |
| ¼ cup caramel ice cream topping | |

*Per serving:* Calories: 511; Total fat: 12g; Saturated fat: 8g; Cholesterol: 43mg; Sodium: 311mg; Carbohydrates: 91g; Fiber: 1g; Sugar: 84g; Protein: 11g.

## How I got pushed into the deep end of the gluten-free pool

Here's my story about how I joined the ranks of the gluten-free.

I didn't aspire to do any of this. I was deeply involved in a successful career, and a mommy first and foremost. But today I'm an accidental author, researcher, and support group founder who was pushed into the deep end of the gluten-free pool and realized I needed to learn to swim. Fast.

Until 1991, my family and I ate a fairly typical American diet. Oh, I tried to keep it nutritious (extra cheese on the spaghetti to add protein), and I was aware of the need to limit fat and calories (scratch the extra cheese), but we didn't spend a lot of time worrying about what we ate or the long-term effects food might have on our bodies. We pretty much took eating for granted.

All that changed in an instant when my first child, Tyler, was about 9 months old and developed what seemed to be chronic diarrhea. The pediatrician chalked it up to the antibiotics Ty was taking for ear infections and told me to call if it hadn't cleared up in a few weeks. Three weeks later, I was back in the pediatrician's office. "Yep, he still has diarrhea," the doctor declared with confidence. "Yeah, I know. That's why I'm here," I mumbled with self-restraint worthy of the Nobel Peace Prize. "Give him foods that will plug him up like crackers and bread — and call me if it hasn't cleared up in a few weeks." *Huh?!?* That's the best you can do? My Pampers bill is higher than your paycheck, my hands are raw from washing them every six minutes, and I do eight loads of laundry a day because everything we own is covered in diarrhea, and you want me to "plug him up" and wait another three weeks? I don't *think* so!

I waited. Not patiently (patience isn't my greatest strength), but I waited. What choice did I have? Three weeks later, after another perfunctory examination of Ty's ears, nose, and throat (did I lead you to believe this problem was *above* the

*(continued)*

*(continued)*

waist, Doctor?!?), he made that "mmhhhmmm" noise that doctors make when they figure out the problem. Yay! We were finally going to get some answers! "Yep. He still has diarrhea." All those years of medical school had really paid off. "Don't worry about it. He's not dehydrated, and he's in the 75th percentile for height and weight. It's nothing to be concerned about." Gee, could the fact that I practically infuse Ty with liquids have anything to do with the fact that he's not dehydrated? And does the fact that he started off in the 99th percentile and has *dropped* to the75 th mean anything? Apparently not. I was instructed not to bring him back for diarrhea, because there was nothing to be concerned about. If I was going to insist on bringing him back, I'd be fired from that pediatric office. I guess they meant it.

Doctor number two agreed with doctor number one. After a quick look in Ty's ears, nose, and throat, he declared that we had a healthy baby boy. "But what about the diarrhea?" I eeked. "Really, it's nothing to worry about. He's a healthy height and weight, he's not dehydrated, and he looks fine to me," he chirped as he raced to his next four-minute appointment. Oh, good. I'm glad he *looks* fine to you. I considered offering to give Doctor Do-Nothing a close *look* at the 22 diarrhea diapers a day that I was changing, but somehow managed to control myself.

In desperation, we changed doctors again, and — long story short — a quick look in the ears, nose, and throat turned up — you guessed it — nothing. By this time, Tyler's belly had grown hugely distended, his arms and legs were wasted to skinny little limbs, his hiney had disappeared completely, and his personality had changed. He had transformed from a lively, energetic toddler to a listless, irritable, clingy, and quiet little boy. It had been nearly a year since the diarrhea first started, and we figured we were just neurotic first-time parents with a mellow kid who pooped a lot.

Eventually, we ended up in the hands of doctor number four. By this time, "realizing" there was nothing wrong with Tyler, I thought nothing of dragging a lifeless baby with a Biafra belly into the pediatrician's office for a routine visit. After looking in Tyler's ears, nose, and throat, he laid Tyler down on his back and thumped on his belly like you might thump a honeydew melon to see if it's ripe. "My goodness," he said with that I'm-alarmed-but-I'm-a-doctor-and-don't-want-to-freak-you-out-so-I'll- talk-in-my-pediatrician—baby-talk-voice-that-will-surely-calm-you tone, "What's going on with his belly? It's very distended." I couldn't answer through the tears of relief.

After testing for cystic fibrosis, blood diseases, and cancer, we finally got the bittersweet diagnosis. "Your son has celiac disease." *Huh*? Is that anything like the flu? Surely a few weeks of antibiotics will wipe it out. "He'll need to be on a gluten-free diet for the rest of his life."

I don't have room here to give the details of the rest of the story, but you can read it in my other books or on my websites. Suffice it to say that the words "for the rest of his life" had a huge impact, and we realized it was time to step up to the plate and do some research and lifestyle and attitude adjustments to help ourselves — and others.

When we were told that Tyler would have to lead a gluten-free lifestyle, we had come to a fork in the road. At first, we were devastated, confused, frustrated, and grief-stricken. But we knew there was another path we could choose — a path that would have a more positive effect on Tyler's life. As we learned to live with the diet and its ramifications, we worked hard to find a way to turn the adversity into a positive force in our lives. More than two decades later, I realize that what we once interpreted as misfortune has actually been a huge blessing in our lives — and most importantly, Tyler agrees.

# Chapter 11

# Breakfast: Don't Leave Home Without It

*I*f you eat dinner at 6 p.m. and wake up at 7 a.m., you'll have fasted for more than 13 hours before you sit down to breakfast. At that point, your body's blood sugar levels are screaming for nourishment. If you're weight conscious, eating breakfast jump-starts your metabolism so it works harder and more efficiently all day. Simply put, never skip breakfast.

Forget the excuse, "I don't have time for breakfast." There are foods that you can take in the car and eat as you commute to work. At the very least, you can grab a piece of fruit, a container of gluten-free yogurt, and a gluten-free health bar. Some foods can be prepared the night before so that, in the morning, you can put them in the oven while you shower, and they're ready by the time you're dressed. Now, did that cover all the "I don't have time for breakfast" excuses? Besides, after making the recipes in this chapter, you'll wake up each morning anticipating your first meal of the day.

TIP

Many of the recipes in this chapter call for a gluten-free flour mixture. See Chapter 9 for our no-fail recipe.

# *Starting the Day the Gluten-Free Way*

Most people climb out of bed, shuffle into the kitchen, and pop some bread into the toaster or pour a bowl of cereal — you can too. You just have to make sure your bread and cereal are gluten-free.

 If you have non-celiacs in the house, you need to be certain that your toast is not contaminated by their toast crumbs. The easiest way to do this is to have two toasters or to use Toast-It! Bags. With these bags, you insert the bread into the bag, and then insert the bag into the toaster. The bag allows heat to penetrate so the bread will toast, but no crumbs or essence of crumbs can cling to the bread. These bags are great to take with you when you're traveling so you can have toast on the road without fear of cross-contamination.

But you are about to realize that breakfast is so much more than mere bread and cereal. However, if you do like cereal to start your day, the following recipe is a good gluten-free option.

# Cinnamon Breakfast Cereal

**Prep time:** 4 min • **Cook time:** 5 min • **Yield:** 2 servings

| *Ingredients* | *Directions* |
|---|---|
| **2 cups cooked brown rice** | **1** Place all the ingredients in the top of a double boiler over boiling water, stirring frequently, for about 5 minutes. |
| **1 cup milk** | |
| **2 tablespoons brown sugar** | |
| **⅛ teaspoon cinnamon** | **2** When the cereal is thoroughly warmed, spoon it into 2 serving bowls. |
| **¾ teaspoon vanilla** | |
| **2 tablespoons maple syrup** | |
| **1 tablespoon butter** | |
| **2 tablespoons raisins** | |
| **⅓ cup toasted pecan pieces** | |

*Per serving:* Calories: 605; Total fat: 25g; Saturated fat: 7g; Cholesterol: 27mg; Sodium: 108mg; Carbohydrates: 88g; Fiber: 6g; Sugar: 39g; Protein: 11g.

*Tip:* To speed things up in the morning, cook the rice the night before or use leftover dinner rice.

*Note:* If you prefer a more liquid cereal, add more warmed milk.

# Adding Sizzle to Your Morning

A little whipping can make an egg amazing. We like to think of egg preparations in terms of the height of the finished product. Here's what we mean:

- ✔ Fried eggs aren't beaten at all; scrambled eggs are just stirred up. When cooked, neither rises much at all.
- ✔ Omelets, whose eggs are given a quick beating, rise a little bit.
- ✔ Frittatas have even more lift.
- ✔ One step above the frittata is the quiche.
- ✔ And the ultimate elevation results in a soufflé.

Take that same egg, scramble it, lay it in a gluten-free flour or corn tortilla, spoon on your choice of toppings, and you've just created a breakfast wrap. Kids love wraps because they're fun to eat and a welcome reprieve from the usual bowl of gluten-free cereal.

## Eggs: Healthier than they're cracked up to be

The egg has been a victim of a lot of criticism in the past couple of decades. Doctors told us eggs are high in cholesterol and, therefore, bad for our hearts. Much of this myth has been dispelled in the past few years. Scientists of yore erred a bit in their initial appraisal of the egg.

Without digressing into a lengthy lecture in chemistry and science, suffice it to say that there are two kinds of cholesterol, one good (HDL) and one bad (LDL). The LDL is the one that sticks to our artery walls and causes all kinds of internal clogging.

Here is the irony: Scientists are now saying that there is *dietary cholesterol* and *blood cholesterol*. Eating a lot of *dietary* cholesterol doesn't increase *blood* cholesterol. According to recent studies, a person who consumes two eggs every day and maintains a low-fat diet doesn't show any increase in blood cholesterol levels. What does raise blood cholesterol is saturated fats. Eggs contain mostly polyunsaturated fat, which can actually lower blood cholesterol.

The risk of being contaminated with harmful bacteria from eggs is extremely low. It's estimated that only 0.005 percent (1 in 20,000) of eggs may be contaminated with salmonella bacteria, but even with a risk that is this low, you should cook eggs to the proper doneness to ensure safety. Cooking an egg to a temperature of 160 degrees kills salmonella.

*Warning:* Never use eggs that are cracked or leaking or stuck to the bottom of the carton. Even if you can't see a crack, an egg that is stuck to the carton, even slightly, may indicate that it has leaked and shouldn't be used.

If you have a recipe that calls for raw eggs, you don't have to throw the recipe out. Consider using gluten-free egg substitutes instead, such as gluten-free refrigerated egg white substitutes or meringue powder. Or you can use pasteurized eggs. They cost a little more, but the risk of salmonella is eliminated.

# Farmer's Skillet Eggs

**Prep time:** 8 min • **Cook time:** 8 min • **Yield:** 4 servings

| *Ingredients* | *Directions* |
|---|---|
| ½ cup sliced mushrooms | *1* Preheat the broiler. Wrap the handle of a 10-inch skillet with foil. |
| 1 green onion, sliced | |
| 2 teaspoons butter | *2* In the skillet, sauté the mushrooms and onions in the butter and oil over medium-high heat, stirring frequently, until the vegetables are tender but not browned. |
| 1 teaspoon olive oil | |
| ½ small zucchini, finely chopped (about ⅓ cup) | |
| 3 slices deli ham (sliced, not shaved), cut into ¼-inch cubes | *3* Stir in the zucchini; cook the vegetables 2 to 3 minutes until the zucchini is tender. |
| 4 large eggs | *4* Stir in the ham. |
| ⅛ teaspoon thyme | |
| ¼ teaspoon dried dill | *5* In a medium bowl, whisk the eggs until the whites and yolk are blended but not foamy. Stir in the thyme, dill, salt, and pepper. Stir in the cheese. |
| ⅛ teaspoon salt | |
| ¼ teaspoon pepper | |
| ¼ cup (1 ounce) shredded Swiss cheese | *6* Pour the egg mixture over the ham and vegetables. Cook over medium-low heat, without stirring, until the mixture begins to set on the bottom and around the edges. As the eggs set, run a rubber spatula around the edge of the skillet, lifting the egg mixture to allow the uncooked portion to flow underneath. Continue doing this until the eggs are almost set. |
| | *7* Set the skillet under the broiler and broil for 2 minutes, or until the eggs are just set. |
| | *8* To serve, cut the omelet in wedges. |

**Per serving:** *Calories: 163; Total fat: 12g; Saturated fat: 5g; Cholesterol: 236mg; Sodium: 439mg; Carbohydrates: 2g; Fiber: 0g; Sugar: 1g; Protein: 12g.*

**Note:** Children often won't eat zucchini — but they won't even taste it in this gorgeous omelet.

# Mixed-Up Omelet

**Prep time:** 10 min  •  **Cook time:** 20 min  •  **Yield:** 4–6 servings

| *Ingredients* | *Directions* |
|---|---|
| 1 tablespoon olive oil | *1* In a 10-inch nonstick skillet, heat olive oil over medium heat. Add potatoes and sauté for 10 to 15 minutes. Add garlic, peppers, and onion. Sauté until vegetables are soft and onion is translucent. Add the herbs, pepper, and salt. |
| 1 large sweet potato, peeled and cut into ½-inch cubes | |
| 2 large garlic cloves, minced | |
| ½ green bell pepper, cored, seeded, and diced | *2* In a medium-size bowl, lightly beat the eggs. Add eggs to the cooked vegetable mixture in the skillet. Stir to combine. |
| ½ red bell pepper, cored, seeded, and diced | |
| 1 small onion, peeled and diced | *3* As the egg mixture begins to set, lift the edges with a silicon or plastic spatula so that the uncooked eggs can flow underneath until the eggs are completely cooked. Cover with a lid and turn the heat on low until the omelet is set, 3 to 5 minutes. |
| 1 teaspoon dried Italian herbs | |
| Fresh ground pepper | |
| ½ teaspoon salt | |
| 6 eggs | |
| 1 tablespoon grated Pecorino or Parmesan cheese | *4* To serve, cut in wedges and sprinkle with cheese. |

**Per serving:** *Calories: 209; Total fat: 11g; Saturated fat: 3g; Cholesterol: 280mg; Sodium: 414mg; Carbohydrates: 16g; Fiber: 2g; Sugar: 0g; Protein: 11g.*

**Note:** Similar to a frittata, this mixed-up omelet can be served warm or at room temperature for breakfast, lunch, or dinner. Refer to Figure 11-1 for how to mince to garlic.

**Vary It!** You can substitute russet potatoes for sweet potatoes and any other favorite vegetables for the peppers.

MINCING GARLIC

HEY! Crush the garlic clove under the blade of a knife.

Pull away the paper-like skin.

Put the clove on the cutting board. Make slices through the clove in one direction, then slice crosswise, to mince!

**Figure 11-1:**
How to mince garlic.

*Illustrations by Elizabeth Kurtzman*

# Pepperoni Frittata

**Prep time:** 10 min • **Cook time:** 5 min • **Yield:** 6 servings

| Ingredients | Directions |
|---|---|
| **1 tablespoon olive oil** | *1* Preheat the broiler. Wrap the handle of a 10-inch nonstick skillet with foil. |
| **1½ cups thinly sliced broccoli florets** | |
| **¼ cup sliced green onion** | *2* Heat the oil in the skillet. Add the broccoli, green onion, salt, pepper, Italian seasoning, thyme, dill, and parsley. Cook the vegetables and seasonings over medium-high heat, stirring, until the broccoli florets are tender-crisp. Sprinkle pepperoni over broccoli. |
| **¼ teaspoon salt** | |
| **¼ teaspoon pepper** | |
| **½ teaspoon dried Italian seasoning** | |
| **¼ teaspoon dried thyme** | *3* In a small bowl, whisk together the eggs, cornstarch, and milk until they're very light. Pour the mixture over the vegetables. |
| **¼ teaspoon dried dill** | |
| **1 tablespoon snipped fresh parsley** | *4* As the eggs begin to set, run a rubber spatula around the edge of the skillet, lifting the egg mixture to allow the uncooked portions to flow underneath. Continue cooking and lifting the edges until the eggs are nearly set. (The top surface will still be moist.) |
| **6 eggs** | |
| **3 tablespoons cornstarch** | |
| **1½ tablespoons milk** | *5* Sprinkle the top of the frittata with cheese. |
| **10 slices pizza pepperoni, chopped** | *6* Place the skillet under the broiler and broil the frittata for 1 to 2 minutes until the top is set and the cheese has melted. Cut the frittata into wedges to serve. |
| **¾ cup shredded Swiss cheese** | |

*Per serving: Calories: 197; Total fat: 13g; Saturated fat: 5g; Cholesterol: 229mg; Sodium: 261mg; Carbohydrates: 10g; Fiber: 1g; Sugar: 1g; Protein: 12g.*

*Vary It!* Use cooked, crumbled sausage in place of the pepperoni. Instead of the broccoli, try asparagus tips. Substitute cheddar or mozzarella cheese for the Swiss cheese.

# Crab Quiche

**Prep time:** 10 min • **Cook time:** 20 min • **Yield:** 6 servings

| Ingredients | Directions |
|---|---|
| Nonstick cooking spray | *1* Preheat the oven to 375 degrees. Spray a 9-inch pie plate with cooking spray. |
| 3 eggs | |
| 2 green onions, chopped | *2* In a large bowl, whisk together the eggs, green onions, yogurt, cornstarch, basil, dill, parsley, salt, and pepper until they're thoroughly blended. |
| ¼ cup plain low-fat yogurt | |
| 2 teaspoons cornstarch | |
| ¼ teaspoon dried basil | *3* Stir in the broccoli, crabmeat, and Romano and Swiss cheeses. |
| ½ teaspoon dried dill | |
| 2 tablespoons fresh parsley, minced | *4* Spread the mixture evenly in the prepared pie plate. |
| ⅛ teaspoon salt | |
| ⅛ teaspoon pepper | *5* Lay the tomato slices neatly across the top of the quiche and then sprinkle them with breadcrumbs. |
| ¾ cup (½ of a 10-ounce box) chopped broccoli, thawed | |
| 4.25-ounce can flaked crabmeat, drained | *6* Bake the quiche, uncovered, at 375 degrees for 20 minutes, or until a knife inserted in the center comes out clean. Let the quiche stand for 5 minutes before cutting. |
| 2 tablespoons grated Romano cheese | |
| ¼ cup (1 ounce) shredded Swiss cheese | |
| 2 plum tomatoes, sliced thin | |
| ¼ cup gluten-free bread crumbs | |

*Per serving:* Calories: 123; Total fat: 6g; Saturated fat: 3g; Cholesterol: 133mg; Sodium: 299mg; Carbohydrates: 7g; Fiber: 1g; Sugar: 2g; Protein: 12g.

*Note:* You can make a gluten-free pie crust for this quiche, but it isn't needed.

*Vary It!* Use a 6-ounce can of salmon in place of the crabmeat with equally excellent results.

# Curried Chard with "Poached" Egg

**Prep time:** 10 min • **Cook time:** 10 min • **Yield:** 4 servings

| *Ingredients* | *Directions* |
|---|---|
| **2 large bunches fresh swiss chard, rinsed** | *1* Remove stems from chard and chop into ½-inch pieces. Layer the chard leaves in a stack and chop into strips. |
| **1 tablespoon olive oil** | |
| **1 large garlic clove, minced** | *2* In a 10-inch nonstick skillet, heat olive oil over medium heat. Add garlic, cumin, ginger, mustard seeds, pepper, and cardamon, and sauté for 1 minute. Add chard stems and sauté until tender, stirring occasionally. Add chard leaves and continue to sauté until tender. |
| **½ teaspoon cumin** | |
| **½ teaspoon ground ginger** | |
| **½ teaspoon yellow mustard seeds** | |
| **⅛ teaspoon fresh black pepper** | *3* Use a large spoon to make four indentations in the cooked chard. Crack open one egg into each indention. Sprinkle with fresh ground pepper. Place a lid over the mixture allow the steam to cook eggs to soft stage, approximately 5 minutes, until egg white solidifies from transparency to opaque. |
| **⅛ teaspoon cardamom** | |
| **4 eggs** | |
| | *4* Divide the contents of the skillet into four servings and serve immediately. |

*Per serving:* Calories: 141, Total fat: 9g, Saturated fat: 2g; Cholesterol: 186mg; Sodium: 341mg; Carbohydrates: 8g; Fiber: 4g; Sugar: 0g; Protein: 9g.

*Tip:* Wash chard leaves and stems before using to remove dirt and sand clinging to them.

*Note:* Swiss chard comes in a few varieties and is a source of many different antioxidants and phytonutrients. It's low in calories, high in fiber — some say it's a vegetable with a PhD!

# Maple Soufflé

**Prep time:** 10 min • **Cook time:** 40 min • **Yield:** 4 servings

| Ingredients | Directions |
|---|---|
| 6 large eggs, separated | *1* Preheat the oven to 350 degrees. |
| 6 tablespoons maple syrup | *2* In a small mixing bowl, use the mixer to whip the egg whites on high speed until soft peaks form. Set the bowl aside. |
| ¼ teaspoon cinnamon | |
| ⅛ teaspoon salt | |
| ¼ cup small-curd cottage cheese | *3* In a large mixing bowl, use the mixer to whip the egg yolks about 3 minutes until they're thick. Whip in the maple syrup, cinnamon, salt, and cottage cheese until blended. |
| 2 tablespoons butter, melted | |
| ⅓ cup sliced almonds | *4* Fold the egg whites into the egg yolk mixture. |
| | *5* Brush the melted butter on the bottom and sides of a 9-x-1½-inch round straight-sided soufflé dish. Pour the egg mixture into the prepared pan. Sprinkle the top with almonds. |
| | *6* Bake for 40 minutes at 350 degrees, or until the top is puffed and lightly browned. |
| | *7* Cut into wedges to serve. |

*Per serving: Calories: 240; Total fat: 13g; Saturated fat: 5g; Cholesterol: 60mg; Sodium: 123mg; Carbohydrates: 16g; Fiber: 1g; Sugar: 13g; Protein: 7g.*

**Tip:** Drizzle a little maple syrup over the top of each piece for a perfect presentation.

# Breakfast Enchilada

**Prep time:** 40 min plus refrigeration time • **Cook time:** 40 min • **Yield:** 2 servings

| Ingredients | Directions |
|---|---|
| ½ cup finely minced cooked ham | *1* In a medium skillet, sauté the ham, green onions, and green pepper in the oil over medium heat, stirring occasionally, until the vegetables are tender, about 10 minutes. |
| 2 sliced green onions | |
| ⅓ cup finely chopped green pepper | *2* Lay out the tortillas. Spoon the ham mixture down the center of each tortilla, dividing the mixture evenly. Sprinkle the cheese on top of the ham mixture. |
| 1 tablespoon olive oil | |
| Two 8-inch tortillas | |
| 6 tablespoons shredded cheddar cheese | *3* Roll up the tortillas and place them in a greased 9-x-6-inch baking dish. |
| 3 eggs | *4* In a medium bowl, whisk the eggs until they're frothy. Add the half-and-half and whisk until the ingredients are blended. |
| ⅓ cup half-and-half | |
| 2 teaspoons gluten-free flour mixture | *5* Add the flour, garlic powder, and hot pepper sauce to the eggs and mix well. |
| ⅛ teaspoon garlic powder | |
| 3 drops hot pepper sauce | *6* Pour the egg mixture over the tortillas. Cover the pan with plastic wrap and chill for at least 1 hour. |
| Salsa | |
| Sour cream | *7* Remove the baking dish from the refrigerator 30 minutes before baking. |
| | *8* Preheat the oven to 350 degrees. |
| | *9* Bake the enchiladas, uncovered, at 350 degrees for 40 minutes, or until the eggs are set and the top is very lightly browned. Serve the enchiladas with salsa and sour cream. |

*Per serving:* Calories: 514; Total fat: 31g; Saturated fat: 12g; Cholesterol: 372mg; Sodium: 979mg; Carbohydrates: 30.7g; Fiber: 3g; Sugar: 32g; Protein: 3g.

*Tip:* For ultimate enjoyment, top the enchiladas with salsa and sour cream.

# Rise and Shine! Breads and Bagels

Ah, bread. Bread is probably the most difficult item to convert success-fully to gluten-free. It's challenging but conquerable! The sweet breads and those that depend on baking soda and baking powder for leavening aren't the problem. They taste every bit as good as their wheat counterparts. The yeast breads, however, get us exasperated at times. Fortunately, you can play tricks with the dough to achieve a delicious loaf of bread.

In Chapter 9, we emphasize that only one gluten-free flour mixture is used throughout this book to make it easier for the baker. You may notice that the bread recipes that follow use the gluten-free flour mixture and then call for additional flours to be used. Here's the reason: Adding cornstarch and/or sor-ghum flour changes the consistency of the bread for the better. Occasionally coconut flour is used for flavor. You can use just the gluten-free flour mix-ture, but your breads won't turn out as well. Light flaxseed meal is also added frequently. Flax not only adds fiber to the bread, but it helps to activate the yeast so your bread is lighter. The light flaxseed meal has virtually no taste, so it doesn't affect the taste of the bread.

## Choosing and prepping yeast

Quick-rising yeast is very effective in some instances, but active dry yeast tends to work better with the alternative flours. Sometimes people *proof* yeast (let it rise) in warm water before adding it to other ingredients to make sure it will work, but most times you can simply mix it in with the dry ingredients.

It's vital when working with yeast that the water (or other liquid) temperature be between 110 to 120 degrees. If the liquid is cooler than that, it may not activate the yeast. If the liquid is warmer than that, it may kill the yeast. When running warm water on your wrist, 115 degrees feels comfortably warm but not hot.

Make sure that all the ingredients are at room temperature before beginning. Adding cold eggs or other cold liquid may keep the yeast from fermenting.

## Working the dough: You don't need Popeye arms

Kneading is an important step in making bread, but not with gluten-free breads. The process of turning the dough on a board activates the gluten in wheat so the bread will rise. Because wheat gluten is absent in the alternative flours, kneading is only done long enough to form a smooth ball from the dough.

However, many gluten-free bread doughs are more like the consistency of cake batter, so they usually need no kneading at all.

Instead of depending on wheat gluten to help the bread rise, you add additional ingredients (something acidic like vinegar) to trick the dough into rising. If you find large holes in the baked loaf of bread, you have added too much *leavening*.

In regular bread preparation, you let the bread rise, punch it down, and then let it rise again. No can-do with gluten-free dough. Because the alternative flours are heavier than wheat flour, gluten-free bread dough only rises once, so after mixing the dough, place it in the container in which you intend to bake it and let it rise.

As bread rises, it shouldn't be exposed to drafts. A trick that works well is to heat your oven to 200 degrees. When it reaches that temperature, turn off the oven and wait 5 minutes, and then place your bread pans in the oven to rise and close the oven door. Usually your dough will only need to rise between 30 to 45 minutes with this method, depending on the kind of yeast used and the size of the loaf.

## Creating the crust

You can get the desired type of crust on your bread by doing one of the following:

✔ For a **shiny crust,** warm 1 tablespoon of sugar with 5 tablespoons of milk just to a simmer, and then brush the liquid on the hot loaves as soon as they come out of the oven.

✔ For a **soft crust,** brush melted butter on the hot, baked loaves of bread, and then cover them with a clean towel to retain the heat.

✔ If you want a **thin, light crust,** place a pan of hot water on the bottom rack of your oven to create moist heat as your bread bakes.

✔ For a **medium crust,** brush milk over the loaves before placing them in the oven, and then brush them again with milk when the bread is about halfway through baking.

✔ **Crunchy crusts** are also possible. Whip an egg white with 1 tablespoon of water until it's frothy, and then brush this on top of the loaves before baking.

✔ Finally, if you like a **hard crust** on your bread, mix together ½ cup of water with 1 teaspoon of salt and brush it on the loaves before placing them in the oven, and then again about halfway through the baking time.

# Troubleshooting breads

It may take several attempts at bread making to get it right, so don't get discouraged if your first try isn't perfect. Here are a few troubleshooting points to keep in mind:

- ✔ If your baked loaf of bread isn't fully cooked inside, the easiest remedy is to bake the dough in two smaller pans next time. If your bread is still mushy inside, often the cause may be due to the oven temperature. Gluten-free products frequently need to be baked at a lower temperature for a longer period of time. If you lower the oven temperature by 25 degrees, that may solve the problem. If the loaf starts to get too dark, cover it with foil halfway through baking. And don't use dark or Teflon-coated baking pans. They may cause the bottom of the bread to burn before the inside is completely baked.

- ✔ Periodically you'll bake a loaf of bread that may suffer from the crumbles. It looks pretty and smells divine, but when you go to cut it, it falls apart. First, do *not* throw out the crumbs. Dry them out and add seasonings to make bread crumbs. The cause of the crumbles may be that the dough was too dry. Next time, slightly reduce the amount of flour used. Add a teaspoon of unflavored gelatin to the dry ingredients to help bind the bread (in addition to the xanthan gum called for in a recipe). Before even trying to cut the loaf, refrigerate it and then slice it with a serrated knife while it's cold.

- ✔ Finally, we address the taste of the bread. Without some precautions, gluten-free bread can easily taste like cardboard. Fortunately, you can add all sorts of things to the dough to avoid this from happening. Substitute some of the water with a liquid that has flavor, like cold brewed coffee, honey, maple syrup, molasses, or fruit juice (pineapple, lemon, orange, or apple). Add extra flavoring (more vanilla or almond flavoring, cinnamon, Italian seasoning, Parmesan, or cheddar cheese). You can add toasted seeds (sesame, poppy, caraway, or sunflower) as well as toasted nuts of all kinds. Toasted coconut or mini chocolate chips are also optional stir-ins, as are minced dried fruits. Try using dark brown sugar in place of granulated sugar. And finally, think about substituting a portion of the gluten-free flour mixture with a flour that has more flavor, such as cornmeal, almond flour, coconut flour, or sweet potato flour.

We've made these adjustments to the recipes that follow. When you convert a wheat bread recipe, experiment several times with the options above until you get a loaf of bread that rises, tastes fantastic, has the ideal crust, and doesn't crumble. You can do it!

# Breakfast Biscuit Bread

**Prep time:** 15 min plus rising time • **Cook time:** 35 min • **Yield:** 1 loaf (12 slices)

| Ingredients | Directions |
| --- | --- |
| Nonstick cooking spray | **1** Preheat the oven to 200 degrees. When the oven reaches that temperature, turn it off. Spray a 4-x-8-inch baking pan with cooking spray. |
| ¼ cup cornstarch | |
| ¼ cup sorghum flour | **2** Place the cornstarch, sorghum flour, gluten-free flour mixture, flaxseed meal, salt, cinnamon, sugar, and yeast in a medium mixing bowl. With a whisk, stir the ingredients to blend thoroughly. |
| ½ cup plus 2 tablespoons gluten-free flour mixture | |
| 1 tablespoon light flaxseed meal | **3** With a rubber spatula, stir in the vinegar, honey, melted butter, egg, egg whites, and buttermilk. |
| ½ teaspoon salt | **4** Stir in the warm water last. |
| ¾ teaspoon cinnamon | **5** Turn on the mixer and slowly increase the speed to high. Beat the batter for 3 minutes. (It will be more of a batter than a dough consistency.) |
| 2½ tablespoons granulated sugar | |
| ¾ teaspoon active dry yeast | **6** Spoon the batter into the prepared baking pan. |
| ½ teaspoon cider vinegar | **7** Cover the pan with wax paper that has been sprayed with cooking spray. Place the pan in the oven to rise for 40 minutes. |
| 1 tablespoon honey | |
| 4 teaspoons melted butter, cooled | **8** Remove the pan from the oven and preheat the oven to 350 degrees. When the oven reaches that temperature, remove the wax paper from the bread. |
| 1 egg, at room temperature | |
| 2 egg whites, at room temperature | **9** Bake the bread at 350 degrees for 35 to 40 minutes, or until baked through. |
| 2 tablespoons buttermilk, at room temperature | **10** Let the bread set for 5 minutes. Then remove the bread from the pan and allow it to cool on a wire rack. |
| ¼ cup warm water (110 degrees) | |

*Per slice:* Calories: 93; Total fat: 2g; Saturated fat: 1g; Cholesterol: 21mg; Sodium: 125mg; Carbohydrates: 17g; Fiber: 1g; Sugar: 4g; Protein: 2g.

# French Baguettes

**Prep time:** 15 min plus rising time • **Cook time:** 40 min • **Yield:** 2 baguettes (10 slices per loaf)

| Ingredients | Directions |
|---|---|
| ¾ cup cornstarch | **1** Preheat the oven to 200 degrees. When the oven reaches that temperature, turn it off. |
| ¼ cup sorghum flour | |
| 1⅓ cups gluten-free flour mixture | **2** Place the cornstarch, sorghum flour, gluten-free flour mixture, flaxseed meal, salt, garlic powder, onion flakes, sugar, and yeast in a large mixing bowl. Blend the ingredients together with a whisk. |
| 2 tablespoons light flaxseed meal | |
| 1 teaspoon salt | **3** Stir in the vinegar, honey, oil, egg, and egg whites. |
| ½ teaspoon garlic powder | |
| 1 teaspoon dried onion flakes | **4** Stir in the warm water last. |
| 2 tablespoons granulated sugar | **5** Turn on the mixer and slowly increase the speed to high. Beat the ingredients for 4 minutes. |
| 1½ teaspoons active dry yeast | |
| 1 teaspoon cider vinegar | **6** Spray the cooking spray on a large baking sheet. |
| 1 tablespoon honey | |
| 2½ tablespoons olive oil | **7** Divide the dough in half. Place half of the dough on one side of the baking sheet. The dough will be very sticky. |
| 1 egg, at room temperature | |
| 2 egg whites, at room temperature | **8** With wet hands, form the dough into a long, thin loaf approximately 11 inches long and 2½ inches wide. |
| ¾ cup warm water (110 degrees) | |
| Nonstick cooking spray | **9** Repeat Step 8 with the remaining dough, placing it on the other side of the baking sheet. |

**10** Cover the loaves with a sheet of wax paper that has been sprayed with cooking spray.

**11** Place the baking sheet in the oven and let the dough rise for 40 minutes.

**12** Remove the baking sheet from the oven. Preheat the oven to 350 degrees.

**13** If you want a crisp crust, stir ½ teaspoon of salt into ¼ cup of water and brush it on top of the loaves. For a hard crust, brush the loaves again with this mixture halfway through baking.

**14** Bake the loaves at 350 degrees for 40 minutes, or until golden and baked through.

*Per slice:* Calories: 94; Total fat: 2g; Saturated fat: 0g; Cholesterol: 11mg; Sodium: 126mg; Carbohydrates: 17g; Fiber: 1g; Sugar: 2g; Protein: 2g.

# Flatbread Wrap

**Prep time:** 15 min • **Cook time:** 15 min • **Yield:** 4 wraps

| *Ingredients* | *Directions* |
|---|---|
| 1 cup plus 2 tablespoons gluten-free flour mixture | *1* In a medium bowl, whisk together 1 cup of the flour mixture, the baking powder, salt, sugar, Italian seasoning, and garlic powder. |
| ½ teaspoon baking powder | |
| ½ (heaping) teaspoon salt | *2* In a small bowl, dissolve the chicken bouillon in the warm water. |
| ½ teaspoon granulated sugar | |
| ½ teaspoon Italian seasoning | *3* With a rubber spatula, blend the water mixture into the flour mixture until a dough forms. |
| ¼ teaspoon garlic powder | |
| ½ teaspoon chicken bouillon granules | *4* Divide the dough into four sections. Roll each section into a ball. |
| ¼ cup warm water (110 degrees) | *5* Sprinkle a sheet of plastic wrap with ¼ teaspoon of the remaining flour mixture, place one of the balls of dough on the plastic wrap, and cover it with a second sheet of plastic wrap. Using a rolling pin, roll the ball into a flat, 7-inch round about ⅛ inch thick. Repeat with the remaining balls of dough. |
| Nonstick cooking spray | |
| | *6* Heat an 8-inch skillet over medium heat and spray it very lightly with the cooking spray. |
| | *7* Place one of the circles of dough in the pan and cook, turning once, for about 3 minutes total, or until it just begins to brown on each side. (If you overcook these, they won't be pliable.) Repeat with the remaining circles of dough. |

*Per serving:* Calories: 145; Total fat: 0g; Saturated fat: 0g; Cholesterol: 0mg; Sodium: 395mg; Carbohydrates: 33g; Fiber: 2g; Sugar: 1g; Protein: 1g.

*Tip:* Make the wraps ahead and freeze them between sheets of wax paper. To thaw and reheat, place the wraps between sheets of damp paper towels and microwave them for a few moments.

*Note:* Fold the wrap in half to create a gyro, or fill and roll for a traditional wrap.

# Zucchini Bread

**Prep time:** 20 min • **Cook time:** 55 min • **Yield:** 1 loaf (10 slices)

| Ingredients | Directions |
|---|---|
| **Nonstick cooking spray** | *1* Preheat the oven to 325 degrees. Spray an 8-x-4-inch baking pan with cooking spray. |
| **2 eggs** | |
| **1 cup granulated sugar** | *2* In a medium mixing bowl, use the mixer to whip together the eggs, sugar, zucchini, oil, vanilla, and mayonnaise. Beat for 3 minutes. |
| **1 cup grated unpeeled zucchini, squeezed dry** | |
| **½ cup corn oil** | *3* In a small bowl, whisk together the cinnamon, flour mixture, salt, baking soda, and baking powder. |
| **1½ teaspoons vanilla** | |
| **1 tablespoon mayonnaise** | |
| **1½ teaspoons cinnamon** | *4* Whisk the dry ingredients into the egg mixture, and then stir in the walnuts until everything is blended. |
| **1½ cups gluten-free flour mixture** | |
| **¼ teaspoon salt** | *5* Pour the batter into the prepared pan. |
| **1 teaspoon baking soda** | *6* Bake the batter at 325 degrees for 55 minutes, or until a toothpick inserted in the center comes out clean. |
| **1 teaspoon baking powder** | |
| **½ cup chopped walnuts** | *7* Let the hot loaf set in the pan for 5 minutes, and then remove the bread and let it cool on a wire rack. |

**Per serving:** *Calories: 322; Total fat: 17g; Saturated fat: 2g; Cholesterol: 43mg; Sodium: 247mg; Carbohydrates: 41g; Fiber: 2g; Sugar: 21g; Protein: 3g.*

**Tip:** When you have too many zucchinis maturing in your garden, make a slew of these breads and freeze them for gift-giving during the holidays.

## Surviving a gluten-free bread disaster

If you do end up with a disastrous loaf of bread at some point, *do not* throw it out! Gluten-free ingredients are far too expensive to simply toss in the trash can, and you put too much effort into your creation. Instead, cut the loaf into slices and lay them on a baking sheet. Bake the slices at 200 degrees for 1 hour, or until the bread is crisp. (The baking time will vary considerably depending on the thickness of the slices and the texture of bread.) Let the slices cool, and then put them into a blender with seasonings to make your own bread crumbs.

If the loaf is semi-salvageable, first cut slices, and then cut those slices into cubes. Toss the bread cubes in a bowl with a little oil and seasonings, and then spread the cubes out on a baking sheet. Bake the cubes at 200 degrees until they're crisp (but not jaw-breaker crisp). Use these cubes as croutons in salads, or freeze them until you're ready to make bread dressing or bread pudding.

# What a Sweet Idea! Pastries and Muffins

Nature provides us with fresh fruits and vegetables to keep us healthy. But pastries and muffins were created to keep us happy.

Because these items are derived primarily from a gluten-free flour base, if you are converting a wheat recipe, you'll need to add extra flavoring in the form of stir-ins (nuts, coconut, fresh, canned, or dried fruit, shredded carrots or zucchini, mashed bananas, applesauce or jars of baby fruit, chocolate chips, or even liqueurs) or added flavoring (extra vanilla, almond, or other liquid flavoring plus additional or increased amounts of spices). Add an extra egg and 1 tablespoon of mayonnaise to help the pastry rise. It also helps to substitute some of the liquid called for in the recipe with something more flavorful, like brewed coffee, juice, or sweetened condensed milk. The recipes in this section already have these adjustments made, so start baking!

# Breakfast Bread Pudding

**Prep time:** 10 min plus refrigeration time • **Cook time:** 20 min • **Yield:** 9 servings

| Ingredients | Directions |
|---|---|
| 4 eggs | *1* In a large bowl, whisk together the eggs, whole milk, cinnamon, vanilla, ½ cup of the brown sugar, and baking powder. |
| ⅔ cup whole milk | |
| ½ teaspoon cinnamon | |
| 4 teaspoons vanilla | *2* Cut the bread slices into small cubes, and then stir them into the egg mixture. Cover the mixture and refrigerate it for at least 2 hours. |
| ½ cup plus 1 tablespoon brown sugar | |
| ¼ teaspoon baking powder | *3* In a small bowl, stir the raisins into the rum. Cover the mixture and let it cure at room temperature for at least 2 hours. |
| 6 slices bread | |
| ¾ cup raisins | |
| 2 tablespoons dark rum | *4* Preheat the oven to 400 degrees. Spray a 9-x-9-inch baking pan with cooking spray. |
| Nonstick cooking spray | |
| 1 banana, sliced thinly | *5* Stir the raisins into the bread mixture. |
| 2 teaspoons cinnamon sugar | |
| 3 tablespoons maple syrup | *6* Spoon half of the soaked bread into the prepared pan. Slice the banana on top of the bread and sprinkle with remaining 1 tablespoon brown sugar. Spoon the remaining bread over the banana slices, pouring any remaining egg mixture on top. Press down gently on the bread cubes to even out the top. |
| | *7* Sprinkle the top of the pudding with cinnamon sugar. |
| | *8* Bake the pudding at 400 degrees for 20 minutes, or until the top is lightly browned. Remove the pudding from the oven and drizzle it with maple syrup. Cool the pudding for 10 minutes before cutting. |

*Per serving:* Calories: 239; Total fat: 5g; Saturated fat: 1g; Cholesterol: 96mg; Sodium: 72mg; Carbohydrates: 43g; Fiber: 2g; Sugar: 29g; Protein: 4g.

*Note:* Because of the soaking time required, assemble this the night before.

*Vary It!* Use orange juice in place of the rum.

# Cranberry Cornmeal Muffins

**Prep time:** 15 min • **Cook time:** 20 min • **Yield:** 16 large muffins

| Ingredients | Directions |
|---|---|
| **Nonstick cooking spray** | **1** Preheat the oven to 400 degrees. Spray muffin tins with cooking spray. |
| ¾ **cup 2 percent milk** | |
| **1 tablespoon lemon juice** | **2** In a small bowl, stir together the milk and lemon juice; set the mixture aside for a few minutes to thicken. |
| **2 eggs** | |
| **1 egg white** | **3** In a mixing bowl, use the mixer to whip the eggs and egg white for 1 minute. |
| ⅓ **cup granulated sugar** | |
| ¼ **cup olive oil** | **4** Add the thickened milk, sugar, oil, vanilla, almond extract, and mayonnaise, and continue to whip for another minute. |
| 1½ **teaspoons vanilla** | |
| ½ **teaspoon almond extract** | |
| **1 tablespoon mayonnaise (not low-fat version)** | **5** In a medium bowl, stir together the flour mixture, coconut flour, cornmeal, baking powder, and salt. |
| ¾ **cup gluten-free flour mixture** | **6** Add the flour mixture to the egg mixture; blend the dry ingredients in thoroughly using a whisk. |
| ¼ **cup coconut flour** | |
| ¾ **cup cornmeal** | **7** Fold in the cranberries and pecans. |
| **3 teaspoons baking powder** | |
| ¼ **teaspoon salt** | **8** Spoon the batter into the prepared muffin tins. |
| 1⅓ **cups dried cranberries** | **9** Bake the batter at 400 degrees for 15 minutes, or until a toothpick inserted in the center comes out clean. |
| ½ **cup chopped, toasted pecans** | |
| | **10** Cool the muffins slightly, and then remove them to a wire rack. |

*Per serving: Calories: 183; Total fat: 8g; Saturated fat: 1g; Cholesterol: 28mg; Sodium: 185mg; Carbohydrates: 27g; Fiber: 2g; Sugar: 12g; Protein: 3g.*

*Tip:* Keep leftover muffins stored in the freezer to keep them from drying out. To thaw, wrap a muffin in wax paper and pop it into the microwave or wrap it in foil and bake at 300 degrees for 15 minutes.

*Note:* With wheat flour muffins, the directions usually say, "Stir the ingredients just until blended." With the gluten-free flours, whip the liquid ingredients first to incorporate air so the finished product will be lighter.

# Banana Chocolate Chip Muffins

**Prep time:** 15 min • **Cook time:** 17 min • **Yield:** 18 muffins

| Ingredients | Directions |
|---|---|
| Nonstick cooking spray | **1** Preheat the oven to 350 degrees. Grease the muffin tins with cooking spray. |
| 2 eggs | |
| ½ cup milk | **2** In a large bowl, beat the eggs slightly with a whisk. |
| ¼ cup vegetable oil | **3** Whisk in the milk and oil. |
| ½ cup granulated sugar | |
| 1 teaspoon vanilla | **4** Whisk in the sugar, vanilla, and bananas. |
| 2 medium ripe bananas, mashed | **5** Sift the flour mixture, salt, baking powder, and baking soda into a small bowl. |
| 1¼ cups gluten-free flour mixture | |
| ½ teaspoon salt | **6** Slowly stir the mixture into the egg mix until everything is blended. |
| ½ teaspoon baking powder | |
| ½ teaspoon baking soda | **7** Stir in the chocolate chips. |
| ½ cup mini semisweet chocolate chips | **8** Fill the greased muffin tins ¾ full with batter. |
| | **9** Bake the muffins at 350 degrees for 17 minutes, or until a toothpick inserted in the center comes out clean. |

*Per serving: Calories: 143; Total fat: 6g; Saturated fat: 2g; Cholesterol: 24mg; Sodium: 121mg; Carbohydrates: 22g; Fiber: 1g; Sugar: 11g; Protein: 2g.*

***Tip:*** Use very ripe bananas for this recipe.

# Corn Muffins

**Prep time:** 8 min • **Cook time:** 12–15 min • **Yield:** 16 muffins

| Ingredients | Directions |
|---|---|
| Nonstick cooking spray | *1* Preheat the oven to 400 degrees. Spray the muffin tins with cooking spray. |
| 1 cup cornmeal | |
| 1 cup gluten-free flour mixture | *2* In a medium bowl, whisk together the cornmeal, flour mixture, brown sugar, granulated sugar, baking soda, and salt. |
| ⅓ cup brown sugar | |
| ½ cup granulated sugar | |
| 2 teaspoons baking soda | *3* In a second medium bowl, whisk together the eggs, buttermilk, oil, mayonnaise, and vanilla. |
| ½ teaspoon salt | |
| 2 eggs | *4* Stir the egg mixture into the flour mixture until the two are thoroughly combined. |
| 1¼ cups buttermilk | |
| ¾ cup corn oil | *5* Spoon the batter into the prepared muffin tins. |
| 1 tablespoon mayonnaise | |
| ½ teaspoon vanilla | *6* Bake the muffins at 400 degrees for 12 to 15 minutes, or until a toothpick inserted in the center comes out clean. |
| | *7* Cool the muffins in the pan for 3 minutes, and then remove them to a wire rack. |

*Per serving:* Calories: 227; Total fat: 12g; Saturated fat: 2g; Cholesterol: 28mg; Sodium: 264mg; Carbohydrates: 27g; Fiber: 1g; Sugar: 12g; Protein: 3g.

# *Whipping Up Pancakes and Waffles*

Nothing warms the tummy on a cold morning like hot pancakes fresh off the griddle. The next time you mix up a bowl of pancake batter, brainstorm and add shredded apples, pears, or zucchini to the batter, or chopped walnuts or pecans, mashed bananas, miniature chocolate chips, or a tablespoon of peanut butter (or all four if you're daring). Substitute brown sugar for the white sugar or coconut milk for the whole milk. If you always serve maple syrup for a topping, surprise your family with new toppings like cherry or strawberry sauce, cinnamon maple butter, blueberry syrup, apple cinnamon syrup, or maple rum syrup. When cooking pancakes, use just enough butter to keep the batter from sticking. Too much butter causes the pancakes to brown before they are cooked through. Or you can lightly brush the pan with a little bit of corn oil instead of using butter.

Creating perfect gluten-free waffles is both an art and a science. Resist the urge to overbeat the batter. Spray both sides of the iron generously with gluten-free nonstick spray. Batter needs room to expand, so only pour in enough batter to just cover the lower cooking grid — too much batter will result in a waffle that has a soggy middle. Cook the waffle at a medium-high setting; too low of a setting results in moisture condensation, and you'll end up with a mushy mess. Despite the temptation, wait at least 3 minutes before opening the iron to check for doneness. When breakfast is over, wash the iron grates, and then season them with a very light coat of corn oil.

## Crepe magic

Crepes are versatile and delicious. To cook crepes ahead, layer the unfilled crepes with wax paper between each crepe. You can wrap them in plastic wrap or slide them into a self-seal bag and refrigerate them for up to three days.

To freeze crepes for up to two months, stack the unfilled crepes between sheets of wax paper. Wrap the stack in foil and then place the stack in a self-seal freezer bag. When you're ready to use the crepes, thaw them in the refrigerator overnight. To reheat thawed crepes in the oven, remove the stack of crepes from the freezer bag, and while they're still wrapped in foil, place the stack on a baking sheet. Bake the crepes in a preheated 350-degree oven for 10 minutes or until they're heated through. To reheat the crepes in the microwave, remove the crepes from the freezer bag and foil. Then place a stack of 4 crepes, separated with wax paper, on a microwave-safe plate. Cover the stack with a damp paper towel and heat on a medium setting for 1½ minutes.

To make dessert crepes, work with the Feather-Light Crepes recipe in this section and use one or more of the following substitutions or additions:

- ✔ Replace ¾ cup of the milk with coconut milk.

- ✔ Replace the granulated sugar with brown sugar.

- ✔ Add 3 tablespoons of chocolate syrup to the batter.

# Baked Apple Pancake

**Prep time:** 20 min • **Cook time:** 30 min • **Yield:** 6 servings

| *Ingredients* | *Directions* |
|---|---|
| **Nonstick cooking spray** | *1* Preheat the oven to 350 degrees. Spray a 9-inch pie plate with cooking spray. |
| **3 tablespoons plus 2 tablespoons butter** | |
| **¼ cup plus 1 tablespoon granulated sugar** | *2* Melt 3 tablespoons of butter in a large nonstick skillet. |
| **¼ cup brown sugar** | *3* Add ¼ cup of granulated sugar, the brown sugar, and 1 teaspoon of cinnamon. Stir constantly until the sugars melt. |
| **1 teaspoon plus ¼ teaspoon cinnamon** | |
| **1 large McIntosh apple, peeled, cored, and sliced thin** | *4* Add the apples and sauté, stirring frequently, until the apples are softened (about 15 minutes). |
| **2 eggs** | *5* Spoon the apples and sauce into the prepared pie pan. |
| **⅓ cup milk** | |
| **⅓ cup gluten-free flour mixture** | *6* In a small mixing bowl, whisk the eggs until they're frothy. Add the milk and whisk until the eggs and milk are blended. |
| **½ teaspoon baking powder** | |
| **⅛ teaspoon salt** | *7* Add the flour mixture, the remaining 1 tablespoon of granulated sugar, the baking powder, the remaining ¼ teaspoon of cinnamon, the salt, the remaining 2 tablespoons of butter, and the vanilla to the egg mixture and continue to whisk until blended. |
| **¼ teaspoon vanilla** | |
| | *8* Pour the batter over the apples. |
| | *9* Bake the pancake at 350 degrees for 30 minutes, or until the pancake is cooked through. Cut the pancake into wedges to serve, spooning the sauce and apples over the top of each individual pancake. |

*Per serving: Calories: 242; Total fat: 12g; Saturated fat: 7g; Cholesterol: 146mg; Sodium: 121mg; Carbohydrates: 32g; Fiber: 2g; Sugar: 24g; Protein: 3g.*

*Tip:* You won't need maple syrup — just spoon some of the apple syrup from the bottom of the pan onto the top of each slice of pancake.

*Note:* The edges of the pancake will rise during baking and then sink to the level of the pancake after you remove it from the oven.

# Pumpkin Waffles

**Prep time:** 10 min • **Cook time:** 24 min (4 min per waffle) • **Yield:** 6 servings

| Ingredients | Directions |
|---|---|
| Nonstick cooking spray | **1** Preheat the waffle iron to the medium-high setting. |
| 2 eggs | |
| 2 egg whites | **2** Spray the waffle iron grates with cooking spray. |
| 3 tablespoons brown sugar | |
| 1¾ cups milk | **3** In a large bowl, whisk together the eggs and egg whites. |
| ½ cup canned pumpkin | **4** Add the brown sugar, milk, pumpkin, and vanilla, and whisk until the ingredients are completely blended. |
| 2 teaspoons vanilla | |
| 1 cup gluten-free flour mixture | **5** Sift the flour mixture, baking powder, baking soda, salt, cinnamon, nutmeg, ginger, and cloves over the egg mixture. Whisk the mixture together just until everything is combined. |
| 2 teaspoons baking powder | |
| 1 teaspoon baking soda | |
| ¼ teaspoon salt | |
| 1½ teaspoons cinnamon | **6** Stir in the walnuts. |
| ½ teaspoon nutmeg | |
| ¼ teaspoon ginger | **7** Pour ¾ cup of batter onto the waffle iron. Cook for 3 minutes, or until the waffle is cooked through and the outside is crisp. Repeat with the remaining batter, remembering to spray the waffle iron with cooking spray each time. |
| ¼ teaspoon ground cloves | |
| ⅓ cup toasted finely chopped walnuts | |

*Per serving:* Calories: 247; Total fat: 12g; Saturated fat: 7g; Cholesterol: 146mg; Sodium: 121mg; Carbohydrates: 32g; Fiber: 2g; Sugar: 24g; Protein: 3g.

*Note:* The exact number of waffles will depend on the size of your waffle iron.

# Feather-Light Crepes

**Prep time:** 5 min • **Cook time:** 10 min • **Yield:** 8 crepes

| *Ingredients* | *Directions* |
|---|---|
| 2 eggs<br><br>1¼ cups whole milk or half-and-half | *1* Preheat the broiler. In a medium bowl, whisk together the eggs and milk (or half-and-half). Add the sugar and whisk to blend it in. |
| 2 tablespoons granulated sugar<br><br>½ cup gluten-free flour mixture<br><br>1 tablespoon melted butter | *2* Stir in the flour mixture until the batter is smooth. Add the melted butter, vanilla, almond flavoring, and salt, stirring with a whisk just until blended. The batter should be the consistency of thin cream. If it's too thick, slowly add more milk as needed. |
| ½ teaspoon vanilla<br><br>¼ teaspoon almond flavoring | *3* Wrap the handle of an 8-inch nonstick skillet with heavy-duty foil. Heat the skillet over medium-low heat on the stove. |
| Dash salt<br><br>3 tablespoons stick butter | *4* Holding the stick of butter with a paper towel, rub the butter over the entire surface of the skillet (do not overgrease the pan). |
|  | *5* Remove the pan from the stove and pour in about 3 tablespoons of batter (a gravy ladle usually works perfectly for this). Tilt the pan quickly so the batter is evenly distributed. Return the pan to the stovetop and cook the batter for about 1 minute. Lift the edge of the crepe with a rubber spatula to see when the underside is just beginning to brown. |
|  | *6* Place the pan under the broiler for 40 seconds, or until the top of the crepe is just beginning to brown. |
|  | *7* Remove the crepe from the pan to wax paper and repeat the process from Step 8 with the remaining batter. It may be necessary to re-butter the pan after the first four crepes. |

*Per serving: Calories: 139; Total fat: 8g; Saturated fat: 5g; Cholesterol: 72mg; Sodium: 93mg; Carbohydrates: 13g; Fiber: 0g; Sugar: 5g; Protein: 3g.*

# Cheese Waffles

**Prep time:** 12 min • **Cook time:** 12 min (3 min per waffle) • **Yield:** 4 servings

| *Ingredients* | *Directions* |
|---|---|
| Nonstick cooking spray | *1* Preheat the waffle iron to its medium setting. |
| 2 green onions, minced | |
| 3 tablespoons minced green pepper | *2* Spray the waffle iron grates with cooking spray. |
| ¼ cup corn oil, plus some for sautéing | *3* In a small skillet over medium-high heat, sauté the onion and green pepper in oil until they're tender but not browned. Remove the pan from heat and let the vegetables cool slightly. |
| 2 eggs | |
| 1 cup milk | |
| ½ cup gluten-free flour mixture | *4* In a medium bowl, whisk together the veggies, ¼ cup of oil, the eggs, and milk. Add the flour mixture, sorghum flour, cornmeal, baking powder, sugar, salt, and pepper, and whisk until the ingredients are thoroughly blended. (Add a little more milk if the mixture is too thick.) |
| ⅓ cup sorghum flour | |
| 2 tablespoons cornmeal | |
| 1 tablespoon baking powder | |
| 2 teaspoons granulated sugar | *5* Stir in the cheese. |
| ¼ teaspoon salt | |
| ⅛ teaspoon pepper | *6* Pour ¾ cup of batter onto the waffle iron. Cook for 3 minutes, or until the waffle is cooked through and the outside is crisp. Repeat with the remaining batter, remembering to spray the waffle iron with cooking spray each time. |
| ¼ cup grated Monterey Jack cheese | |

*Per serving:* *Calories: 308; Total fat: 21g; Saturated fat: 5g; Cholesterol: 118mg; Sodium: 517mg; Carbohydrates: 38g; Fiber: 2g; Sugar: 6g; Protein: 10g.*

*Note:* The exact number of waffles will depend on the size of your waffle iron.

*Vary It!* Add some bacon crumbles to the batter and you have a breakfast. Make them as directed and you have the perfect "bed" for sloppy joes. Lay a slice of cheese on top of a waffle and stick it in a toaster oven for a luscious toasted cheese sandwich. Or add a little cumin and cayenne to the batter, then spread 1 waffle with refried beans, sprinkle it with a little cheese and a dollop of salsa, and top with a second waffle — tacos were never like this!

# Peachy French Toast

**Prep time:** 8 min • **Cook time:** 10 min • **Yield:** 4 servings

| *Ingredients* | *Directions* |
|---|---|
| 15-ounce can sliced peaches with syrup | *1* Coarsely chop the peaches into a small saucepan. Add the syrup from the peaches to the pan. |
| 1 tablespoon honey | |
| 1 tablespoon plus 4 teaspoons butter | *2* Stir in the honey, 1 tablespoon of butter, brown sugar, maple flavoring, and ¼ teaspoon of cinnamon. Heat over medium heat until the butter has melted. |
| 1 tablespoon brown sugar | |
| ¼ teaspoon maple flavoring | *3* In a small bowl, stir together the cornstarch and water until the cornstarch is dissolved. Stir this into the peach mixture. |
| ¼ teaspoon plus ¼ teaspoon cinnamon | |
| 2 teaspoons cornstarch | *4* Cook over medium heat, stirring constantly, until the mixture thickens (about 4 to 5 minutes). |
| 1 tablespoon water | |
| 6 eggs | *5* In a medium shallow bowl, whisk together the eggs, vanilla, ¼ teaspoon of cinnamon, and milk. |
| 1 teaspoon vanilla | |
| ¾ cup milk | *6* Melt 2 teaspoons of butter in a large skillet over medium heat. |
| 8 slices white bread | |
| | *7* Dip 4 slices of bread, one slice at a time, into the egg mixture. Drain for a moment, and then cook the slices in a skillet, turning once, until they're browned on both sides. |
| | *8* Melt the remaining 2 teaspoons of butter in the skillet and repeat Step 7 with the remaining 4 slices of bread. |
| | *9* To serve, spoon the warm peach syrup over slices of French toast. |

*Per serving:* Calories: 470; Total fat: 20g; Saturated fat: 9g; Cholesterol: 381mg; Sodium: 430mg; Carbohydrates: 58g; Fiber: 3g; Sugar: 32g; Protein: 15g.

*Note:* You need to have porous gluten-free bread to make this recipe. The Breakfast Biscuit Bread in this chapter is ideal.

# Chapter 12

# Brilliant Brunches, Luscious Lunches

## In This Chapter

▶ Splitting the difference and serving brunch

▶ Fixing foods that travel well

▶ Savoring hot and cold sandwiches with *bread!*

▶ Getting the inside scoop on wraps, pitas, and pizzas

▶ Changing the pace with casseroles

*T*ry and say the word *brunch* without emoting an audible sigh of satisfaction and conjuring images of luxury and overindulgence. Brunch is usually a feast of fancy drawn out over a ridiculously long and relaxing timeframe, with far too many calories for normal human consumption.

Certainly not limited to the Sunday variety, brunch and lunch present the perfect opportunity to decompress with a midday meal to give you that boost you need before launching into the rest of your day. With just a few tweaks and twists, you can enjoy a gluten-free brunch or lunch that's every bit as decadent (or not!) and delicious as those that aren't gluten-free.

# Breaking for Brunches

Overslept? Or are you getting a late start? Either way, you missed breakfast, which means it's time for *brunch*. Brunch invokes the anticipation of fancier foods that can amuse and arouse your appetite. Brunches are for cultivated connoisseurs and aficionados with refined tastes (people who like to eat good food). Just mentioning brunch denotes a wow factor.

You're likely to find most any concoction offered at a brunch. Sometimes the fare consists primarily of breakfast foods, but it often has lunch-type offerings, such as beef, chicken, or seafood with sides and even dessert. The plethora of choices is what makes brunches fun.

# Make-Ahead Brunch Casserole

**Prep time:** 20 min  •  **Cook time:** 35 min  •  **Yield:** 6 servings

| *Ingredients* | *Directions* |
|---|---|
| **Nonstick cooking spray** | *1* Preheat the oven to 375 degrees. Lightly spray a 9-x-9-inch baking dish with cooking spray. |
| **3 large Idaho potatoes, boiled, peeled, and diced** | |
| **5 hard-boiled eggs, peeled and diced** | *2* Place the diced potatoes, eggs, ham, green pepper, and onion in the baking dish. |
| **¾ pound low-salt ham, cut into ½-inch cubes** | *3* Sprinkle the parsley, pepper, and 1 cup of cheese on top; using a spoon, toss the ingredients lightly to distribute the cheese evenly. |
| **¼ green pepper, minced** | |
| **½ medium onion, minced** | |
| **2 tablespoons chopped fresh parsley** | *4* In a small bowl, stir together the melted butter, cornstarch, and sour cream (the mixture will be thick). Spoon tablespoonfuls of the mixture on top of the casserole. With the back of the spoon, smooth the topping to cover the casserole evenly. |
| **¼ teaspoon pepper** | |
| **1 cup plus 2 tablespoons grated sharp cheddar cheese** | |
| **2 tablespoons butter, melted** | *5* Sprinkle the top with the remaining 2 tablespoons of cheese and paprika. |
| **2½ tablespoons cornstarch** | |
| **8-ounce container sour cream** | *6* Bake the casserole at 375 degrees for 35 minutes. Let the dish set for 5 minutes before serving. |
| **Paprika** | |

*Per serving:* Calories: 524; Total fat: 28g; Saturated fat: 10g; Cholesterol: 281mg; Sodium: 722mg; Carbohydrates: 42g; Fiber: 4g; Sugar: 8g; Protein: 26g.

*Tip:* Assemble this dish the day before, and just pop it in the oven before your friends arrive.

*Note:* This recipe is for a 9-x-9-inch dish, but you can easily double the ingredients to fit a 9-x-13-inch pan for a larger crowd.

*Note:* Some non-stick cooking sprays contain flour. Check the label carefully!

# Potato Tomato Pie

**Prep time:** 15 min • **Cook time:** 65 min • **Yield:** 8 servings

| Ingredients | Directions |
|---|---|
| Nonstick cooking spray | **1** Preheat the oven to 400 degrees. Spray a 9-inch pie plate with cooking spray. |
| 2 cups firmly packed grated raw potatoes | |
| ¼ teaspoon salt | **2** Place the raw potatoes in a colander or sieve. Sprinkle them with salt and let them set for 5 minutes. |
| 2 eggs | |
| ¼ cup grated onion | **3** In a medium bowl, whisk the eggs. Squeeze out the excess water from the potatoes and add them to the eggs. Stir in the onion. |
| 3 or 4 medium tomatoes, sliced ⅛-inch thick | |
| ½ teaspoon oregano | **4** Put the mixture into the prepared pie plate. Using the back of a spoon, pat the mixture onto the bottom and sides of the pan. |
| ¼ teaspoon pepper | |
| 1 teaspoon Italian seasoning | |
| 8 slices bacon, cooked crisp and crumbled | **5** Bake the crust at 400 degrees for 35 minutes. Remove the pan from the oven and reduce the oven temperature to 350 degrees. |
| ¾ cup grated Parmesan cheese | |
| ¾ cup mayonnaise | **6** Layer half of the tomato slices onto the bottom of the baked crust. Sprinkle with half of the pepper and Italian seasoning and half of the bacon. Repeat the layer with the remaining tomatoes, pepper, Italian seasoning, and bacon. |
| ⅓ cup seasoned bread crumbs | |
| | **7** In a small bowl, stir together the cheese and mayonnaise. Drop this mixture in dollops on top of the tomatoes and then spread it carefully to cover the top of the pie. |
| | **8** Sprinkle the bread crumbs on top of the pie. Bake the pie uncovered at 350 degrees for 30 minutes, or until the bread crumbs begin to brown. |

*Per serving: Calories: 222; Total fat: 15g; Saturated fat: 4g; Cholesterol: 76mg; Sodium: 645mg; Carbohydrates: 14g; Fiber: 1g; Sugar: 3g; Protein: 9g.*

***Note:*** You can serve this delicious pie at a brunch, as a side dish for dinner, and even as a main entree with a tossed salad.

# Ham with Glazed Bananas

**Prep time:** 5 min • **Cook time:** 5 min • **Yield:** 4 servings

| *Ingredients* | *Directions* |
|---|---|
| 3 tablespoons plus 1 tablespoon butter | *1* Melt 3 tablespoons of butter in a nonstick medium skillet. Stir in the brown sugar until it melts. |
| 3 tablespoons brown sugar | |
| ¼ cup dark corn syrup | *2* Stir in the corn syrup and cinnamon and bring it to a gentle simmer. Slice the bananas into the syrup and simmer for 2 minutes. |
| ½ teaspoon cinnamon | |
| 2 large bananas, peeled | *3* In a medium skillet, melt 1 tablespoon of butter. Add the ham pieces and brown quickly on each side, turning once. |
| 8-ounce ham steak, cut into 4 pieces | |
| | *4* Place the ham slices on a serving dish and top with the banana glaze. |

*Per serving:* *Calories: 335; Total fat: 14g; Saturated fat: 8g; Cholesterol: 53mg; Sodium: 786mg; Carbohydrates: 43g; Fiber: 2g; Sugar: 25g; Protein: 13g.*

*Tip:* Select fairly firm bananas so they don't get too soft when cooked.

*Note:* If the ham you select has skin or rind encircling it, cut it off before preparing this dish.

# Potato Nests with Shrimp

**Prep time:** 20 min • **Cook time:** 20 min • **Yield:** 8 servings

| *Ingredients* | *Directions* |
|---|---|
| **Nonstick cooking spray** | *1* Preheat the oven to 450 degrees. Coat 8 cupcake tins with cooking spray. |
| **4 medium russet potatoes, shredded** | |
| **¼ teaspoon plus ¼ teaspoon salt** | *2* In a medium bowl, toss together the shredded potatoes, ¼ teaspoon of salt, and the melted butter until the potatoes are evenly coated. Press the mixture onto the bottom and sides of the prepared cupcake tins. Bake the nests at 450 degrees for 15 to 20 minutes until golden. |
| **3 tablespoons melted butter** | |
| **1 tablespoon olive oil** | |
| **¼ cup chopped onions** | |
| **¾ cup sliced fresh mushrooms** | *3* Heat the oil in a medium saucepan over medium-high heat; sauté the onions and mushrooms until they're lightly browned. Stir in the milk, cream cheese, parsley flakes, ¼ teaspoon of salt, pepper, and pimento. Stir the mixture until the cheese melts. Stir in the shrimp and wine, simmering just until the ingredients are warmed. Serve in the potato nests. |
| **¼ cup whole milk** | |
| **8 ounces cream cheese, cubed** | |
| **2 tablespoons dried parsley flakes** | |
| **⅛ teaspoon pepper** | |
| **2 tablespoons chopped pimento** | |
| **1 pound small cooked shrimp** | |
| **¼ cup dry white wine** | |

*Per serving: Calories: 314; Total fat: 17g; Saturated fat: 10g; Cholesterol: 269mg; Sodium: 213mg; Carbohydrates: 22g; Fiber: 1g; Sugar: 2g; Protein: 16g.*

# Midday Munchables, Gluten-Free Style

A human being can only consume so many peanut butter and jelly sandwiches before the body screams for something new for lunch. The primary issue for celiacs is that the bread needed to make sandwiches is often — ahem — less than adequate in the taste department. (That was as tactful as I could be, considering many gluten-free breads resemble crumbly cardboard.) Lucky for you, this book contains recipes for excellent breads (see Chapters 9 and 11).

Gluten-free lunches seem to be a challenge for many people. Rest assured that your choices are vast.

Variety is the key. Switch foods and alter combinations to make lunch an event of anticipation. One day add deviled or hard-boiled eggs; the next day add salsa and gluten-free tortilla chips. Include veggies as often as possible, whether it's carrot sticks with dip or celery stuffed with peanut butter. If time is a factor, add no-fuss items like applesauce, gelatin cups, or flavored yogurt; or pack a few gluten-free crackers to have with cheese slices or to spread with hummus. For a treat, take a sandwich made from gluten-free sweet bread slices spread with cream cheese.

## Meals on the move

If you work, you probably have little time in the morning to dawdle in the kitchen preparing a homemade bag lunch. For kids on a gluten-free diet, the problem is compounded because many children are picky eaters. But with a little preplanning and unlimited ingenuity, you can create many viable alternatives, even if you're on the run.

### Miracles of the microwave

What *did* we do without microwaves? Fortunately, most workplaces and even schools have microwaves that employees or teachers can use. These appliances can be a lifesaver when you've made something at home and need to warm it up for your midday meal. Other gluten-free foods conducive to being warmed in a microwave include pizza, lasagna, eggplant parmigiana, crustless quiche, and twice-baked potatoes.

One idea is to make your own "lunchables" from dinner leftovers. Nearly every grocery store carries divided, plastic, lidded containers that are ideal for making these handy lunches. To prevent spoilage, freeze your meal in the container so you take a frozen package with you in the morning; by lunchtime, it will be thawed and ready to heat.

If you're making mashed potatoes for dinner, bake the potatoes (instead of boiling them); remove most of the insides (also referred to as "guts") to make the mashed potatoes, and leave the skins intact. Then make your own potato skins topped with cheddar cheese, sliced green onions, and crumbled bacon (Chapter 18 has a potato skins recipe if you need a little more direction). Potato skins make a fun lunch for kids and adults.

Another fun microwavable lunch is a hot dog topped with American cheese and wrapped in a corn tortilla (wrap it all in wax paper to heat in the microwave). Tamales, quesadillas, and Chinese stir-fry add variety to your lunch and warm easily in the microwave, too.

### Think about a Thermos

If you think a Thermos is just for coffee, think again. Ah, so you think you're quite the adventurer because you've been brave enough to spoon chili or stew into a Thermos? Now think even further outside the box — be daring! Pack a gluten-free bun and spoon sloppy joe mix into the insulated container. By the way, many sloppy joe mixes available at the grocery store — even generics — are gluten-free.

You can also fill a Thermos with boiling water and add corn on the cob, or one or two hot dogs. A Thermos is great for taco meat (spoon it on top of a salad at lunchtime), pork and beans, hot dog slices and beans, or sausage in barbecue sauce. Rice dishes and gluten-free pasta entrees — everything from Spanish rice and beans, to gluten-free pasta marinara, to fettuccini Alfredo, to macaroni and cheese — hold well in a Thermos.

## Quickie cold lunches

If you're cool with cold, there's no end to your lunch selections. For entrees, here are just a few suggestions. Remember, creativity is key:

- Baked or fried chicken or chicken wings
- Cold poached salmon, plain or spread with mayonnaise
- Shrimp with cocktail sauce
- Cold sliced steak, chicken, or sushi
- Tomato stuffed with tuna fish
- Cottage cheese with fruit

## Satisfying salads

Salads are gaining popularity as a lunch entree, whether it's a (gluten-free, of course) pasta salad, shrimp or crab salad, chicken Caesar salad, or chicken pineapple salad. You can also enjoy the traditional potato salad made with mayonnaise and a hint of mustard, or a Greek potato salad made with green pepper, onion, olive oil, and cider vinegar. A chef salad is an excellent way to use up leftovers in the refrigerator. And let's not forget healthy bean salad. (Chapter 19 features salad recipes.)

If the salad is your main dish, treat yourself to an antipasto of marinated cubes of pepperoni, shredded chicken, cheese, olives, tomato wedges, artichoke hearts, and pepperoncini.

Craving croutons on your salad? Try tortilla chips instead. You can also check out several varieties of gluten-free salad toppings in the veggie section of your grocery store.

## Hot or cold sandwiches

Oh, sure, so the days of throwing together a sandwich with cheap and easy-to-find bread may be a thing of the past — but prepare to be amazed because you have plenty of sandwich options, even in the gluten-free world.

It's time to try new innovations with old favorites. The common favorites — chicken breast sandwich, toasted cheese sandwich, tuna sandwich, and sloppy joes — have been modified, altered, enhanced, disguised, and transformed into totally new creations of savory sustenance.

Keep these tips in mind:

- If you want something small to have with your sandwich, try coleslaw or marinated vegetables.
- If you enjoy sandwiches made on gluten-free bread, break the routine of deli lunchmeats with meatloaf, egg salad, or Reuben sandwiches.

Okay, I'm the first to admit that gluten-free bread is — ahem — a matter of taste. Either you do or you don't like gluten-free breads. So if you don't want the bread, don't worry. You can improvise and make a sandwich out of just about anything else. Try wrapping lunchmeat around a piece of string cheese — or, if you're more daring, add a piece or two of marinated asparagus before wrapping. Make toothpick kabobs of cubes of lunchmeat, cheese, pickles, and olives.

# Tuna Fish Sandwich Like No Other

**Prep time:** 8 min • **Cook time:** 3 min • **Yield:** 4 servings

| *Ingredients* | *Directions* |
|---|---|
| 4 slices olive oil bread | **1** Preheat the broiler. Place the bread slices in a 9-x-13-inch baking dish. |
| ¼ green pepper, cut into thin julienne strips | |
| ⅛ red onion, sliced thin | **2** On each slice of bread, layer the green pepper, onion, spinach leaves, and tomato slices, dividing evenly. |
| ½ cup baby spinach leaves | |
| 2 small plum tomatoes, sliced thin | **3** In a small bowl, blend the pepper, Italian seasoning, tuna, and Italian dressing. Spoon the mixture on top of the tomato slices. |
| ⅛ teaspoon pepper | |
| ¼ teaspoon Italian seasoning | **4** Cut the artichoke hearts in half. Lay 4 halves on each sandwich. |
| 6.5-ounce can water-pack chunk tuna, drained | |
| 2 teaspoons Italian dressing | **5** Lay 1 slice of pepper cheese on top of each sandwich. |
| 8 artichoke hearts | |
| 4 slices pepper cheese | **6** Broil the sandwiches about 3 minutes or just until the cheese is melted. |

*Per serving: Calories: 429; Total fat: 15; Saturated fat: 9g; Cholesterol: 40mg; Sodium: 632mg; Carbohydrates: 50g; Fiber: 3g; Sugar: 9g; Protein: 24g.*

**Note:** Try this filling on bread, in a gluten-free pita or tortilla, or even spoon it atop shredded lettuce. You won't want to go back to the old tuna-and-mayo rendition.

# *Best-Ever Sloppy Joes*

**Prep time:** 15 min • **Cook time:** 10 min • **Yield:** 4 servings

| *Ingredients* | *Directions* |
|---|---|
| 1 tablespoon olive oil | **1** In a medium skillet over medium-high heat, brown the ground beef, onion, and green pepper in oil, breaking up the meat with a fork. |
| 1 pound lean ground beef | |
| 1 medium onion, diced | |
| ¼ green pepper, diced | **2** Stir in the chili powder, cayenne pepper, paprika, cumin, mustard, garlic powder, salt, pepper, brown sugar, vinegar, Worcestershire sauce, and tomato sauce and simmer for 10 minutes, stirring often. |
| 1 teaspoon chili powder | |
| ¼ teaspoon cayenne pepper | |
| 1 teaspoon paprika | |
| ½ teaspoon cumin | |
| 1 teaspoon yellow mustard | |
| ½ teaspoon garlic powder | |
| ¼ teaspoon salt | |
| ¼ teaspoon pepper | |
| 1 tablespoon brown sugar | |
| 2 teaspoons cider vinegar | |
| 2 tablespoons Worcestershire sauce | |
| 8-ounce can tomato sauce | |

*Per serving:* *Calories: 257; Total fat: 10g; Saturated fat: 3g; Cholesterol: 68mg; Sodium: 829mg; Carbohydrates: 16g; Fiber: 3g; Sugar: 9g; Protein: 3g.*

*Note:* Double, triple, or quadruple this recipe when you host a big crowd. Spoon several heaping spoonfuls of hamburger mix on top of a toasted gluten-free bun.

# Creating Wraps and Other Sandwich Containers

Do you like wraps? If you can't find a premade loaf of gluten-free bread to your liking and you haven't had time to bake your own bread, don't despair. There are other viable sandwich "containers."

If you haven't tried a peanut butter and jelly sandwich made on gluten-free waffles, you have a taste-treat awaiting you. Purchase corn tortillas made from either yellow or white corn. Corn taco shells, precooked of course, are a crisp, fun holder for a multitude of fillings. Pancakes and crepes make wonderful wraps. And lettuce leaves are the ideal holders for lunchmeat and cheese. (If you feel daring, use Belgian endive leaves; they're shaped like boats and make a neat container for tuna and chicken salads.)

If you'd like, avoid the wrap altogether and pack a sandwich filling (like tuna or egg salad) in a container and take along a gluten-free muffin. Gluten-free crackers are also an alternative, and they're now available in many different flavors and textures. You can probably find them at your neighborhood grocery store.

Corn tortillas are available just about anywhere. Even the new gluten-free "flour" tortillas are excellent, and you can find them online or in most health food stores, usually in the frozen-foods section. After you bring them home, keep them refrigerated if you plan to use them within the week, or freeze them. To soften the tortillas so they don't crack when you wrap them, place them between two sheets of dampened paper towels and microwave them for a few seconds.

---

## Eata pita

Okay, you won't find them in every grocery store, but gluten-free pitas *are* available. If you can't find them, don't worry — you can make a good homemade version. Because the alternative flours are heavier, you may not always be able to cut open the pocket of the pita without destroying the integrity of the bread (which means it very well may crumble and fall apart). The good news is that you can make a marvelous pita flatbread, sans pocket, that is thin enough so you can place the filling on the bread, and then fold the bread in half to form a sandwich (the Mediterranean equivalent of a taco). Flip to Chapter 11 for a good flatbread recipe.

---

# Antipasto Lettuce Wraps

**Prep time:** 6 min  •  **Cook time:** None  •  **Yield:** 4 servings

| *Ingredients* | *Directions* |
|---|---|
| 2 tablespoons olive oil | *1* In a medium bowl, whisk together the olive oil, vinegar, garlic powder, pepper, and oregano. Add the onion, green pepper, red peppers, tuna fish, pepperoni, and artichokes and stir to blend. |
| 2 tablespoons cider vinegar | |
| ¼ teaspoon garlic powder | |
| ⅛ teaspoon pepper | |
| ¾ teaspoon dried oregano | *2* Spoon the mixture into 8 endive leaves to form boat sandwiches. |
| 1 small onion, minced | |
| ¼ green pepper, chopped | |
| 3 red peppers, roasted and sliced thin (or use canned, prepared red roasted peppers) | |
| 6.5-ounce can tuna fish, drained | |
| 2 ounces pizza pepperoni, slices halved | |
| 6-ounce jar marinated artichokes, drained and cut in half | |
| 8 Belgian endive leaves | |

*Per serving:* Calories: 232; Total fat: 17g; Saturated fat: 3g; Cholesterol: 28mg; Sodium: 720mg; Carbohydrates: 6g; Fiber: 1g; Sugar: 1g; Protein: 15g.

# Turkey Roll-Ups

**Prep time:** 10 min, plus 2 to 6 hr refrigeration time • **Cook time:** None • **Yield:** 4 servings

| Ingredients | Directions |
|---|---|
| 10-inch gluten-free tortilla | **1** Spread the mayonnaise on one side of the tortilla. Along one edge, layer the turkey and cheese on top of the mayonnaise. Along that same edge, lay out the peppers and cucumber. Sprinkle the spinach leaves over all. |
| 1 tablespoon mayonnaise | |
| 2 ounces deli turkey breast, sliced thin | |
| 2 ounces provolone cheese, sliced thin | **2** Tightly roll up the tortilla. Wrap it in a damp paper towel, then in wax paper, and refrigerate for several hours. |
| 2 red peppers, roasted and sliced (or use canned, prepared red roasted peppers) | |
| 1 small cucumber, sliced very thin | **3** When you're ready to serve the roll-up, remove the paper towel and wax paper, and slice the tortilla into 8 slices. |
| ½ cup baby spinach leaves | |

*Per serving:* Calories: 135; Total fat: 6g; Saturated fat: 3g; Cholesterol: 26mg; Sodium: 291mg; Carbohydrates: 10g; Fiber: 1g; Sugar: 2g; Protein: 11g.

# Reuben Quesadillas

**Prep time:** 5 min • **Cook time:** 5 min • **Yield:** 6 servings

| Ingredients | Directions |
|---|---|
| Three 10-inch gluten-free tortillas, cut in half | **1** Spread 3 of the tortilla halves with ½ teaspoon of mustard. |
| 1½ teaspoons hot mustard | **2** Divide the corned beef in thirds; lay 1 portion on each of 3 halves of the tortilla. |
| 8 ounces deli corned beef, sliced thin | |
| 8-ounce can sauerkraut, drained and rinsed | **3** Divide the sauerkraut in thirds; lay 1 portion on top of the corned beef on each tortilla. |
| 6 slices low-fat Swiss cheese | **4** Lay 2 slices of Swiss cheese on top of the sauerkraut on each quesadilla. |
| | **5** Cover each quesadilla with the remaining 3 tortilla halves. |
| | **6** Cut each tortilla semicircle in half to make a total of 6 halves. |
| | **7** Place the quesadillas in a large skillet that has been prewarmed over medium-high heat, and toast the quesadillas on each side until the tortillas are lightly browned and the cheese is melted. |

*Per serving:* Calories: 232; Total fat: 10g; Saturated fat: 3g; Cholesterol: 47mg; Sodium: 7,143mg; Carbohydrates: 16g; Fiber: 1g; Sugar: 1g; Protein: 24g.

*Note:* These quesadillas are great eaten fresh off the griddle, but you can also make them ahead and pack them in a bag for lunchtime.

*Vary It!* You can substitute different ingredients for the contents of the quesadilla, using pastrami in place of the corned beef and/or provolone cheese in place of Swiss. If you aren't a fan of sauerkraut, substitute cole slaw.

# Broiled Veggie Tortillas

**Prep time:** 15 min • **Cook time:** 7 min • **Yield:** 4 servings

| Ingredients | Directions |
|---|---|
| 1 tablespoon olive oil | **1** Preheat the broiler. |
| ¼ teaspoon minced garlic | |
| ¼ green pepper, cut into thin strips | **2** In a large skillet, sauté the garlic and vegetables in olive oil on high heat until they're tender crisp, about 3 minutes. Stir in the parsley flakes, oregano, Italian seasoning, salt, and pepper. |
| ½ small zucchini, sliced | |
| ¼ medium onion, sliced thin | |
| ½ small portobella mushroom, cut in half and sliced thin | **3** Reassemble the tortilla wedges together to form a circle on a baking sheet. |
| ½ teaspoon dried parsley flakes | |
| ¼ teaspoon dried oregano | **4** Spoon the veggies evenly over the tortilla wedges and then sprinkle with feta cheese. |
| ¼ teaspoon Italian seasoning | |
| Dash of salt | **5** Broil for 7 minutes or until the tortillas are crisp. |
| ⅛ teaspoon pepper | |
| 10-inch rice flour tortilla, cut into 4 wedges | |
| ¼ cup crumbled feta cheese | |

*Per serving:* Calories: 100; Total fat: 7g; Saturated fat: 2g; Cholesterol: 8mg; Sodium: 192mg; Carbohydrates: 8g; Fiber: 1g; Sugar: 2g; Protein: 3g.

*Vary It!* You can easily adapt this recipe for a wrap. Instead of cutting the tortilla into wedges, spoon the vegetables onto two whole tortillas and then roll each one up. After baking, cut each tortilla wrap in half.

Jumpstarting your day with a gluten-free breakfast is so easy. Try the Pumpkin Waffles with a side of Cranberry Cornmeal Muffins and Breakfast Biscuit Bread (all in Chapter 11).

Your children may be picky eaters, but eating gluten-free is easy for everyone. Mom and Dad can eat the Parmesan Chicken with Fresh Tomato Salsa (see in Chapter 15), and the kids can share a Three Cheese Pizza or Reuben Quesadillas (both in Chapter 13).

If you want a heartier, gluten-free lunch on a cold day, you can make the Cheesy Corn Chowder (see Chapter 20) and a Taco Salad in Tortilla Shells (refer to Chapter 13).

Hosting a party and need some gluten-free finger foods? No worries. Cook up some Speedy Taco Wings (flip to Chapter 13) and Cajun Stuffed Mushrooms and Roulade Canapé (all in Chapter 18).

Ready for an intimate meal with your special someone? Fix a gluten-free dinner, starting with Spinach Mandarin Salad (see Chapter 10) and move on to the main course with Glazed Filet Mignon with Bleu Cheese (refer to Chapter 16) and a side of French Baguettes (check out Chapter 11).

Want a vegetarian and gluten-free lunch? Choose the Spinach Pie and Cranberry and Yams (both in Chapter 17).

Eating gluten-free doesn't mean you have to skimp on snacks. Make some easy Honey Cinnamon Grahams and Trail Mix Bars (both in Chapter 21).

Everyone loves dessert, and you can whip up some delectable, gluten-free dishes your entire family will love. Pumpkin Cheesecake, Whoopee Pies, and Strawberry Almond Torte are all great choices (refer to Chapter 22).

# *Eating Pizza (No Foolin')*

When you first thought of cooking gluten-free, visions of bread and spaghetti floating away filled your mind. Chances are, the next looming image was pizza. Dispel those negative thoughts because you can have all three! You can make gluten-free pizza to your liking with thick or thin crust, but you'll need to add extra flavoring, usually in the form of Italian seasoning.

Thin crust? Thick crust? You decide. The recipe in this section is for a thicker crust. If you prefer a thinner crust pizza, use a larger pan and roll the dough thinner. The challenge with gluten-free pizza dough is in the spreading. To get a light textured crust, the dough must be sticky to work with. You can add extra flour if you want to roll out the dough, but the baked crust won't be as light as one that isn't rolled. When spreading the crust in the pan, dip your fingers in warm water to keep the dough from sticking to your hands.

# Three-Cheese Pizza

**Prep time:** 15 min • **Cook time:** 25 min • **Yield:** 6 servings

| Ingredients | Directions |
|---|---|
| 2 teaspoons sugar | **1** Preheat the oven to 425 degrees. In a small bowl, dissolve the sugar and yeast in warm water. Set aside for 5 minutes. |
| 1 packet (2½ teaspoons) quick rising yeast | |
| ⅔ cup warm water (115 degrees) | **2** In a medium mixing bowl, whisk together the flour mixture, milk powder, salt, baking powder, gelatin, Italian seasoning, garlic powder, and 1 teaspoon of the Romano cheese. |
| 1⅓ cup gluten-free flour mixture | |
| ¾ cup nonfat dry milk powder | |
| ½ teaspoon salt | **3** In another small bowl, whisk together 1 tablespoon of olive oil, the vinegar, and honey. Add the oil mixture to the flour mixture and stir until well blended. Add the yeast water to the flour mixture, and use the electric mixer to beat the mixture on high speed for 3 minutes. The dough should be very soft and moist. |
| ½ teaspoon baking powder | |
| 1 teaspoon unflavored gelatin | |
| 1 teaspoon Italian seasoning | |
| ¼ teaspoon garlic powder | |
| 1 teaspoon plus 2 tablespoons grated Romano cheese | **4** Grease the bottom of a 12-inch pizza pan with ½ teaspoon of olive oil and then sprinkle it with cornmeal. With dampened hands, press the dough into the bottom of the pan, building up the sides a bit to hold in the toppings. |
| 1 tablespoon plus ½ teaspoon olive oil | |
| 1 teaspoon cider vinegar | **5** Bake the dough at 425 degrees for 10 minutes and then remove it from the oven and put on the toppings. First sprinkle the feta cheese, then the mozzarella, then the remaining 2 tablespoons of the Romano cheese on top of the crust. Return the pizza to the oven and bake it at 425 degrees for an additional 15 minutes, or until the top is nicely browned. |
| 1 teaspoon honey | |
| 1 tablespoon cornmeal | |
| 4 ounces feta cheese, crumbled | |
| 1 cup shredded mozzarella cheese | |

*Per serving: Calories: 306; Total fat: 10g; Saturated fat: 6g; Cholesterol: 30mg; Sodium: 517mg; Carbohydrates: 39g; Fiber: 2g; Sugar: 8g; Protein: 14g.*

**Tip:** For a pizza with a thinner crust, use a baking sheet; for a deep-dish pizza, use an 11-x-7-inch pan.

# Crafting Quick Midday Casseroles

As much as Americans enjoy their sandwiches at lunchtime, sometimes you're ready for something different. When the hungries hit at noontime, the casserole recipes in this section can lend variety to your nourishment fare and leave your tummy feeling full and content.

Casseroles became popular in America during World War I when certain food items were scarce. Leftovers were chopped up and mixed with whatever else was available, and then put in a glass or metal pan and baked. The virtues of these easy-to-prepare meals are many.

You can prepare the ingredients ahead of time and then slide the pan in the oven just before you're ready to eat. Casseroles are flexible because they can encompass leftovers and often use inexpensive meats. And these one-pan dishes can be anything from a vegetable conglomeration (for example, the much-overused but still-popular green bean casserole) to main dishes and even desserts.

Here are some casserole hints that will make your life easier:

- ✔ When making a casserole, make two. It's just as easy to double the ingredients and then freeze half so you have a spare on those days when you don't have time to cook. Preferably you'll have time to let the frozen casserole thaw in the refrigerator overnight before baking. If you're baking the casserole from a frozen state, you may need to almost double the baking time. And be very careful about freezing casseroles in glass dishes. If a glass casserole dish is cold and is set on a hot oven rack, the dish can crack.

- ✔ If you're cooking for a small brood and don't want to buy a whole head of cauliflower, broccoli, or whatever because you'll have too much left over, pick up just the amount you need from the salad bar available at most grocery stores.

- ✔ Fresh herbs tend to lose their flavor during prolonged baking at high heat. If your casserole will bake for more than 20 minutes, it may be better to use dried herbs instead.

- ✔ To convert almost any casserole to *au gratin,* just stir in some shredded cheese and then mix together some grated cheese, gluten-free bread crumbs, and a little melted butter to sprinkle on top before baking.

# Pepperoni Squares

**Prep time:** 15 min • **Cook time:** 40 min • **Yield:** 6 servings

| Ingredients | Directions |
|---|---|
| Nonstick cooking spray | **1** Preheat the oven to 400 degrees. Spray a 9-x-9-inch baking dish with cooking spray. |
| 1 tablespoon olive oil | |
| ½ cup chopped onion | **2** In a small skillet, sauté the onions and green pepper in oil over medium heat, stirring often, until the vegetables are soft. |
| ⅓ cup chopped green pepper | |
| 2 eggs | **3** In a medium mixing bowl, use the mixer to whip together the eggs and milk. Add the flour and beat the mixture until it's smooth and thickened. Stir in the reserved onion and green pepper, parsley flakes, red pepper flakes, mozzarella cheese, salt, pepper, Italian seasoning, and pepperoni. |
| ¾ cup whole milk | |
| ¾ cup gluten-free flour mixture | |
| 1½ tablespoons dried parsley flakes | |
| ⅛ teaspoon red pepper flakes | |
| ½ cup shredded mozzarella cheese | **4** Transfer the mixture to the prepared baking pan and bake it at 400 degrees for 40 minutes. Cut into 6 pieces. |
| ⅛ teaspoon salt | |
| Dash pepper | **5** In a microwave-safe bowl, warm the spaghetti sauce to serve as a dipping sauce for the Pepperoni Squares. |
| ½ teaspoon Italian seasoning | |
| 2 ounces pizza pepperoni, slices quartered | |
| 1 cup spaghetti sauce | |

*Per serving:* Calories: 229; Total fat: 11g; Saturated fat: 3g; Cholesterol: 84mg; Sodium: 510mg; Carbohydrates: 25g; Fiber: 4g; Sugar: 7g; Protein: 8g.

*Tip:* If you cut the pieces smaller (24 pieces per pan), you can serve the squares as an appetizer.

*Note:* These squares can be prepared the night before, covered, and refrigerated. Just before serving, pop them in the oven.

# Enchilada Casserole

**Prep time:** 15 min • **Cook time:** 20 min • **Yield:** 6 servings

| *Ingredients* | *Directions* |
|---|---|
| Nonstick cooking spray | *1* Preheat the oven to 350 degrees. Spray a 7-x-11-inch baking pan with cooking spray. |
| 8-ounce can tomato sauce | |
| ⅓ cup water | *2* In a large skillet over medium-high heat, stir together the tomato sauce, water, and hot pepper sauce. Bring it to a boil, then lower the heat and let it simmer for 3 minutes. Remove the skillet from the heat and let the sauce cool slightly. |
| 5 drops hot pepper sauce | |
| ½ medium onion, diced | |
| 1 clove garlic, minced | |
| ½ cup diced green pepper | *3* In a small skillet, sauté the onions, garlic, and green pepper in the oil over medium heat until the vegetables are softened but not browned. Stir frequently. Remove the skillet from the heat and let the veggies cool. |
| 2 teaspoons olive oil | |
| 3 tablespoons fresh chopped parsley | |
| ⅛ teaspoon salt | *4* In a medium bowl, stir together the onion mixture, parsley, salt, pepper, chili powder, oregano, cumin, Monterey Jack cheese, and ½ cup of cheddar cheese. |
| ⅛ teaspoon pepper | |
| 2½ teaspoons chili powder | |
| ½ teaspoon dried oregano | *5* Dip each tortilla quickly into the tomato sauce to coat both sides. Lay the tortilla on a flat surface and spread with 1 tablespoon of the refried beans. |
| ½ teaspoon cumin | |
| 1 cup shredded Monterey Jack cheese | *6* Spoon the cheese mixture on top of the beans, dividing evenly among the 6 tortillas. |
| ½ cup plus 2 tablespoons shredded sharp cheddar cheese | *7* Roll the tortillas and arrange them in the prepared baking dish. Pour the remaining tomato sauce over the tortillas, and then sprinkle them with the remaining 2 tablespoons of cheddar cheese. |
| Six 9-inch corn tortillas | |
| 6 tablespoons refried beans | |
| | *8* Cover the pan with foil and bake the enchiladas at 350 degrees for 20 minutes. |

*Per serving: Calories: 239; Total fat: 13g; Saturated fat: 7g; Cholesterol: 29mg; Sodium: 619mg; Carbohydrates: 21g; Fiber: 5g; Sugar: 3g; Protein: 12g.*

***Tip:*** When dipping the tortillas in the tomato sauce, do it quickly or the tortillas will get so soft they may fall apart.

***Note:*** Keep these enchiladas covered in the refrigerator to pop in the oven, toaster oven, or microwave.

# Macaroni and Sausage Casserole

**Prep time:** 20 min • **Cook time:** 30 min • **Yield:** 8 servings

| *Ingredients* | *Directions* |
|---|---|
| Nonstick cooking spray | **1** Preheat the oven to 325 degrees. Spray a 9-x-13-inch baking dish with cooking spray. |
| 1 pound sausage (regular or spicy) | |
| 1 medium onion, diced | **2** In a large skillet, brown the sausage and onion over medium-high heat, breaking up the meat with a fork. Remove the skillet from the heat and drain off the fat. |
| 3 cups pasta shells | |
| 8-ounce jar processed cheese | **3** Boil the pasta in water in a large saucepan until it's barely tender and then drain. Return the pasta to the saucepan and immediately stir in the cheese so it melts. |
| 18-ounce can cream of mushroom soup | |
| ¼ teaspoon pepper | **4** Stir in the sausage, soup, and pepper. |
| ¾ cup gluten-free bread crumbs | **5** Spoon the mixture into the prepared baking dish. |
| 2 tablespoons melted butter | **6** In a small bowl, stir together the bread crumbs and melted butter. Sprinkle this over the macaroni and sausage. |
| | **7** Bake the casserole at 325 degrees for 30 minutes until hot and bubbly and the bread crumbs start to brown a little. |

*Per serving: Calories: 333; Total fat: 17g; Saturated fat: 9g; Cholesterol: 51mg; Sodium: 1,233mg; Carbohydrates: 31g; Fiber: 1g; Sugar: 4g; Protein: 15g.*

# Chapter 13

# Diving into the Melting Pot: Ethnic Dishes

## In This Chapter

▶ Seeking gluten-free recipes with an Asian flair

▶ Tapping into Mexican spices and flavors

▶ Delivering gluten-free Italian dishes that won't disappoint

*J*ust because you maintain a gluten-free lifestyle doesn't mean you can't savor delicious dishes from around the world. Many ethnic foods are traditionally gluten-free, and many more can be easily adapted to fit your gluten-free needs. If your favorite recipes have lost their luster, you may need to break out your passport and explore some new flavors. Often laden with fresh vegetables and spices, ethnic foods can be a wonderful alternative to your standard gluten-free fare. So grab your sauté pan and prepare for take-off.

When using any sauces, we suggest you carefully read the ingredients.

## Asian-Style Gluten Free

Grabbing some quick Chinese take-out typically isn't an option for people who avoid gluten. Those delightful wontons, noodles, and dumplings are often made from wheat flour. And that flour also coats many of the tempting fried items on the menu. What about the sauces? You guessed it. Soy and other sauces in restaurants often contain wheat.

The recipes that follow allow you to enjoy Asian foods at home, without fear of gluten or cross-contamination. Before you get started, take some time to look for gluten-free versions of some common Asian condiments at Asian markets, specialty stores, and gluten-free suppliers.

# General Tso's Sirloin Kebabs

**Prep time:** 10 min • **Cook time:** 12 min • **Yield:** 4 servings

| Ingredients | Directions |
|---|---|
| ¼ cup gluten-free hoisin sauce | **1** In a small glass bowl, mix together the hoisin sauce, soy sauce, vinegar, sugar, garlic chili sauce, oil, ginger, garlic, and red pepper flakes. Add meat to the marinade and refrigerate for 2 hours. |
| 2 tablespoons gluten-free soy sauce | |
| 2 tablespoons rice vinegar | **2** If using bamboo skewers, soak in water for at least 30 minutes to prevent the skewers from burning on the grill. Preheat gas grill on high. |
| 1 tablespoon sugar | |
| 2 teaspoons garlic chili sauce | |
| 1 tablespoon canola oil | **3** Remove beef from refrigerator and bring to room temperature for 30 minutes. Doing so allows meat to cook more evenly. |
| 1 tablespoon minced ginger | |
| 2 garlic cloves, minced | |
| 1 tablespoon red pepper flakes | **4** To assemble the kebabs, oil the skewers using nonstick cooking spray and place the marinated beef on skewers. Grill 10 to 12 minutes, rotating 90 degrees every 4 minutes to evenly cook the beef. Let kebabs rest for 4 minutes after grilling is complete. |
| 2 pounds sirloin, cut into 2-inch cubes | |
| Metal or bamboo skewers | |
| Nonstick cooking spray | |

*Per serving: Calories: 478; Total fat: 29g; Saturated fat: 10g; Cholesterol: 135mg; Sodium: 789mg; Carbohydrates: 8g; Fiber: 1g; Protein: 43g.*

**Tip:** Several good cuts of meat are good to use for kebobs. If your budget isn't a concern, substitute beef tenderloin. For more economical cuts, try the sirloin, flank, flat iron, or skirt. Choose cuts that are about 1¼ inches thick.

**Note:** Hoisin sauce doesn't always contain wheat, but it can. Be sure to read labels carefully.

**Vary It!** Skewer your favorite vegetables, bell peppers, onions, zucchini, mushrooms, and so on, drizzle with marinade, and cook separately from meat.

# Lemongrass-Infused Wild Salmon

**Prep time:** 10 min • **Cook time:** 10 min • **Yield:** 4 servings

| Ingredients | Directions |
|---|---|
| **Four 7-inch pieces lemongrass, bruised with meat mallet** | *1* Preheat gas grill to 350 degrees. |
| **1 teaspoon olive oil**<br><br>**Four 4-ounce wild salmon fillets with skin attached**<br><br>**Freshly ground pepper** | *2* Spear lemongrass through the length of each salmon fillet just as you would a kebob skewer. Rub each fillet with ¼ teaspoon olive oil. Dust with freshly ground pepper and salt, if desired. |
| **2 lemons, cut in half**<br><br>**¼ cup roughly chopped cilantro** | *3* Cook salmon on heated grill for 10 minutes skin side down. Cook lemons on grill, skin side down, and rotate so the skin is lightly charred and pulp is softened. |
| | *4* Serve the lemongrass-skewered salmon with skin removed and with a grilled lemon half and chopped cilantro. |

*Per serving:* Calories: 242; Total fat: 8g; Saturated fat: 1g; Cholesterol: 97mg; Sodium: 128mg; Carbohydrates: 5g; Fiber: 1g; Sugar: 0g; Protein: 37g.

*Tip:* When purchasing lemongrass, look for firm stalks. You can purchase lemongrass fresh or in frozen packets at local grocery stores or Asian markets. Bruising the lemongrass releases the aroma and infuses the salmon with a wonderful flavor component.

*Note:* Lemongrass (refer to Figure 13-1) is a rough, stalky plant that adds a lemon fragrance and flavor; it's frequently used in Thai cooking.

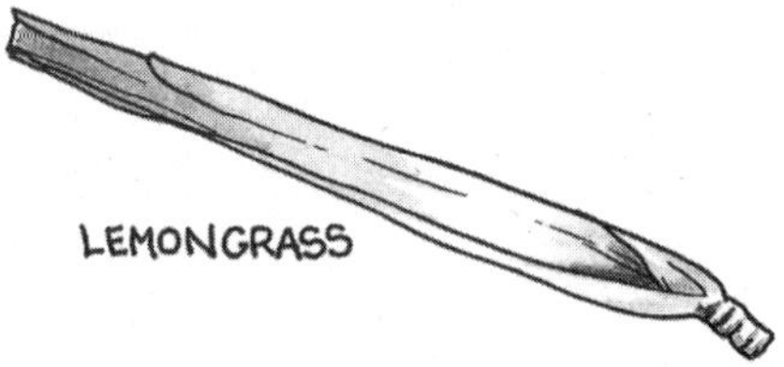

**Figure 13-1:**
Look for
lemongrass
stalks that
are firm and
unblemished.

LEMONGRASS

*Illustrations by Elizabeth Kurtzman*

# Vegetable Stir Fry with Tofu

**Prep time:** 10 min • **Cook time:** 10 min • **Yield:** 4 to 6 servings

| Ingredients | Directions |
|---|---|
| 8 ounces extra-firm tofu, drained well | **1** Remove moisture from tofu by wrapping it in a clean kitchen towel, applying gentle pressure to squeeze out the excess liquid. Cut into ½-inch cubes and pat with the towel to remove any additional liquid. Lightly dust tofu with cornstarch to help with browning when stir-fried. |
| 2 tablespoons gluten-free soy sauce | |
| 2 tablespoons gluten-free hoisin sauce | |
| 1 tablespoons balsamic vinegar | **2** In a small bowl combine the soy sauce, hoisin sauce, balsamic vinegar, garlic chile sauce, and cornstarch. |
| ½ tablespoons garlic chile sauce | |
| 1 teaspoon cornstarch | **3** Heat 1 tablespoon sesame oil in wok skillet over high heat. Add tofu and gently stir until tofu browns slightly, about 4 minutes. Using a slotted spoon, remove tofu from skillet and place into a bowl. |
| 2 tablespoons sesame oil | |
| 2 garlic cloves, minced | |
| 2 tablespoons peeled minced fresh ginger | **4** Add additional sesame oil and stir fry the garlic and ginger for 30 seconds. Add broccoli, asparagus, and snow peas and stir fry until crisp-tender, about 3 to 4 minutes. Return tofu to skillet. |
| 2 cups broccoli florets | |
| 6 asparagus spears, trimmed and cut into 2-inch long pieces | **5** Stir in the sauce and simmer 1 minute or until sauce is mixed well into the vegetables and thickens slightly. |
| 4 ounces snow peas | |

*Per serving:* Calories: 172; Total fat: 11g; Saturated fat: 2g; Cholesterol: 0mg; Sodium: 689mg; Carbohydrates: 11g; Fiber: 3g; Protein: 10g.

*Tip:* There is no limit to the number of different combinations of vegetables you can use. The key is to chop the vegetables in similar sizes for uniformity in cooking.

*Note:* Tofu is a versatile, nutritious, high-quality protein substitute for meat. Serve with steamed brown rice.

# Yakitori Chicken

**Prep time:** 10 min • **Cook time:** 6 min • **Yield:** 4 servings

| *Ingredients* | *Directions* |
|---|---|
| ⅓ cup gluten-free soy sauce | *1* Preheat gas grill to 350 degrees. |
| 6 tablespoons sugar | |
| 2 tablspoons sake or dry white wine | *2* In a medium saucepan combine soy sauce, sugar, sake or wine, and cornstarch until well blended. Set aside. |
| 1 tablespoon cornstarch | |
| 6 boneless skinless chicken thighs, each cut into six chunks | *3* Thread the chicken thighs and green onions onto 6-inch wooden skewers. Brush generously with the sauce and grill 5 to 6 minutes or until the chicken is cooked but still moist. |
| 1 bunch green onions, cut into 2-inch pieces | |
| | *4* In a small saucepan, bring to boil any leftover sauce. Serve chicken skewers with yakitori sauce. |

**Per serving:** *Calories: 279; Total fat: 9g; Saturated fat 2g; Cholesterol: 74mg; Sodium: 1,270mg; Carbohydrates: 22g; Fiber: 1g; Protein: 26g.*

**Tip:** This Japanese-inspired recipe makes a great main dish or appetizer.

**Note:** Soaking the wooden skewers in water for at least 30 minutes before threading the chicken will prevent them from burning on the grill.

# Asian Pork Salad

**Prep time:** 10 min plus refrigeration time • **Cook time:** 8 min • **Yield:** 2 servings

| *Ingredients* | *Directions* |
|---|---|
| Dressing (see the following recipe) | *1* Place the pork, 1 tablespoon of olive oil, 2 teaspoons of soy sauce, garlic, cayenne pepper, ginger, mint, and lemon juice in bowl. Blend the ingredients well, and then cover and refrigerate for 3 hours to marinate the meat. |
| ½ pound pork tenderloin, cut into thin slices, then julienned | |
| 1 tablespoon plus 2 teaspoons olive oil | |
| 2 teaspoons plus 2 teaspoons soy sauce | *2* Heat 2 teaspoons of olive oil in a large skillet or wok over medium heat. Remove the pork from the marinade (discarding the marinade) and sauté the pork until no pink shows (about 2 minutes). |
| 1 clove garlic, minced | |
| ¼ teaspoon cayenne pepper | |
| ¼ teaspoon ginger | |
| ¼ teaspoon dried mint | *3* Add the snow peas, green pepper, onions, and parsley to the skillet and sauté for 1½ minutes on high heat. (The vegetables should be crisp.) Drizzle 2 teaspoons of soy sauce over the pork mixture and toss. Remove from heat. |
| 3 tablespoons fresh lemon juice | |
| 8 snow peas | |
| ¼ green pepper, cut in half, then julienned | |
| 1 onion, sliced | *4* Place the watercress on two dinner plates, dividing evenly. Spoon the pork and vegetables on top. Whisk the dressing to mix and then drizzle it on top of the salads. Sprinkle the salads with sesame seeds. |
| 4 sprigs fresh parsley, chopped | |
| 3 cups (1 bunch) watercress, trimmed | |
| 1 teaspoon sesame seeds | |

## Dressing

| | |
|---|---|
| ½ teaspoon brown mustard | *1* In a small bowl, whisk together the mustard, soy sauce, vinegar, oil, pepper, and cayenne pepper. Cover the dressing and refrigerate it until needed. |
| 1½ teaspoons soy sauce | |
| 1 tablespoon balsamic vinegar | |
| 2 tablespoons olive oil | |
| ⅛ teaspoon pepper | |
| Dash cayenne pepper | |

*Per serving: Calories: 496; Total fat: 33g; Saturated fat: 6g; Cholesterol: 106mg; Sodium: 1,050mg; Carbohydrates: 13g; Fiber: 2g; Sugar: 5g; Protein: 38g.*

# *Taking Gluten-Free South of the Border*

Mexican food is a wonderful option for people who require a gluten-free diet. To begin with, traditional Mexican food is essentially free of gluten. Beans, corn, and ancient grains such as rice and amaranth form the foundation of the Mexican diet. Add in an appetizing array of chiles, spices, lean meats, seafood, vegetables, and fruits, and you have enough ingredients to create a nearly endless combination of gluten-free healthy meals.

Can't stomach the wheat flour tortilla used in the burrito recipe you've been dying to try? Simply replace it with a corn tortilla and you're ready to go. Not sure if the chips from the local restaurant were fried in the same oil used to fry wheat tortillas? Then make your own, using the recipe included in this chapter.

Mexican foods can fit the bill for breakfast, lunch, and dinner. Test out these recipes, and then feel free to substitute a different bean, grain, vegetable, or lean protein to create an entirely new recipe. You'll be happy you did!

# Halibut with Tomato Avocado Salsa

**Prep time:** 10 min • **Cook time:** 20 min • **Yield:** 4 servings

| Ingredients | Directions |
|---|---|
| 1 ripe tomato, thinly sliced | **1** To prepare the salsa, combine tomatoes, onions, and cilantro in a medium bowl. |
| ¼ cup thinly sliced red onion | |
| 2 tablespoons fresh cilantro, chopped | **2** In a separate small bowl, whisk together oil, vinegar, garlic, cumin, salt, and pepper and pour over the salsa mixture. Gently toss to coat the ingredients with the dressing. Cover and chill for an hour. |
| 1 medium avocado, peeled and cut into slices | |
| 1 tablespoon olive oil | |
| 1 tablespoon white wine vinegar | **3** Heat olive oil and butter in a large skillet over medium to medium-high heat. Add fish and cook until lightly browned about 4 to 5 minutes, turn and cook until fish is opaque and flakes easily with a fork about 2 to 3 more minutes. Remove from skillet and place on a dish. |
| 1 garlic clove, minced | |
| ⅛ teaspoon cumin | |
| Salt and pepper, to taste | **4** Just before serving, add avocado slices to the salsa and serve with the halibut. |
| 1 tablespoon olive oil | |
| 1 tablespoon butter | |
| Four 4-ounces halibut fillets | |

*Per serving:* Calories: 250; Total fat: 15g; Saturated fat: 4g; Cholesterol: 43mg; Sodium: 211mg; Carbohydrates: 7g; Fiber: 4g; Protein: 25g.

*Tip:* With a little practice, anyone can make fish dee-lish! Cooking times vary greatly depending on the thickness of the fish. Thicker fish like halibut may take 4 to 5 minutes per side. The general rule is 10 minutes of cooking per inch of thickness. For thicker fish, cover the pan with a lid to make sure the inside of the fish is cooked throughout or complete the cooking process in a pre-heated oven at 400 degrees for 5 minutes.

*Note:* Using both olive oil and butter to sauté the fish provides a flavorful blend.

*Vary It!* For an added flavor component, add sliced mango or peaches to the salsa.

# Hot Taco Bake

**Prep time:** 5 min • **Cook time:** 40 min • **Yield:** 3 cups

| Ingredients | Directions |
|---|---|
| **Nonstick cooking spray** | **1** Preheat the oven to 325 degrees. Using the nonstick cooking spray, grease a 9-inch-square baking dish. |
| **½ onion, minced** | |
| **¼ green pepper, minced** | **2** In a small skillet, slowly sauté the onion and green pepper in oil over medium heat until they're soft. Remove from the heat. |
| **1 tablespoon olive oil** | |
| **16 ounces cream cheese, softened** | **3** Using a mixer, whip the cream cheese until it's light. Add the sour cream and continue to whip until the mixture is blended and smooth. |
| **16 ounces sour cream** | |
| **9-ounce can bean dip** | **4** Whip in the bean dip and taco seasoning. Stir in the cheddar cheese, onions, and green pepper. |
| **1.25-ounce package taco seasoning mix** | |
| **1 cup shredded cheddar cheese** | **5** Spoon the mixture into the prepared baking dish. |
| **½ cup grated hot pepper cheese** | **6** Sprinkle the pepper cheese on top. |
| | **7** Bake the dip at 325 degrees for 25 minutes, or until it's lightly browned on top. |

*Per serving:* Calories: 286; Total fat: 27g; Saturated fat: 16g; Cholesterol: 72mg; Sodium: 524mg; Carbohydrates: 6g; Fiber: 0g; Sugar: 1g; Protein: 8g.

**Tip:** Spread any leftover dip on gluten-free corn tortillas and warm them in the microwave or oven for lunch or a quick snack.

# Taco Salad in Tortilla Shells

**Prep time:** 1 hr • **Cook time:** 10 min • **Yield:** 4 servings

| *Ingredients* | *Directions* |
|---|---|
| 4 tortilla shells (see the following recipe) | **1** Make the tortilla shells and set them aside. |
| 1 pound lean ground beef | **2** In a large skillet, brown the beef in the oil over medium-high heat, breaking up the meat with a fork. Stir in the taco seasoning and water. Add the kidney beans and simmer the mixture gently until the moisture has been absorbed, stirring occasionally. Remove the skillet from the heat. |
| 1 tablespoon olive oil | |
| 1.25-ounce envelope taco seasoning mix | |
| 1 cup water | |
| 8-ounce can light red kidney beans, rinsed and drained | **3** Cut the lettuce crosswise into thin strips and place it in a large bowl. Add the green onions, tomatoes, cheese, ground beef, and dressing; toss the ingredients to blend well. |
| 1 small head iceberg lettuce | |
| 3 green onions, sliced thin | |
| 3 plum tomatoes, diced | **4** Serve the salad in the tortilla shells. |
| 1 cup shredded cheddar cheese | |
| ½ cup Italian dressing | |

## Tortilla Shells

| Four 8-inch corn tortillas | **1** Preheat the oven to 400 degrees. Wrap the tortillas in a damp paper towel. Warm them in the microwave for 15 seconds to soften. |
|---|---|
| Nonstick cooking spray | **2** Spray the outside of a 6- or 7-inch round glass bowl or baking dish (large custard cups work great) with the cooking spray. Mold 1 tortilla over the bottom of the inverted bowl or baking dish. |
| | **3** Bake the tortilla at 400 degrees for 15 minutes, or until the tortilla is very crisp and lightly browned. |
| | **4** Carefully remove the shell from the bowl and set it aside to cool. Repeat Steps 3 and 4 with the remaining tortillas. |

*Per serving:* Calories: 645; Total fat: 39g; Saturated fat: 13g; Cholesterol: 105mg; Sodium: 1,415mg; Carbohydrates: 39g; Fiber: 6g; Protein: 37g.

# South-of-the-Border Cheese Ball

**Prep time:** 5 min plus refrigeration time • **Cook time:** None • **Yield:** 8 servings

| Ingredients | Directions |
|---|---|
| 8 ounces cream cheese, softened<br><br>2 tablespoons salsa<br><br>⅓ cup shredded Monterey Jack cheese<br><br>½ envelope taco seasoning mix<br><br>⅓ cup crushed Homemade Tortilla Chips | **1** In a medium mixing bowl, use the mixer to blend together the cream cheese, salsa, Monterey Jack cheese, and seasoning mix until they're thoroughly blended (about 30 seconds). Place the crushed chips on a piece of plastic wrap.<br><br>**2** With a rubber spatula, scoop the cheese onto the crushed chips and smooth it into a ball. Roll the ball over the chips until it's covered with chips. Wrap the cheese ball in a fresh piece of plastic wrap and refrigerate it for 2 hours until it's firm. |

*Per serving:* Calories: 145; Total fat: 12g; Saturated fat: 7g; Cholesterol: 35mg; Sodium: 484mg; Carbohydrates: 5g; Fiber: 0g; Sugar: 1g; Protein: 4g.

# Homemade Tortilla Chips

**Prep time:** 5 min • **Cook time:** 10–12 min • **Yield:** 8 servings

| Ingredients | Directions |
|---|---|
| Nonstick cooking spray<br><br>Four 6-inch corn tortillas<br><br>4 teaspoons olive oil<br><br>Salt for seasoning | **1** Preheat the oven to 400 degrees. Spray a baking sheet with cooking spray. Lightly brush both sides of each tortilla with the olive oil. With a clean pair of scissors, a knife, or a sharp pizza cutter, cut each tortilla into 8 wedges. Place the wedges in a single layer on the baking sheet. Sprinkle each wedge with a dash of salt.<br><br>**2** Bake the tortilla wedges at 400 degrees for 10 to 12 minutes, or until the chips are crisp and light golden, turning the chips once halfway through baking. Transfer the chips to paper towels and allow them to cool completely. Store the unused portion at room temperature in an airtight container. |

*Per serving:* Calories: 46; Total fat: 3g; Saturated fat: 0g; Cholesterol: 0mg; Sodium: 625mg; Carbohydrates: 5g; Fiber: 1g; Sugar: 0g; Protein: 1g.

# Speedy Taco Wings

**Prep time:** 5 min • **Cook time:** 20 min • **Yield:** 20 pieces

| Ingredients | Directions |
|---|---|
| ¼ cup olive oil | **1** Preheat the oven to 400 degrees. Lightly oil an 8-x-11-inch baking dish. |
| 20 pieces disjointed chicken wings | **2** Pour the oil into a self-seal bag. Add the chicken pieces, seal the bag, and push the pieces around until they're evenly coated with oil. |
| 1.25-ounce package taco seasoning mix | |
| ¼ teaspoon cayenne pepper | **3** Add the taco seasoning mix, cayenne pepper, Cajun seasoning, and chili powder to another self-seal bag. |
| ¾ teaspoon Cajun seasoning | |
| ½ teaspoon chili powder | **4** Remove the oil-coated chicken pieces from their bag and add them to the seasoning bag; push (or shake) the pieces around until they're evenly coated with the dry mix. Place the chicken in the prepared baking dish. |
| | **5** Bake the wings at 400 degrees for 20 minutes, or until the chicken pieces are cooked through and the tops are beginning to brown. |

*Per serving:* Calories: 136; Total fat: 11g; Saturated fat: 2g; Cholesterol: 22mg; Sodium: 443mg; Carbohydrates: 3g; Fiber: 0g; Sugar: 0g; Protein: 5g.

*Tip:* For those who want to bump up the heat a degree or two, add a little extra cayenne and chili powder to the mix.

# *Italian Favorites: Hold the Gluten!*

What's the first thing that comes to mind when you think of Italian food? Pasta, you say? It's true that pasta, traditionally made from wheat flour, forms the basis of many beloved Italian dishes. If you travel to Italy, you'll be happy to find that many people are aware of celiac, so getting amazing gluten-free Italian fare isn't out of the question.

But what about cooking Italian at home? Fortunately, gluten-free pastas — zitis, pennes, spaghettis, lasagnas, and more — are now widely available and entirely palatable. Test out a few brands, find your favorite, and gather up your garlic and tomatoes.

Don't restrict your Italian fare to pasta-based menus. Plenty of traditional Italian dishes are free of pasta. Think cheeses, grilled vegetables, fresh seafood, cured meats, and sauces to suit every taste.

## Advisory labels: Sometimes more (information) is less (helpful)

You've seen the advisory labels: "This product manufactured in a facility that produces wheat"; it's right next to the "gluten-free" designation. Or, "This product made on shared equipment that also processes wheat ingredients." What about the labels that say "gluten-free" and then say "This product may contain wheat"? Huh?

Companies are trying to be helpful (and to cover their hineys liability-wise), but sometimes the extra information adds to the confusion.

So what *do* you do if a product says it's gluten-free but manufactured in a facility that produces wheat products? There's not an easy answer.

The truth of the matter is that all manufacturers in North America have good manufacturing policies (GMPs) that require them to thoroughly clean all equipment between product lines. In other words, if they make a gluten-containing product and then the next product on the line is gluten-free, they have to clean all equipment really well before making the change.

Is there a chance that a tiny particle of gluten could get left behind on the manufacturing line? Yes. Is there a chance that you'll buy the box of cereal that contains that little bit of gluten? Sure. Is there a chance that you, the celiac in the family, will be the one to eat that little gluten particle (and the surrounding particles that have been contaminated)? Yep. Admittedly, those chances are remote.

# Eggplant Rollatini with Marinara Sauce

**Prep time:** 10 min • **Cook time:** 18 min • **Yield:** 8 servings

### Ingredients

2 medium eggplants, sliced lengthwise into 16 slices, ¼-inch thick

Salt

Nonstick cooking spray

12 ounces lowfat ricotta cheese

8 ounces cream cheese

1 cup chopped fresh baby spinach

2 garlic cloves, minced

½ teaspoon oregano

½ teaspoon basil

1 egg

Freshly ground pepper

1 jar, favorite marinara sauce

1 cup lowfat mozzarella cheese, shredded

¼ cup grated parmesan cheese

### Directions

1. Arrange eggplant slices on a rack over a large baking pan. Sprinkle with salt and set aside for an hour to remove any bitter juices. Pat dry with paper towels. Preheat a large grill pan over kitchen stove or pre-heated gas grill and generously spray with cooking spray. Grill eggplant slices in batches until tender and lightly browned, about 3 minutes per side. Be careful not to tear the slices. Remove and cool to room temperature.

2. In a medium bowl, combine ricotta cheese, cream cheese, spinach, garlic, oregano, basil, egg, salt, and pepper.

3. Preheat oven to 350 degrees. Lightly spray a 13-x-9-2-inch glass baking pan with cooking spray. Gently spread cheese mixture evenly over eggplant slices. Roll up eggplant slices using your fingers to keep the filling from spilling out. Lay each roll in baking pan, seam-side down.

4. Top the eggplant rolls with the marinara sauce and bake for 15 to 18 minutes. Sprinkle mozzarella and parmesan cheeses over top and broil an additional 3 minutes or until cheese is bubbly and begins to brown.

*Per serving:* Calories: 269; Total fat: 17g; Saturated fat: 10g; Cholesterol: 76mg; Sodium: 781mg; Carbohydrates: 17g; Fiber: 4g; Protein: 14g.

*Tip:* When purchasing eggplant, look for deep purple color, a glossy shine, and no brown spots. Plump eggplants tend to be juicier. Choose one that is firm and heavy for its size.

*Note:* This is a lower-calorie alternative to the classic breaded and fried eggplant rollatini. The cheese mixture will be fairly thin if using lowfat ricotta and cream cheeses, but it firms up during baking.

# Herbed Shrimp Scampi

**Prep time:** 15 min • **Cook time:** 10 min • **Yield:** 4 servings

| *Ingredients* | *Directions* |
|---|---|
| 2 tablespoons butter | *1* Heat butter and oil in a large skillet, add garlic slices, and sauté on medium heat until fragrant, about a minute. |
| 1 tablespoon olive oil | |
| 6 garlic cloves, thinly sliced | |
| ½ cup white wine | *2* Add the wine and boil on high heat for 2 to 3 minutes. Add shrimp and cook for 2 to 3 minutes. Turn shrimp and add the lemon, lemon zest, parsley, chives, and tarragon. Cook for one more minute until flavors blend. Don't overcook shrimp, or they will become tough. Shrimp should be uniformly pink when cooking is complete. Garnish with parsley sprigs before serving. |
| 1½ pounds large raw shrimp, peeled and deveined | |
| ½ fresh squeezed lemon | |
| ¼ teaspoon lemon zest | |
| 1 teaspoon dried parsley | |
| 1 teaspoon dried chives | |
| ½ teaspoon dried tarragon | |
| Fresh parsley sprigs | |

*Per serving: Calories: 219; Total fat: 11g; Saturated fat: 4g; Cholesterol: 267mg; Sodium: 292mg; Carbohydrates: 2g; Fiber: 0g; Protein: 28g.*

**Tip:** Because this recipe is made very quickly, have all the ingredients organized, measured, and ready to use when the cooking begins.

**Note:** This savory meal is a huge hit. Serve with brown rice or with gluten-free spaghetti or linguine, made from quinoa. Refer to Figure 13-2 about how to clean and devein shrimp.

## CLEANING AND DEVEINING SHRIMP

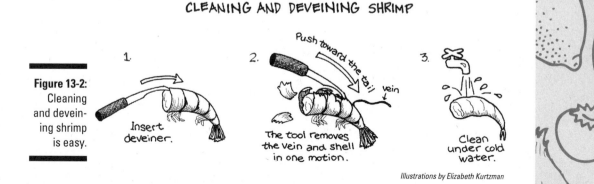

**Figure 13-2:** Cleaning and deveining shrimp is easy.

1. Insert deveiner.

2. Push toward the tail. vein. The tool removes the vein and shell in one motion.

3. Clean under cold water.

*Illustrations by Elizabeth Kurtzman*

# Italian Beef Vegetable Soup

**Prep time:** 15 min • **Cook time:** 35 min • **Yield:** 10 servings

| Ingredients | Directions |
| --- | --- |

### Ingredients

¾ pound 90 percent lean ground beef

1 medium onion, chopped

1 teaspoon minced garlic

2 tablespoons olive oil

2 cups beef broth

5 cups water

2 teaspoons beef bouillon

14.5-ounce can diced tomatoes

8-ounce can kidney beans, undrained

½ small head cabbage, shredded

2 stalks celery, sliced thin

1 large carrot, sliced thin

1 small zucchini, cut into small cubes

2 tablespoons dried parsley flakes

¼ teaspoon pepper

1 teaspoon salt (add more salt to taste if needed)

1 teaspoon Italian seasoning

1½ cups uncooked pasta (elbow macaroni, noodles, broken spaghetti, so on)

### Directions

*1* In a Dutch oven or large saucepan over medium-high heat, brown the beef, onion, and garlic in olive oil, breaking the meat up with a fork. Drain off the excess fat.

*2* Stir in the remaining ingredients except the pasta. Heat to boiling.

*3* Reduce the heat to medium-low. Cover and simmer the soup for 20 minutes.

*4* Add the pasta and cook the soup 10 minutes more, or until the pasta is tender but not mushy.

*Per serving:* Calories: 238; Total fat: 10g; Saturated fat: 3g; Cholesterol: 41mg; Sodium: 1,031mg; Carbohydrates: 20g; Fiber: 5g; Sugar: 3g; Protein: 18g.

*Tip:* If you plan to freeze the soup, don't add the pasta because it may get mushy when you thaw it.

# Spaghetti and Meatball Soup

**Prep time:** 20 min • **Cook time:** 20 min • **Yield:** 4 servings

| Ingredients | Directions |
|---|---|
| **4 teaspoons pesto sauce** | *1* Drain off the oil that has collected at the top of the pesto before measuring the pesto. Place the pesto in a medium bowl. |
| **½ pound lean ground beef** | |
| **½ onion, chopped** | |
| **1 clove garlic, minced** | *2* Add the ground beef to the bowl and mix it with the pesto until the ingredients are completely blended. Roll the mixture into tiny meatballs (no wider than a nickel). Set aside. |
| **½ cup carrots, sliced thin** | |
| **1 tablespoon olive oil** | |
| **2 tablespoons chopped fresh parsley** | *3* In a large saucepan, sauté the meatballs, onion, garlic, and carrots in the oil, over medium-high heat, turning the meat frequently, until the vegetables are tender and the meat is cooked through. |
| **¼ teaspoon salt** | |
| **¼ teaspoon pepper** | |
| **⅔ cup spaghetti sauce** | *4* Add the parsley, salt, pepper, and spaghetti sauce; bring to a boil over medium-high heat. Lower heat to medium-low, cover the pan, and gently simmer for 15 minutes. |
| **Three 14.5-ounce cans chicken broth** | |
| **¼ pound spaghetti** | *5* In a medium saucepan, bring the broth to a boil. Break the spaghetti into fourths and add it to the broth. Cook the spaghetti over medium-high heat for 5 minutes, or just until the pasta is barely tender. |
| **4 tablespoons grated Parmesan cheese** | |
| | *6* Add the spaghetti and broth to the meatball mixture and simmer for 3 minutes. Spoon the soup into bowls and sprinkle with the cheese. |

*Per serving:* Calories: 253; Total fat: 10g; Saturated fat: 5g; Cholesterol: 53mg; Sodium: 2,091mg; Carbohydrates: 6g; Fiber: 7g; Sugar: 12g; Protein: 23g.

*Note:* Serve this favorite with a large tossed salad, and you have a complete dinner.

# Italian Stuffed Cabbage

**Prep time:** 55 min • **Cook time:** 1 hr • **Yield:** 8 servings

| *Ingredients* | *Directions* |
|---|---|

**Ingredients**

1 large cabbage

1 zucchini

1 carrot

2½ cups uncooked rice

2 medium onions, minced

½ bunch fresh parsley, minced

½ teaspoon garlic powder

1 teaspoon Italian seasoning

2 teaspoons salt

1 teaspoon pepper

½ teaspoon cumin

½ teaspoon cinnamon

2 drops hot pepper sauce

¾ cup water

¼ cup olive oil

Two 26-ounce jars spaghetti sauce

**Directions**

*1* Cut the core out of the cabbage. Place the cabbage, core down, in a large saucepan. Add about 3 cups of water and steam the cabbage, covered, until the outer leaves turn bright green. Remove the softened leaves, and then return the cabbage to the pot and repeat until all the cabbage leaves have been removed.

*2* Preheat the oven to 350 degrees.

*3* Shred the zucchini and carrot into a large bowl. Add the remaining ingredients except the spaghetti sauce and cabbage leaves. Stir to mix well. Stir ½ cup of the spaghetti sauce into the rice mixture.

*4* Stuff each cabbage leaf with 3 tablespoons of the rice mixture. (Use slightly more rice mixture for the larger cabbage leaves and slightly less mixture for the small, inside cabbage leaves.) Fold in one side of the leaf to cover the filling, and then roll the cabbage.

*5* Spread 1 cup of the spaghetti sauce on the bottom of a 9-x-13-inch baking dish. Lay the cabbage rolls in the pan, seam side down. Pour 2½ cups of the spaghetti sauce over the top of the rolls.

*6* Cover the pan with foil and bake the rolls at 350 degrees for 1 hour, adding a little water if needed.

*7* Warm the remaining 2 cups of spaghetti sauce to pour over the rolls just before serving.

*Per serving:* Calories: 431; Total fat: 10g; Saturated fat: 1g; Cholesterol: 581mg; Sodium: 909mg; Carbohydrates: 78g; Fiber: 8g; Sugar: 15g; Protein: 11g.

***Note:*** Long-grain rice works best in these rolls. Pack the cabbage loosely, allowing room for the rice to expand.

# Spaghetti Marinara

**Prep time:** 10 min • **Cook time:** 25 min • **Yield:** 4 servings

| *Ingredients* | *Directions* |
|---|---|
| 1½ tablespoons virgin olive oil | *1* Heat the oil in a large saucepan over medium heat. Sauté the onions, carrots, and garlic until tender, stirring frequently (about 5 minutes). |
| 2 medium onions, chopped | |
| ¼ cup grated carrots | |
| 3 cloves garlic, finely minced | *2* Stir in the tomatoes, tomato sauce, parsley, basil, oregano, cinnamon, salt, pepper, and sugar. Heat the sauce to boiling, and then reduce the heat to low. Cover and simmer the sauce for 20 minutes. |
| 28-ounce can crushed tomatoes | |
| 8-ounce can tomato sauce | |
| 2 tablespoons chopped fresh parsley | *3* Prepare the spaghetti as the package directs. Spoon the marinara sauce over the cooked pasta. |
| ½ teaspoon dried basil | |
| ½ teaspoon dried oregano | |
| ¼ teaspoon cinnamon | |
| ¼ teaspoon salt | |
| ¼ teaspoon pepper | |
| 2 teaspoons sugar | |
| 12-ounce box rice spaghetti | |

*Per serving:* Calories: 414; Total fat: 6g; Saturated fat: 1g; Cholesterol: 0mg; Sodium: 606mg; Carbohydrates: 82g; Fiber: 6g; Sugar: 9g; Protein: 5g.

*Tip:* Many tomato-based dishes taste better the next day, and this marinara sauce is no exception. If you have the time, make the sauce the day before, and cover and refrigerate the pan to allow the flavors to blend before reheating and spooning it onto your pasta.

*Note:* Figure 13-3 shows how to chop parsley.

## CHOPPING PARSLEY & OTHER FRESH HERBS

**Figure 13-3:**
Fresh herbs
can add
flavor to a
dish.

1. Rinse and dry well.

2. chop roughly

*NOTE: For herbs like rosemary and thyme, remove and chop leaves. Discard thick stem.

3. gather and chop some more. Use rocking motion. move knife around.

*Illustrations by Elizabeth Kurtzman*

# Italian Hamburger Pasta Casserole

**Prep time:** 15 min • **Cook time:** 60 min • **Yield:** 10 servings

| Ingredients | Directions |
|---|---|
| **1 pound pasta shells or elbow macaroni** | **1** Preheat the oven to 350 degrees. |
| **2 tablespoons olive oil** | **2** In a large saucepan, boil the pasta, stirring occasionally, until the pasta is barely tender (about 6 minutes). Rinse it under cold running water, and then drain in a colander. |
| **2½ pounds lean ground beef** | |
| **2 medium onions, diced** | |
| **3 cloves garlic, minced** | **3** Add the olive oil to the same saucepan, and brown the beef, onions, and garlic over medium-high heat, breaking up the meat with a fork. |
| **3 tablespoons minced fresh parsley** | |
| **¾ teaspoon cinnamon** | **4** Stir the parsley, cinnamon, basil, salt, pepper, diced tomatoes and juice, tomato sauce, and 1 cup of water into the meat mixture and simmer, stirring often, for 3 minutes. Stir in the pasta and mix to blend. |
| **¾ teaspoon dried basil** | |
| **½ teaspoon salt** | |
| **¼ teaspoon pepper** | |
| **14.5-ounce can diced tomatoes with juice** | **5** Spoon the mixture into a 9-x-13-inch pan. Sprinkle the top with cheese. |
| **Two 15-ounce cans tomato sauce** | |
| **1 cup water** | **6** Bake the dish at 350 degrees for 1 hour. |
| **½ cup grated Parmesan cheese** | |

*Per serving: Calories: 404; Total fat: 21g; Saturated fat: 4g; Cholesterol: 73mg; Sodium: 766mg; Carbohydrates: 47g; Fiber: 3g; Sugar: 5g; Protein: 27g.*

# Chapter 14

# Something's Fishy 'Round Here

## In This Chapter

▶ Catching some tips for preparing fish

▶ Sticking to simple seasonings and sauces

▶ Serving creative seafood dishes

**S**ome people think fish is fish. But oh, how wrong they are. Think of the options. Do you want to cook it with dry heat (baking, barbecuing, blackening, bronzing, broiling, microwaving), or use moist heat (steaming, poaching), or fry the fish (deep-frying, pan-frying)? When you've made up your mind about how to cook it, then you're confronted with further queries: Should it be marinated? Stuffed? Breaded? Basted? Glazed? Served with a sauce?

Before you become totally overwhelmed with choices, take a look at some of the recipes in this chapter and realize that fish can make a fabulous dish!

## Reeling in Compliments with Fish and Seafood Dishes

Unlike meat, fish is naturally tender and requires short cook times at a high temperature. All fish and seafood are naturally gluten-free. Below are some general guidelines for cooking fish:

✔ Measure fish at its thickest part.

✔ Allow 10 minutes of cook time per inch of thickness for fresh fish.

✔ Allow 20 minutes of cook time per inch of thickness for frozen fish.

✔ Fish is ready when it's opaque but still juicy. Sometimes if you cook a filet until it flakes easily with a fork, it will be overdone and dried out.

Raw fish is *translucent*, kind of like frosted glass. You certainly can't look through it, but it's not solid either. Cooked fish is *opaque* and solid, meaning you can't see through it at all.

✔ Baking fish in an aluminum pan can create a chemical reaction that leaves the fish tasting acidic. It's best to bake fish in a glass or stainless steel pan.

✔ *Do not overcook* or the fish will become tough.

Fish is loaded with great nutrients, such as healthy Omega-3s and protein, but nearly all fish and shellfish contain traces of mercury as well. For most people, the risk from mercury isn't of concern, but pregnant women, nursing mothers, and young children would be prudent to avoid those fish that contain higher levels of mercury. Those fish include shark, swordfish, king mackerel, and tilefish. Fish and shellfish low in mercury include shrimp, canned light tuna, salmon, Pollock, and catfish. Albacore ("white" tuna) has more mercury than canned light tuna.

# Broiling, Baking, and Poaching Fish

Preparing fish by baking, broiling, and poaching it are healthy ways to serve it to your family and friends. This section focuses on several easy recipes.

The good news: Fish is a highly nutritious food commodity. It provides protein, far fewer calories than meat, and is rich in Omega-3 fatty acids. (Isn't it odd that we're always being told to stay away from fatty foods, yet certain fatty acids are good for us?)

Omega-3 has many health benefits including lowering triglycerides and helping to prevent heart disease and blood clots; improving brain function; helping with high blood pressure, diabetes, strokes, depression, arthritis, allergies, circulation problems, ADHD, Alzheimer's disease, skin disorders, and gout; and lowering the risk of osteoporosis in post-menopausal women. The primary source for this fatty acid is fatty fish, such as salmon, mackerel, sardines, and herring. Opt to buy fish that comes from the deep sea (as opposed to farm-raised) so it will be as pollutant-free as possible.

# Sesame Pretzel Fish

**Prep time:** 10 min • **Cook time:** 20 min • **Yield:** 4 servings

| Ingredients | Directions |
|---|---|
| **Nonstick cooking spray** | *1* Preheat the oven to 400 degrees. Spray a 9-x-13-inch baking dish with cooking spray. |
| **Two 2.65-ounce bags sesame pretzel rings** | *2* Puree 1 bag of pretzels at a time in a blender; empty the crumbs into a gallon-size self-seal plastic bag. |
| **½ teaspoon salt** | |
| **¼ teaspoon pepper** | *3* Add the salt, pepper, dill, and garlic powder to the plastic bag; seal the bag and shake well to mix the ingredients. |
| **¾ teaspoon dried dill** | |
| **¼ teaspoon garlic powder** | |
| **½ cup fresh lemon juice (about 3 whole lemons)** | *4* In a shallow bowl, whisk together the lemon juice and brown mustard. |
| **1½ tablespoons brown mustard** | *5* Rinse the filets and pat them dry. Place the filets in the lemon-mustard mixture and let them marinate for 3 minutes. |
| **Four 5-ounce fillets of bass** | |
| | *6* Remove the bass and place the filets in the bag with the crumbs. Seal the bag and shake it to coat the filets evenly. |
| | *7* Place each piece of fish in a single layer in the prepared baking dish and bake the fillets at 400 degrees for 20 minutes. |

*Per serving: Calories: 403; Total fat: 16g; Saturated fat: 5g; Cholesterol: 129mg; Sodium: 963mg; Carbohydrates: 24g; Fiber: 2g; Sugar: 2g; Protein: 39g.*

**Tip:** Ground pretzels, especially ones with sesame seeds, make an excellent coating for oven-baked chicken, too!

**Note:** The fish may be prepared ahead, covered with plastic wrap, and refrigerated until you're ready to bake it.

**Vary It!** If bass is not available, you can substitute orange roughy. Orange roughy is not as thick as bass, so you may have to reduce the baking time.

# Salmon with Mustard Dill Sauce

**Prep time:** 5 min  •  **Cook time:** 15 min  •  **Yield:** 4 servings

| *Ingredients* | *Directions* |
|---|---|
| 1 teaspoon plus 3 tablespoons olive oil | *1* Preheat the oven to 350 degrees. |
| Four 5-ounce wild salmon filets with the skin removed | *2* Lightly oil an 8-x-11-inch baking dish with 1 teaspoon of olive oil. Rinse and pat the filets dry, and place the fish in a single layer in the dish. |
| ½ teaspoon dried dill | |
| ¼ teaspoon crushed red pepper flakes | *3* Combine the dill, red pepper flakes, oregano, salt, garlic, almonds, onion, lemon juice, brown mustard, pepper, and 3 tablespoons of olive oil in a blender. Puree the ingredients for 10 seconds, scrape down the blender's sides with a spatula, and then puree for 10 more seconds. |
| ¼ teaspoon dried oregano | |
| ¼ teaspoon salt | |
| ¼ teaspoon minced garlic | |
| 3 tablespoons slivered almonds | *4* Spread the sauce over the fish, dividing evenly. |
| 2 green onions, chopped | |
| 2 tablespoons fresh lemon juice (about 1 whole lemon) | *5* Bake the filets at 350 degrees for about 15 minutes or until a fork inserted in the thickest part of the salmon turns easily. |
| 1 teaspoon brown mustard | |
| ¼ teaspoon pepper | |

*Per serving:* Calories: 392; Total fat: 25g; Saturated fat: 4g; Cholesterol: 101mg; Sodium: 243mg; Carbohydrates: 3g; Fiber: 1g; Sugar: 1g; Protein: 38g.

*Tip:* Wild salmon is deeper in color and has a much richer taste than farm-raised salmon.

*Note:* Before preparing this dish, remove the skin from the salmon by using a very sharp, thin knife.

# Poached Salmon Piccata

**Prep time:** 5 min • **Cook time:** 10 min • **Yield:** 2 servings

| Ingredients | Directions |
|---|---|
| ¾ cup water | *1* Place the water, sherry, lemon juice, bouillon granules, capers, salt, pepper, parsley flakes, dill, mint, and butter in a medium skillet over high heat. Bring the mixture to a boil. |
| ¼ cup sherry | |
| 2 teaspoons fresh lemon juice | |
| ½ teaspoon chicken bouillon granules | *2* Reduce the heat to medium and add the salmon. Cover the skillet and simmer the filets for 7 to 8 minutes (cook 10 minutes per inch of thickness at the thickest part) or until the fish flakes easily with a fork. (You won't need to turn the fish over during cooking.) |
| 1 tablespoon capers, rinsed and drained | |
| ⅛ teaspoon salt | |
| ⅛ teaspoon pepper | |
| 1 teaspoon dried parsley flakes | *3* Remove the fish from the skillet with a wide spatula to prevent the salmon from breaking apart. Discard the remaining liquid in the pan. |
| ¼ teaspoon dried dill | |
| ¼ teaspoon dried mint flakes | |
| 1 tablespoon butter | |
| Two 5-ounce pieces wild salmon filets, thawed and skin removed | |

*Per serving: Calories: 282; Total fat: 15g; Saturated fat: 5g; Cholesterol: 92mg; Sodium: 701mg; Carbohydrates: 3g; Fiber: 0g; Sugar: 1g; Protein: 28g.*

*Tip:* Serve this dish over a bed of gluten-free noodles or on a bed of cooked spinach.

*Note:* Some bouillon contains modified wheat starch. Read labels carefully!

# Trying Seafood in Crepes and Casseroles

The recipes in this section provide more creative ways to get fish in your meals. And more fish is a good thing. Fish and seafood are lower in saturated fat, total fat, and calories than comparable portions of meat or poultry.

Oysters are the least-consumed seafood even though they are loaded with zinc, which has been proven to be an aphrodisiac. Rumor has it that Casanova, the infamous 18th-century lover, ate 50 oysters for breakfast every day!

# Salmon Crepes

**Prep time:** 15 min • **Cook time:** 10-15 min • **Yield:** 4 servings

| Ingredients | Directions |
|---|---|
| Nonstick cooking spray | *1* Preheat the oven to 400 degrees. Using the cooking spray, grease a 9-x-9-inch baking dish. |
| 1½ tablespoons butter | *2* In a medium saucepan, sauté the onion in butter over medium heat until the onion is soft but not browned. |
| 1 green onion, sliced thin | *3* Remove the pan from the heat. |
| 1 tablespoon cornstarch | *4* In a small bowl, stir together the cornstarch, salt, pepper, thyme, dill, and half-and-half until well blended, and then add it to the butter and onions in the pan. Stir until blended. |
| ½ teaspoon salt | |
| ⅛ teaspoon pepper | |
| ⅛ teaspoon dried thyme | *5* Return the pan to the heat and cook the contents over medium heat, stirring constantly, until the mixture has thickened. Remove the pan from the heat. |
| ⅛ teaspoon dried dill | |
| ¾ cup half-and-half | *6* In a medium bowl, whip the egg with a whisk. Very slowly, drizzle the half-and-half mixture into the egg, whisking constantly, until ¾ of the *roux* (the half-and-half mixture) has been incorporated. Stir the egg mixture into the remaining roux in the pan. Cook 1 minute over medium heat, stirring constantly, and then remove the pan from the heat. |
| 1 egg | |
| 2 teaspoons sherry | |
| 6-ounce can salmon, drained | *7* Pour ¾ of the sauce into a medium bowl. Stir the sherry into the remaining sauce in the pan and set it aside. |
| 4-ounce can mushroom stems and pieces, drained | *8* Stir the salmon and mushrooms into the bowl with the reserved sauce. |
| 8 crepes (see the recipe in Chapter 9) | *9* Place a heaping tablespoon of the salmon mixture down the center of each crepe. Roll up the crepes, jelly-roll style, and place them in a single layer in the prepared baking dish. Pour the remaining sauce over the tops of the crepes, and then sprinkle with cheese. |
| 1 tablespoon grated Romano cheese | |
| | *10* Bake the crepes at 400 degrees for 10 to 15 minutes, or until they're heated through. |

*Per serving of 2 crepes:* Calories: 217; Total fat: 15g; Saturated fat: 9g; Cholesterol: 122mg; Sodium: 473mg; Carbohydrates: 9g; Fiber: 1g; Sugar: 2g; Protein: 13g.

# Seafood Sole

**Prep time:** 15 min • **Cook time:** 30 min • **Yield:** 4 servings

| Ingredients | Directions |
|---|---|
| **Nonstick cooking spray** | *1* Preheat the oven to 400 degrees. Lightly grease a 9-x-9-inch baking dish with cooking spray. |
| **1 tablespoon butter** | |
| **½ cup onion, chopped** | *2* Melt the butter in a large saucepan; add the onions and mushrooms and sauté them over medium heat until they're soft. Stir in the shrimp and crabmeat and heat the mixture. |
| **7-ounce can sliced mushrooms, drained** | |
| **½ pound fresh, cooked medium shrimp, cut in half** | |
| **6-ounce can lump crabmeat, drained** | *3* Rinse the filets and pat them dry. Sprinkle the filets with salt, pepper, and paprika, and lay them in the prepared baking dish. Spoon the shrimp mixture over the filets. |
| **Four 6-ounce sole or flounder filets** | |
| **¼ teaspoon salt** | |
| **¼ teaspoon pepper** | *4* In a medium bowl, stir together the soup, bouillon granules, and cornstarch until the ingredients are blended. Stir in the cheese and parsley flakes. Pour the mixture over the casserole. |
| **¼ teaspoon paprika** | |
| **18-ounce can ready-to-serve cream of mushroom soup** | |
| **¼ teaspoon chicken bouillon granules** | *5* Bake the casserole at 400 degrees for 30 minutes. |
| **2 teaspoons cornstarch** | |
| **¼ cup shredded sharp white cheddar cheese** | |
| **1 tablespoon dried parsley flakes** | |

*Per serving:* Calories: 418; Total fat: 16g; Saturated fat: 7g; Cholesterol: 178mg; Sodium: 1,414mg; Carbohydrates: 13g; Fiber: 1g; Sugar: 2g; Protein: 54g.

*Tip:* If you prepare this dish for company, you may opt to stuff each piece of fish with the seafood mixture, and then roll it up, secure it with a toothpick, and pour the sauce over the top before baking.

*Note:* Be sure to use lump crabmeat because imitation crabmeat usually isn't gluten-free.

# Seafood au Gratin

**Prep time:** 15 min • **Cook time:** 30 min • **Yield:** 6 servings

| Ingredients | Directions |
|---|---|
| Nonstick cooking spray | *1* Preheat the oven to 325 degrees. Grease a 9-x-13-inch glass baking dish with cooking spray. |
| 3 tablespoons butter | |
| 2 tablespoons cornstarch | *2* In a medium saucepan, melt the butter. |
| ¼ cup plus 1¾ cups half-and-half | *3* In a small bowl, stir the cornstarch together with ¼ cup of the half-and-half until the mixture is smooth. Stir this into the butter in the pan. |
| ¼ teaspoon salt | |
| 1 teaspoon dried parsley flakes | |
| ⅛ teaspoon dried red pepper flakes | *4* Add the remaining half-and-half, salt, parsley, red pepper flakes, and dried onion to the cornstarch mixture. Over medium heat, cook the mixture, stirring constantly with a whisk, until the mixture has thickened. |
| 1 teaspoon minced dried onion | |
| ¾ cup shredded cheddar cheese | *5* Stir in the cheddar cheese until it melts. Remove from heat. |
| ¼ cup sherry | |
| 14-ounce can quartered artichoke hearts | *6* Drain the artichoke hearts, reserving the liquid. Stir the sherry and the artichoke juice into the sauce in the saucepan. |
| Juice from artichokes | |
| ¾ pound crabmeat pieces | |
| ½ pound raw shrimp, peeled and deveined | *7* Place the artichoke hearts, crabmeat, shrimp, and scallops in the prepared baking dish. |
| ½ pound sea scallops, sliced into medallions | *8* Pour the cream sauce over the seafood. Sprinkle the top with almonds, Parmesan cheese, and very lightly with paprika. |
| ⅓ cup slivered almonds | |
| ¼ cup grated Parmesan cheese | |
| Paprika to taste | *9* Bake the seafood at 325 degrees for 30 minutes. |

*Per serving:* Calories: 461; Total fat: 27g; Saturated fat: 15g; Cholesterol: 183mg; Sodium: 667mg; Carbohydrates: 16g; Fiber: 4g; Sugar: 1g; Protein: 37g.

*Tip:* Don't substitute milk for the half-and-half, or the sauce won't be as thick and rich.

*Note:* Use real crabmeat; the imitation crabmeat may not be gluten-free.

# Tuna Broccoli Casserole

**Prep time:** 15 min • **Cook time:** 25 min • **Yield:** 6 servings

### Ingredients

Nonstick cooking spray

2 cups rice seashell pasta

2 tablespoons cornstarch

1 teaspoon chicken bouillon granules

1 teaspoon dried minced onion flakes

¼ teaspoon dried thyme

1 tablespoon dried parsley flakes

¼ teaspoon pepper

⅛ teaspoon salt

12-ounce can tuna packed in water, drained

4-ounce jar chopped pimiento, drained

18-ounce can cream of mushroom soup

3 tablespoons whole milk

10-ounce box frozen chopped broccoli, thawed

½ cup plus ¾ cup shredded Monterey Jack cheese

¼ cup seasoned gluten-free bread crumbs

¼ teaspoon paprika

### Directions

1   Preheat the oven to 400 degrees. Using the cooking spray, grease a 9-x-9-inch baking dish.

2   In a medium saucepan, cook the pasta according to package directions, and then rinse and drain it.

3   In a large bowl, stir together the cornstarch, bouillon granules, onion flakes, thyme, parsley flakes, pepper, and salt. Add the pasta, tuna, pimiento, soup, milk, broccoli, and ½ cup of the cheese to the bowl. Stir to mix well.

4   Spoon the mixture into the prepared baking dish.

5   In a small bowl, stir together the remaining ¾ cup of cheese, bread crumbs, and paprika. Sprinkle this mixture on top of the casserole.

6   Bake the casserole at 400 degrees for 25 minutes.

*Per serving: Calories: 385; Total fat: 13g; Saturated fat: 7g; Cholesterol: 40mg; Sodium: 406mg; Carbohydrates: 41g; Fiber: 3g; Sugar: 3g; Protein: 26g.*

**Tip:** Because companies change their recipes and ingredients regularly, check the label ingredients to make sure the soup is gluten-free before you purchase it.

**Note:** You can assemble this dish ahead of time, cover and refrigerate it, then bake it at dinnertime.

# Chapter 15

# Tastes Like Chicken: Poultry Dishes

*A* barbecued chicken leg is hot off the grill, dripping with sauce, and sitting on your plate. You're starving, and the aroma is activating all your sensory glands. Are you *really* going to use your fork and knife? Or are you going to dive down with both hands and pick it up? According to Emily Post, "Birds are not eaten with the fingers in company!" Fortunately, Miss Manners counters with the advice that hands can definitely be used in the enjoyment and consumption of said bird. (Like any of us really cares what either of them has to say!)

Few foods are as versatile as chicken. First, you need to decide what kind of chicken to buy — free-range or farm-raised, light meat or dark meat, whole chickens or separate parts, diced or shredded or strips, fresh or frozen, pre-marinated or plain, bone-in or boned. After you've made these decisions, then you have to figure out how you're going to prepare the bird. It can be grilled, stewed, baked, roasted, stuffed, broiled, boiled, oven-fried, deep-fried, pan-fried, microwaved, or cooked in a slow cooker. With all these choices, picking just one can be difficult.

The recipes in this chapter come to your rescue. We have taken America's favorite food and dressed it up in new ways. Now the only decision you have to make is which of these recipes you're going to make first!

# Flocking to Baked, Broiled, and Pan-Fried Dishes

Short of the chop-everything-into-one-baking-dish-and-cover-with-gluten-free-cream-of-mushroom-soup casseroles, the most common ways to prepare chicken are baked, broiled, and pan-fried. Here are some new ways to re-create the chicken dinner.

# Honey Broiled Chicken

**Prep time:** 8 min • **Cook time:** 35 min • **Yield:** 4 servings

| *Ingredients* | *Directions* |
|---|---|
| **Nonstick cooking spray** **Four 6-ounce bone-in chicken thighs** | *1* Preheat the broiler. Spray a 9-x-9-inch baking dish with nonstick spray. |
| **Juice from 1 lemon** | *2* Place the chicken, skin side up, in the baking dish. Squeeze the lemon juice over the chicken. |
| **4 tablespoons butter** **½ teaspoon salt** **¼ teaspoon pepper** **½ teaspoon garlic powder** | *3* Melt the butter in a small saucepan. Remove the saucepan from the heat and stir in the salt, pepper, and garlic powder. Spoon the butter sauce over the chicken thighs. |
| **5 teaspoons sugar** **2 tablespoons brown mustard** | *4* Broil the chicken for 20 minutes, turning once. |
| **4 teaspoons honey** | *5* In a small bowl, stir together the sugar, mustard, and honey. Brush half of the mixture over the chicken pieces and return to the broiler for 10 minutes. Turn the chicken pieces over, brush with the remaining sauce, and broil for 5 minutes more. |

*Per serving: Calories: 201; Total fat: 13g; Saturated fat: 8g; Cholesterol: 65mg; Sodium: 638mg; Carbohydrates: 11g; Fiber: 0g; Sugar: 11g; Protein: 8g.*

*Tip:* Use bone-in chicken pieces so the meat stays moist during broiling.

*Tip:* If you opt to put the chicken on the grill, baste frequently with pan juices.

*Note:* Figure 15-1 shows how you can juice a lemon.

HOW TO JUICE A LEMON

**Figure 15-1:** Juicing a lemon is easy.

Cut a lemon in half across the middle.

Hold a half in one hand at an angle. Use a fork to apply pressure and squeeze out the juice!

*Illustrations by Elizabeth Kurtzman*

# Sizzling Chicken and Walnuts

**Prep time:** 15 min • **Cook time:** 10 min • **Yield:** 4 servings

| *Ingredients* | *Directions* |
|---|---|
| 3 boneless and skinless chicken breasts, cut into bite-size strips | *1* In a large wok skillet, heat oil over medium-high heat and sauté chicken for about 3 minutes or until browned. Remove from pan. |
| 2 tablespoons peanut oil | |
| 3 green onions, cut in diagonal slices | *2* Add onions and celery and sauté quickly. Add chicken back to pan. Add butter, walnuts, and lemon zest. Cook uncovered for several minutes while continuing to stir. |
| 2 medium celery sticks, cut in diagonal slices | |
| ½ to 1 tablespoon butter | *3* Add soy sauce and lemon juice. Stir until chicken is coated. |
| ¾ cup walnut halves | |
| 1 teaspoon lemon zest | *4* Serve with cooked brown rice. |
| 2 tablespoons gluten-free soy sauce | |
| 1 tablespoon fresh lemon juice | |
| 2 cups cooked brown rice | |

*Per serving:* Calories: 424; Total fat: 24g; Saturated fat: 4g; Cholesterol: 59mg; Sodium: 540mg; Carbohydrates: 27g; Fiber 4g; Sugar: 0g; Protein: 27g.

*Tip:* When stir-frying, it's best to have all your ingredients prepped ahead and ready to use because the cooking takes no time to do. Don't overcrowd your dish with too many ingredients to get the perfect searing.

*Note:* Walnuts are high in alpha-linolenic acid, a heart healthy Omega-3 fatty acid that may help prevent heart attacks.

# Corn Chip Chicken

**Prep time:** 10 min • **Cook time:** 45 min • **Yield:** 5 servings

| Ingredients | Directions |
|---|---|
| 9.75-ounce bag corn chips | *1* Preheat the oven to 375 degrees. |
| ¼ teaspoon pepper | |
| ½ teaspoon Cajun seasoning | *2* Pour half of the corn chips into a blender and purée; pour the fine crumbs into a self-seal plastic bag. Repeat with the second half of corn chips. |
| ¼ teaspoon garlic powder | |
| 1 teaspoon paprika | *3* Add the pepper, Cajun seasoning, garlic powder, and paprika to the corn chips and mix well to distribute the spices evenly. |
| 4 tablespoons melted butter | |
| 5 whole chicken legs (leg and thigh) | *4* Dip one chicken piece into the melted butter, and then place it in the bag. Seal the bag and shake it to coat the chicken with crumbs. Repeat with the remaining chicken pieces. |
| | *5* Place the chicken in an 8-x-11-inch baking dish. |
| | *6* Bake the chicken at 375 degrees for 40 to 45 minutes, or until the chicken is just cooked through. (You don't need to turn the chicken pieces during cooking.) |

*Per serving (breaded without skin):* Calories: 630; Total fat: 35g; Saturated fat: 37g; Cholesterol: 170mg; Sodium: 540mg; Carbohydrates: 32g; Fiber: 4g; Sugar: 0g; Protein: 41g.

*Tip:* You can bread the chicken ahead, cover it, and refrigerate it until baking time.

*Vary It!* This recipe uses chicken legs, but you can use the pieces your family likes best.

# Herbes de Provence Chicken

**Prep time:** 10 min • **Cook time:** 50 min • **Yield:** 4 servings

| *Ingredients* | *Directions* |
|---|---|
| ½ **pound fingerling potatoes, cut in half** | *1* Preheat oven to 425 degrees. Line a large baking pan with silicon baking mat or parchment paper. |
| **6 shallots, peeled and cut in half** | |
| **4 Roma tomatoes, halved** | *2* Combine carrots and potatoes and place on the baking pan. Spritz with cooking spray. Sprinkle with 1 tablespoon Herbs de Provence. Roast in the oven for 20 minutes. Gently toss, then add shallots and tomatoes and roast an additional 10 minutes. Toss in the beans and roast for an additional 5 minutes. Remove from oven, place on a large platter, and keep warm. |
| **2 cups baby carrots, halved** | |
| **2 cups French green beans (herticot verts)** | |
| **Nonstick olive oil cooking spray** | |
| **1 tablespoon olive oil** | *3* Rub chicken thighs and legs with remaining Herbs de Provence, sea salt, and pepper. Place chicken on the same baking pan used to roast vegetables. Roast for 30 to 35 minutes or until chicken is done. |
| **2 tablespoons Herbs de Provence** | |
| **Sea salt and fresh ground pepper to taste** | *4* Serve chicken with roasted vegetables. |
| **4 bone-in, skinless chicken thighs and legs** | |

*Per serving: Calories 456: Total fat: 18g; Saturated fat: 4g; Cholesterol: 139mg; Sodium: 322mg; Carbohydrates: 31g; Fiber: 6g; Sugar: 0g; Protein: 44g.*

*Tip:* You can substitute chicken breasts, but because of the low fat content and no liquid in the recipe, the chicken may become dry during the roasting process. Reduce cooking time to prevent overcooking. Use a probe thermometer to achieve internal temperature of 165 degrees.

*Note:* Herbes de Provence are traditional dried herbs that are typically grown in the hills of southern France. Most grocery stores sell them as a blend in the spice aisle. Some of the herbs in the blend are a combination of thyme, chervil, rosemary, savory, lavender, tarragon, marjoram, oregano, mint, and bay leaves.

# Creole Chicken

**Prep time:** 10 min • **Cook time:** 50 min • **Yield:** 4 servings

| *Ingredients* | *Directions* |
|---|---|
| 1 tablespoon olive oil | *1* Preheat the oven to 350 degrees. |
| 2 cloves garlic, minced | |
| 1 medium onion, thinly sliced | *2* In a medium skillet over medium heat, sauté the garlic, onion, celery, and green pepper in oil, stirring frequently, until tender (about 4 minutes). |
| 2 ribs celery, thinly sliced | |
| ½ green pepper, finely diced | *3* Stir in the parsley flakes, tomato sauce, water, bay leaves, salt, and cayenne pepper. Simmer 2 more minutes. |
| 1 tablespoon dried parsley flakes | |
| 8-ounce can tomato sauce | *4* Place the chicken in a 9-x-9-inch baking dish. Pour the sauce over the chicken. |
| 1 cup water | |
| 2 bay leaves | *5* Bake the chicken at 350 degrees for 35 minutes and then cover with foil and bake another 15 minutes until the chicken is very tender. |
| ½ teaspoon salt | |
| ⅛ rounded teaspoon cayenne pepper | |
| Four 5-ounce bone-in skinless chicken breasts | |

*Per serving:* Calories: 194; Total fat: 5g; Saturated fat: 0g; Cholesterol: 68mg; Sodium: 707mg; Carbohydrates: 8g; Fiber: 2g; Sugar: 5g; Protein: 29g.

*Tip:* If you like really spicy hot food, add more cayenne pepper.

# Parmesan Chicken with Fresh Tomato Salsa

**Prep time:** 15 min • **Cook time:** 15 min • **Yield:** 4 servings

| Ingredients | Directions |
|---|---|
| Four 4-ounce boneless skinless chicken breasts | **1** On a cutting board and using the meat mallet, pound the thicker portion of each chicken breast to make the thickness of the pieces uniform. |
| 8 teaspoons sherry | |
| ¼ teaspoon plus ¼ teaspoon pepper | **2** Pour the sherry into a shallow bowl. |
| 2 cups coarsely shredded Parmesan cheese (do not use canned grated cheese) | **3** Mix ¼ teaspoon of pepper, the cheese, and bread crumbs together on a sheet of wax paper. |
| ⅓ cup bread crumbs | **4** Dip each chicken breast in the sherry, moistening both sides, and then press the breasts firmly into the cheese mixture, covering both sides of each breast. Use a meat mallet to help the cheese adhere to the meat. |
| 1 tablespoon plus 3 tablespoons olive oil | |
| ½ medium onion, chopped | **5** In a medium skillet over medium heat, sauté the onion, green pepper, and garlic in 1 tablespoon of olive oil, stirring frequently, until the vegetables are tender. Stir in the Italian seasoning, salt, ¼ teaspoon of pepper, tomatoes, and parsley. Continue cooking until the mixture is heated through. |
| ½ small green pepper, chopped | |
| ½ teaspoon minced garlic | |
| 2 teaspoons Italian seasoning | **6** Preheat a large nonstick skillet over medium-high heat. Add 3 tablespoons of oil. Set the breasts in the skillet and cook 5 to 6 minutes per side, until the cheese is light golden and the chicken is cooked through. |
| ¼ teaspoon salt | |
| 4 plum Roma tomatoes, chopped | |
| 2 tablespoons minced fresh parsley | **7** Remove the breasts from the skillet and set on paper toweling to drain the excess oil. |
| | **8** To serve, place the chicken breasts on a serving platter and spoon the tomato salsa over the chicken breasts. |

*Per serving:* Calories: 449; Total fat: 26g; Saturated fat: 10g; Cholesterol: 83mg; Sodium: 1,034mg; Carbohydrates: 61g; Fiber: 1g; Sugar: 2g; Protein: 38g.

**Tip:** To get the cheese coating to stick to the chicken, pound the cheese in with the flat side of a meat mallet.

# Stuffed Rock Cornish Game Hens

**Prep time:** 25 min • **Cook time:** 1½ hr • **Yield:** 4 servings

| Ingredients | Directions |
|---|---|
| **1 cup rice** | *1* Put the rice in a small bowl and cover it with water. Let it soak for several hours, and then rinse the rice in a strainer under cold water until the water runs clear. Drain. Preheat the oven to 500 degrees. |
| **2 Rock Cornish game hens, halved** | |
| **2 tablespoons olive oil** | *2* Rub the oil over the hens, inside and out. Place the hens in a 9-x-13-inch baking dish, cut side down. Sprinkle them with ¼ teaspoon of salt and ¼ teaspoon of pepper, and the paprika. Cut 1 tablespoon of the butter into small pieces and place it on top of the hens. Pour 2 cups of the chicken broth and the sherry into the pan around the hens. |
| **¼ teaspoon plus ¼ teaspoon salt** | |
| **¼ teaspoon plus ¼ teaspoon pepper** | |
| **½ teaspoon paprika** | |
| **1 tablespoon plus 2 tablespoons butter** | *3* Bake the hens at 500 degrees for 5 minutes, and then lower the heat to 350 degrees and continue baking for 15 minutes. Cover the hens with foil and bake for 25 minutes more, or until the leg twists easily. |
| **5 cups chicken broth, divided** | |
| **½ cup sherry** | *4* In a medium saucepan, sauté the onion and almonds in 2 tablespoons of butter over medium heat, stirring frequently, until the onion has softened. Add the roasted red pepper, 1 cup of chicken broth, ¼ teaspoon each of salt and pepper, dill, mint, and parsley. Bring to a boil. |
| **2 green onions, sliced thin** | |
| **3 tablespoons slivered almonds** | |
| **1 large red pepper, roasted and chopped** | *5* Lower the heat and stir in the rinsed, drained rice. Cover the pan and cook about 15 minutes, or until the moisture is absorbed. Remove from the heat. |
| **¼ teaspoon dried dill** | |
| **¼ teaspoon dried mint** | |
| **2 teaspoons dried parsley flakes** | *6* In a small saucepan, stir together 2 cups of chicken broth, the half-and-half, cornstarch, and mustard. Using a whisk, stir until the mixture is smooth. Stir in the cheese and cook, stirring constantly, over medium heat until the sauce thickens. |
| **½ cup half-and-half** | |
| **2 tablespoons cornstarch** | |
| **2 teaspoons brown mustard** | *7* To serve, place a compressed mound of rice on each dish. Place a hen half on top, and then spoon the sauce over the top. |
| **2 ounces (about ½ cup) shredded Swiss cheese** | |

*Per serving: Calories: 871; Total fat: 52g; Saturated fat: 19g; Cholesterol: 217mg; Sodium: 1,853mg; Carbohydrates: 49g; Fiber: 3g; Sugar: 2g; Protein: 39g.*

# *Making Poultry Casseroles That Will Fly Off the Plate*

Think of casseroles as energy conservation. You bake everything in one pot, so you usually only have to clean one pot after dinner. You don't have to dish out a vegetable, a starch, and an entree — with one large spoon you can serve up an entire meal.

Casseroles also fall into the category of food conservation and utilization. Do you have two carrots at the bottom of your vegetable bin that are starting to dry out and one last green onion that's starting to outlive its prime? Chop them up, sauté them in a little oil until they're soft, and then add them to any casserole. It's a much wiser alternative than waiting two more days and then throwing them out. Other ingredients that are prime candidates for adding to casseroles include that partially used bag of peas in the back of your freezer, the last cube of gluten-free chicken bouillon that's been sitting in your cupboard since 2003, and bits of fresh spinach that are left in the bag from that spinach salad you made four days ago. This section provides you with some chicken casseroles. Feel free to swap out ingredients as you experiment.

If you're looking for something besides gluten-free bread crumbs to top your casseroles, try crushed Funyuns, crushed corn chips or potato chips, crushed gluten-free cereals, crumbled bacon, shredded cheese (add this toward the end of the baking time), gluten-free cracker crumbs, or chopped nuts.

# Company Chicken

**Prep time:** 10 min • **Cook time:** 50 min • **Yield:** 6 servings

| *Ingredients* | *Directions* |
|---|---|
| 6 large chicken thighs | *1* Preheat the oven to 375 degrees. |
| 18-ounce can cream of mushroom soup (not condensed) | *2* Place the chicken thighs in an 8-x-11-inch baking dish. |
| 1½ cups plus ½ cup shredded sharp cheddar cheese | *3* In a medium bowl, stir together the soup, 1½ cups of cheese, taco seasoning mix, and milk. Spoon the mixture over the chicken. |
| 1.25-ounce package taco seasoning mix | |
| ½ cup milk | *4* Sprinkle with crushed crackers. |
| 2 cups crushed crackers | *5* Cover the pan with foil and bake the casserole at 375 degrees for 40 minutes. |
| | *6* Remove the foil and sprinkle the casserole with the remaining ½ cup of cheese. Return the dish to the oven to bake for 10 minutes more, or until the cheese has melted. |

*Per serving:* Calories: 298; Total fat: 20g; Saturated fat: 11g; Cholesterol: 49mg; Sodium: 661mg; Carbohydrates: 15g; Fiber: 1g; Sugar: 4g; Protein: 14g.

# Slow Cooker Chicken with Spinach and Mushrooms

**Prep time:** 5 min • **Cook time:** 8 hr • **Yield:** 4 servings

| *Ingredients* | *Directions* |
|---|---|
| Two 10-ounce boxes frozen, chopped spinach, thawed | *1* Stir together all the ingredients, except the chicken, in the slow cooker. |
| 8-ounce can sliced mushrooms, with liquid | |
| 18-ounce can cream of mushroom soup | *2* Add the chicken thighs and stir them in so they're covered with the sauce. |
| ¼ cup sherry | |
| 1 packet dry onion soup mix | *3* Cover and cook on low for 8 hours. |
| ½ teaspoon pepper | |
| ¼ teaspoon dried thyme | |
| Four 5-ounce skinless chicken thighs | |

*Per serving:* Calories: 401; Total fat: 9g; Saturated fat: 2g; Cholesterol: 63mg; Sodium: 1,520mg; Carbohydrates: 19g; Fiber: 6g; Sugar: 4g; Protein: 21g.

# Grecian Chicken with Pasta

**Prep time:** 15 min • **Cook time:** 1 hr, 15 min • **Yield:** 5 servings

| *Ingredients* | *Directions* |
|---|---|
| **3 tablespoons butter** | *1* Preheat the oven to 350 degrees. |
| **3½-pound chicken, cut into serving pieces** | *2* Sauté the chicken pieces and onions in the butter in a large skillet over medium-high heat until the chicken is browned on both sides. Transfer the chicken and onions to a roasting pan. |
| **1 onion, chopped** | |
| **Two 8-ounce cans tomato sauce** | |
| **2 cups chicken broth** | *3* Stir in the tomato sauce, chicken broth, white wine, cinnamon, salt, and pepper. Bake the chicken at 350 degrees for 1 hour, or until the chicken is very tender. (If the chicken gets too brown before it's cooked through, cover the pan with foil for the remainder of the baking time.) |
| **¼ cup white wine** | |
| **2 teaspoons cinnamon** | |
| **½ teaspoon salt** | |
| **¼ teaspoon pepper** | |
| **1 pound spaghetti (or other pasta)** | *4* Boil the spaghetti in a large saucepan of boiling water until the pasta is just barely tender, and then drain. |
| **3 tablespoons grated Parmesan cheese** | *5* When the chicken is tender, stir the spaghetti into the chicken and sauce and return the pan to the oven for 15 minutes, stirring the spaghetti every 5 minutes. (You may need to add a little water to the sauce.) |
| | *6* Remove the casserole from the oven and sprinkle the top with cheese. |

*Per serving:* Calories: 904; Total fat: 41g; Saturated fat: 14g; Cholesterol: 171mg; Sodium: 1,112mg; Carbohydrates: 84g; Fiber: 4g; Sugar: 5g; Protein: 43g.

*Tip:* Don't cook the spaghetti as long as the package directs because the pasta is also baked after it's boiled. The gluten-free pastas tend to get mushy when overcooked.

# Moroccan Chicken with Sweet Potatoes

**Prep time:** 10 min • **Cook time:** 90 min • **Yield:** 8 servings

| Ingredients | Directions |
|---|---|
| 2 tablespoons canola oil | *1* Heat oil in a Dutch oven, add turmeric, and sauté chicken breasts and thighs for 8 to 12 minutes, until evenly brown, stirring frequently. |
| Pinch ground turmeric | |
| 1 pound bone-in, skinless chicken breasts | |
| 1 pound bone-in, skinless chicken thighs | *2* Reduce heat to low. Add onion, pepper, paprika, cayenne pepper, and cumin with a cup of water, just enough to cover the meat. Add sweet potatoes. Cover Dutch oven tightly and cook for 15 minutes. |
| 1 large onion, chopped | |
| 1 jalapeño pepper, seeded and chopped | |
| 1½ teaspoons paprika | *3* Preheat the oven to 350 degrees. Place Dutch oven in preheated oven and cook for 60 to 90 minutes until meat is very tender, adding water to keep the stew moist. |
| Pinch cayenne pepper | |
| ½ teaspoon cumin | |
| 1 cup water | *4* Stir the parsley and cilantro into the meat and add tablespoon of water if the stew appears dry. |
| 1 pound sweet potatoes, peeled and chopped | |
| 3 tablespoons fresh parsley, chopped | |
| 3 tablespoons fresh cilantro, chopped | |
| Freshly ground pepper, to taste | |

*Per serving:* Calories: 189; Total fat: 9g; Saturated fat: 2g; Cholesterol: 54mg; Sodium: 54mg; Carbohydrates: 11g; Fiber: 2g; Sugar: 0g; Protein: 18g.

*Note:* Turmeric, paprika, and cumin are typical spices used in Moroccan cooking. This exotic style is delicious and has lots of great health benefits.

# Chapter 16

# Meat Matters

## In This Chapter

▶ Using caution when buying meat

▶ Seeking out steaks, chops, ribs, and more

▶ Shaping ground meats into meals

If you're a vegetarian or cooking for one, you can skip this chapter and head to Chapter 17. But for those meat-and-potatoes people, or even those who love a healthy, veggie-filled lifestyle but enjoy the protein-packed punch of a tasty lean meat, read on.

The recipes in this chapter delve into the delights of beef, pork, and lamb. Sorry, but there are no recipes for buffalo, venison, antelope, wild turkey, or alligator, but being the fan I am of interesting foods, we suggest finding a recipe for your favorite off-beat meat and modifying it to be gluten-free if you're up for the challenge. If you need help modifying recipes, take a look at Chapter 8 for some pointers. And if you're looking for seafood and chicken recipes, see Chapters 14 and 15, respectively.

## Gluten-Free . . . If You're Game

Yes, meat is gluten-free . . . initially. If you buy roasts, chops, or any other whole piece of meat, you don't need to be concerned from a gluten standpoint. If, however, you pick up a package of marinated beef kebabs or pre-seasoned pork tenderloin, you'll need to check what ingredients have been used in the marinade and seasonings.

 When you buy meat from the deli department, be careful. Most of the premium meats sold there are solid meat, but some of the less expensive brands may use extenders. *Extenders* are inexpensive fillers and binders that can include wheat; they can enhance the flavor of processed meats, but they're primarily added to expand and extend the product. These fillers must be listed on the label, and manufacturers must list wheat on the label — so if you're reading carefully, you'll find it.

And then there's the enigma surrounding ground meats. If you pick up a package that says "ground beef," wouldn't you assume it was just beef that was ground up? Well, that may not necessarily be so. Some (granted, not many) meat processors add fillers that contain wheat products to their ground meats. Again, the ingredients in the fillers must be listed on the package ingredient label, but you still have to read the label to make sure it's safe for you to eat.

# Eyeing the Main Attractions: Beef, Pork, and Lamb

Three grades of beef are sold in grocery stores: prime, choice, and select.

- ✔ **Prime** is juicier and more tender than the other two grades because it has the most *marbling* (a fancy word for "fat specks").

- ✔ **Choice** beef is moderately marbled and generally slightly more "mature" than prime beef. It's the most popular grade purchased because it isn't as expensive as prime and it's more tender than select.

- ✔ **Select** is the leanest, so ultimately it's the healthiest, but because it has the least amount of marbling, it's usually tougher, less juicy, and less flavorful.

On one hand you have tender, juicy, flavorful; on the other hand you have healthier. And then you have the beef that's in the middle of the road. It's really a matter of preference.

Pork today is 35 percent to 50 percent leaner than it was just 30 years ago. Unfortunately, pork dries out when it's overcooked, primarily because of the lower fat content. You can avoid overcooking pork by paying close attention to the internal temperature with an accurate instant-read thermometer. Pork is cooked through when the thermometer registers 160 degrees. Always let the meat *rest* (that's a fancy word for letting it sit for a few minutes after it's cooked) before serving or carving so the juices can be reabsorbed into the center.

If you aren't partial to the taste of lamb, chances are you tasted mutton. Meat from older sheep is called *mutton,* and most people think it tastes disgusting, whereas the taste of spring lamb is succulent, delicious, and moist. When buying leg of lamb, you may find it challenging to figure out how much you need because of the bone. You're safe if you buy 1 pound for every two people to be served.

# Beef Pot Roast a la Mushrooms

**Prep time:** 10 min • **Cook time:** 3 hr • **Yield:** 4 servings

| *Ingredients* | *Directions* |
|---|---|
| 2 pounds lean chuck steak, cut into 1-inch cubes | *1* Preheat the oven to 350 degrees. |
| ⅛ teaspoon plus ⅛ teaspoon salt | *2* Place the steak cubes in a 9-x-9-inch baking pan. Add ⅛ teaspoon of salt, ¼ teaspoon of pepper, the chopped parsley, onions, soy sauce, water, beef broth, Italian salad dressing, and garlic. Cover the pan securely with heavy-duty foil. |
| ¼ teaspoon plus ⅛ teaspoon pepper | |
| 3 tablespoons chopped parsley | |
| 2 green onions, sliced | |
| 2 tablespoons gluten-free soy sauce | *3* Roast the steak at 350 degrees for 3 hours. |
| 1 cup water | |
| 14.5-ounce can beef broth | *4* Melt the butter in a large skillet. Add the mushrooms, ⅛ teaspoon of salt, ⅛ teaspoon of pepper, and the minced parsley and sauté on high heat, stirring often, until the mushrooms are browned and glazed. |
| 2 tablespoons Italian salad dressing | |
| 1 clove garlic, minced | |
| 2 tablespoons butter | |
| 16 ounces fresh mushroom slices | *5* To serve, spoon the beef onto a plate, and then spoon the mushrooms on top. |
| 1 tablespoon minced parsley | |

***Per serving:*** *Calories: 421; Total fat: 23g; Saturated fat: 10g; Cholesterol: 163mg; Sodium: 1,382mg; Carbohydrates: 4g; Fiber: 1g; Sugar: 2g; Protein: 47g.*

***Tip:*** You can also prepare this meat in a slow cooker — just be sure to reduce the water to ¼ cup.

***Note:*** If you prefer to leave the roast whole instead of cubed, add a half-hour to the roasting time. Let the whole roast cool, and then cut it into thin slices.

***Note:*** Figure 16-1 shows to how to trim and slice mushrooms.

## HOW TO TRIM AND SLICE MUSHROOMS

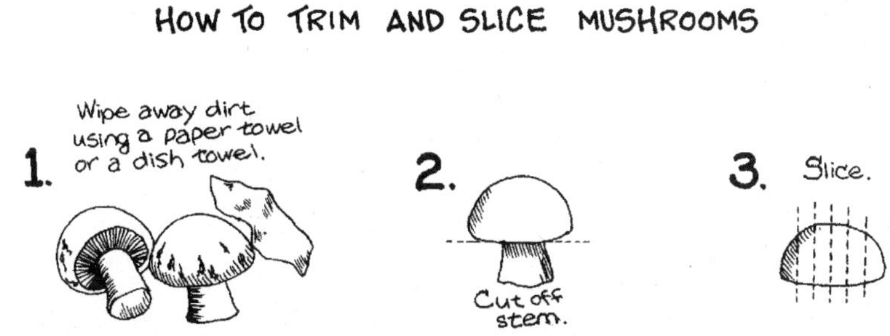

**Figure 16-1:** Slicing mushrooms.

**1.** Wipe away dirt using a paper towel or a dish towel.

**2.** Cut off stem.

**3.** Slice.

*Illustrations by Elizabeth Kurtzman*

# Glazed Filet Mignon with Blue Cheese

**Prep time:** 7 min • **Cook time:** 10 min • **Yield:** 4 servings

| Ingredients | Directions |
|---|---|
| ¼ **teaspoon salt** | *1* In a small bowl, stir together the salt, pepper, paprika, cumin, garlic powder, and cayenne pepper. |
| ¼ **teaspoon pepper** | |
| ⅛ **teaspoon paprika** | *2* Rub the spices onto both sides of the steaks. |
| ⅛ **teaspoon cumin** | |
| ⅛ **teaspoon garlic powder** | *3* In the same small bowl, combine the soy sauce, vinegar, and wine. Set the mixture aside. |
| ⅛ **teaspoon cayenne pepper** | |
| **Four 4-ounce filet mignons** | *4* Heat a nonstick skillet over medium-high heat. |
| **2 tablespoons gluten-free soy sauce** | *5* Melt the butter in the skillet, and then add the steaks. Cook for 1 minute on each side to brown. |
| **2 teaspoons balsamic vinegar** | |
| **2 teaspoons dry red wine** | *6* Reduce the heat to medium and cook for 3 minutes. |
| **2 tablespoons butter** | |
| **4 tablespoons blue cheese** | *7* Turn the steaks. Pour the soy mixture over the meat and continue to cook for 3 to 4 more minutes (depending on the thickness of the steaks and the desired doneness). |
| | *8* Spoon 1 tablespoon of the blue cheese on top of each steak. Cover the pan with a lid to seal in the steam until the cheese begins to melt. |

*Per serving:* Calories: 336; Total fat: 21g; Saturated fat: 10g; Cholesterol: 117mg; Sodium: 880mg; Carbohydrates: 2g; Fiber: 0g; Sugar: 1g; Protein: 33g.

*Note:* This recipe calls for blue cheese. Some blue cheese, like Gorgonzola, is made from mold grown on wheat bread, but many brands of blue cheese are now made synthetically and contain no wheat mold. Shropshire, Frigo, and Kraft are just three of the gluten-free blue cheeses on the market, but still check the ingredient label every time you purchase the cheese to be sure the product is still gluten-free.

# Glazed Corned Beef

**Prep time:** 10 min • **Cook time:** 2 hr, 50 min • **Yield:** 4 servings

| *Ingredients* | *Directions* |
|---|---|
| **2½-pound lean corned beef brisket** | *1* Put the corned beef brisket in a large saucepan or Dutch oven. Add enough water to cover. Add the onion, bay leaves, pepper, garlic, and cloves. |
| **2 onions, peeled and quartered** | |
| **2 bay leaves** | *2* Bring to a boil; reduce the heat, cover, and simmer for 2 hours and 45 minutes, or until the meat is very tender. |
| **¼ teaspoon pepper** | |
| **1 clove garlic, quartered** | *3* In a small saucepan, stir together the corn syrup and mustard. Bring to a boil; reduce the heat and simmer for 5 minutes, stirring occasionally. Let the glaze cool. |
| **3 whole cloves** | |
| **½ cup dark corn syrup** | *4* Preheat the broiler. |
| **1 tablespoon brown mustard** | *5* Remove the brisket from the water and discard the water and vegetables. |
| | *6* Trim the excess fat from the beef and place the beef in a broiler pan. |
| | *7* Spoon the glaze over the top of the meat. |
| | *8* Broil the brisket for 3 to 4 minutes, or until the meat is heated through. Watch the meat closely and remove it from the broiler as soon as it's glazed. |

*Per serving: Calories: 704; Total fat: 42g; Saturated fat: 13g; Cholesterol: 153mg; Sodium: 3,313mg; Carbohydrates: 38g; Fiber: 1g; Sugar: 13g; Protein: 42g.*

*Tip:* If you want to save time at dinnertime, you can simmer the corned beef ahead of time, and then slice it and set it in a broiler pan that is lined with foil. Shape the foil closely around the meat slices to keep the slices as close as possible and shaped in a loaf. Just before serving, spoon the glaze over the meat and broil until the meat has warmed and is glazed.

# Smoky Sweet Grilled Pork Tenderloin

**Prep time:** 10 min plus refrigeration time • **Cook time:** 15 min • **Yield:** 4 servings

| Ingredients | Directions |
|---|---|
| One 1-pound pork tenderloin | *1* Trim off any excess fat and silver skin on the pork tenderloin. Rub down the entire tenderloin with the canola oil. |
| 1 tablespoon canola oil | |
| 2 teaspoons smoked paprika | *2* Combine the smoked paprika, red pepper, brown sugar, cumin, pepper, cocoa powder, and salt. Rub the seasonings into the pork tenderloin and refrigerate for 3 to 4 hours. |
| ¼ teaspoon crushed red pepper | |
| 1 to 2 teaspoons brown sugar | *3* Remove the tenderloin from refrigerator and let sit at room temperature while preheating the grill to medium high. |
| 1 teaspoon cumin | |
| 1 teaspoon freshly ground pepper | *4* Spray the tenderloin with cooking spray. Place the tenderloin in the center of the grill grate. Cover and cook 12 to 14 minutes, turning 4 times after 3 to 4 minutes each side. Check the internal temperature using a probe thermometer to 145 to 150 degrees. If it needs additional cooking to reach the internal temperature, turn off the grill and let it sit on the grates for a few more minutes. |
| ½ teaspoon cocoa powder | |
| ½ teaspoon salt | |
| | *5* Remove to a cutting board and slice into medallions before serving. |

*Per serving:* Calories: 215; Total fat: 11g; Saturated fat: 3g; Cholesterol: 78mg; Sodium: 346mg; Carbohydrates: 4g; Fiber: 1g; Protein: 25g.

*Tip:* To remove the silver skin, place the tip of the knife under the silvery skin and slice with the sharp edge of the knife blade angled upward to keep the membrane tight as you cut. Cutting the silver skin prevents the roast from shrinking and cooking unevenly.

*Note:* Lean and tender, pork tenderloin is perfect for grilling. It's low in carbs, relatively economical, and a great source of protein. The goal in grilling is for the pork to be well seared, juicy, and fully cooked, without being dry.

# Pork Chops with Caramelized Onions

**Prep time:** 20 min plus marinating time • **Cook time:** 10 min • **Yield:** 4 servings

| *Ingredients* | *Directions* |
|---|---|
| **Four ¾-inch thick pork chops** | *1* Place the pork chops and wine in a gallon-size self-seal bag and marinate the meat for 2 hours in the refrigerator. |
| **½ cup marsala wine** | |
| **Nonstick cooking spray** | *2* Preheat the broiler. Spray an 8-x-11-inch baking dish with cooking spray. |
| **¼ teaspoon salt** | *3* Remove the chops from the marinade and sprinkle them with salt and pepper. Set them in the prepared baking dish. |
| **⅛ teaspoon pepper** | |
| **8 slices bacon** | *4* In a large skillet, cook the bacon, drain it on paper toweling, and then crumble it. Reserve 2 tablespoons of the bacon drippings. |
| **1 large white onion, sliced thin** | |
| **7-ounce can sliced mushrooms, drained** | *5* Add the onions and mushrooms to the drippings in the skillet and cook over medium heat, stirring occasionally, until the onions begin to soften. |
| **1 teaspoon brown sugar** | *6* Stir the brown sugar into the skillet and cook for 5 minutes longer, or until the onions are completely browned. |
| **⅓ cup hot water** | *7* In a small bowl, stir together the water and bouillon until the cube has dissolved. Add this to the onions and boil until the liquid is reduced by half, scraping up any browned bits from the bottom of the skillet. |
| **1 chicken bouillon cube** | |
| | *8* Stir in the bacon. |
| | *9* Broil the pork chops for about 5 minutes per side, or just until the meat is cooked through and the internal temperature reaches 160 degrees. |
| | *10* Spoon the onion-mushroom mixture over the pork chops to serve. |

*Per serving: Calories: 529; Total fat: 38g; Saturated fat: 14g; Cholesterol: 128mg; Sodium: 1,320mg; Carbohydrates: 5g; Fiber: 1g; Sugar: 2g; Protein: 37g.*

*Tip:* Watch the cook time closely with these pork chops so they remain moist and tender.

# Baked Pork Chops

**Prep time:** 10 min  •  **Cook time:** 2 hr  •  **Yield:** 4 servings

| *Ingredients* | *Directions* |
|---|---|
| **Four ¾-inch thick bone-in pork chops** | **1** Preheat the oven to 350 degrees. |
| **½ teaspoon salt** <br> **¼ teaspoon pepper** | **2** Sprinkle both sides of the pork chops with salt and pepper. In a large skillet, brown the chops in oil over medium-high heat. |
| **2 tablespoons olive oil** <br> **8-ounce can tomato sauce** | **3** After the chops are browned, place them in a shallow baking dish. |
| **1 cup water** <br> **½ cup diced celery** <br> **½ cup diced onion** | **4** In a small bowl, stir together the tomato sauce, water, celery, onion, brown sugar, and mustard; pour the mixture over the chops. |
| **1 tablespoon brown sugar** <br> **1 teaspoon yellow mustard** <br> **¼ teaspoon cinnamon** | **5** Cover the pan with foil and bake the chops at 350 degrees for 45 minutes. Then uncover them and continue baking for 45 minutes more, or until the chops are so tender that they almost fall apart. |

*Per serving: Calories: 544; Total fat: 27g; Saturated fat: 8g; Cholesterol: 172mg; Sodium: 761mg; Carbohydrates: 9g; Fiber: 2g; Sugar: 7g; Protein: 62g.*

***Tip:*** When you serve the pork chops, you should have some sauce in the pan to spoon over the chops. If, during cooking, you see that the sauce is drying out and being absorbed too much, you may need to add a little water. Don't add more than 1 cup of water at a time. If you're baking in a glass dish, make sure the water being added is very hot because adding cold water can cause the dish to break.

***Note:*** In most cases when you overcook pork chops, they become tough. This dish is the exception. The longer you bake this dish, the more tender the meat becomes, until it gets so tender that it falls off the bone.

***Note:*** Figure 16-2 shows how you can dice celery.

QUICK AND EVEN DICING (CARROTS, POTATOES, OR CELERY)

WE ARE ALL PEELED

1. SLICE YOUR VEGETABLES LENGTHWISE INTO EVEN THICKNESSES.

2. STACK THE SLICES ONE ON TOP OF ANOTHER. MAKE EVEN, PARALLEL CUTS. NOW, YOU HAVE LONG, THIN PIECES.

3. TO DICE, MAKE PARALLEL CUTS, EVENLY, ACROSS THE LONG PIECES AND YOU ARE ALL DICED!

**Figure 16-2:** Dicing veggies is easy.

*Illustrations by Elizabeth Kurtzman*

# Best Spare Ribs You'll Ever Eat!

**Prep time:** 1 hr • **Cook time:** 40 min • **Yield:** 4 servings

| *Ingredients* | *Directions* |
| --- | --- |
| **1 tablespoon brown sugar** | *1* Early in the day (or the day before), put the sugar and vinegar in a large Dutch oven. Reduce over medium heat about 8 minutes until the vinegar and sugar form a syrup. (Watch carefully because the syrup will suddenly darken in color.) |
| **¼ cup cider vinegar** | |
| **5 cups water** | |
| **1 tablespoon beef bouillon granules** | *2* Immediately add the water and bouillon granules. Stir in the molasses, ketchup, dry mustard, Worcestershire sauce, cloves, chili powder, and cayenne pepper. Bring it to a boil. |
| **2 tablespoons molasses** | |
| **¼ cup ketchup** | *3* Cut each slab of ribs into smaller sections. Add them to the saucepan and simmer for 20 minutes. |
| **2 teaspoons dry mustard** | |
| **1 teaspoon gluten-free Worcestershire sauce** | *4* Remove the pan from the heat. Remove the ribs and place them in a dish. Cover and refrigerate. |
| **⅛ teaspoon cloves** | |
| **½ teaspoon chili powder** | *5* Cook the liquid over medium heat until it becomes thick and syrupy (about 25 minutes), stirring constantly during the last 5 minutes. |
| **¼ teaspoon cayenne pepper** | |
| **3 pounds baby back ribs (2 slabs)** | *6* Remove the pan from the heat and pour the sauce into a bowl. (Yield will be about 1 cup of basting sauce.) Cool the sauce, then cover and refrigerate it. |
| | *7* Before dinner, preheat the oven to 350 degrees. |
| | *8* Place the ribs on a nonstick baking dish, with the underside facing up. |
| | *9* Baste well with the sauce and bake at 350 degrees for 20 minutes. Turn the ribs over and baste generously. Continue to bake for 20 to 25 minutes. |

*Per serving: Calories: 607; Total fat: 28g; Saturated fat: 10g; Cholesterol: 218mg; Sodium: 673mg; Carbohydrates: 16g; Fiber: 0g; Sugar: 13g; Protein: 67g.*

# Lamb Chops with Tiered Topping

**Prep time:** 15 min • **Cook time:** 42 min • **Yield:** 6 servings

| Ingredients | Directions |
|---|---|
| 1 tablespoon minced garlic | *1* Preheat the oven to 350 degrees. Line an 8-x-11-inch baking dish with foil, leaving enough overhang to cover the pan after it's filled. |
| 3 tablespoons minced fresh mint (leaves only) | |
| ¼ cup minced fresh parsley | *2* In a small bowl, use a fork to mash together the garlic, mint, parsley, soy sauce, and 2 tablespoons of the butter. |
| 2 tablespoons gluten-free soy sauce | |
| 2 tablespoons plus 2 tablespoons butter, softened | *3* Place the lamb chops in the lined baking dish. |
| Six 4-ounce loin lamb chops | *4* Cover the tops of the chops with the herb mixture, dividing the mixture evenly. If any herb sauce remains in the bowl, drizzle it over the chops. |
| 6 thick lemon slices, seeds removed | |
| 6 large, firm white mushroom caps | *5* Lay 1 lemon slice on top of each chop. |
| ⅛ teaspoon salt | *6* Melt the remaining 2 tablespoons of butter; roll the mushroom caps in butter to coat. Set one cap on top of each lamb chop. |
| ¼ teaspoon pepper | |
| 6 tablespoons shredded mozzarella cheese | *7* Sprinkle the chops with salt and pepper. |
| | *8* Seal the foil. Bake the chops at 350 degrees for 40 minutes. |
| | *9* Remove the chops from the oven and turn on the broiler. Fold back the foil. Sprinkle the cheese on top of the chops. Broil for 2 minutes, or until the cheese has melted. |

*Per serving:* Calories: 308; Total fat: 28g; Saturated fat: 13g; Cholesterol: 75mg; Sodium: 530mg; Carbohydrates: 5g; Fiber: 1g; Sugar: 2g; Protein: 15g.

# Lamburgers with Tzatziki Sauce

**Prep time:** 10 min • **Cook time:** 12 min • **Yield:** 4 servings

| *Ingredients* | *Directions* |
|---|---|
| **4 tablespoons plain Greek yogurt** | *1* Preheat gas grill on high. |
| **2 tablespoons cucumber, finely minced** | *2* In a small bowl, make the tzatziki sauce by blending together the yogurt, cucumber, garlic, 1 teaspoon lemon zest, and dill. Refrigerate. |
| **1 teaspoon minced garlic** | |
| **1 teaspoon plus 1 teaspoon lemon zest** | *3* In mixing bowl, combine ground lamb, herbs, 1 teaspoon lemon zest, bread crumbs, salt, and pepper until well blended. Divide mixture and gently shape into four 1-inch burger patties. |
| **½ teaspoon dried dill** | |
| **1 pound ground lamb** | |
| **1 teaspoon dried basil** | *4* Transfer burgers to hot grill and cook for 4 to 5 minutes each side until browned and cooked through. Let sit for 5 minutes. |
| **½ teaspoon dried chives** | |
| **½ teaspoon dried rosemary** | |
| **½ teaspoon dried thyme** | *5* Place burgers on burger buns and top with tzatziki sauce, spinach, tomato, and red onion. |
| **½ cup bread crumbs made from gluten free bread** | |
| **Salt and pepper, to taste** | |
| **Gluten-free burger buns** | |
| **1 cup baby spinach** | |
| **1 tomato, sliced** | |
| **1 small red onion, sliced** | |

*Per serving: Calories: 635; Total fat: 32g; Saturated fat: 8g; Cholesterol: 76mg; Sodium: 340mg; Carbohydrates: 62g; Fiber: 3g; Sugar: 0g; Protein: 25g.*

*Tip:* A loosely packed patty makes a juicier burger. When cooking, flip only once to prevent losing more juices than necessary.

*Vary It!* If you have difficulty finding ground lamb, choose a shoulder cut or lamb stew meat and have your butcher trim and grind it.

*Note:* Cook time may vary a bit depending on the size of the shanks.

# Barbecue Lamb Shanks

**Prep time:** 15 min • **Cook time:** 2 hr • **Yield:** 4 servings

| Ingredients | Directions |
|---|---|
| 4 lamb shanks, about ½ pound each | *1* Preheat the oven to 325 degrees. |
| ¼ teaspoon paprika | *2* Sprinkle the lamb shanks with paprika, garlic powder, salt, and pepper. |
| ¼ teaspoon garlic powder | |
| ¾ teaspoon salt | *3* In a large skillet or Dutch oven over medium-high heat, brown the shanks on all sides in the oil. Transfer the meat to an 8-x-11-inch baking dish. |
| ¼ teaspoon pepper | |
| 2 tablespoons olive oil | |
| ½ cup ketchup | *4* Stir the ketchup, water, brown sugar, onion, vinegar, mustard, and Worcestershire sauce into the skillet, scraping any browned bits from the bottom of the pan. Spoon this mixture on top of the lamb shanks and cover the baking dish with foil. |
| ½ cup water | |
| 1 tablespoon brown sugar | |
| 1 large onion, chopped | |
| 1 tablespoon cider vinegar | *5* Bake at 325 degrees for 2 hours, or until the meat is very tender. |
| ½ teaspoon dry mustard | |
| ¼ teaspoon gluten-free Worcestershire sauce | |

*Per serving: Calories: 627; Total fat: 44g; Saturated fat: 20g; Cholesterol: 161mg; Sodium: 878mg; Carbohydrates: 15g; Fiber: 1g; Sugar: 12g; Protein: 42g.*

## The pros of eating plenty of protein

Do you ever wonder what all the hype is about protein? Well for one thing, cells are made up mostly of protein. For another, protein helps the body resist disease. And we know that every adult needs a minimum of 1 gram of protein for every 10 pounds of body weight to keep from slowly breaking down our tissues. And then there's the fact that protein helps maintain our energy levels throughout the day. Okay, so maybe protein *is* good for us.

Beef, pork, chicken, fish, beans, and other high-protein foods can help you feel full for a longer period of time, and the body uses up more energy to digest these proteins (that's good). But just because protein is good for us, doesn't mean you should eat unlimited amounts. Too much protein can weaken our bones and can sometimes be tough on the kidneys (that's bad).

# Mixing Up Meals with Ground Meats

Bad news and good news . . . Ground meats have issues that aren't associated with whole cuts of meats. In whole cuts, the interior of the meat is essentially sterile; bacteria are isolated to the surface. When meat is ground, bacterial contamination from the surface can be distributed throughout the meat.

Now the good news: Ground meat is now *irradiated* (zapped with rays), which kills the bacteria. And if you cook the meat properly as described in the following recipes, you won't have anything to worry about.

When buying ground meats, ask the butcher if the meat has had fillers added. Some stores add wheat-based fillers to ground hamburger. Sausage is always questionable, so read the label ingredients carefully.

# BBQ Meatloaf

**Prep time:** 15 min • **Cook time:** 55 min • **Yield:** 4 servings

| Ingredients | Directions |
|---|---|
| Nonstick cooking spray | *1* Preheat the oven to 350 degrees. Spray a 9-x-9-inch baking dish with cooking spray. |
| 2 tablespoons olive oil | |
| ½ cup onion, minced | *2* Over medium heat, sauté the onions, green pepper, and garlic in oil in a large skillet, stirring frequently, until the vegetables are tender and very lightly browned. |
| ½ cup green pepper, minced | |
| 1 clove garlic, minced | |
| ½ cup fresh parsley, chopped | *3* Stir in the parsley, bouillon granules, and water. Simmer, stirring, until the liquid has been absorbed. Remove the skillet from the heat and let it cool slightly. |
| ½ teaspoon beef bouillon granules | |
| 2 tablespoons water | |
| 1 egg | *4* In a medium bowl, whisk together the egg, Worcestershire sauce, and soy sauce. Add the ground beef, salt, pepper, and sautéed vegetables. Combine until well mixed. |
| 1 teaspoon gluten-free Worcestershire sauce | |
| 1 teaspoon gluten-free soy sauce | *5* Mix in the cheese and crushed crackers. |
| 1 pound lean ground beef | *6* Transfer the meat mixture to the baking dish. Shape the meat into a loaf about 3 inches thick; smooth the top. |
| ¼ teaspoon salt | |
| ¼ teaspoon pepper | *7* Brush the top of the loaf with the barbecue sauce. |
| ½ cup shredded cheddar cheese | |
| ⅓ cup crushed crackers | *8* Bake at 350 degrees for 55 minutes, or until the center of the loaf is no longer pink. Let the loaf stand for 5 minutes before slicing. |
| 3 tablespoons barbecue sauce | |

*Per serving:* Calories: 398; Total fat: 23g; Saturated fat: 8g; Cholesterol: 137mg; Sodium: 738mg; Carbohydrates: 18g; Fiber: 1g; Sugar: 7g; Protein: 29g.

*Tip:* The easiest way to crush the crackers for this recipe is to put them in a plastic bag and use a rolling pin.

*Note:* You can portion the meat mixture into four muffin tins for individual meat pies. The muffin-sized loaves only take about 40 minutes to bake at 350 degrees.

# Meatballs in Lemon Sauce

**Prep time:** 15 min • **Cook time:** 35 min • **Yield:** 4 servings

| Ingredients | Directions |
|---|---|
| **1 pound lean ground beef** | **1** In a medium bowl, mix together the ground beef, onion, salt, pepper, parsley, mint, and rice. |
| **1 small onion, minced** | |
| **¼ teaspoon salt** | **2** Shape the mixture into balls a little smaller in size than a ping-pong ball. You'll have about 24 meatballs. |
| **¼ teaspoon pepper** | |
| **2 tablespoons chopped fresh parsley** | **3** Dust the meatballs lightly in cornstarch. |
| **½ teaspoon dried mint** | **4** Place the meatballs in a Dutch oven and add enough water to cover them. Add the oil. Bring the water to a boil, and then lower the heat to medium-low and let the meatballs simmer for 30 minutes. |
| **¼ cup uncooked rice** | |
| **3 tablespoons cornstarch** | |
| **1 tablespoon olive oil** | |
| **2 eggs** | **5** In a medium mixing bowl, use the mixer to whip the eggs for 2 minutes. Add the lemon juice. |
| **Juice of 1 lemon** | |
| **Salt to taste** | **6** Remove the pan with the meatballs from the stove. |
| | **7** Add ⅔ of the meatball broth, in a slow steady stream, to the eggs, whipping constantly. Taste the sauce; add salt to taste. |
| | **8** Pour the lemon sauce over the meatballs and the remaining sauce in the Dutch oven and cook for 2 minutes over very low heat. (Don't permit the mixture to boil or the eggs will curdle.) Serve immediately. |

*Per serving:* Calories: 337; Total fat: 13g; Saturated fat: 5g; Cholesterol: 188mg; Sodium: 248mg; Carbohydrates: 18g; Fiber: 1g; Sugar: 1g; Protein: 35g.

*Vary It!* If you're mentally prepared to break all previous culinary boundaries, you can substitute ground lamb for the ground beef.

# Meatballs in Wine Sauce

**Prep time:** 15 min • **Cook time:** 40 min • **Yield:** 4 servings

| Ingredients | Directions |
|---|---|
| 2 slices porous bread, toasted | **1** Crumble the toast into a medium bowl. Add the ground beef, egg, salt, pepper, and garlic. Mix thoroughly. |
| 1 pound lean ground beef | |
| 1 egg | **2** Form the meat mixture into small balls, and then roll into football-shaped ovals. You should have about 24 meatballs. |
| ¼ teaspoon salt | |
| ¼ teaspoon pepper | |
| 2 cloves garlic, minced | **3** In a large skillet over medium heat, brown the meatballs in butter, turning frequently. |
| 2 tablespoons butter | |
| 3 ounces (½ of a 6-ounce can) tomato paste | **4** Add the tomato paste, sugar, red wine, and water, cover, and simmer for 30 minutes, adding more water only if needed. |
| ½ teaspoon sugar | |
| ½ cup red wine | |
| 1½ cups water | |

*Per serving:* Calories: 310; Total fat: 14g; Saturated fat: 7g; Cholesterol: 137mg; Sodium: 478mg; Carbohydrates: 12g; Fiber: 2g; Sugar: 4g; Protein: 26g.

*Tip:* Use the most porous gluten-free bread you can find for toasting.

*Note:* This is one recipe where you can't take a shortcut by substituting garlic powder for the cloves of garlic.

# Marinated Kielbasa

**Prep time:** 5 min plus marinating time • **Cook time:** 10 min • **Yield:** 4 servings

| Ingredients | Directions |
|---|---|
| 1½ tablespoons dark corn syrup | *1* Place the corn syrup, oil, ginger, mustard, Worcestershire sauce, and soy sauce in a gallon-size self-seal bag. Swish it around to blend the ingredients. |
| 2 teaspoons olive oil | |
| ¼ teaspoon powdered ginger | |
| 1 teaspoon brown mustard | *2* Add the kielbasa to the bag. Seal the bag and push the sausage around so it's evenly covered with marinade. |
| 1 teaspoon gluten-free Worcestershire sauce | |
| 1 teaspoon gluten-free soy sauce | *3* Refrigerate the sausage for at least 1 hour. |
| 1 pound kielbasa links | *4* Preheat the broiler. |
| | *5* Remove the kielbasa from the bag and place it on a broiler pan. Drizzle the marinade over the top of the meat. |
| | *6* Broil the meat for approximately 10 minutes, turning several times, until the kielbasa is barely charred on the outside and cooked through. |

*Per serving:* Calories: 298; Total fat: 22g; Saturated fat: 7g; Cholesterol: 79mg; Sodium: 137mg; Carbohydrates: 11g; Fiber: 0g; Sugar: 2g; Protein: 15g.

*Note:* Always read the ingredients of any package you buy, but this holds especially true when buying sausage because some fillers used in making sausage contain wheat and wheat byproducts.

# Chapter 17

# Making Memories with Meatless Dishes

## In This Chapter

▶ Creating side dishes for every season

▶ Mixing and mashing potatoes and pastas

▶ Making veggies the main course, of course

Meatless dishes are perceived to be a challenge on a gluten-free diet because so many vegetarian or vegan dishes use pasta. The good news is that *lots* of really great gluten-free pastas are available; the other good news is that veggies are gluten-free! All of them! Here we talk veggies, starting with the incredible side dishes you can make with very little effort.

## Veggin' Out with Side Dishes

Side dishes with veggies add flavor, nutrition, and color to a dinner plate. For a festive presentation, sprinkle the dish with minced parsley before putting the vegetables on the plate. If you want to get really wild and crazy, add some edible flowers, like nasturtiums.

Cooking vegetables is somewhat of an art, and Connie and I have some helpful hints to help you make the best of your veggies. Here are a few suggestions to keep in mind:

- ✔ All vegetables that grow above ground can start cooking in boiling water.

- ✔ For those that grow beneath the ground (beets, turnips, and so on), start in cold water.

- ✔ Many vegetables can be grilled (leeks, onions, asparagus, eggplant, and so on). Just slather them with a little olive oil and some seasonings before grilling.

- ✔ Salted eggplant absorbs less fat than unsalted eggplant when it's fried or sautéed. Sprinkle the slices with salt and place them in a colander in the sink. Let them set for 30 minutes, and then rinse the slices in cool water and pat them dry with paper towels.

- ✔ Peeled sweet potatoes can be substituted for white potatoes in many recipes.

- ✔ Whether you steam, grill, roast, stir-fry, or pan-fry your veggies, try to include them in as many meals as possible.

By adding a tossed salad, some of the selections in this section can double as a meatless entree. Check out Figure 17-1 for some ideas of vegetables you can eat.

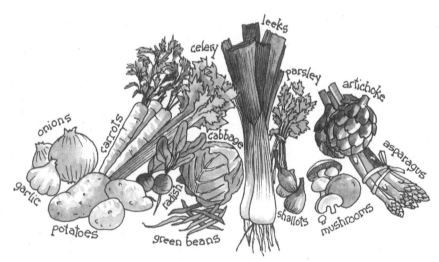

**Figure 17-1:**
Your veggie options are endless.

*Illustrations by Elizabeth Kurtzman*

# Broccoli Cauliflower Combo

**Prep time:** 8 min • **Cook time:** 30 min • **Yield:** 6 servings

| Ingredients | Directions |
|---|---|
| **Nonstick cooking spray** | *1* Preheat the oven to 350 degrees. Spray a 9-x-9-inch baking dish with cooking spray. |
| **10-ounce box frozen cauliflower** | *2* Place the cauliflower and broccoli in a medium saucepan and cover the vegetables with water. |
| **Two 10-ounce boxes frozen broccoli** | *3* Bring the water to a boil, and then simmer the vegetables for 2 minutes. |
| **2 tablespoons slivered almonds** | |
| **1½ cups processed cheese** | *4* Drain the vegetables in a colander, and then transfer them to the prepared baking dish. |
| **18-ounce can cream of mushroom soup** | *5* Sprinkle the almonds over the vegetables. |
| **1 cup plus 1 cup crushed Funyuns** | *6* In a small mixing bowl, stir together the cheese, soup, and 1 cup of crushed Funyuns; pour the mixture over the broccoli and cauliflower. |
| | *7* Sprinkle the remaining 1 cup of crushed Funyuns on top of the casserole. |
| | *8* Bake the vegetables at 350 degrees for 30 minutes. |

*Per serving:* Calories: 288; Total fat: 17g; Saturated fat: 7g; Cholesterol: 23mg; Sodium: 948mg; Carbohydrates: 25g; Fiber: 6g; Sugar: 6g; Protein: 12g.

*Note:* Crumbled Funyuns are used for the topping on this casserole. As of the writing of this book, Funyuns (sold in the chips aisle) are gluten-free. Should the ingredients on the package change, you can use crushed potato chips instead.

# Glazed Carrots with Walnuts

**Prep time:** 5 min • **Cook time:** 8 min • **Yield:** 4 servings

| Ingredients | Directions |
|---|---|
| **3 cups baby carrots** | **1** Put the carrots in a medium saucepan and cover them with water. Boil until they're tender but not mushy. Drain. |
| **2 tablespoons butter** | |
| **3 tablespoons chopped walnuts** | |
| **1½ tablespoons brown sugar** | **2** While the carrots are draining, melt the butter in the same saucepan and add the walnuts. |
| **¼ teaspoon cinnamon** | **3** Sauté the nuts for 1 minute, and then add the brown sugar, cinnamon, salt, and pepper. Stir to combine. |
| **⅛ teaspoon salt** | |
| **⅛ teaspoon pepper** | **4** Stir in the carrots until they're evenly coated with the glaze. |

*Per serving: Calories: 140; Total fat: 9g; Saturated fat: 4g; Cholesterol: 15mg; Sodium: 112mg; Carbohydrates: 141g; Fiber: 2g; Sugar: 11g; Protein: 1g.*

***Vary It!*** You can use pecans in place of the walnuts and pure maple syrup in place of the brown sugar.

# Spinach Pie

**Prep time:** 15 min • **Cook time:** 45 min • **Yield:** 12 servings

| *Ingredients* | *Directions* |
|---|---|
| Nonstick cooking spray<br><br>3 tablespoons butter<br><br>1 medium onion, chopped<br><br>3 large eggs<br><br>16-ounce container small curd cottage cheese<br><br>1 cup grated mozzarella cheese<br><br>1 cup grated Parmesan cheese<br><br>¼ teaspoon salt<br><br>½ teaspoon pepper<br><br>1 teaspoon dried dill<br><br>10-ounce box frozen chopped spinach, thawed and squeezed dry | *1* Preheat the oven to 350 degrees. Spray a 9-inch pie plate with cooking spray.<br><br>*2* Melt the butter in a large skillet over medium heat. Add the onion and sauté until tender, about 8 minutes.<br><br>*3* In a large bowl, whisk the eggs lightly.<br><br>*4* Stir in the cottage cheese, mozzarella, Parmesan cheese, salt, pepper, and dill.<br><br>*5* Stir in the onions and spinach until everything is well blended.<br><br>*6* Spoon the mixture into the prepared pie plate.<br><br>*7* Bake the pie at 350 degrees for 45 minutes, or until a knife inserted near the center comes out clean. If the pie begins to brown too much on top before being cooked through, cover it with a piece of foil.<br><br>*8* Let the pie rest for 10 minutes before cutting it into 12 wedges. |

*Per serving:* Calories: 177; Total fat: 11g; Saturated fat: 7g; Cholesterol: 81mg; Sodium: 484mg; Carbohydrates: 4g; Fiber: 1g; Sugar: 1g; Protein: 16g.

*Tip:* You can prepare this dish ahead, cover and refrigerate it, and then bake it just before dinner. After removing the dish from the oven, let it set for 10 minutes before cutting.

# Stuffed Acorn Squash

**Prep time:** 15 min • **Cook time:** 1 hr • **Yield:** 2 servings

| *Ingredients* | *Directions* |
|---|---|
| **1 large acorn squash, halved and seeded** | **1** Preheat the oven to 375 degrees. |
| **1 cup water** | **2** Place the squash, cut side down, on a small baking dish. |
| **2 tablespoons butter, melted** | |
| **½ teaspoon bottled lemon juice** | **3** Pour the water onto the bottom of the dish and bake the squash at 375 degrees for 35 minutes. Remove the squash from the oven and discard the water in the pan. |
| **¼ teaspoon cinnamon** | |
| **2 tablespoons brown sugar** | **4** In a bowl, stir together the butter, lemon juice, cinnamon, brown sugar, apple, and pecans. |
| **1 medium red or golden delicious apple, peeled, cored, and chopped fine** | **5** Mound the apple mixture on top of the squash halves, dividing evenly. |
| **2 tablespoons chopped pecans** | **6** Place the squash back in the baking dish, cut side up, and continue baking it at 375 degrees for another 30 to 35 minutes or until the flesh is tender when poked with a fork. If the top browns too much, cover it with foil during the last 15 minutes of baking. |

*Per serving: Calories: 294; Total fat: 14g; Saturated fat: 8g; Cholesterol: 30mg; Sodium: 94mg; Carbohydrates: 45g; Fiber: 5g; Sugar: 20g; Protein: 3g.*

*Tip:* The easiest way to half the squash is to take a strong, pointed knife and first make jabs that cut through the skin around the center of the vegetable. Then take a butcher knife and press down along the "jabbed" line.

*Note:* Figure 17-2 shows how to core an apple before you chop it.

## HOW TO CORE AN APPLE

**Figure 17-2:** Coring an apple.

Run a paring knife clockwise around the core (leaving ¼" at the bottom)...

...and pop out the core!

*Illustrations by Elizabeth Kurtzman*

# Cranberries and Yams

**Prep time:** 15 min • **Cook time:** 20 min • **Yield:** 4 servings

| Ingredients | Directions |
| --- | --- |
| **Nonstick cooking spray** | **1** Preheat the oven to 450 degrees. Spray a baking sheet with cooking spray. |
| **2 large yams, peeled** | |
| **¼ teaspoon cinnamon** | **2** Cut each yam in half crosswise, and then into wedges. |
| **¼ teaspoon plus ⅛ teaspoon salt** | **3** In a plastic, self-seal bag, combine the cinnamon, ¼ teaspoon of salt, cumin, pepper, and garlic powder. |
| **¼ teaspoon cumin** | |
| **⅛ teaspoon pepper** | **4** Add the yams. Seal the bag and shake it until the yams are evenly coated. |
| **¼ teaspoon garlic powder** | |
| **2 tablespoons dried cranberries** | **5** Lay the yam wedges in a single layer on the prepared baking sheet. |
| **2 teaspoons butter** | **6** Bake the yams at 450 degrees for 30 to 35 minutes, or until the wedges are very tender, turning the yams once during baking. |
| **1 large pear, peeled, cored, and cut into ½-inch cubes** | **7** While the yams bake, place the cranberries in a bowl of hot water to soak and soften for 5 minutes. Drain. |
| **¼ cup coarsely chopped pecans** | |
| **¼ teaspoon ginger** | **8** Melt the butter in a large nonstick skillet. |
| **1 teaspoon brown sugar** | **9** Add the pears and pecans and sauté them over medium heat until the pears are tender and golden, about 4 minutes, stirring frequently. |
| **½ teaspoon balsamic vinegar** | |
| | **10** Stir in the cranberries, ginger, brown sugar, vinegar and remaining ⅛ teaspoon of salt, and heat until the sauce is warmed. |
| | **11** To serve, spoon the cranberry sauce over the yams. |

*Per serving:* Calories: 186; Total fat: 7g; Saturated fat: 2g; Cholesterol: 5mg; Sodium: 279mg; Carbohydrates: 31g; Fiber: 5g; Sugar: 13g; Protein: 2g.

# Carrot and Zucchini Latkes

**Prep time:** 15 min • **Cook time:** 10 min • **Yield:** 6 latkes

| Ingredients | Directions |
| --- | --- |
| ½ **pound carrots** | **1** Grate the carrots, zucchini, and onion using the large holes of a box grater. |
| **1 medium zucchini** | |
| **1 small onion** | **2** Place the vegetables in the center of several thicknesses of paper toweling. Bring up the ends of the toweling and twist them together to form a pouch. Holding the pouch over the sink, squeeze out the excess moisture from the vegetables. |
| **1 egg** | |
| **1 tablespoon plus 1 teaspoon cornstarch** | |
| ¼ **teaspoon salt** | |
| ¼ **teaspoon pepper** | **3** Place the vegetables in a medium bowl. Add the egg, cornstarch, salt, pepper, dill, Romano cheese, and bread crumbs, and mix well. |
| ¼ **teaspoon dried dill** | |
| **1 tablespoon grated Romano cheese** | **4** Heat the oil in a large skillet over medium heat. |
| ¼ **cup Italian seasoned bread crumbs** | **5** For each latke, spoon 1 large spoonful of the mixture carefully into the pan. Immediately use the side and back of the spoon to form the mixture into a flat round. Cook about 4 minutes per side, or until browned. |
| **2 tablespoons olive oil** | |
| | **6** Remove the latke from the skillet; drain on a paper towel. Repeat with the remaining mixture. |

*Per serving: Calories: 204; Total fat: 11g; Saturated fat: 2g; Cholesterol: 72mg; Sodium: 345mg; Carbohydrates: 23g; Fiber: 3g; Sugar: 5g; Protein: 5g.*

*Tip:* The gluten-free bread crumbs in the recipe are readily available at most health food stores. The bread crumbs will stay fresher longer if you keep the unused portion in the freezer.

*Note:* The only thing that these latkes are missing is a dollop of sour cream on top. Enjoy these latkes as a side dish, or serve several as a main entree.

# Roasted Asparagus with Mustard Dressing

**Prep time:** 6 min • **Cook time:** 15 min • **Yield:** 4 servings

| Ingredients | Directions |
|---|---|
| **1 bunch thin asparagus (approximately 28 stalks)** | **1** Preheat the oven to 400 degrees. |
| **1 tablespoon plus 3 tablespoons olive oil** | **2** Wash the asparagus, and break off and discard the tough ends. Place the stalks in a baking dish. |
| **2 tablespoons brown mustard** | |
| **¼ teaspoon salt** | **3** Drizzle the stalks with 1 tablespoon of oil and toss to coat evenly. Spread the asparagus in a single layer. |
| **⅛ teaspoon pepper** | |
| **1 tablespoon balsamic vinegar** | **4** Bake the asparagus at 400 degrees for 10 minutes, or until they're almost tender-crisp. |
| **1 teaspoon sugar** | |
| | **5** In a small bowl, whisk together the remaining 3 tablespoons of oil, mustard, salt, pepper, vinegar, and sugar. |
| | **6** Pour the mustard glaze over the asparagus and return it to the oven for 5 minutes. |

**Per serving:** Calories: 160; Total fat: 14g; Saturated fat: 2g; Cholesterol: 0mg; Sodium: 237mg; Carbohydrates: 7g; Fiber: 1g; Sugar: 4g; Protein: 3g.

**Tip:** Cover and refrigerate any leftovers because they're also amazing when served cold.

# Packing Some Punch with Pastas and Starches

While veggies may be good for us, face it — nothing beats a great bowl of pasta or a side of potatoes. We're talking good, stick-to-your-ribs foods here. The gluten-free pastas taste every bit as good as traditional wheat pasta if you take a little care with the preparation. When boiling gluten-free pasta, add a little oil to the pot of water. Oil helps prevent the pasta from sticking together. Also add some salt. Salt raises the temperature of the boiling water, enabling the pasta to cook more quickly without falling apart.

The alternative flour pastas and macaronis become gooey and mushy if you overcook them. As soon as they're *al dente* (a fancy word for "just about tender"), remove the pan from the stove, drain off the water, and then rinse the pasta under cold running water (unless a recipe directs otherwise).

To serve the pasta with a sauce, add some sauce to the pot you used to cook the pasta and bring it to a boil. Add the rinsed and drained pasta, and then heat, stirring occasionally, just until the strands are hot, and serve immediately. If you're going to use the pasta in a casserole that will be baked, you don't need to reheat the pasta after you drain it.

The variety of alternative pastas available is increasing almost daily. Corn and rice are still the mainstays. Corn pasta is a bit coarser and grainier, takes a little longer to cook, and has a more distinctive taste. It also holds together better. Rice pasta has no distinctive taste, so it absorbs the sauce's flavor. It cooks more quickly than the corn-based products, so you need to pay close attention when it nears al dente. If it's overcooked, it can fall apart — but cooked al dente, it's fabulous.

Although rice and corn are the most common alternative pastas on the grocery shelves, you can also buy gluten-free pasta that's made from the following flours:

- White sweet potato
- Milo
- Water chestnut
- Arrowroot
- Yam
- Lotus
- Cassava

✔ Quinoa

✔ Amaranth

✔ Buckwheat

✔ Lentil

After corn and rice pasta, lentil definitely weighs in as the next most popular. It's darker in color, but the taste is very good and it resists the mushy factor. Quinoa pasta is pretty widely available these days, too, and is *loaded* with nutrition! (See Chapter 9 for the lowdown on most of these flours.)

Buckwheat pasta often has wheat flour added to it. Don't assume the buckwheat pasta is pure buckwheat. Be sure to read the label!

# Parmesan Potatoes

**Prep time:** 5 min • **Cook time:** 40 min • **Yield:** 4 servings

| Ingredients | Directions |
|---|---|
| 4 medium to large unpeeled red-skinned potatoes, cut in quarters lengthwise | *1* Preheat the oven to 375 degrees. |
| 3 tablespoons olive oil | *2* Place the potatoes in an 8-x-11-inch baking dish. |
| ¼ teaspoon garlic powder | *3* Pour the oil over the potatoes. Sprinkle the garlic powder, Romano cheese, salt, pepper, and Italian seasonings over the potatoes. |
| 2 tablespoons grated Romano cheese | |
| ⅛ teaspoon salt | |
| ⅛ teaspoon pepper | *4* Bake the potatoes at 375 degrees uncovered for 40 minutes, or until tender. |
| ¼ teaspoon Italian seasoning | |

*Per serving: Calories: 202; Total fat: 11g; Saturated fat: 2g; Cholesterol: 1mg; Sodium: 366mg; Carbohydrates: 25g; Fiber: 2g; Sugar: 2g; Protein: 0g.*

***Vary It!*** You can substitute dried dill for the Italian seasoning, melted butter for the oil, and Romano cheese for the Parmesan.

# Buckwheat Stuffed Bell Peppers

**Prep time:** 20 min • **Cook time:** 1 hr • **Yield:** 6 servings

| Ingredients | Directions |
|---|---|
| 1 cup roasted buckwheat (kasha) groats, rinsed well | **1** Preheat oven to 350 degrees. In a medium saucepan, add the vegetable stock. Bring to boil over medium-high heat. Add kasha to the boiling water and stir well with a wooden spoon. Reduce the heat to simmer, cover pan, and cook until all the liquid is absorbed, about 10 to 15 minutes. |
| 1½ cups vegetable stock | |
| 2 tablespoons olive oil, divided | |
| ½ red bell pepper, diced | |
| 1 cup baby spinach | **2** In a medium skillet, add 1 tablespoon olive oil and red bell pepper and sauté on high heat for 2 minutes. Remove from heat and combine peppers with spinach, edamame, corn, chia seeds, pepper, and salt. Add mixture to the cooked buckwheat. |
| 2 cups frozen edamame, thawed | |
| 1 cup frozen corn, thawed | |
| ¼ cup chia seeds | |
| Fresh ground pepper and salt to taste | |
| 6 whole bell peppers, combination of red, green, and yellow, cored with tops removed | **3** Rub remaining oil over bell peppers. Prebake the peppers in a glass baking pan for 15 minutes to soften. Remove from oven and fill the peppers with the kasha mixture, pressing firmly to fill the cavity. Place in baking pan, cover with foil, and bake for an additional 40 minutes. |
| 6 tablespoons rice vinegar | |
| 3 tablespoons gluten-free soy sauce | |
| 2 tablespoons sesame oil | **4** In a small glass bowl, whisk together the rice vinegar, soy sauce, sesame oil, cilantro, ginger, and sugar. Drizzle sauce over peppers when ready to serve. |
| 2 tablespoons chopped fresh cilantro | |
| 1 tablespoon fresh ginger, peeled and minced | |
| ½ teaspoon sugar | |

*Per serving:* Calories: 341; Total fat: 14g; Saturated fat: 2g; Cholesterol: 0mg; Sodium: 839mg; Carbohydrates: 45g; Fiber: 10g; Sugar: 0g; Protein: 13g.

*Tip:* Many grocery stores now carry buckwheat. Even though it doesn't naturally contain gluten, grains can be contaminated in the farming and production processes. Also sometimes vegetable stock can have gluten-containing ingredients, such as malt, malt flavoring, or hydrolyzed wheat protein, so read labels.

*Note:* With a delicious nutty flavor, buckwheat is easy to cook and super nutritious. It's loaded with fiber, and low in saturated fat, cholesterol, and sodium. Don't overcook buckwheat, or it will become mushy.

# The Ultimate Macaroni and Cheese

**Prep time:** 30 min • **Cook time:** 30 min • **Yield:** 9 servings

| *Ingredients* | *Directions* |
|---|---|
| **Nonstick cooking spray** <br> **8-ounce box rice penne pasta** | *1* Preheat the oven to 350 degrees. Spray a 9-x-9-inch baking dish with cooking spray. |
| **2 cups milk** | *2* In a medium saucepan, cook the pasta as the package directs, boiling only for 6 minutes. Rinse and drain the pasta. |
| **½ cup whipping cream** <br> **4 tablespoons butter** | |
| **1 teaspoon salt** | *3* In the same saucepan, stir together the milk and whipping cream. Remove ½ cup of the milk mixture and set it aside. |
| **¾ cup shredded Romano cheese, divided** | |
| | *4* Bring the remaining milk mixture to a simmer and add the drained pasta. |
| | *5* Cook the milk and pasta over medium heat, stirring frequently, about 10 minutes, or until the mixture thickens and most of the milk is absorbed. |
| | *6* Add the butter and salt and stir until the butter melts. |
| | *7* In the prepared baking dish, layer half of the macaroni, and then half of the cheese. Repeat the layers. |
| | *8* Pour the reserved milk over the top of the pasta. |
| | *9* Bake the pasta at 350 degrees for 30 minutes, or until the top begins to brown around the edges. Let the dish cool for 10 minutes before slicing. |

*Per serving:* Calories: 227; Total fat: 12g; Saturated fat: 7g; Cholesterol: 36mg; Sodium: 326mg; Carbohydrates: 23g; Fiber: 0g; Sugar: 3g; Protein: 7g.

**Tip:** You can assemble this dish ahead and freeze it (thaw it before baking), or you can cover and refrigerate it until shortly before dinner.

# Twice-Baked Sweet Potatoes

**Prep time:** 15 min • **Cook time:** 90 min • **Yield:** 4 servings

| Ingredients | Directions |
|---|---|
| **2 large sweet potatoes or yams, cut in half lengthwise** | *1* Preheat the oven to 375 degrees. |
| **Nonstick cooking spray** | *2* Put the halves of the potatoes together to form a whole potato, and wrap each potato in foil. |
| **3 tablespoons milk** | |
| **3 tablespoons maple syrup** | *3* Bake the potatoes at 375 degrees for about 1 hour until they're tender but not mushy. |
| **½ teaspoon vanilla** | *4* Cool the potatoes slightly, and then scoop out the centers, leaving enough potato to hold the shape of the skin. Place the scooped-out centers in a large mixing bowl. |
| **¼ teaspoon salt** | |
| **1 egg** | |
| **3 tablespoons gluten-free flour mixture (see Chapter 9 for the recipe)** | *5* Lower the oven temperature to 325 degrees. Spray an 8-x-11-inch baking dish with cooking spray. |
| **3 tablespoons brown sugar** | *6* Using a mixer, whip the potato pulp until it's smooth. Add the milk, maple syrup, vanilla, salt, and egg, and continue to whip until the pulp is light and fluffy. |
| **3 tablespoons butter, melted** | |
| **3 tablespoons finely chopped pecans** | *7* Spoon the filling into the potato shells, dividing evenly. |
| | *8* Place the shells in the prepared baking dish. |
| | *9* In a small bowl, use a fork to blend together the flour mixture and brown sugar. Add the butter and continue to blend with the fork until the dry ingredients are evenly moistened. |
| | *10* Stir in the pecans. |
| | *11* Crumble sugar mixture over the potatoes. Bake the potatoes at 325 degrees for 30 minutes. |

*Per serving:* Calories: 384; Total fat: 21g; Saturated fat: 7g; Cholesterol: 77mg; Sodium: 238mg; Carbohydrates: 46g; Fiber: 3g; Sugar: 22g; Protein: 5g.

*Tip:* Sweet potatoes have a relatively low glycemic index (see Chapter 4 for more info), making them far healthier for you than white potatoes.

# Mashed Potatoes with Caramelized Onions

**Prep time:** 25 min • **Cook time:** 20 min • **Yield:** 4 servings

| Ingredients | Directions |
|---|---|
| **2 tablespoons olive oil**<br><br>**1 cup sliced onions**<br><br>**½ teaspoon brown sugar**<br><br>**4 large Idaho potatoes**<br><br>**¼ cup butter, softened**<br><br>**1 teaspoon salt**<br><br>**¼ teaspoon pepper**<br><br>**¾ cup milk**<br><br>**⅔ cup shredded white sharp cheddar cheese** | *1* In a large skillet, heat the oil. Stir in the onions and brown sugar, and cook over medium heat for about 10 minutes, or until the onions are browned and glazed, stirring frequently. |
| | *2* Peel the potatoes. Cut each potato in half crosswise, and then cut each half into quarters. |
| | *3* Place the potatoes in a large saucepan and cover them with water. Bring the water to a boil and boil for 20 minutes, or until the potatoes are tender. Drain. |
| | *4* Place small batches of potatoes in a ricer and rice the potatoes into a mixing bowl. If you don't have a ricer, place the potatoes in the mixing bowl and whip the potatoes smooth with the mixer. Add the butter, salt, and pepper, and blend well. |
| | *5* Add the milk to the potatoes and whip until they're light and fluffy. |
| | *6* Whip in the onions and cheese just until they're evenly distributed and blended. |
| | *7* Either serve the potatoes immediately or transfer the mixture to a casserole dish that has been sprayed with nonstick cooking spray, cover, and refrigerate. To reheat the potatoes, bake the covered casserole at 400 degrees for 20 minutes. |

*Per serving:* Calories: 536; Total fat: 26g; Saturated fat: 13g; Cholesterol: 55mg; Sodium: 814mg; Carbohydrates: 66g; Fiber: 6g; Sugar: 6g; Protein: 12g.

*Vary 1t!* If you want even richer potatoes, use half-and-half in place of the milk.

# Serving Vegetable Dishes as the Main Attraction

Anyone who is vegan or vegetarian has already discovered some of the fascinating and delectable things that can be done with vegetables. A meat-and-potatoes person may need a little more convincing that it's possible to fill an empty stomach *and* enjoy the meal with no meat present. This section includes a few entrees that will convince anyone that meat isn't needed to satisfy the tummy at mealtime.

If you're innovative, select a vegetable large enough to stuff. Hollow it out, chop up the center, and sauté with onions and green pepper. Add "something" (rice, pasta, and/or veggies) to the onions and peppers, restuff the vegetable, and top it off with gluten-free bread crumbs, shredded cheese, or a sauce, and then bake. Each time you opt to do this, select a different veggie for the shell, a different filling, and a different topping.

Gluten-free lasagna noodles are another source for creativity. *Parboil* (partially cook by boiling) the noodles *slightly,* and then drain. (If the noodles are fully cooked, they'll fall apart when you assemble the casserole.) Don't rinse the noodles because they need to keep the starch intact for a cohesive finished product. If you use enough sauce in the casserole, you don't even need to parboil. Simply lay the noodles in a pan, top with a filling of your choice, repeat the layers, spread with a sauce, and bake.

# Quinoa-Stuffed Tomatoes

**Prep time:** 30 min • **Cook time:** 20 min • **Yield:** 4 servings

| *Ingredients* | *Directions* |
|---|---|
| 4 large tomatoes | *1* Preheat the oven to 350 degrees. |
| 1 cup water | *2* Cut ½ inch off the stem side of each tomato and discard the lid. Hollow out the insides. |
| 2 teaspoons butter | |
| 2 teaspoons olive oil | *3* Place the tomato shells in a 9-x-9-inch baking dish, cut side down. |
| ½ teaspoon minced garlic | *4* Pour the water around the tomatoes, cover the dish with foil, and bake the tomatoes at 350 degrees for 15 to 20 minutes until the skins are slightly softened but firm enough to hold their shape. Remove the tomatoes from the oven and drain off the hot water. |
| 2 green onions, minced | |
| ½ teaspoon salt | |
| ¼ teaspoon pepper | |
| ½ teaspoon dried dill | *5* In a large nonstick saucepan, sauté the garlic and onions in the butter and oil over medium-high heat until the onion is tender, stirring frequently. |
| ¼ teaspoon dried thyme | |
| ¼ teaspoon dried mint | *6* Stir in the salt, pepper, dill, thyme, mint, and parsley. |
| 2 teaspoons dried parsley flakes | *7* Add the chicken broth and bring it to a boil. |
| 14-ounce can chicken broth | *8* Lower the heat to medium-low, stir in the quinoa, cover the pan, and simmer the broth slowly for 20 minutes, or until the broth has been absorbed and the quinoa is tender. |
| ½ cup uncooked quinoa | |
| 2 tablespoons fresh lemon juice | *9* With a fork, stir in the lemon juice and spinach until everything is well combined. Stir in the feta cheese. |
| 10-ounce box frozen chopped spinach, thawed and drained well | *10* Stuff the tomatoes with the quinoa mixture. Cover the pan with foil. |
| 3 tablespoons crumbled feta cheese | *11* Bake the stuffed tomatoes at 350 degrees for 20 minutes. |

*Per serving:* *Calories: 222; Total fat: 10g; Saturated fat: 4g; Cholesterol: 17mg; Sodium: 815mg; Carbohydrates: 28g; Fiber: 6g; Sugar: 7g; Protein: 11g.*

*Tip:* Select large, ripe (but not too soft) tomatoes for this recipe because, after they're baked, they need to be firm enough to hold their shape, yet soft enough to cut easily with a fork. You don't use the tomato pulp in this recipe, so place the pulp in a self-seal bag to use in a stew or pasta sauce another day.

# *Spinach Lasagna*

**Prep time:** 35 min • **Cook time:** 45 min • **Yield:** 6 servings

| *Ingredients* | *Directions* |
|---|---|
| ½ cup hot water | *1* Preheat the oven to 350 degrees. |
| 1 chicken bouillon cube | |
| 1 medium onion, chopped | *2* In a small bowl, stir together the hot water and bouillon cube until the cube dissolves. |
| 2 teaspoons minced garlic | |
| 1 tablespoon olive oil | *3* In a medium saucepan over medium heat, sauté the onion and garlic in oil until tender, stirring frequently. |
| 2½ cups spaghetti sauce | |
| ¾ teaspoon Italian seasoning | *4* Stir in the broth (bouillon cube and water), spaghetti sauce, Italian seasoning, and pepper; simmer slowly for 15 minutes. |
| ¼ teaspoon pepper | |
| 1½ cups gluten-free small curd cottage cheese | *5* In a medium bowl, stir together the cottage cheese, yogurt, Romano cheese, and spinach. |
| ½ cup plain yogurt | |
| ¼ cup grated Romano cheese | *6* In a medium saucepan, boil the noodles according to the package directions, boiling only for 10 minutes. Drain the water and rinse the noodles very quickly with cold water so they're cool enough to handle (you want them to retain their starch). |
| 10-ounce box frozen chopped spinach, thawed and squeezed dry | |
| 8-ounce box lasagna noodles | |
| 1½ cups shredded mozzarella cheese | *7* Spread ¼ of the sauce in an 8-x-11-inch baking dish. Lay 1 layer of noodles on top of the sauce. Spread ½ of the spinach mixture over the noodles, and then ⅓ of the mozzarella. Repeat the layers, ending with the sauce and mozzarella. |
| | *8* Bake the lasagna uncovered at 350 degrees for 45 minutes. Let the lasagna set for 10 minutes before cutting. |

*Per serving:* Calories: 388; Total fat: 14g; Saturated fat: 6g; Cholesterol: 29mg; Sodium: 911mg; Carbohydrates: 45g; Fiber: 5g; Sugar: 8g; Protein: 22g.

*Tip:* Take care not to overcook the noodles when parboiling them.

# Cheese-Stuffed Zucchini

**Prep time:** 20 min • **Cook time:** 45 min • **Yield:** 4 servings

| *Ingredients* | *Directions* |
|---|---|
| Nonstick cooking spray | *1* Preheat the oven to 350 degrees. Spray a 9-x-9-inch baking dish with cooking spray. |
| 2 medium zucchini, each cut in half lengthwise | |
| 2 teaspoons olive oil | *2* Carefully remove the pulp from each zucchini half, leaving a ¼-inch thick shell. Chop the pulp. |
| 1 cup finely chopped onion | |
| 1 cup finely chopped green pepper | *3* Heat the oil in a large nonstick skillet. Add the onion, green pepper, and garlic. Sauté over medium heat, stirring frequently, until the vegetables are soft (about 5 minutes). |
| 2 cloves garlic, minced | |
| 1 cup finely chopped plum tomatoes | *4* Stir the tomatoes, zucchini pulp, oregano, parsley, salt, pepper, dill, and mint into the onion mixture. Reduce the heat and cook over medium-low heat for 5 minutes, stirring occasionally. Remove from the heat; cool for 5 minutes. |
| ¾ teaspoon dried oregano | |
| ¼ cup chopped fresh parsley | |
| ¼ teaspoon salt | |
| ¼ teaspoon pepper | *5* Stir in the cheese. |
| ¼ teaspoon dried dill | |
| ¼ teaspoon dried mint | *6* Stuff each zucchini shell with about ½ cup of the onion mixture. Sprinkle the tops with bread crumbs. |
| ¾ cup crumbled feta cheese | |
| 4 teaspoons Italian seasoned bread crumbs | *7* Set the zucchini "boats" in the prepared baking dish. |
| | *8* Bake the zucchini at 350 degrees for 30 minutes, or until the bread crumbs are lightly browned and the shells are tender. |

*Per serving:* Calories: 165; Total fat: 9g; Saturated fat: 5g; Cholesterol: 25mg; Sodium: 610mg; Carbohydrates: 17g; Fiber: 4g; Sugar: 7g; Protein: 7g.

*Tip:* You can also serve this as a side dish.

*Note:* If you grow your own zucchini, try stuffing the flowers from the plant before the vegetable begins to develop. Pick the flowers when they are large, wash them well, and then stuff and bake them.

# Part III
# Dishes to Enjoy Before, After, or Any Time

The 5th Wave                    By Rich Tennant

"Jane finally teach Boy how to cook.
Before that, him just eat cheetah.
Too much fast food not good."

# In this part . . .

We explore new and intriguing recipes outside of the usual three square meals a day: beyond toast for breakfast, beyond that sandwich at lunch, and certainly beyond the typical dinner. The pages are jammed with tempting appetizers, salads, soups, snacks, and desserts.

# Chapter 18

# Appetizing Appetizers

## In This Chapter

▶ Knowing what to serve when

▶ Whipping up some can't-resist dips and grab-and-go goodies

▶ Serving hot munchies straight from the oven

Appetizers, hors d'oeuvres, starters, anti-pasto, gustus, mezethes, tapas, maza, mezze, zakuski, dim sum, smorgasbord . . . an appetizer by any other name is still an appetizer.

It seems a little ironic that we *eat* to build an appetite, but that's the idea. Appetizers are small servings of foods served before a meal to whet the appe-tite, or they can be served alone to enable people to dawdle over small serv-ings of different dishes. Serving appetizers stretches out a social gathering while guests circulate, talk, bond, and mingle. This chapter gives you several gluten-free appetizers you can serve before your next meal or gathering.

## Choosing the Right Appetizers for the Occasion

Conjure up in your mind all those appetizers you've been offered at parties over the years. Celery sticks with plain cream cheese. Crackers with spray cheese. Chips and dip made from sour cream and onion soup mix. Herring in dill sauce. Aren't you tired of these things? Wouldn't you rather serve something with more character and spice? Something a bit more memorable? Bland appetizers merely fill the belly, whereas appetizers with pizzazz actu-ally assault the senses and get guests craving more.

Be creative in your food choice. Balance hot and cold dishes, rich and mild foods, and try to include at least one vegetarian offering. Assortment is the key. Pick foods that are party-friendly — people will most likely be walking around, so you don't want to serve foods that are too sticky, messy, or greasy. Better choices are items that people can pick up easily and eat with two fingers.

Here are a few ideas to get your creative juices flowing:

- Consider serving something where people can participate, like assembling their own mini-tacos on corn tortillas or in corn taco shells and adding their own toppings, fillings, or condiments.

- Rice papers (available at Asian markets), when soaked in water for 2 minutes, become very pliable and make the perfect wrapper for appetizers. You can use these wrappers to make mini-Reuben wraps with pastrami and Swiss cheese and a dab of gluten-free brown mustard (to be served hot or cold). Or spread the rice papers with cream cheese, and then top with gluten-free chunky salsa, shredded lettuce, crisp-cooked bacon, and some guacamole. Roll them up for one delicious appetizer.

- A great assemble-ahead appetizer is eggplant pizza. Brown slices of eggplant in your broiler, top with a small amount of gluten-free spaghetti sauce, sprinkle with Italian seasoning, and then top off with a slice of provolone cheese. Pop it in the microwave to melt the cheese, and it's ready to serve.

- In the summertime, make use of your grill. Early in the day, assemble mini-kebabs (shrimp, chicken, beef, veggies), or wrap mushrooms in bacon and brush them with gluten-free barbecue sauce. Let your friends grill their own appetizers.

To add some sanity to the day of the party, choose appetizers that you can make ahead and store in the refrigerator or freezer until it's time to serve them. If guests are coming for dinner, choose lighter appetizers so people don't fill up on them, but prepare enough so that your guests stay busy munching and meandering in the living room or family room (so they'll stay out of your kitchen and let you work at plating the dinner). Plan on about four appetizers per person. If you're offering two appetizers, that would average two of each selection per person. If you're only serving appetizers, then you'd better make a bit larger quantity of each. Figure on eight to nine pieces per guest.

If you're hosting a party, chances are that most of your guests aren't on a gluten-free diet. But hey, it's your party! Make gluten-free appetizers that everyone can enjoy!

# *Taking a Dip with Cold Appetizers*

If you're planning an event that will last an entire afternoon or evening, keep in mind that some foods shouldn't remain at room temperature for longer than two hours at the most. When serving foods that need refrigeration (dips, deviled eggs, meats or seafood, anything with mayonnaise), put out partial amounts and refill the platter from the refrigerated stash.

In the case of cold dips, an easy way to keep them cool longer is to set the dip bowl into a slightly larger bowl that has been filled with ice. Or think outside the bowl. Spoon the dip into a hollowed-out small head of cabbage, squash, or large green or red pepper, and then set this into the bowl with ice.

Although you can't gauge exactly how much chips and dip your friends will consume, a pretty good approximation is to have ¼ cup of chip dip per person when other snacks are also served.

Here we provide four tasty recipes for cold appetizers that are sure to be a hit.

## A blast from the past for nutrition that lasts

They may have been a little stinky, but our Paleolithic ancestors were remarkably healthy. They were lean, fit, and didn't get the plethora of diseases that we get today. In fact, anthropological studies show they were lean, had good aerobic capacity, low cholesterol, low blood pressure, and better insulin metabolism. Healthwise, they rank right up there with today's elite and highly trained athletes.

In contrast, most of today's humans are a mess. We eat too much, we eat the wrong foods, we're fat, and we have lots and lots of diseases, some of which we're inventing as we go. More people are overweight than aren't, and it's killing us. Heart and blood-vessel disease is a leading killer; high blood pressure, high cholesterol, diabetes, and obesity are all epidemic.

*Tip:* You can find lots of detailed information about the Paleolithic diet on the Internet by doing a quick search on your favorite search engine.

# Shrimp Deviled Eggs

**Prep time:** 10 min • **Cook time:** 11 min • **Yield:** 6 servings

| Ingredients | Directions |
|---|---|
| 3 eggs | **1** Place the eggs in a single layer in a medium saucepan with enough cold water to cover them. Add a teaspoon of salt to the pan to help prevent the eggshells from cracking. Bring the water to a boil over high heat. As soon as the water starts to boil, let the eggs cook for exactly 11 minutes, and then remove the pan from the heat. Set the pan in the sink and run cold water over the eggs to stop them from further cooking. |
| 1 teaspoon plus dash of salt | |
| 8 large cocktail shrimp, cooked and deveined | |
| 2 tablespoons plus 1 teaspoon mayonnaise | |
| ¼ teaspoon mustard | **2** Dice the shrimp and set them aside. |
| ¼ teaspoon dried dill | **3** Peel the eggs and cut them in half lengthwise. Carefully remove the yolks and place them in a medium bowl. Set the egg whites aside. |
| ¼ teaspoon lemon juice | |
| ⅛ teaspoon pepper | |
| Paprika | **4** Mash the yolks with the back of a fork. Add the mayonnaise, mustard, dill, lemon juice, pepper, and a dash of salt and stir until the mixture is smooth. |
| | **5** Stir in the shrimp until it's evenly distributed. |
| | **6** With a small spoon, refill the egg white halves, mounding the yolk mixture on top. |
| | **7** Sprinkle the tops lightly with paprika, cover, and refrigerate until serving time. |

*Per serving: Calories: 68; Total fat: 5g; Saturated fat: 1g; Cholesterol: 122mg; Sodium: 116mg; Carbohydrates: 2g; Fiber: 0g; Sugar: 1g; Protein: 5g.*

# Feta Supreme Spread

**Prep time:** 5 min plus refrigeration time • **Cook time:** None • **Yield:** 2 cups

| Ingredients | Directions |
|---|---|
| **8 ounces feta cheese** | **1** With a fork, crumble the feta in a medium bowl. |
| **1½ tablespoons fresh lemon juice (1 lemon)** | **2** Add the lemon juice, red wine vinegar, olive oil, oregano, garlic powder, cumin, and pepper and continue to blend with a fork until everything is mixed. |
| **1 tablespoon red wine vinegar** | |
| **3 tablespoons olive oil** | |
| **½ teaspoon dried oregano** | **3** Cover the bowl with plastic wrap and refrigerate the spread for several hours. |
| **¼ teaspoon garlic powder** | |
| **⅛ teaspoon cumin** | |
| **¼ teaspoon pepper** | |

*Per serving:* Calories: 121; Total fat: 11g; Saturated fat: 5g; Cholesterol: 25mg; Sodium: 316mg; Carbohydrates: 2g; Fiber: 0g; Sugar: 1g; Protein: 4g.

*Tip:* Make this spread ahead so it has plenty of time for the flavors to blend.

*Note:* Slather this spread on gluten-free pita wedges or gluten-free crackers to make an easy appetizer. You can also use it as a sandwich spread or sprinkled over a Greek salad.

# Roulade Canapé

**Prep time:** 5 min plus refrigeration time  •  **Cook time:** None  •  **Yield:** 24 pieces

| Ingredients | Directions |
|---|---|
| 3 ounces cream cheese, softened | **1** Cut the ham and turkey slices the same sizes (approximately the size of a slice of bread). |
| 1 cup baby spinach leaves, rinsed | **2** Spread cream cheese on each of the ham slices, dividing evenly. |
| 2 whole roasted red peppers, each cut in half | **3** Place 1 slice of turkey on top of each ham slice. |
| 4 slices deli ham | **4** Spread the spinach leaves on top of the turkey slices, and then place a red pepper half at one end of each slice. |
| 4 slices deli turkey | **5** Starting at the narrow end of the meat, roll each into a roulade. |
| | **6** Wrap each individual roulade tightly in plastic wrap and refrigerate for 4 or more hours. |
| | **7** To serve, remove the plastic wrap and cut each roulade into 6 rounds with a serrated knife. Place the pieces, cut side up, on a platter. |

*Per serving: Calories: 47; Total fat: 3g; Saturated fat: 2g; Cholesterol: 15mg; Sodium: 181mg; Carbohydrates: 1g; Fiber: 0g; Sugar: 1g; Protein: 4g.*

*Tip:* These directions call for slicing the roulades (rolled slices of meat stuffed with filling) to convert them to canapés (another fancy word for appetizer), but this concoction also makes a great lunch.

# Crabmeat Dip

**Prep time:** 10 min plus refrigeration time • **Cook time:** None • **Yield:** 2 cups

| *Ingredients* | *Directions* |
|---|---|
| 4.5-ounce can crabmeat, drained and flaked | *1* In a medium bowl, stir together all the ingredients, mixing well to blend thoroughly. |
| 1 hard-boiled egg, shelled and minced | |
| ¼ cup mayonnaise | *2* Cover and chill the dip for at least 2 hours for flavors to blend. |
| ¼ cup sour cream | |
| 1 teaspoon lemon juice | |
| ½ teaspoon dry mustard | |
| ¼ teaspoon dried dill | |
| 1 green onion, minced | |
| ¼ teaspoon Worcestershire sauce | |
| ½ teaspoon dried parsley flakes | |
| ¼ teaspoon salt | |
| ⅛ teaspoon pepper | |

*Per serving:* Calories: 88; Total fat: 7g; Saturated fat: 2g; Cholesterol: 59mg; Sodium: 284mg; Carbohydrates: 3g; Fiber: 0g; Sugar: 1g; Protein: 4g.

# Serving Up Some Hors D'oeuvres from the Oven

The hot appetizers in this section are perfect for any occasion. Whether you're having a formal cocktail party at home (does anyone still have those?) or friends over to watch a game on TV, or you're going to a picnic or tailgate party, these offerings will impress your friends. Appetizers bring cohesiveness to any gathering. People gather around the food, so make sure that the food is absolutely irresistible!

## Gluten-free fights Father Time

Can gluten-free make wrinkles flee? Possibly! According to many experts, gluten-free is the way to be if you're trying to turn back the wrinkled hands of time or stave off symptoms of menopause. Anti-aging specialists often tell patients to avoid wheat, and especially refined flours, to improve the quality of skin and erase wrinkles. One of the best known experts in his field, Dr. Nicholas Perricone, maintains that wheat and other high glycemic load foods provoke an inflammatory response that causes our skin to age more quickly. He says that avoiding foods like wheat can actually help *reverse* the aging process.

Wheat-based foods are also implicated in symptoms of menopause, such as hot flashes, night sweats, headaches, fatigue, and mood swings. Patients are often advised to give up wheat to alleviate menopausal symptoms.

# Baked Potato Skins

**Prep time:** 15 min • **Cook time:** 60 min • **Yield:** 12 servings

| *Ingredients* | *Directions* |
|---|---|
| **6 medium russet potatoes** | *1* Preheat the oven to 400 degrees. |
| **2 tablespoons butter** | |
| **1 teaspoon minced garlic** | *2* Rinse each potato and then cut it in half. Put the two halves back together and wrap the potato in foil. Repeat with the remaining potatoes. Put them on the oven rack and bake for 45 minutes. Let the potatoes cool for 15 minutes. (***Note:*** Leave the oven on because you'll put the skins back in to reheat them and melt the cheese.) |
| **⅛ teaspoon pepper** | |
| **4 ounces crumbled blue cheese** | |
| **3 slices bacon, cooked crisp and crumbled** | |
| **3 tablespoons seasoned bread crumbs** | *3* Remove the foil. Using a small spoon, scoop out the centers of each potato half. |
| **2 tablespoons grated Parmesan cheese** | *4* In a small skillet, melt the butter. Add the garlic and pepper and sauté them in the butter over medium heat. Using a pastry brush, brush the inside of each potato half with the butter mixture. |
| | *5* Sprinkle the blue cheese inside of each potato half and then top with the bacon crumbles. |
| | *6* In a small bowl, stir together the bread crumbs and Parmesan cheese; sprinkle the mixture on top of the bacon. |
| | *7* Place the potato skins on a baking sheet and bake at 400 degrees for 15 minutes, or until the skins are hot and crisp. |

*Per serving:* Calories: 172; Total fat: 33g; Saturated fat: 5g; Cholesterol: 26mg; Sodium: 424mg; Carbohydrates: 15g; Fiber: 2g; Sugar: 1g; Protein: 8g.

***Tip:*** When scooping out the potato center, don't go all the way to the skin. Leave an inner lining of potato so it can hold its shape. You won't need the pulp, so spoon the scooped-out centers into a self-seal bag to make potato pancakes at another time.

# Tortilla Sticks

**Prep time:** 5 min • **Cook time:** 8 min • **Yield:** 20 pieces

| Ingredients | Directions |
|---|---|
| 2 (8-inch) rice flour tortillas | **1** Preheat oven to 400 degrees. Spray a nonstick cookie sheet with nonstick spray. |
| 2 tablespoons butter, melted | |
| 3 tablespoons grated Parmesan cheese | **2** Brush one side of each tortilla with the melted butter, then sprinkle with the cheese, garlic powder, and Italian seasoning. Press toppings into the tortillas so they will adhere. |
| ⅛ teaspoon garlic powder | |
| ¼ teaspoon Italian seasoning | |
| | **3** With a clean pair of scissors, cut each tortilla into 10 (¾-inch wide) strips. Place strips on the baking sheet. |
| | **4** Bake for 8 minutes or until strips are light golden and crisp. |

*Per serving:* Calories: 26; Total fat: 2g; Saturated fat: 0.8g; Cholesterol: 4mg; Sodium: 35mg; Carbohydrates; 2. Fiber: 0g; Sugar: 0g; Protein: 1g

*Note:* These sticks are perfect for snacking hot from the oven, but they're also the perfect accompaniment for soups or a pasta dinner.

*Vary It!* Tortilla sticks are also tasty when sprinkled with sesame seeds before baking.

# Artichoke Squares

**Prep time:** 10 min • **Cook time:** 35 min • **Yield:** 16 pieces

| Ingredients | Directions |
|---|---|
| 3 tablespoons olive oil | **1** Preheat the oven to 325 degrees. Oil an 8-inch-square baking dish. |
| 8 green onions, sliced thin | |
| ½ teaspoon minced garlic | **2** Add the olive oil to a small skillet and sauté the onion and garlic over medium heat until they're soft. Let the mixture cool slightly. |
| 4 eggs | |
| ½ teaspoon dried mint | |
| 1 teaspoon dried dill | **3** With a whisk, whip the eggs in a large bowl until they're frothy. Stir the mint, dill, and Worcestershire sauce into the eggs. |
| 1 teaspoon gluten-free Worcestershire sauce | |
| 15-ounce can artichoke quarters, drained and chopped | **4** Stir in the artichokes, cheese, onions, and garlic. |
| 1 cup shredded Swiss cheese | **5** Smooth the mixture into the prepared baking dish. Sprinkle the bread crumbs over the top. |
| 3 tablespoons seasoned bread crumbs | |
| | **6** Bake at 325 degrees for 35 minutes, or until the bread crumbs are lightly browned. |
| | **7** Let the dish cool slightly before cutting. |

*Per serving:* Calories: 76; Total fat: 6g; Saturated fat: 2g; Cholesterol: 59mg; Sodium: 64mg; Carbohydrates: 3g; Fiber: 1g; Sugar: 1g; Protein: 4g.

*Tip:* Don't buy marinated artichokes or this dish will be too bitter.

*Note:* You can assemble these squares ahead of time, they bake by themselves while you prepare for company, and you usually don't need forks to enjoy them.

# Cajun Stuffed Mushrooms

**Prep time:** 15 min • **Cook time:** 35 min • **Yield:** 24 mushroom caps

| Ingredients | Directions |
|---|---|
| Nonstick cooking spray | **1** Preheat the oven to 350 degrees. Line an 8-x-11-inch baking dish with foil; spray the foil with nonstick cooking spray. |
| 24 large mushrooms | |
| ½ pound spicy sausage | |
| 1 cup chopped onion | **2** Clean the mushrooms, removing the stems. Set the caps aside. Chop the stems. |
| ¼ cup minced green pepper | |
| ½ teaspoon garlic powder | **3** In a large skillet, brown the sausage, onion, green pepper, and mushroom stems over medium heat, breaking the meat up with a fork. Stir in the garlic powder, Cajun seasoning, parsley flakes, and cumin. |
| ¾ teaspoon Cajun seasoning | |
| 2 teaspoons dried parsley flakes | |
| ½ teaspoon cumin | **4** Pile the stuffing into the mushroom caps. Set the caps, stuffing side up, in the prepared baking dish. |
| 1 cup mayonnaise | |
| ¾ cup grated Parmesan cheese | **5** In a small bowl, stir together the mayonnaise and Parmesan cheese. Spoon the mixture on top of each mushroom cap. |
| | **6** Bake the mushrooms at 350 degrees for 35 minutes, or until the cheese is golden. |

*Per mushroom: Calories: 8; Total fat: 7g; Saturated fat: 2g; Cholesterol: 7mg; Sodium: 143mg; Carbohydrates: 1g; Fiber: 0g; Sugar: 1g; Protein: 2g*

**Tip:** If you thrive on five-alarm foods that virtually disintegrate your taste buds, then use gluten-free hot sausage and add more Cajun seasoning.

# Chapter 19

# Salads with Pizzazz

## In This Chapter

▶ Tossing the varietal veggies

▶ Making fruit fun

▶ Slipping in some meat

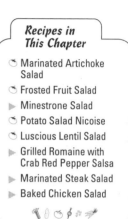
**A**dmittedly, this chapter *has* to be one of the easiest to write. After all, most salads are naturally gluten-free, aren't they? Seriously, when was the last time you shopped for salad-makin's and had to read a label — other than croutons and toppings, of course. "Ingredients: carrot." Hmmm, better look that one up to make sure it's on the approved list of gluten-free ingredients. *Not!*

Best of all, fruits and veggies — aka salad makin's — are a great source of nutrition. Loaded with antioxidants, vitamins, and minerals, they're also a great source of fiber and even water.

In this chapter, I show you lots of ways to jazz up a salad with fruits, veggies, and other ingredients you may not have thought to add to the mix. I also offer some ideas for making gluten-free salads that would otherwise be on the no-no list and show you how to incorporate meat into your salads for a little extra protein and flavor.

If you're making meatloaf, stuffed peppers, sweet breads, or muffins, shred some carrots and/or zucchini into them. They'll add flavor and moisture, and you'll be getting more vitamins without much extra effort. You can add chopped green pepper and onion to almost any meat, casserole, or vegetable dish.

## Viewing Fruit and Vegetable Options

Before you even begin to create a salad, you have to make choices. What kind of lettuce will you select? Will it be iceberg (which has almost no nutritional value), leaf lettuce, spinach, spring field greens, or something more exotic like watercress or Bibb lettuce? A good rule of thumb to remember is that the darker the green, the better it is for you.

When making a fruit salad, begin by placing a handful of crisp greens on a dish, and then use your imagination. Experiment by adding the less common fruits like pomegranate seeds, sliced dates, black raspberries, grapefruit sections, sliced persimmons, or mango cubes.

For vegetable salads, you can jazz up a salad by

- ✔ Replacing the cucumber with zucchini
- ✔ Substituting sliced roasted red peppers for the tomatoes
- ✔ Using feta cheese crumbles instead of shredded cheddar or mozzarella cheese
- ✔ Tossing in kalamata olives in place of the ripe olives

Think of some of the alternative options offered at salad bars. Why not borrow some of these ideas to spruce up your own salads? You can include

- ✔ Marinated asparagus tips or artichoke hearts
- ✔ Peas or snow pea pods
- ✔ Diced beets
- ✔ Teeny cubes of ham or shredded tuna
- ✔ Marinated beans (green, kidney, black, navy)
- ✔ Corn kernels
- ✔ Nuts (walnuts, pecans, cashews, almonds)
- ✔ Raw cauliflower or broccoli
- ✔ Sprouts (alfalfa or bean)
- ✔ Seeds (poppy, sesame, sunflower)

Life is full of decisions. When you have your salad assembled, what are you going to use for dressing? For a fruit salad, whisk 1 tablespoon of jam into gluten-free Italian dressing and drizzle it over the salad. When tossing a veggie salad, you can choose from a wide variety of gluten-free salad dressings on the market.

No dressing in the cupboard or refrigerator? Not to worry. One of the best salad dressings is still a blend of olive oil and vinegar with seasonings.

# Marinated Artichoke Salad

**Prep time:** 5 min plus refrigeration time • **Cook time:** None • **Yield:** 6 servings

| Ingredients | Directions |
|---|---|
| **7.5-ounce jar marinated artichokes, reserve juice** | **1** Combine the artichokes, mushrooms, tomato, and broccoli in a large bowl. |
| **8-ounce jar marinated button mushrooms, reserve juice** | **2** In a small bowl, whisk together the juices from the artichokes and mushrooms, the salt, pepper, dill, oregano, mint, and oil. Pour the dressing over the vegetables and toss to coat evenly. |
| **1 large tomato, cut into chunks** | |
| **3 cups broccoli florets** | |
| **¼ teaspoon salt** | **3** Cover and refrigerate the salad for several hours to allow the flavors to blend. |
| **¼ teaspoon pepper** | |
| **¼ teaspoon dried dill** | |
| **¼ teaspoon dried oregano** | |
| **⅛ teaspoon dried mint** | |
| **3 tablespoons olive oil** | |

*Per serving: Calories: 95; Total fat: 7g; Saturated fat: 1g; Cholesterol: 0mg; Sodium: 265mg; Carbohydrates: 7g; Fiber: 3g; Sugar: 2g; Protein: 3g.*

*Note:* Marinated salads need "bonding" time in the refrigerator to meld all the flavors together.

# Frosted Fruit Salad

**Prep time:** 20 min • **Cook time:** None • **Yield:** 8 servings

| Ingredients | Directions |
|---|---|
| ⅓ cup sweetened condensed milk | *1* In a large mixing bowl, whip together the condensed milk, cream cheese, marmalade, and vanilla using the electric mixer, until the ingredients are fluffy and well blended. |
| 3 ounces cream cheese, softened | |
| 2 tablespoons orange marmalade | |
| ½ teaspoon vanilla | *2* Drain the peaches and pineapple well using a sieve or a colander. |
| 15.25-ounce can sliced peaches, cut in thirds | |
| 8-ounce can crushed pineapple | *3* Stir the peaches, pineapple, walnuts, strawberries, blueberries, and kiwi into the cream cheese mixture until the salad is blended. |
| ½ cup coarsely chopped walnuts | |
| ½ pint fresh strawberries, hulled and sliced | |
| ½ pint fresh blueberries | |
| 3 ripe kiwis, peeled and sliced | |

*Per serving: Calories: 233; Total fat: 10g; Saturated fat: 3g; Cholesterol: 16mg; Sodium: 55mg; Carbohydrates: 33g; Fiber: 3g; Sugar: 27g; Protein: 4g.*

# Minestrone Salad

**Prep time:** 15 min  •  **Cook time:** 8 min plus refrigeration time  •  **Yield:** 8 servings

| *Ingredients* | *Directions* |
|---|---|

½ cup rice pasta shells

3 tablespoons olive oil

2 tablespoons cider vinegar

1 tablespoon balsamic vinegar

1 tablespoon dried parsley flakes

¾ teaspoon dried oregano

½ teaspoon dried basil

½ teaspoon dried mint flakes

¼ teaspoon salt

¼ teaspoon pepper

½ teaspoon sugar

15.5-ounce can light red kidney beans, rinsed and drained

1 carrot, sliced thin

1 medium zucchini, sliced thin

½ green pepper, chopped

1 medium yellow onion, sliced thin

⅛ pound pepperoni, slices halved

*1* In a medium saucepan, boil the pasta according to the package directions; drain.

*2* In a large bowl, whisk together the oil, vinegars, parsley, oregano, basil, mint, salt, pepper, and sugar. Add the pasta and the kidney beans, carrot, zucchini, green pepper, onion, and pepperoni. Toss well to coat the pasta and veggies evenly with the dressing.

*3* Cover the salad and refrigerate it for several hours to allow the flavors to blend.

*Per serving: Calories: 149; Total fat: 8g; Saturated fat: 2g; Cholesterol: 8mg; Sodium: 318mg; Carbohydrates: 15g; Fiber: 4g; Sugar: 2g; Protein: 4g.*

*Tip:* Don't rinse the pasta if you want the dressing to stick to it.

*Note:* This tasty salad should be made ahead and then refrigerated to allow the flavors to blend.

# Potato Salad Nicoise

**Prep time:** 35 min • **Cook time:** 15 min plus refrigeration time • **Yield:** 4 servings

| *Ingredients* | *Directions* |
|---|---|
| **16 small white gourmet potatoes or small red-skinned potatoes** | **1** Place potatoes in a medium saucepan. Cover with water and bring to a boil. Boil for 20 minutes or until potatoes are just fork tender. Rinse in cold water to cool them down. When cool, slide off the skins and discard skins. |
| **4 eggs** | |
| **2 cups frozen, cut green beans** | |
| **2 green onions, sliced thin** | **2** Place eggs in a small saucepan. Cover with water and bring to a boil. Boil for 11 minutes and then remove eggs to a colander and rinse well with cold water. When cool enough to handle, peel eggs, discarding shells. Quarter eggs and set aside. |
| **4 Roma tomatoes, sliced** | |
| **12 pitted black olives** | |
| **1 teaspoon brown mustard** | |
| **¼ teaspoon garlic powder** | **3** Place the beans in a medium saucepan and cover them with water. Bring the beans to a boil and cook them until they're fork tender; rinse the beans in cold water and then drain them. Place the beans in a large bowl. |
| **¼ teaspoon salt** | |
| **¼ teaspoon pepper** | |
| **2 teaspoons dried parsley flakes** | **4** Quarter the potatoes and add them to the beans. Peel the eggs and quarter them; set the eggs aside. Add the green onions, tomatoes, and olives to the bowl. |
| **½ teaspoon Italian seasoning** | |
| **2 tablespoons cider vinegar** | |
| **¼ cup olive oil** | **5** In a small bowl, whisk together the mustard, garlic powder, salt, pepper, parsley flakes, Italian seasoning, vinegar, and oil; pour the dressing over the potato mixture and gently blend to distribute the dressing evenly. Cover the potato salad and refrigerate it for 2 hours. |
| **Croutons (see the following recipe)** | |
| | **6** Just before serving, toss in the croutons (see the following recipe) and garnish with the egg wedges. |

## Gluten-Free Croutons

⅛ teaspoon salt

⅛ teaspoon pepper

¼ teaspoon Italian seasoning

¼ teaspoon garlic powder

1 teaspoon grated Romano cheese

2 tablespoons olive oil

3 slices bread

**1** Preheat the oven to 300 degrees. In a medium bowl, whisk together the salt, pepper, Italian seasoning, garlic powder, cheese, and oil.

**2** Cut the bread into ½-inch cubes. Add the bread cubes to the bowl and toss them until the oil mixture is evenly distributed.

**3** Spoon the bread cubes onto a baking sheet and bake them at 300 degrees for 35 minutes, or until the bread is toasted, stirring occasionally. Watch closely so that the cubes don't burn.

*Per serving: Calories: 570; Total fat: 28g; Saturated fat: 5g; Cholesterol: 212mg; Sodium: 657mg; Carbohydrates: 68g; Fiber: 10g; Sugar: 7g; Protein: 15g.*

*Note:* The beauty of this salad is that you can make it ahead, cover it, and refrigerate it until serving time.

# Luscious Lentil Salad

**Prep time:** 10 min • **Cook time:** 15 min plus refrigeration time • **Yield:** 4 servings

| Ingredients | Directions |
|---|---|
| ⅓ **pound lentils** | **1** Place the lentils in a small saucepan and cover with water. Bring the water to a rolling boil, and boil about 15 minutes, or until the lentils are tender but not mushy. Rinse the lentils under cold water, and then drain. |
| **3 tablespoons olive oil** | |
| **2 tablespoons balsamic vinegar** | |
| ¼ **teaspoon salt** | |
| ⅛ **teaspoon pepper** | **2** Place the lentils in a medium bowl. Add the oil, vinegar, salt, pepper, dill, mint, oregano, onion, green pepper, celery, carrot, and parsley to the bowl. Stir the lentils well to coat them evenly. |
| ¼ **teaspoon dried dill** | |
| ⅛ **teaspoon dried mint flakes** | |
| ¼ **teaspoon dried oregano** | **3** Cover the salad and refrigerate it for 2 hours to allow the flavors to blend. |
| **1 small onion, chopped** | |
| ¼ **green pepper, chopped** | |
| **1 rib celery, sliced thin** | |
| ½ **carrot, sliced thin** | |
| **1 tablespoon chopped fresh parsley** | |

*Per serving: Calories: 168; Total fat: 10g; Saturated fat: 1g; Cholesterol: 0mg; Sodium: 163mg; Carbohydrates: 15g; Fiber: 5g; Sugar: 4g; Protein: 5g.*

# Combining Greens with Meats

Unadorned, lettuce is just a side dish that periodically appears near your plate at lunch or dinner. Even though additional ingredients can be added to the lettuce, some people still relegate salads to summer buffets and lunches for those on diets. It's time to reevaluate that thinking. By adding meat and some fiber (sunflower seeds, poppy seeds, sesame seeds, tomatoes, raw baby zucchini, or even flax seed), a salad suddenly becomes a hearty, healthy, great-tasting meal in a bowl.

If the lettuce gets soggy in the refrigerator storage bin, perk it up by adding lemon juice to a bowl of cold water and soak it for an hour in the refrigerator.

## Gluten-free — indulgently!

All this talk about good nutrition is meant to provide you with guidelines for a healthy approach to the gluten-free lifestyle. Having made my point about the importance of good nutrition, I think it's also important to point out that it's okay to live a little — indulge from time to time! *Not* in gluten, of course — but in something yummy and decadent, whatever that means to you. No matter which approach you take to the gluten-free lifestyle, you need to find a balance that works for you for the long haul.

# Grilled Romaine Salad with Crab Red Pepper Salsa

**Prep time:** 10 min • **Cook time:** 10 min • **Yield:** 4 servings

| Ingredients | Directions |
|---|---|
| 2 heads romaine lettuce, washed and dried thoroughly | **1** Preheat grill to high heat. Place whole red bell pepper on grill grates and turn until entire pepper is charred and blistered. Place pepper in a brown paper bag and let stand for 5 minutes. Peel the skin from the pepper, discard the seeds and core. Rinse under cold water to remove residue. Chop the red pepper and place in a small glass bowl. |
| Nonstick olive oil cooking spray | |
| 1 large red bell pepper | |
| 2 green onions, trimmed and sliced | **2** Gently toss the chopped red peppers with the green onions, cilantro, lime juice, olive oil, and crab meat. Set aside. |
| ½ cup chopped fresh cilantro | |
| 1 tablespoon lime juice | |
| ½ tablespoon olive oil | **3** Cut each head of romaine lengthwise into two pieces with the core intact. Lightly spray the romaine with olive oil spray and place on grill for 2 to 3 minutes each side until very lightly charred. Romaine will be slightly wilted and lightly brown. |
| 1 cup fresh lump crabmeat | |
| Freshly ground pepper, to taste | |
| | **4** Place the grilled romaine lettuce on individual plates and top with the crab red pepper salsa. |

*Per serving:* Calories: 77; Total fat: 4g; Saturated fat: 0g; Cholesterol: 18mg; Sodium: 186mg; Carbohydrate: 9g; Fiber: 3g; Sugar: 0g; Protein: 7g.

*Tip:* To save time, use store-bought roasted red bell peppers. Roasting peppers and letting them rest in a paper bag allows them to sweat, which makes it easier to remove the charred skin. Roasting give them a smoky, rich, sweet flavor.

*Note:* This salad needs no dressing but you could drizzle one of your favorite oil and vinegar based dressings over top.

*Vary It!* Omit crab red pepper salsa and instead sprinkle romaine with chopped tomatoes and goat cheese. Top with balsamic vinaigrette.

# Marinated Steak Salad

**Prep time:** 10 min plus refrigeration time • **Cook time:** 15 min • **Yield:** 8 servings

| Ingredients | Directions |
|---|---|
| 3 tablespoons gluten-free soy sauce | *1* In a small bowl, whisk together the soy sauce, balsamic vinegar, ginger, water, and oil. |
| 3 tablespoons balsamic vinegar | |
| ¼ teaspoon ginger | *2* Pour half of the mixture into a self-seal plastic bag. Cover the remaining mixture in a bowl and refrigerate it. |
| ¼ cup water | |
| 2 tablespoons olive oil | *3* Place the steak in the self-seal plastic bag with the marinade, turning to coat. Seal the bag and marinate the meat in the refrigerator for 2 hours. |
| 1½ pound well-trimmed beef sirloin steak, 1 inch thick | |
| 6 cups baby spinach leaves | *4* Preheat the broiler. |
| ½ cup thin, diagonally cut carrot slices | *5* Remove the steak from the marinade and place the meat on a broiler pan. Broil the steak for 15 minutes (medium rare) or to desired doneness, turning once. Let the meat stand 5 minutes, and then carve it into thin slices. |
| ½ cup thinly sliced cucumber | |
| ½ cup thinly sliced radishes | |
| 1 cup small broccoli florets | |
| 24 pea pods, blanched | *6* Distribute the spinach leaves evenly onto 8 salad dishes. Top with the carrot, cucumber, and radish slices. Sprinkle the salads with the broccoli and place the pea pods on the salads. |
| 4 teaspoons sesame seeds | |
| | *7* Sprinkle the salads with the reserved dressing. Top with the steak slices and then sprinkle with the sesame seeds. |

*Per serving: Calories: 245; Total fat: 13g; Saturated fat: 5g; Cholesterol: 62mg; Sodium: 468mg; Carbohydrates: 5g; Fiber: 2g; Sugar: 2g; Protein: 27g.*

***Tip:*** To get the most flavor from this salad, marinate the steak early in the morning or overnight so it will absorb all the essence of the seasonings.

***Note:*** Although this recipe is even better when the steak is grilled over an open fire, using the broiler is a good alternative.

# Baked Chicken Salad

**Prep time:** 10 min  •  **Cook time:** 30 min  •  **Yield:** 4 servings

| Ingredients | Directions |
|---|---|
| 2 boneless, skinless chicken breasts, cooked | *1* Preheat the oven to 350 degrees. Grease a 9-inch-square baking dish. |
| 1 cup chopped celery | |
| ¼ cup slivered almonds | *2* Cut the cooked chicken breasts into ½-inch cubes, and place them in a large bowl. |
| 3 tablespoons chopped green pepper | |
| 1 teaspoon dried parsley flakes | *3* Add the celery, almonds, green pepper, parsley, onion, and mayonnaise to the bowl. Using a rubber spatula, mix until the ingredients are well combined. |
| ¼ cup chopped onion | |
| 1¼ cup mayonnaise | *4* Spoon the mixture into the prepared pan. Sprinkle potato chips over the top. |
| 1 cup crushed potato chips | |
| | *5* Bake the chicken salad at 350 degrees for 30 minutes. |

*Per serving:* Calories: 490; Total fat: 33g; Saturated fat: 5g; Cholesterol: 70mg; Sodium: 662mg; Carbohydrates: 26g; Fiber: 2g; Sugar: 6g; Protein: 24g.

*Tip:* You can used boiled, broiled, fried, grilled, or roasted chicken breast in this recipe — whatever you have on hand or leftover from a previous meal.

*Vary It!* You can use buttered gluten-free bread crumbs in place of the potato chips.

# Chapter 20

# Slurpilicious Soups

## In This Chapter

▶ Singing soup's goodness

▶ Getting hearty: Soups that'll stick to your ribs

▶ Trying some lighter, healthier fare

▶ Sipping on stand-alone meals: Chili, chowders, and stews

*W*hoever invented soups was a genius. What other food concoction allows you to dump almost anything into some water, cover it, and let it cook all by itself, and then call it a meal?

Soup is the ideal solution for gardeners. In late summer, when you have more vegetables than you know what to do with, when you can't even *give* away all that stuff hanging off vines and popping up through the ground, consider chopping up that yield and making a huge pot of soup. Soup is a cornucopia of nutrition and tastes.

# No Glutens and Swimming with Flavor

As the old-time theme song from one of the large soup companies used to say about soup, MMMMM . . . MMMMM . . . GOOD! If you steam vegetables to serve as a side dish, the water used to steam them (which is overflowing with nutrients from these veggies) is poured down the drain. With soup, all the nutrients that these natural foods exude during cooking remain in the broth, and you just know that has to be healthy and good for you.

If soups have one drawback, it's that for the broths to be palatable, it seems like you have to dump in half the salt shaker. Still, you have options. The best option is to reduce the amount of salt used and use more herbs and spices for flavoring. Here are some tips for using herbs and spices:

- ✔ Fresh herbs are much more potent and impart more flavor than dried ones, so less is needed. But fresh herbs vary greatly in strength and the amount of flavor they exude.

- ✔ Dominant, strong flavors include cardamom, curry, ginger, hot peppers, black pepper, mustard, rosemary, cloves, and sage.

- ✔ Medium flavors are found in basil, celery seed, cumin, dill, fennel, tarragon, garlic, marjoram, mint, oregano, thyme, and turmeric.

- ✔ Then there are herbs that you can use by the bushelful. They add a very mild flavor, like parsley, chives, and chervil.

- ✔ Usually ¼ teaspoon of dried or powdered herbs equals ¾ to 1 teaspoon of fresh herbs that are cut or crumbled.

The recipes that follow can help you think beyond chicken noodle (albeit gluten-free noodle) soup. We don't mean to demean or berate chicken soup. At the first sign of a sniffle or sneeze, chances are you reach for chicken soup and hot tea. The medicinal effects of this soup are more than just an old wives' tale. Chicken soup has been prescribed for the common cold as far back as the ancient Egyptians.

If your soup is too thin for your liking, stir in a small amount of gluten-free instant potato flakes to thicken it up almost instantly. If it's too greasy, lay a few lettuce leaves on top of the broth to absorb the fat. And if you plan to freeze the soup, hold off adding any pasta to it until you thaw and reheat it, or the gluten-free pasta may get too soft and fall apart.

# Making Broths and Hearty Soups

When you make rice or quinoa, using chicken broth instead of water infuses it with wonderful flavor. Use a small amount of broth instead of butter or oil to sauté vegetables. As for that take-home doggie bag from an Asian restaurant, adding a little broth is perfect for reheating a stir-fry. Instead of adding water to casseroles and roasts, use broth. Use broth as a base for gravies and au jus. Boil your gluten-free pasta in broth instead of water and taste what a difference it makes. Are you boiling chicken? Or boiling potatoes for a potato salad? Boiling them in chicken broth increases their flavor quotient. For added flavor and moisture, replace the water with broth when making your Thanksgiving stuffing (gluten-free, of course). Don't forget to use broth to baste the turkey. And the next time you make muffins, substitute chicken broth for the milk. Don't wrinkle up your face. Just try it!

You also have meal-in-a-bowl soups, the hearty soups that fill your kitchen with cozy and tantalizing aromas as they cook. Nutritionists believe that a hot, hearty soup satisfies hunger because it tends to be eaten slowly.

# Hearty Chicken Broth

**Prep time:** 10 min • **Cook time:** 1½ hr • **Yield:** 6 servings

| *Ingredients* | *Directions* |
|---|---|
| **10 cups water** | *1* Combine all the ingredients in a large stockpot. |
| **1½ pounds chicken wings (about 6 wings)** | *2* Bring the water to a boil, and then reduce the heat and simmer, uncovered, for 1½ hours. (When the water begins to boil, don't skim the surface of the broth.) |
| **4 thin-skinned potatoes, unpeeled, cut in quarters** | |
| **1 medium onion, quartered** | |
| **8 fresh mushrooms** | *3* Strain the soup into a large pot or bowl, removing all the solids. Let the broth cool. |
| **2 leeks, trimmed and cut into 4 sections** | |
| **2 carrots, cut in large chunks** | *4* Keep the broth refrigerated, covered, up to 3 days. Before reheating the broth, skim off and discard any congealed fat that has collected on top of the broth. You can also freeze the broth until you're ready to use it. |
| **2 ribs celery, cut in thirds** | |
| **2 cloves garlic, cut in half** | |
| **3 sprigs fresh parsley** | |
| **½ teaspoon dried dill weed** | |
| **1½ teaspoons salt** | |
| **5 peppercorns** | |
| **1 bay leaf** | |
| **1 clove** | |

*Per serving:* Calories: 238; Total fat: 8g; Saturated fat: 2g; Cholesterol: 38mg; Sodium: 685mg; Carbohydrates: 30g; Fiber: 4g; Sugar: 3g; Protein: 12g.

*Tip:* After you strain the soup, pick out the potatoes, cut them up, and make a potato salad by adding green pepper, onion, salt, pepper, oregano, olive oil, and a dash of cider vinegar. You can also pick out the chicken wings, sprinkle them with salt, pepper, and lemon juice, and enjoy them either warm or cold.

*Note:* Make this broth and then freeze it in ice cube trays or small plastic containers.

# Thai Soup with Shrimp

**Prep time:** 10 min  •  **Cook time:** 10 min  •  **Yield:** 4 servings

| *Ingredients* | *Directions* |
|---|---|
| 1 cup water | *1* Place water in Dutch oven and heat to boiling. Add lemongrass, lime leaves, and ginger root and boil for 4 minutes. Add red pepper flakes, fish sauce, garlic chili paste, and mushrooms, and continue cooking another 1 to 2 minutes. Reduce heat to low, add coconut milk and simmer for another 5 minutes to allow flavors to blend. |
| 2 stalks lemongrass, bruised with meat mallet and cut into 2-inch pieces | |
| 4 fresh kaffir lime leaves, each cut into 3 pieces, or 2 tablespoons lime juice | |
| 2-inch piece of fresh ginger root, cut into thin slices | *2* Turn heat on high to boiling and add shrimp. Boil for 3 minutes until shrimp is opaque in color. Add lime juice. Garnish with Thai basil when ready to serve. |
| ½ to 1 teaspoon red pepper flakes | |
| 3 tablespoons fish sauce | |
| 1 teaspoon garlic chili paste | |
| 4 baby portobello mushrooms, thinly sliced | |
| 1 cup light coconut milk | |
| 1 pound large shrimp, shelled and deveined | |
| 1 tablespoon fresh lime juice | |
| Thai basil, garnish | |

*Per serving: Calories: 172; Total fat: 5g; Saturated fat: 3g; Cholesterol: 168mg; Sodium: 1,265mg; Carbohydrates: 11g; Fiber: 2g; Protein: 22g.*

*Tip:* When purchasing lemongrass, look for firm stalks. You can purchase lemongrass fresh or in frozen packets at local grocery stores or Asian markets. Bruising the lemongrass and tearing the kaffir lime leaves releases the aroma and flavors into the soup. While you're perusing that Asian market, experience the joy of gluten-free goodies galore! Rice and tapioca pastas abound, and they're far less expensive than their domestic counterparts.

*Note:* Lemongrass, fresh ginger root, and lime leaves are a trio of flavors that are very distinctive of Thai cooking. They're typically left in the soup for amazing flavor when served but generally not eaten. Be sure to warn guests.

*Vary It!* Substitute thinly sliced chicken breast in place of the shrimp. Allow more time for cooking when you add the mushrooms and raw chicken.

*Vary It!* This soup can be strained to remove the ginger root, kaffir leaves, and lemongrass before serving.

# Spicy Chicken Soup

**Prep time:** 10 min • **Cook time:** 35 min • **Yield:** 6 servings

| Ingredients | Directions |
|---|---|
| 2 tablespoons olive oil | **1** In a large saucepan over medium-high heat, sauté the onion, garlic, and green pepper in oil until they're soft, stirring frequently. |
| 1 medium onion, chopped | |
| 2 cloves garlic, minced | |
| ¼ cup minced green pepper | **2** Stir in the drained green chilies, tomatoes with their juice, broth, salt, pepper, Worcestershire sauce, chili powder, cumin, and hot pepper sauce. Cover the saucepan and simmer the soup for 20 minutes. |
| 4-ounce can chopped green chilies, drained | |
| 15-ounce can diced tomatoes | |
| Four 10.5-ounce cans chicken broth | **3** Cut the chicken into ½-inch cubes. Stir them into the soup and simmer for 5 minutes. |
| ¼ teaspoon salt | |
| ½ teaspoon pepper | **4** Stir the cheese into the soup, stirring until it's melted. |
| 2 teaspoons Worcestershire sauce | |
| ½ teaspoon chili powder | |
| 1 teaspoon ground cumin | |
| ¼ teaspoon hot pepper sauce | |
| 2 boneless, skinless chicken breasts, boiled until tender | |
| 3 ounces processed cheese | |

*Per serving:* Calories: 252; Total fat: 11g; Saturated fat: 3g; Cholesterol: 76mg; Sodium: 1,994mg; Carbohydrates: 9g; Fiber: 2g; Sugar: 6g; Protein: 28g.

*Tip:* You can adjust how hot this soup is by increasing or decreasing the amount of chili powder and hot pepper sauce you use.

*Vary It!* Just before serving, try stirring in ⅓ cup of gluten-free sour cream for variety; this addition adds even more flavor to the soup.

# Lamb and Rice Soup

**Prep time:** 10 min • **Cook time:** 1¾ hr • **Yield:** 6 servings

| Ingredients | Directions |
|---|---|
| 1 tablespoon olive oil | **1**   In a large saucepan over medium heat, sauté the celery and onion in oil slowly, stirring often, until the vegetables are softened. |
| ¾ cup chopped celery | |
| 1 onion, chopped | |
| 1½ pounds lamb bone-in shoulder steak | **2**   Add the lamb, water, parsley, and bouillon cubes. |
| 8 cups water | **3**   Bring the liquid to a boil, and then lower the heat to medium-low, cover the pan, and simmer for 1½ hours until the lamb is very tender. |
| 2 tablespoons minced fresh parsley | |
| 2 chicken bouillon cubes | **4**   Remove the lamb and cut the meat into tiny pieces. Discard the bones and any fat. Add the lamb to the saucepan. |
| ¾ teaspoon salt | |
| ¼ teaspoon pepper | **5**   Stir in the salt, pepper, and rice. Cover the pan and simmer the soup for 15 minutes until the rice is tender. |
| ⅓ cup uncooked rice | |
| 3 eggs, at room temperature | **6**   In a large mixing bowl, use the electric mixer to whip the eggs for 3 minutes. Add the lemon juice. |
| 3 tablespoons fresh lemon juice | |
| | **7**   Very gradually, drizzle the hot broth from the soup into the eggs, whipping the mixture on high to blend. (The easiest way to add the broth to the eggs is to tip the pan slightly so the broth comes to the top and then dip it out with a soup ladle.) When the bowl feels warm to the touch, lower the mixer speed to medium and continue slowly adding most of the broth from the saucepan. |
| | **8**   Slowly pour the egg mixture back into the saucepan with the lamb, stirring constantly. Simmer the soup on low for 1 minute, stirring constantly. Serve immediately. |

*Per serving:* Calories: 231; Total fat: 12g; Saturated fat: 4g; Cholesterol: 154mg; Sodium: 655mg; Carbohydrates: 11g; Fiber: 1g; Sugar: 2g; Protein: 19g.

*Tip:* Add the hot broth slowly to the eggs to prevent curdling.

# Going Vegetarian: Meatless Marvels

Anyone who's ever been on a diet undoubtedly at some point has eaten cabbage soup. Although cabbage is certainly a healthy vegetable, don't neglect the other great options of vegetable soups available to you. Scientists have provided evidence that consuming a lot of vegetables and beans may reduce stress levels, help fight cancer and heart disease, and fight free radicals. But aside from all this technical stuff, vegetable soups taste great!

# Cream of Mushroom Soup

**Prep time:** 20 min • **Cook time:** 10 min • **Yield:** 4 servings

| Ingredients | Directions |
|---|---|
| **2 tablespoons butter** | **1** In a medium skillet, sauté the onion, garlic, celery, and mushrooms in the butter over medium heat until the onions are translucent and soft (about 6 minutes), stirring frequently. |
| **1 small onion, chopped** | |
| **1 clove garlic, chopped** | |
| **1 celery stalk, sliced thin** | |
| **8-ounce can mushroom stems and pieces (reserve liquid)** | **2** Add 1½ cups of the broth and simmer until the vegetables are very soft (about 10 minutes). |
| **Two 14.5-ounce cans vegetable broth** | **3** In a medium bowl, stir the cornstarch into the remaining broth until smooth. |
| **1½ tablespoons cornstarch** | |
| **2 tablespoons grated Parmesan cheese** | **4** Put the vegetable mixture, the remainder of the broth, the cheese, salt, and pepper into a blender. Cover and puree. (Alternative method: You can blend the mixture with a wand blender until it's smooth.) Spoon the mixture into a medium saucepan. |
| **1 teaspoon salt** | |
| **½ teaspoon pepper** | |
| **1¼ cups half-and-half** | **5** Add the reserved mushroom liquid. |
| **2 tablespoons sherry** | **6** Heat the soup over medium heat, stirring constantly, until the mixture thickens. |
| | **7** Stir in the half-and-half and simmer until the soup is warmed. Don't allow the mixture to boil. |
| | **8** Remove the soup from the heat and stir in the sherry. |

*Per serving:* Calories: 234; Total fat: 15g; Saturated fat: 10g; Cholesterol: 45mg; Sodium: 1,157mg; Carbohydrates: 17g; Fiber: 2g; Sugar: 4g; Protein: 5g.

*Tip:* Everyone on a gluten-free diet seems to be in search of a suitable substitute for condensed cream of mushroom soup to use in casseroles. To convert this recipe to a condensed version, add an additional ½ teaspoon cornstarch and use only 1 can of vegetable broth.

# Three Bean Soup

**Prep time:** 10 min • **Cook time:** 1 hr • **Yield:** 6 servings

| *Ingredients* | *Directions* |
|---|---|
| 3 tablespoons olive oil<br><br>1 cup chopped onion<br><br>1 clove garlic, minced<br><br>1 cup chopped celery<br><br>1 cup chopped carrot<br><br>½ cup chopped green pepper<br><br>¼ cup fresh chopped parsley | *1* In a large saucepan, sauté the onion, garlic, celery, carrots, green pepper, and parsley in the oil over medium heat, stirring often, until the vegetables are soft. |
| 15.5-ounce can navy beans, rinsed and drained | *2* Place ⅓ of the navy beans in a small bowl and mash them with the back of a fork. |
| 15.5-ounce can black beans, rinsed and drained<br><br>15.5-ounce can light kidney beans, rinsed and drained<br><br>1 bay leaf<br><br>1¼ teaspoon salt<br><br>¼ teaspoon pepper<br><br>8-ounce can tomato sauce<br><br>6 cups water | *3* Stir the mashed beans plus the remaining navy beans, black beans, kidney beans, bay leaf, salt, pepper, tomato sauce, and water into the saucepan. Stir to blend. Bring the ingredients to a boil, and then lower the heat and simmer, covered, for one hour. Remove the bay leaf before serving. |

*Per serving:* Calories: 277; Total fat: 8g; Saturated fat: 1g; Cholesterol: 0mg; Sodium: 1,452mg; Carbohydrates: 41g; Fiber: 14g; Sugar: 6g; Protein: 13g.

*Tip:* Using canned beans in this recipe cuts down on the prep time of this soup without cutting down on taste. By mashing a few of the beans, the soup becomes thicker.

# Spinach Lentil Soup

**Prep time:** 20 min • **Cook time:** 50 min • **Yield:** 6 servings

| Ingredients | Directions |
|---|---|
| **1 pound brown lentils** | *1* Place the lentils in a large saucepan and cover them with water. Cook the lentils on high until the water comes to a boil. Remove the pan from the heat and drain the lentils in a colander. Rinse them well under cold running water and drain again. |
| **8 cups water** | |
| **2 tablespoons olive oil** | |
| **½ cup chopped celery** | |
| **⅓ cup chopped carrots** | *2* In the same saucepan, over medium heat, sauté the celery, carrots, onion, and garlic in the oil. Stir the mixture frequently until the vegetables are tender but not browned. |
| **1 large onion, chopped** | |
| **1 clove garlic, minced** | |
| **3 sprigs fresh parsley, chopped** | *3* Add the lentils, parsley, bay leaves, spinach, and 8 cups of water. Bring the contents to a boil, skimming off any foam as needed. |
| **2 bay leaves** | |
| **10-ounce box chopped spinach, thawed** | *4* Lower the heat, cover the pan, and simmer for 40 minutes, or until the lentils are very soft, adding more water if needed. |
| **8 cups water** | |
| **8-ounce can tomato sauce** | |
| **1¼ teaspoon salt** | *5* Stir in the tomato sauce, salt, pepper, and vinegar. Continue to simmer the soup for 10 minutes. Discard the bay leaves before serving. |
| **¼ teaspoon pepper** | |
| **2 teaspoons cider vinegar** | |

*Per serving: Calories: 155; Total fat: 5g; Saturated fat: 1g; Cholesterol: 0mg; Sodium: 698mg; Carbohydrates: 22g; Fiber: 8g; Sugar: 5g; Protein: 8g.*

*Tip:* Adding a teeny amount of cider vinegar makes all the difference in the world in the taste of this creation. If the tomato sauce and salt are added too early, the lentils may not cook thoroughly.

# Waist-Slimming Cabbage Soup

**Prep time:** 15 min • **Cook time:** 1 hr • **Yield:** 12 servings

| *Ingredients* | *Directions* |
|---|---|
| 6 medium onions, chopped | *1* Place all the ingredients in a large saucepan. |
| 2 cloves garlic, minced | |
| 1 large green pepper, seeded and chopped | *2* Bring the ingredients to a rapid boil, and then reduce the heat, cover the pan, and let the soup simmer for 1 hour. |
| 14.5-ounce can diced tomatoes with juice | |
| 1 medium head of cabbage, cored and chopped | *3* Discard the bay leaves before serving. |
| ½ bunch parsley, chopped | |
| 3 large carrots, sliced thin | |
| 8 stalks celery, sliced thin | |
| 1 package onion soup dry mix | |
| ½ teaspoon salt | |
| ¼ teaspoon pepper | |
| 4 cups chicken bouillon | |
| 1 cup water | |
| 2 bay leaves | |

*Per serving:* Calories: 78; Total fat: 2g; Saturated fat: 0g; Cholesterol: 0mg; Sodium: 540mg; Carbohydrates: 16g; Fiber: 5g; Sugar: 7g; Protein: 3g.

# Chili, Chowders, and Stews: A More Filling Chow

Did you know (or even care) that the name *chowder* is French for "cauldron"? Chowders are soups that are thickened with milk. Although milk is good, using half-and-half is even better — it makes thicker and richer soups.

As for chili, each part of the country claims to have the best chili — whether it's Real Texas Chili, Authentic Cincinnati Chili, West Virginia's Real McCoy Chili, or California Turkey Chili (how can Turkey Chili be *real* chili?). Despite all these claims, the very best chili recipe doesn't come from any of these states or locales. The very best chili is the recipe for Unrivaled Chili in this section!

If you're confused about the difference between a stew and a soup, you're not alone. Most people think the only difference is that a stew is a little thicker, if you will, but there are a few other differences, too. Soups can be served warm or cold, while stews are nearly always served warm. Stews are usually slow-cooked, while soups can be made quickly. It really doesn't matter what it's called — if you're looking for great gluten-free recipes that come in a bowl and get eaten with a spoon, this section is for you.

# Unrivaled Chili

**Prep time:** 10 min • **Cook time:** 20 min • **Yield:** 6 servings

| Ingredients | Directions |
|---|---|
| 1 tablespoon olive oil | *1* In a large saucepan over medium-high heat, sauté the ground beef, green pepper, onion, celery, and garlic in the oil, breaking the meat up with a fork as it cooks. |
| 1 pound 90 percent lean ground beef | |
| ½ medium green pepper, chopped | |
| 1 medium onion, chopped | *2* Stir in the remaining ingredients except the cheese. Bring the ingredients to a boil, and then reduce the heat. Cover the pan and simmer, stirring occasionally, for 15 to 20 minutes, until the broth thickens. |
| 1 rib celery, chopped | |
| 2 cloves garlic, minced | |
| 8-ounce can tomato sauce | |
| 15-ounce can diced tomatoes | *3* Stir in the cheese until it's melted. |
| 1½ cups water | |
| 15-ounce can kidney beans with liquid | |
| 15-ounce can black beans, rinsed and drained | |
| 1½ teaspoons chili powder | |
| 1 teaspoon cumin | |
| ¼ teaspoon cayenne pepper | |
| ½ teaspoon salt | |
| ¼ teaspoon pepper | |
| ¼ cup grated Parmesan cheese | |

*Per serving:* Calories: 329; Total fat: 10g; Saturated fat: 4g; Cholesterol: 49mg; Sodium: 1,039mg; Carbohydrates: 34g; Fiber: 10g; Sugar: 7g; Protein: 26g.

*Tip:* This chili is beyond mouth warming and tongue tingling. After an initial tasting, you can add more chili powder or a few drops of gluten-free hot pepper sauce if you like your tongue to blister and swell and your throat to be on fire.

*Note:* You can adorn your bowl with a dollop of sour cream, chopped green onions, cheddar cheese, or whatever you like.

# Cheesy Corn Chowder

**Prep time:** 10 min • **Cook time:** 20 min • **Yield:** 4 servings

| Ingredients | Directions |
|---|---|
| 4 strips bacon | *1* In a large saucepan, fry the bacon until it's crisp. Drain the bacon on paper toweling. |
| 1 tablespoon olive oil | |
| ½ cup minced onions | *2* Add the oil, onion, green pepper, and garlic to the bacon drippings in the pan. Sauté the vegetables slowly for 5 minutes, until they're soft but not browned. |
| ¼ cup green pepper, minced | |
| 1 clove garlic, minced | |
| 10-ounce box frozen corn, thawed | *3* Add the corn, broth, salt, pepper, oregano, and thyme. Bring the mixture to a boil, and then reduce the heat. Cover and simmer for 2 minutes. |
| 2½ cups chicken broth | |
| 1 teaspoon salt | *4* In a medium bowl, whisk together the half-and-half and cornstarch. Stir it into the corn mixture. Cook the soup over low heat, stirring constantly, until the mixture thickens slightly (about 6 minutes). Don't allow the mixture to boil. Crumble the bacon, and then stir in the bacon pieces and cheese until the cheese is completely melted. |
| ⅛ teaspoon pepper | |
| ¼ teaspoon dried oregano | |
| ¼ teaspoon dried thyme | |
| 1½ cups half-and-half | |
| 1 tablespoon cornstarch | |
| ¼ cup shredded sharp cheddar cheese | |

*Per serving:* Calories: 305; Total fat: 20g; Saturated fat: 10g; Cholesterol: 50mg; Sodium: 1,211mg; Carbohydrates: 24g; Fiber: 2g; Sugar: 1g; Protein: 11g.

*Vary It!* Some like it hot, and some don't. If you like spicy foods, add ⅛ teaspoon cayenne pepper to this chowder for extra pizzazz.

# Seafood Chowder

**Prep time:** 35 min plus resting time • **Cook time:** 35 min • **Yield:** 6 servings

| *Ingredients* | *Directions* |
|---|---|
| ½ teaspoon butter | *1* In a large saucepan, melt the butter, and then sauté the bacon bits over medium-high heat. When the bacon is crisp, add the onion and celery and cook, stirring frequently, until the vegetables are tender (about 5 minutes). |
| 2 slices bacon, minced | |
| 1 cup onion, minced | |
| 1 cup celery, chopped | |
| Two 14.5-ounce cans chicken broth | *2* Add the broth; bring it to a boil. |
| ½ teaspoon dried thyme | *3* Add the thyme, salt, pepper, parsley flakes, garlic powder, and potatoes. Stir in the broccoli and simmer until the broccoli is tender. |
| ¼ teaspoon salt | |
| ¼ teaspoon pepper | |
| 1 teaspoon dried parsley flakes | |
| ¼ teaspoon garlic powder | *4* Drain the clams and set them aside, reserving the juice. |
| 2 medium potatoes, boiled, peeled, and diced | |
| 2 cups broccoli florets, cut into small pieces | *5* In a medium bowl, whisk the cornstarch into the reserved clam juice. Add the bottled clam juice. Stir the cornstarch mixture into the vegetable mixture and bring it to a boil. Reduce the heat. Stir in the half-and-half and simmer for 20 minutes. |
| 6.5-ounce can clams, liquid reserved | |
| 1½ tablespoons cornstarch | |
| 8-ounce bottle clam juice | |
| 1½ cups half-and-half | *6* Stir in the clams, shrimp, crabmeat, sherry, and cheese. Cook the chowder over low heat until the cheese is melted. |
| 4.25-ounce can crabmeat | |
| ¼ pound fresh, shelled, cooked baby shrimp | *7* Set the chowder aside for 1 hour, covered, to allow the flavors to blend. Place the pan over low heat to slowly reheat. Don't allow the chowder to boil. |
| ½ cup sherry | |
| ½ cup grated Romano cheese | |

*Per serving:* Calories: 321; Total fat: 17g; Saturated fat: 9g; Cholesterol: 180mg; Sodium: 1,078mg; Carbohydrates: 25g; Fiber: 3g; Sugar: 4g; Protein: 18g.

*Vary It!* Although this chowder calls for clams and crabmeat, no one will be the wiser if you use scallops and shrimp or any combination of seafood you like.

*Vary It!* Avoid imitation crabmeat because it nearly always contains wheat.

# Hobo Stew

**Prep time:** 10 min • **Cook time:** 7hr • **Yield:** 6 servings

| *Ingredients* | *Directions* |
|---|---|
| 1 to 1½ pounds stew meat | *1* Preheat oven to 250 degrees. |
| 1 large russet potato, peeled and cut into large cubes | |
| 1 large sweet potato, peeled and cut into large cubes | *2* Combine all ingredients in a 3-quart Dutch oven and place in oven for 6 to 7 hours. Don't lift lid until baking is complete. |
| 1 small package baby carrots | |
| 1 large onion, sliced | |
| 2½ pound can diced tomatoes | |
| 1 cup tomato juice | |
| 2 slices gluten-free bread | |
| Dash salt | |
| ¾ tablespoon sugar | |
| 1 tablespoon arrowroot flour or other thickening agent, such as cornstarch | |

**Per serving:** *Calories: 308; Total fat: 8g; Saturated fat: 2g; Cholesterol: 47mg; Sodium: 543mg; Carbohydrates: 42g; Fiber: 6g; Sugar: 0g; Protein: 19g.*

**Tip:** Stew can also be made in a slow cooker and cooked on the low temperature setting for 7 to 8 hours or on the high setting for 3 to 4 hours.

**Note:** Sweet potatoes are a wonderful addition to a more traditional stew. They're nutritious, they contain a large amount of beta carotene, and they have a low glycemic index — plus, they're easy on the budget.

# Chapter 21

# Stupendous Snacks

As "into" nutrition as I am, I'm still a snacker. Pretty much all day long, I'm eating, so it's important to have handy, quick snacks, sans gluten, of course. Because we live in a society where snacks usually consist of crackers, cookies, or pretzels, it may seem at first as though gluten-free snacks would be hard to come by. But there's so much good news to convey about gluten-free snacking that the only problem is where to begin.

People today lead busy lifestyles, so we're usually grabbing snack foods to save time — so snacks-on-the-run are key. But snacking is more than just a time-saver. And while it sometimes has a bad rap, it turns out snacking may actually be *good* for you.

A study done throughout 12 European countries showed that people who eat more frequently, but don't consume more overall calories, are actually healthier than those who eat three square meals a day. (Hooray for snacking!) Some elderly people have poor appetites, so snacking more frequently enables them to get the nutrition they need. Snackers also tend to eat throughout the day (as opposed to throughout the evening), so their bodies have time to burn off the calories before bedtime.

And finally, the more you snack, the more your body has to work to digest all that food — and that uses up more energy. Aren't all the health experts telling us we should expend more energy? So eating must be good for us, and eating often must be better. Nibbling between meals lessens the hunger pangs, preventing gorging at mealtime. (Okay, okay, I know that *what* you're snacking on is an important consideration, but this is the *snack* chapter, not the weight-loss chapter, so read on for some delicious gluten-free snack recipes.)

# Snackin' Healthy

No matter what your age, you should be aware of a couple of rules when it comes to snacking. Know the ingredients in snacks you buy off the grocery shelf. For a general healthy rule, try to stay away from Olestra, artificial sweeteners, and anything hydrogenated (trans fats) or with MSG (those things don't have gluten in them; they're just bad for you).

When you read the list of ingredients, if a word has more than three syllables and is hard to pronounce, it's probably not good for you. Most likely it's a chemical additive and not something you should eat. You're better off sticking with natural ingredients.

If you're watching your weight, beware of bowls and bags. Mindlessly reaching into a large bag of chips or large bowl of popcorn usually ends up in overindulgence and tight jeans. On the other hand, if you have these snacks pre-portioned into snack-size self-seal bags or small serving plates, the degree of debauchery is limited to the amount of goodies you can squeeze into one little bag or onto one little plate.

One idea for snacking is to make your own gluten-free granola and trail mix. Have bags of cherries or grapes handy. Gluten-free crackers with cheese are always good. Keep a supply of gluten-free pretzels for the snack drawer. A single-serving container of gluten-free yogurt with fruit is a healthy alternative. You can find several brands of gluten-free tortilla chips in the grocery stores — add some salsa and you have a terrific snack. And it's always fun to munch on popcorn.

# Cool Snacks for Chillin' Out

Everybody loves to snack, whether it's to curb the midafternoon grumbellies, to eat something small to get you through the evening after an early dinner, or to make car trips or airline flights more pleasant. Snacking for people on a gluten-free diet, though, requires a bit more planning than for most people.

Some snacks require advance preparation because they need to be refrigerated or frozen. This section digs into some of the options.

# Pudding Pops

**Prep time:** 10 min • **Cook time:** 8 min plus cooling and freezing time • **Yield:** 12 servings

| *Ingredients* | *Directions* |
|---|---|
| 2½ **cups 2 percent milk** | **1** Pour the milk into a medium saucepan. |
| **3.4-ounce package cook-and-serve chocolate pudding mix** | **2** Stir in the pudding mix and sugar, and heat the ingredients, stirring constantly, until the mixture comes to a boil. |
| ¼ **cup sugar** | |
| ¾ **cup nondairy whipped topping, thawed** | **3** Lower the heat to medium and cook, stirring constantly, for 2 minutes. |
| **12 wooden sticks or plastic spoons** | **4** Remove the pan from the heat and allow the pudding mixture to cool for 30 minutes, stirring several times. |
| | **5** Fold in the whipped topping. |
| | **6** Spoon the mixture into 12 molds, cupcake tins, or paper cups; insert the wooden sticks or plastic spoons into the center of the pops. Freeze until firm. |

*Per serving: Calories: 87; Total fat: 2g; Saturated fat: 2g; Cholesterol: 4mg; Sodium: 67mg; Carbohydrates: 15g; Fiber: 0g; Sugar: 12g; Protein: 2g.*

# Almond Hummus

**Prep time:** 10 min plus refrigeration time • **Cook time:** None • **Yield:** 1½ cups

| Ingredients | Directions |
|---|---|
| Nonstick cooking spray | *1* Over medium heat, sauté the almonds in a small skillet that has been sprayed with cooking spray. Stir frequently until the almonds are browned. |
| ¼ cup blanched slivered almonds | |
| 15-ounce can garbanzo beans, rinsed and drained | *2* Place the almonds into a blender and puree until smooth. Then add the remaining ingredients, pureeing until smooth. You may need to scrape down the sides of the blender during this process. Depending on your personal taste, you may want to add more lemon juice. |
| 2 tablespoons olive oil | |
| ½ teaspoon dried dill | |
| 1 teaspoon cumin | |
| 2 tablespoons fresh chopped parsley | *3* Spoon the mixture into a serving bowl. Cover and refrigerate the hummus for several hours to allow the flavors to blend. |
| ¼ teaspoon salt | |
| ¼ teaspoon pepper | |
| 3 tablespoons fresh lemon juice | |
| ¼ teaspoon chicken bouillon granules | |
| ¼ cup water | |

*Per serving:* Calories: 149; Total fat: 9g; Saturated fat: 1g; Cholesterol: 0mg; Sodium: 186mg; Carbohydrates: 14g; Fiber: 3g; Sugar: 3g; Protein: 6g.

*Note:* Spread this hummus on gluten-free crackers, on flatbread, or even on a sandwich topped with roasted red peppers, chopped kalamata olives, and crumbled feta cheese.

# Fixing Salts and Sweets to Satisfy Your Munchies

Two hours after dinner, are you or a member of your family standing in front of the refrigerator, with the door wide open, trying to figure out what to eat next? Do you find yourself staring at the fridge for several minutes at a time? Don't get depressed; get determined. When you feel a snack attack coming on, you still have time to prepare a hot snack. Snacking definitely need not be dreary. You can make some of the selections in this section at the last minute, when the impulse hits. You can make others ahead and store them so your cache is always full.

## My snack nightmare doesn't have to be yours

My first gluten-free shopping experience was harrowing. It was the summer of 1991, and my then-toddler son Tyler had just been diagnosed with celiac disease. The hospital dietitian was no help at all, sending me home with a tattered list of 7,498 things that Tyler would never again be able to eat, and three things he could: rice, corn, and potatoes. Great. Toddlers love rice, corn, and potatoes.

Keep in mind this was ages ago — there was no Internet; there were no books on the subject, and there weren't any support groups. I was on my own to figure out the intricacies of the gluten-free diet — toddler-style.

Mustering all the strength a good mommy feels she needs to have, I faked a smile and asked Tyler, "What sounds good for a snack?" "Kwackers," he said. I didn't remember crackers being on the "forbidden" side of the tattered sheet, so off to our local grocery store we went. That's where the strong-mommy act ended and reality set in.

The cracker aisle isn't the best place to start if you're gluten-free because it's an exercise in futility. Row after row of varieties I had never noticed before seemed to be screaming a sing-songy taunt, "You can't eat us, ha ha ha ha ha ha." "But you're whole grain! Aren't you nutritious?!?" I wondered. The crackers didn't answer. They just continued to mock.

Three hours, five rows, and gallons of tears later, I ended up in the chips aisle. As I continued to read labels and compare ingredient after ingredient to the 7,498 things Tyler couldn't eat, I stumbled onto a bag of Fritos. You know — normal-every-day-food-that-comes-in-a-normal-looking-package Fritos. Normal-looking packages are important to kids. I couldn't believe my eyes — I reread the label 14 times, before crying with joy, "You can *eat* these, Baby, you can *eat* them!" People in the store stared. I hugged passersby and didn't care. There was something he could eat.

# Better Than S'mores!

**Prep time:** 5 min • **Cook time:** 4 min • **Yield:** 8 servings

| Ingredients | Directions |
|---|---|
| **Four 8-inch gluten-free tortillas** | *1* Spread 2 tortillas with the peanut butter. |
| **¼ cup crunchy peanut butter** | *2* Spread the marshmallow cream on top of the peanut butter, dividing evenly between the two tortillas. |
| **¼ cup marshmallow cream** | |
| **1 banana** | *3* Slice the banana fairly thin and place the slices on top of the marshmallow cream, dividing evenly between the two tortillas. |
| **½ cup semisweet chocolate pieces** | |
| **Nonstick cooking spray** | *4* Sprinkle the bananas with the chocolate pieces. |
| | *5* Place the remaining two tortillas on top of each of the "sandwiches" and then cut each into 4 wedges. |
| | *6* Spray a nonstick skillet with cooking spray. Heat the pan for 45 seconds on high heat. |
| | *7* Place each tortilla "sandwich" in the pan and cook on high for 1 to 2 minutes until the bottom is lightly browned. |
| | *8* Spray the top of each "sandwich" with the cooking spray, and then turn them over and cook the second side until it's lightly browned. Serve warm. |

*Per serving:* Calories: 191; Total fat: 9g; Saturated fat: 3g; Cholesterol: 0mg; Sodium: 141mg; Carbohydrates: 26g; Fiber: 2g; Sugar: 19g; Protein: 4g.

*Tip:* Be sure to eat this snack as soon as it comes out of the pan (actually, let it cool just a tad so you don't burn your tongue). If you reheat this, the tortillas will become like leather.

# Trail Mix Bars

**Prep time:** 10 min • **Cook time:** 10 min • **Yield:** 24 servings

| Ingredients | Directions |
|---|---|

*Ingredients*

½ **cup sesame seeds**

½ **cup sunflower seeds**

½ **cup coconut**

½ **cup slivered almonds**

½ **cup raisins**

½ **teaspoon cinnamon**

2½ **tablespoons butter**

2 **tablespoons honey**

2 **tablespoons brown sugar**

**Nonstick cooking spray**

*Directions*

*1* In a small, dry skillet, heat the sesame seeds over medium heat, stirring often, until they're lightly browned. Place the browned seeds in a medium bowl. Repeat with the sunflower seeds, then the coconut, and then the almonds.

*2* Stir the raisins and cinnamon into the seed mixture.

*3* In a small saucepan, warm the butter, honey, and brown sugar over medium heat to soft-ball stage, or 238 degrees on a candy thermometer. At this temperature, a small amount of this syrup dropped into cold water will form a soft, flexible ball. If you remove the ball from the water, it will flatten like a pancake after a few moments in your hand.

*4* Pour the syrup over the seed mixture. Using a rubber spatula, blend the ingredients well to coat evenly.

*5* Press the mix into a 9-inch-square pan that has been sprayed with cooking spray and let it cool slightly.

*6* Cut the trail mixture into 24 pieces before the bars have completely cooled. Store the bars in an airtight container.

*Per serving:* Calories: 91; Total fat: 6g; Saturated fat: 2g; Cholesterol: 3mg; Sodium: 16mg; Carbohydrates: 8g; Fiber: 1g; Sugar: 6g; Protein: 2g.

*Vary It!* In place of the raisins (or in addition to the raisins), you can use dried cranberries, cut-up dates, or dried apricots.

# Honey Cinnamon Grahams

**Prep time:** 10 min • **Cook time:** 9–11 min • **Yield:** 24 crackers

| *Ingredients* | *Directions* |
|---|---|
| ¾ **cup gluten-free flour mixture** | *1* Preheat the oven to 325 degrees. |
| ¼ **cup coconut flour** | *2* In a medium bowl, whisk together the flour mixture, coconut flour, salt, cinnamon, and baking powder. |
| ½ **teaspoon salt** | |
| ½ **teaspoon cinnamon** | |
| **1 teaspoon baking powder** | *3* In a large mixing bowl, use the mixer to whip together the butter, honey, sugar, vanilla, and milk. |
| ¼ **cup butter, softened** | *4* Slowly add the dry ingredients to the butter mixture. Mix on medium speed until blended. (You may have to add a few more drops of milk if the dough won't hold together. The dough should be pliable.) |
| **2 tablespoons honey** | |
| ⅓ **cup brown sugar** | |
| **1 teaspoon vanilla** | |
| **1 tablespoon milk** | *5* Lightly spray 2 baking sheets with the cooking spray. |
| **Nonstick cooking spray** | *6* On a sheet of plastic wrap, roll out the dough with a rolling pin to ¼-inch thick. Cut the dough into 2-inch squares and place the crackers on the prepared baking sheets. |
| **1 teaspoon cinnamon sugar** | |
| | *7* Prick the top of each cracker several times with the tines of a fork. |
| | *8* Sprinkle the tops with cinnamon sugar. |
| | *9* Bake the crackers at 325 degrees for 9 to 11 minutes until the edges are barely beginning to brown. Remove the crackers to a wire rack to cool. Store in an airtight container. |

*Per serving:* Calories: 69; Total fat: 2g; Saturated fat: 1g; Cholesterol: 5mg; Sodium: 85mg; Carbohydrates: 14g; Fiber: 1g; Sugar: 8g; Protein: 0g.

*Tip:* Watch the crackers closely in the oven. You want to bake them until the edges are just beginning to show signs of browning. Overbaking causes these crackers to get too hard.

*Note:* If you keep your coconut flour in the freezer, it may pack together. Take it out of the freezer the night before you plan to use it.

# Perky Popcorn

**Prep time:** 20 min  •  **Cook time:** 35 min  •  **Yield:** 10 cups

| Ingredients | Directions |
|---|---|
| 2½ quarts (10 cups) popped popcorn | *1* Preheat the oven to 250 degrees. |
| ¾ cup pecan pieces | *2* Combine the popcorn and pecans in a large roasting pan that has been sprayed with cooking spray. |
| Nonstick cooking spray | |
| 1 cup brown sugar | *3* In a medium saucepan, stir together the brown sugar, water, butter, salt, and corn syrup. |
| ½ cup water | |
| ¼ cup butter | *4* Cook the syrup over medium heat, stirring occasionally with a wooden spoon, until the mixture comes to a full boil. |
| ¼ teaspoon salt | |
| ¼ cup light corn syrup | *5* Insert a candy thermometer into the pan, making sure the bulb at the bottom doesn't touch the bottom of the saucepan. |
| ¼ teaspoon baking soda | |
| | *6* Continue cooking the syrup until it reaches 238 degrees, soft-ball stage. (This will take 3 to 5 minutes.) |
| | *7* Remove the pan from the heat. Stir in the baking soda. The mixture will thicken immediately. |
| | *8* Pour the mixture over the popcorn and pecans, stirring until all the popcorn is coated. |
| | *9* Bake the popcorn at 250 degrees for 35 minutes, stirring every 10 minutes. |
| | *10* Remove the popcorn from the roasting pan and spread it out on wax paper to cool completely. |
| | *11* When the popcorn is cool, break it into pieces and store it in a tightly covered container. |

*Per serving:* Calories: 235; Total fat: 11g; Saturated fat: 4g; Cholesterol: 12mg; Sodium: 137mg; Carbohydrates: 35g; Fiber: 2g; Sugar: 24g; Protein: 2g.

# Spicy Almonds

**Prep time:** 15 min • **Cook time:** 15 min • **Yield:** 3 cups

| Ingredients | Directions |
|---|---|
| ¼ cup butter | **1** Preheat the oven to 350 degrees. |
| 2 tablespoons Worcestershire sauce | **2** Melt the butter in a medium saucepan. |
| 2 tablespoons soy sauce | **3** Remove the pan from the heat and stir in the Worcestershire sauce, soy sauce, cumin, salt, garlic powder, pepper, and sugar. |
| 1 teaspoon cumin | |
| 1 teaspoon coarse salt | |
| 1 teaspoon garlic powder | **4** Add the almonds and stir until they are evenly coated. |
| ½ teaspoon cayenne pepper | **5** Transfer the mixture to a shallow baking sheet. |
| ½ teaspoon sugar | |
| 3 cups whole almonds | **6** Bake the almonds at 350 degrees for 15 minutes, stirring once halfway through baking. |
| | **7** Let the almonds cool thoroughly before storing in an airtight container. |

*Per serving: Calories: 247; Total fat: 22g; Saturated fat: 4g; Cholesterol: 10mg; Sodium: 417mg; Carbohydrates: 8g; Fiber: 4g; Sugar: 2g; Protein: 8g.*

**Tip:** For added decadence, sprinkle the hot almonds with ½ teaspoon of coarse salt as soon as they come out of the oven. They should keep for up to 3 weeks in an airtight container.

# Cheesy Crisps

**Prep time:** 7 min • **Cook time:** 30 min • **Yield:** 36 crackers

| *Ingredients* | *Directions* |
|---|---|
| Nonstick cooking spray<br><br>1½ cups spiced flax crackers<br><br>1½ cups shredded sharp cheddar cheese<br><br>¼ cup water | *1* Preheat the oven to 325 degrees. Spray a baking sheet with cooking spray. |
| | *2* Place the crackers in a food processor and grind them to a fine meal. |
| | *3* Add the cheese and water. Continue to process until the ingredients are well blended and a dough is formed. |
| | *4* Remove the dough and form it into a ball. |
| | *5* Place the dough between two sheets of plastic wrap and roll it out to ¼-inch thickness. |
| | *6* Transfer the dough to the prepared baking sheet. |
| | *7* Using a knife or pastry wheel, cut the dough into small squares or diamonds; don't separate or spread the pieces apart. |
| | *8* Bake the dough at 325 degrees for 30 minutes, or until the crackers are crisp and the edges are just beginning to brown. |
| | *9* Remove the crackers from the oven and let them set for 3 minutes. Then break or cut the crackers along the lines and remove them to a cooling rack. |

**Per cracker:** *Calories: 24; Total fat: 2g; Saturated fat: 1g; Cholesterol: 5mg; Sodium: 37mg; Carbohydrates: 0g; Fiber: 0g; Sugar: 0g; Protein: 1g.*

**Tip:** To measure the 1½ cups of crackers, break the whole crackers into bits and squish them into a measuring cup.

**Note:** The crackers used in this recipe were Foods Alive Mexican Harvest Flax Crackers.

# Chapter 22

# Decadent Desserts

*Y*ou've probably heard the saying "Life is short. Eat dessert first." Let's get real here and acknowledge that the most important food group is really dessert. Sure it's feasible to serve cheese and grapes for dessert, but that doesn't contain nearly the amount of sugar needed to satisfy a genuinely refined sweet tooth. Nor does it contain nearly enough calories to qualify as decadent. Dessert really should be an indulgence, something to anticipate, and something that you certainly don't have to be hungry to consume and thoroughly enjoy.

Desserts are a reflection of our society (this is the philosophical part of the book). Years ago, lime gelatin infused with crushed pineapple and miniature marshmallows constituted dessert. Today our tastes have become refined as we enjoy tiramisu, caramel turtle pecan cheesecake, and baklava sundaes (yeah, even if you're gluten-free!), just to name a few.

Why is dessert so important? Because dessert makes us happy. That's the good news. The bad news is that an odd phenomenon occurs when we consume too many desserts — our jeans shrink.

Contemplate this conundrum and look at the true problems. No one has totally ruined her health by consuming a bite of a luscious dessert. The real health culprits are the continual diet of high-fat foods, lack of exercise, and skipping meals, and then gorging.

Many desserts are made with fats (butters, shortening, oil). Using margarine as a butter substitute isn't the solution because margarine contains fat, too. If you're health conscious, when baking cakes, you often can replace half of the fat in a recipe with applesauce or use ¾ cup vegetable or olive oil for each cup of butter. Olive oil and vegetable oil are fats, but they are a healthier choice compared to butter, shortening, or margarine.

Some decadent-tasting desserts are actually quite low in calories and fat. The Liqueur Cups in this chapter have only 166 calories per serving with just 5 grams of fat. The Chocolate Cranberry Cookies have 56 calories with 2 grams of fat. And all desserts have fewer calories when you only eat half a piece!

# Pies and Cobblers You Can't Resist

Gluten-free pie crusts have been a challenge to many newly diagnosed celiacs. They needn't be. They can be easy to make, no matter how flaky you are. First, you don't even need a dough pie crust for many recipes. Crushed gluten-free cookies or nut crusts often work as a viable substitute.

For double-crust fruit pies, you can follow a few tricks for a successful gluten-free crust:

- ✔ Use ice-cold ingredients (butter or shortening, water or milk).

- ✔ Roll out the pastry between two sheets of plastic wrap (instead of wax paper), and sprinkle the plastic wrap with confectioners' sugar (instead of gluten-free flour mixture or cornstarch). Roll the dough thin. If the pie crust is too thick, it may not bake completely on the bottom.

- ✔ Moisten the edge of the bottom crust with water before placing the second crust on top. The moistened edge helps create a good seal after the two crusts are crimped together.

If you have any dough scraps left over, make a snack out of them — cut the dough into squares (or any shape you like), lightly butter them, sprinkle them with cinnamon sugar, and bake until they're golden.

The whole is worth more than the sum of its parts. If you look up the definition of *cobbler*, you'll find it described as "A deep-dish fruit pie with a top crust." That's it? This definition is missing the description of the aroma of the cobbler as it bakes and the scent drifts through the house. Nowhere in the definition does it describe how your heart begins to palpitate stronger as your fork cuts through the crisp crust, anticipating that first bite. Nor does it take into account the gratification and fulfillment you feel when that first bite of cobbler tantalizes your taste buds. The definition definitely does not do justice to the ever-popular cobbler.

# Coconut Lemon Chiffon Pie

**Prep time:** 5 min • **Refrigeration time:** 2 hr • **Yield:** 12 servings

| *Ingredients* | *Directions* |
|---|---|
| 1½ cups shredded coconut | *1* In a medium bowl, stir together the coconut and sugar. Gradually stir in the melted butter. Press the mixture evenly over the bottom and sides of a lightly oiled 9-inch pie plate. Refrigerate the crust until it's firm (about 1 hour). |
| ½ cup confectioners' sugar | |
| 3 tablespoons butter, melted | |
| 14-ounce can sweetened condensed milk | |
| 6-ounce can frozen lemonade, thawed | *2* In a large bowl, stir together the condensed milk, lemonade, and whipped topping until no streaks remain. Spoon the filling into the chilled pie crust. |
| 8 ounces (1 small container) nondairy whipped topping, thawed | *3* Spoon the ice cream topping into a small, microwave-safe bowl, and heat the topping in the microware until it's fairly liquid, stirring frequently. Drizzle the topping over the filling. |
| 3 tablespoons fudge ice cream topping | |
| 8 thin slices fresh lemon | *4* Refrigerate the pie until the filling thickens, at least 1 hour. Before serving, put the lemon slices around the edge of the topping. |

*Per serving:* Calories: 299; Total fat: 12g; Saturated fat: 9g; Cholesterol: 16mg; Sodium: 88mg; Carbohydrates: 45g; Fiber: 1g; Sugar: 40g; Protein: 3g.

*Tip:* Toasting the coconut before making the crust lends a different, almost nutty flavor to the crust because the heat releases the natural oils.

*Vary It!* If chocolate isn't your most favorite thing in life (although how could it not be?), you can drizzle the top of the pie with whisked raspberry jam instead of the fudge topping.

# Peanut Butter Custard Pie

**Prep time:** 25 min • **Bake time:** 10 min plus refrigeration time • **Yield:** 8 servings

| Ingredients | Directions |
|---|---|
| Nonstick cooking spray | **1** Preheat the oven to 375 degrees. Spray an 8-inch pie plate with cooking spray. |
| 7.2-ounce box gluten-free shortbread cookies | |
| ¼ cup plus ½ cup creamy peanut butter | **2** Break the cookies in a plastic self-seal bag. Use a rolling pin to crush the cookies until they're finely ground. Transfer the cookies to a medium bowl. |
| 2 tablespoons plus 2¼ teaspoons cornstarch | |
| 1½ cups water | **3** Add ¼ cup of peanut butter. Using a rubber spatula, mix the cookies and peanut butter until they're thoroughly blended. |
| 14-ounce can sweetened condensed milk | |
| 3 egg yolks, lightly beaten | **4** Press the mixture onto the bottom and up sides of the prepared pie plate. The mixture will be sticky. Use the back of a wet spoon to help spread the crust, or dip your fingers in confectioners' sugar to spread the crust with your hands. |
| 2 tablespoons unsalted butter | |
| 1 teaspoon vanilla | |
| ½ of 11.75-ounce jar hot fudge sauce | **5** Bake the crust at 375 degrees for 10 minutes. Remove the crust from the oven and cool completely. |
| | **6** In a large mixing bowl, whisk all the cornstarch into the water until it dissolves. |
| | **7** Stir in the condensed milk and egg yolks. |
| | **8** Add the remaining ½ cup of peanut butter, and use the mixer to whip the ingredients on low speed for 45 seconds. |

***9*** Pour the mixture into a medium saucepan. Bring the mixture to a boil, stirring constantly with a whisk. Lower the heat to medium-high and continue cooking and stirring the mixture until it has thickened. Remove the mixture from the heat.

***10*** Stir in the butter and vanilla.

***11*** Cool the filling slightly before pouring it into the pie crust.

***12*** Warm the jar of hot fudge topping in the microwave (remove the lid first). Pour ½ of the jar onto the top of the pie and smooth it evenly over the top with the back of a spoon.

***13*** When the pie filling and topping are completely cooled, cover the pie and chill it for at least 4 hours.

*Per serving:* Calories: 605; Total fat: 33g; Saturated fat: 13g; Cholesterol: 48mg; Sodium: 214mg; Carbohydrates: 97g; Fiber: 3g; Sugar: 55g; Protein: 14g.

# Posh Pineapple Pie

**Prep time:** 15 min • **Bake time:** 30 min • **Yield:** 8 servings

## Ingredients

¾ cup plus 2 teaspoons granulated sugar

1 tablespoon butter

3 tablespoons cornstarch

¼ teaspoon cinnamon

20-ounce can crushed pineapple with juice

2 tablespoons milk

1 teaspoon fresh lemon juice

Double recipe Double-Crust Gluten-Free Pie Crust (see the following recipe)

1 egg white

1 tablespoon water

2 teaspoons brown sugar

## Directions

**1** Preheat the oven to 425 degrees.

**2** Prepare a double recipe of the Gluten-Free Pie Crust as directed in the recipe that follows.

**3** In a medium saucepan, stir together ¾ cup of granulated sugar, the butter, cornstarch, cinnamon, pineapple with juice, milk, and lemon juice.

**4** Cook the mixture over medium heat, stirring constantly, until it thickens, and then continue to stir as the mixture boils for 1 more minute. Remove the pan from the heat and let the mixture cool slightly.

**5** Pour the mixture into the prepared pie crust, and then cover it with the top crust. Cut slits in the top crust for air vents.

**6** In a small bowl, whisk together the egg white and water. Brush it over the top of the pie.

**7** Sprinkle the pie with 2 teaspoons of granulated sugar and the brown sugar.

**8** Bake the pie at 425 degrees for 30 minutes, or until the crust is golden.

*Per serving: Calories: 438; Total fat: 16g; Saturated fat: 3g; Cholesterol: 4mg; Sodium: 2mg; Carbohydrates: 39g; Fiber: 2g; Sugar: 36g; Protein: 1g.*

# Gluten-Free Pie Crust

**Prep time:** 15 min • **Bake time:** 30 min • **Yield:** 8 servings

| Ingredients | Directions |
|---|---|
| **2 cups sifted gluten-free flour mixture** | *1* In a medium bowl, sift together the flour mixture, sugar, and salt. |
| **¼ cup sugar** | |
| **½ teaspoon salt** | *2* In a small bowl, combine the oil, water, and vanilla. |
| **½ cup corn oil** | |
| **4 tablespoons ice-cold water** | *3* Pour the liquid mixture into the center of the flour mixture. With a rubber spatula, stir the dough well until it holds together. |
| **½ teaspoon vanilla** | |
| **1 tablespoon confectioners' sugar** | *4* With your hands, knead the dough until it forms a smooth ball. |
| | *5* Sprinkle the confectioners' sugar onto a sheet of plastic wrap. Set the ball on the sugar and turn the dough to coat it. Cover it with a second sheet of plastic wrap. |
| | *6* With a rolling pin, roll out the dough into an 11-inch circle. |
| | *7* Place the dough in a greased 9-inch pie plate. Scallop the edges. |

*Per serving: Calories: 287; Total fat: 14g; Saturated fat: 2g; Cholesterol: 0mg; Sodium: 146mg; Carbohydrates: 39g; Fiber: 2g; Sugar: 7g; Protein: 0g.*

*Tip:* When making a double-crust pie, double this recipe and follow the directions for the filling recipe.

# Best-Ever Apple Cobbler

**Prep time:** 10 min • **Bake time:** 40 min • **Yield:** 10 servings

| *Ingredients* | *Directions* |
|---|---|
| **Nonstick cooking spray** | *1* Preheat the oven to 350 degrees. Spray a 10-inch pie plate with cooking spray. |
| **7 cups peeled, thinly sliced Red or Golden Delicious apples (6 to 7 apples)** | |
| **¼ cup plus ½ cup brown sugar** | *2* Place the apple slices in a medium bowl. Stir in ¼ cup of brown sugar, the granulated sugar, cornstarch, ¼ teaspoon of salt, ½ teaspoon of cinnamon, the nutmeg, and lemon juice. |
| **½ cup granulated sugar** | |
| **2 tablespoons cornstarch** | |
| **¼ teaspoon plus ¼ teaspoon salt** | *3* Spoon the mixture into the prepared pie plate. |
| **½ teaspoon plus ½ teaspoon cinnamon** | *4* In a small bowl, mix together with a fork the remaining ½ cup of brown sugar, ¼ teaspoon of salt, ½ teaspoon of cinnamon, the flour mixture, almond meal, and pecans. Stir in the butter until the mixture is evenly moistened. Crumble the mixture on top of the apples. |
| **¼ teaspoon nutmeg** | |
| **2 teaspoons bottled lemon juice** | |
| **½ cup gluten-free flour mixture** | |
| **½ cup almond meal** | *5* Bake the pie at 350 degrees for 40 minutes. |
| **1 cup chopped pecans** | |
| **6 tablespoons butter, melted** | |

*Per serving:* *Calories: 345; Total fat: 18g; Saturated fat: 5g; Cholesterol: 18mg; Sodium: 173mg; Carbohydrates: 41g; Fiber: 3g; Sugar: 34g; Protein: 3g.*

*Tip:* Pie plates vary in how many cups of filling they can hold. If you don't have a 10-inch pie plate, you can use a 9-x-9-inch pan or a deep-dish 9-inch pie plate.

*Note:* For added decadence, drizzle the top of the warm pie with a sugar glaze (a mixture of sifted confectioners' sugar, vanilla, milk, and a dash of cinnamon).

*Vary It!* You can use canned gluten-free blueberry, cherry, or peach pie fillings in place of the apple pie filling.

# Crafting Cookies and Cakes from Scratch

Everyone loves cookies of all shapes, sizes, and flavors. Gluten-free cookies require just a bit more effort, but the results will be every bit as good as their wheat counterparts. When converting a wheat-based cookie recipe to gluten-free, you need to increase the leavening agent (usually gluten-free baking powder or baking soda) and the flavoring (add more vanilla or almond flavoring), and it's wise to add something that will add flavor; perhaps try toasted chopped nuts, chocolate pieces, toasted coconut, or dried fruits. You may want to substitute part of the liquid with juice, brewed coffee, or even a liqueur. When rolling out dough for cut-out cookies, sprinkle your rolling surface with confectioners' sugar instead of dusting it with gluten-free flour. (Using the flour mixture may make the cookies too dry.)

Gluten-free cookies don't stay fresh as long as wheat-based cookies, so you should either freeze them until they're needed, or sit down and eat every last one of them as soon as they're removed from the oven!

Here are a few tips for keeping your cookies at their best:

- ✔ If you made crispy cookies that are now several days old and are starting to lose their crunch, recrisp them by laying them on a baking sheet and heating them in a 300-degree oven for 3 to 4 minutes.

- ✔ If you made soft cookies that are now drying out, wrap a few in a damp paper towel and microwave them for a few seconds.

Many of the cookie issues regarding conversions apply to cakes as well. The alternative flours are heavier than wheat flour so they won't rise as much unless you add some extra stuff. As with cookies, you'll need to increase the amount of leavening and flavoring. It also helps to add an extra egg (both to help keep the cake moist and for leavening). Gluten-free pastries in general turn out better if you use whole milk rather than low-fat or skim milk. But because you're lucky enough to have this book, the recipes here already have all of those adjustments made.

To keep a layer cake in place on the cake plate, place a dab of frosting on the plate before placing the bottom layer. This holds the cake in place while you frost it. One more tip: If you plan to adorn your creation with shaved chocolate curls, white or milk chocolate makes better chocolate shavings because they're softer and curl more easily.

# Whoopie Pies

**Prep time:** 25 min  •  **Cook time:** 15 min  •  **Yield:** 10 pies

| Ingredients | Directions |
|---|---|
| Nonstick cooking spray | **1** Preheat the oven to 350 degrees. Lightly spray two baking sheets with cooking spray. |
| ¼ cup butter, softened | |
| ⅔ cup brown sugar | **2** In a large mixing bowl, use the mixer to cream together the butter, brown sugar, egg, and vanilla. In another bowl, stir together the cocoa, flour mixture, baking powder, baking soda, and salt. Stir in the grated chocolate. |
| 1 egg | |
| 1 teaspoon vanilla | |
| 2 tablespoons pure cocoa | |
| 1 cup gluten-free flour mixture | **3** Add the dry ingredients alternately with milk to the butter mixture, beating until the mixture is smooth. The batter will become very thick. |
| ¾ teaspoon baking powder | |
| 1 teaspoon baking soda | **4** Drop 2 tablespoons of batter onto the baking sheets. Using the back of a spoon that has been dipped in hot water, flatten the batter into a thin circle about 1½ inches in diameter. Repeat with the remaining dough. These cookies puff up but won't spread very much. You should have a total of 20 rounds. |
| ¼ teaspoon salt | |
| 3 ounces (6 squares) dark chocolate, grated | |
| ½ cup whole milk | |
| Whoopie Pie Filling (see the following recipe) | **5** Bake the dough at 350 degrees for 15 minutes, or until the rounds are firm to the touch. Cool the rounds on a wire rack. |
| | **6** Spread about 2 tablespoons of filling (see the following recipe) on half of the rounds, and then top the filling with the remaining rounds, pressing down gently to distribute the filling evenly. |

## Whoopie Pie Filling

| | |
|---|---|
| ½ cup butter, softened | **1** In a medium bowl, use the mixer to whip together all the ingredients until they're well blended. |
| ¾ cup sifted confectioners' sugar | |
| 1 cup marshmallow cream | |
| 1 teaspoon vanilla | |

*Per serving:* Calories: 369; Total fat: 18g; Saturated fat: 11g; Cholesterol: 60mg; Sodium: 346mg; Carbohydrates: 47g; Fiber: 9g; Sugar: 26g; Protein: 2g.

# Chocolate Cranberry Cookies

**Prep time:** 10 min plus refrigeration time • **Cook time:** 12 min • **Yield:** 54 cookies

| *Ingredients* | *Directions* |
|---|---|
| 2 ounces (2 squares) unsweetened chocolate | *1* In a medium saucepan, melt the chocolate and shortening over medium-low heat, stirring occasionally. |
| ¼ cup vegetable shortening or butter | |
| 1 cup granulated sugar | *2* Remove the pan from the heat and whisk in the sugar and vanilla. Whisk in the eggs, one at a time. |
| 2½ teaspoons vanilla | |
| 2 eggs | *3* In a large bowl, sift together the flour mixture, cornstarch, baking powder, and salt. |
| 1 cup gluten-free flour mixture | |
| 2 tablespoons cornstarch | *4* Stir the chocolate mixture into the flour mixture with a rubber spatula. Stir in the chocolate chips and cranberries. Refrigerate the dough for 2 hours. |
| 3 teaspoons baking powder | |
| ½ teaspoon salt | |
| ½ cup semisweet chocolate chips | *5* Preheat the oven to 350 degrees. |
| ½ cup dried cranberries | *6* Roll the dough into 1-inch balls, and then roll the balls in the confectioners' sugar to coat. Place the dough balls 2 inches apart on the baking sheets that have been lightly sprayed with cooking spray. The cookies will spread during baking. |
| ½ cup confectioners' sugar | |
| Nonstick cooking spray | |
| | *7* Bake the cookies at 350 degrees for 12 minutes. The cookies will be soft; let them rest on the baking sheets for 2 minutes before transferring them to a wire rack to cool. |

*Per serving:* Calories: 56; Total fat: 2g; Saturated fat: 1g; Cholesterol: 8mg; Sodium: 52mg; Carbohydrates: 9g; Fiber: 0g; Sugar: 6g; Protein: 1g.

*Note:* These cookies stay moist and freeze well.

*Vary It!* Forego rolling the cookies in the confectioners' sugar before baking, and when the cookies have cooled, frost them with a chocolate glaze instead.

# Chocolate Raspberry Bars

**Prep time:** 15 min plus refrigeration time • **Cook time:** 30 min • **Yield:** 12 bars

| Ingredients | Directions |
|---|---|
| Nonstick cooking spray | *1* Preheat the oven to 350 degrees. Spray a 9-x-9-inch baking dish with cooking spray. |
| ½ cup softened butter | |
| ¼ cup brown sugar | *2* In a large mixing bowl, use the mixer to whip the butter, brown sugar, and cinnamon together until they're creamy. |
| ½ teaspoon cinnamon | |
| ¾ cup gluten-free flour mixture | *3* Whip in the flour mixture and salt. |
| ⅛ teaspoon salt | *4* Using the back of a spoon, smooth ⅔ of the mixture in the bottom of the prepared baking dish. |
| 1 cup semisweet chocolate chips | |
| | *5* Bake the crust at 350 degrees for 12 minutes. |
| 8-ounce can sweetened condensed milk | *6* In a microwave-safe bowl, microwave the chocolate pieces and condensed milk for 1 minute; the chocolate should get soft and begin to melt. Stir the mixture to melt the remaining chocolate pieces. Spread the mixture over the partially baked crust. Refrigerate the baking dish for 20 minutes to set the chocolate layer. |
| ⅓ cup raspberry preserves | |
| ⅓ cup coconut | |
| | *7* Spread the preserves over the chocolate mixture. |
| | *8* Mix the coconut into the remaining flour mix, blending well. With your fingers, flatten out bits of dough and lay them on top of the preserves, partially covering the top of the chocolate mixture. |
| | *9* Using the back of a wet spoon, smooth out any lumps in the topping. |
| | *10* Bake the bars at 350 degrees for 30 minutes, or until the top crust is lightly browned. Cool the bars before cutting. |

*Per serving:* Calories: 334; Total fat: 19g; Saturated fat: 11g; Cholesterol: 29mg; Sodium: 126mg; Carbohydrates: 37g; Fiber: 2g; Sugar: 34g; Protein: 9g.

*Tip:* When spreading the bottom crust in the pan, dip the spoon in very warm water to keep the dough pliable.

# Chocolate Fleck Cake

**Prep time:** 15 min • **Cook time:** 35 min • **Yield:** 18 servings

| *Ingredients* | *Directions* |
|---|---|
| Nonstick cooking spray | *1* Preheat the oven to 350 degrees. Spray a 9-x-13-inch baking dish with cooking spray. |
| 1¾ cups gluten-free flour mixture | |
| 1 tablespoon baking powder | *2* Sift the flour mixture, baking powder, baking soda, and salt into a small bowl. Set aside. |
| 2 teaspoons baking soda | |
| ½ teaspoon salt | *3* In a large mixing bowl, use the mixer to cream the butter until it's fluffy. |
| ½ cup butter, softened | |
| 2 cups sugar | *4* Add the sugar and vanilla and continue whipping the ingredients until the sugar has been absorbed. |
| 1 tablespoon vanilla | |
| 4 eggs | *5* Whip in the eggs, one at a time, and then whip in the sour cream and chocolate. |
| 1 cup sour cream | |
| 3 ounces (3 squares) bittersweet chocolate, grated | *6* Add the flour mixture alternately with the water and milk until the batter is well blended and then spoon the batter into the prepared baking dish. |
| ¾ cup cold water | |
| ½ cup milk | |
| Fudge Icing (see the following recipe) | *7* Bake the batter at 350 degrees for 35 minutes or until a toothpick inserted in the center comes out clean, and then cool the cake on a wire rack before frosting. |

*Per serving, unfrosted: Calories: 259; Total fat: 12g; Saturated fat: 7g; Cholesterol: 72mg; Sodium: 349mg; Carbohydrates: 37g; Fiber: 1g; Sugar: 23g; Protein: 3g.*

## Fudge Icing

| | |
|---|---|
| ¼ cup butter | *1* Melt the butter in a medium saucepan. Remove it from the heat. |
| ½ cup cocoa | |
| 2 teaspoons vanilla | *2* Using a spoon, stir in the cocoa and vanilla until the ingredients are blended. |
| 3 cups sifted confectioners' sugar | |
| | *3* Stir in the confectioners' sugar until it's blended and the frosting is smooth and spreadable. |

*Per serving, frosting only: Calories: 92; Total fat: 2g; Saturated fat: 1g; Cholesterol: 2mg; Sodium: 18mg; Carbohydrates: 20g; Fiber: 0g; Sugar: 19g; Protein: 0g.*

# Surprising Guests with Fancy Finales

When you're preparing a meal for a really special occasion, you want to serve something that will earn ohhhs and ahhhs. The dessert recipes in this section can elicit all sorts of praise, but only after your guests get over their delight at all the trouble you went to for them. (Truthfully, some of these desserts are surprisingly easy, but no one needs to know that.)

The platter you use to serve the dessert makes a difference. Think about it. Doesn't pudding taste better when it's served in a champagne goblet rather than out of a plastic bowl? The extra effort you take to add finishing touches to both the platter and the dessert will enhance the total effect.

Decorate the plate, but also decorate the dessert. Picture a piece of cheese-cake served on its side on a chipped, everyday dish. Now picture that same piece of cheesecake set upon an attractive glass dish that has been drizzled with raspberry syrup and melted white chocolate or dusted with cocoa. Which presentation is more appealing? If you have a frosted cake, use a damp paper towel to pick up chopped nuts or coconut and adhere them to the side of the cake. If you're serving a chocolate cake, load the top with thickly shaved chocolate curls. Even before your guests taste the wonderful dessert, their sense of sight will appreciate the effort you went to and will stimulate their desire to consume your divine creation.

## Higher glycemic index isn't always a bad thing

Sometimes people *want* a quick rise in their blood sugar. Serious athletes often pay close attention to the glycemic index of foods they eat so they can have optimal energy available when they need it.

Usually before a competition they'll eat foods with a lower glycemic index so that energy is released more slowly.

During a competition they may try to eat a balance of high and low GI foods; the low GI foods will provide sustained energy, and the high GI foods will provide a quick burst.

When they're finished, athletes will often eat high GI foods to quickly restore depleted energy stores.

# No-Bake Lemon Squares

**Prep time:** 10 min • **Freezer time:** About 3 hr • **Yield:** 9 servings

| Ingredients | Directions |
|---|---|
| 1⅔ cups gluten-free lemon cookie crumbs (about 12 cookies pureed in a blender) | **1** In a small bowl, use a fork to blend the cookie crumbs, sugar, and butter. |
| 2 tablespoons granulated sugar | **2** Pat the crumbs into a 9-inch square pan, reserving ¼ cup for the topping. |
| 3½ tablespoons butter, melted | **3** Put the frosting, cottage cheese, and sour cream into a large mixing bowl. Use the mixer to beat the ingredients on high until they're well blended. |
| 1 can ready-to-spread lemon frosting | |
| 1 cup small-curd cottage cheese | **4** Spoon the cream mixture on top of the crust. |
| 1 cup sour cream | **5** Sprinkle the reserved crumbs on top of the cream mixture. |
| | **6** Cover the pan with foil and freeze for at least 3 hours. Remove the squares from the freezer 20 minutes before cutting and serving. |

*Per serving: Calories: 456; Total fat: 27g; Saturated fat: 14g; Cholesterol: 47mg; Sodium: 308mg; Carbohydrates: 59g; Fiber: 1g; Sugar: 42g; Protein: 4g.*

*Tip:* Pamela's Lemon Shortbread Cookies are perfect for this recipe. There are nine cookies in a 7.25-ounce box, so two boxes will be needed . . . and that leaves you with six extra cookies to snack on or pack in lunches.

*Vary It!* Not crazy about lemon? Use chocolate cookies for the base and gluten-free canned chocolate frosting in the mix.

# Pumpkin Cheesecake

**Prep time:** 20 min • **Cook time:** 1 hr • **Yield:** 9 servings

| Ingredients | Directions |
|---|---|
| 1½ cups gingersnap crumbs (an 8-ounce package of cookies pureed in a blender) | *1* Preheat the oven to 350 degrees. |
| ½ cup finely chopped pecans | *2* In a small bowl, mix together the gingersnap crumbs, pecans, and butter with a fork. Press the crust mixture onto the bottom and 1½ inches up the sides of a 9-inch springform pan. Bake the crust at 350 degrees for 10 minutes. When the crust is finished baking, turn the oven temperature down to 325 degrees. |
| ½ cup melted butter | |
| Two 8-ounce packages cream cheese, softened | |
| ½ cup plus ¼ cup granulated sugar | *3* In a large mixing bowl, use the mixer to whip together the cream cheese, ½ cup of sugar, and vanilla until they're well blended. |
| 1 teaspoon vanilla | |
| 3 eggs | *4* Add the eggs, one at a time, until they're blended into the batter. |
| 1 cup canned pumpkin | |
| ¾ teaspoon cinnamon | *5* Reserve 1 cup of the batter and set it aside. |
| ¼ teaspoon nutmeg | *6* To the remaining batter in the bowl, add the remaining ¼ cup of sugar, pumpkin, cinnamon, nutmeg, and ginger. Using the mixer, blend well. |
| ¼ teaspoon ginger | |
| | *7* Spoon the batters alternately on top of the crust. Using a knife, cut through the batter to marbleize. |
| | *8* Bake the batter at 325 degrees for 1 hour, or until the top of the cheesecake is dry and the edges are just beginning to brown. |
| | *9* Run a knife around the edge of pan, and then let the cake cool completely. |
| | *10* When the cheesecake is thoroughly cooled, remove the side of the pan and transfer the cake to a serving dish. Cover and refrigerate. |

**Per serving:** *Calories: 454; Total fat: 36g; Saturated fat: 19g; Cholesterol: 155mg; Sodium: 316mg; Carbohydrates: 29g; Fiber: 2g; Sugar: 26g; Protein: 7g.*

**Tip:** Make sure the cheesecake cools completely before refrigerating it to avoid the top from cracking or getting weepy (where moisture condenses on top of the cheesecake).

# Strawberry Almond Torte

**Prep time:** 15 min • **Cook time:** 25 min • **Yield:** 12 servings

| Ingredients | Directions |
|---|---|
| Nonstick cooking spray | **1** Preheat the oven to 350 degrees. Spray two 9-inch cake pans with cooking spray. |
| 2 cups gluten-free flour mixture | |
| ½ teaspoon salt | **2** In a medium bowl, sift together the flour mixture, salt, baking soda, and baking powder. Set aside. |
| 1 teaspoon baking soda | |
| 3 teaspoons baking powder | **3** In a large mixing bowl, use the mixer to cream ½ cup of butter and the sugar together until they're fluffy. Add the eggs, one at a time, mixing well. |
| ½ cup plus ⅓ cup butter, softened | |
| 1¼ cups granulated sugar | **4** Blend in the vanilla, mayonnaise, and orange juice. (The mixture may look curdled.) |
| 4 eggs | |
| 2 teaspoons vanilla | **5** Slowly add the dry ingredients alternately with 1 cup of milk, blending well. |
| 2 tablespoons mayonnaise | |
| 2 tablespoons orange juice | **6** Spread the batter in the prepared pans. Bake the batter at 350 degrees for 25 minutes, or until a toothpick inserted in the center comes out clean. Cool the cakes completely before filling the layers. |
| 1 cup plus 1 to 2 tablespoons whole milk | |
| 4 ounces almond paste | **7** Break the almond paste into small pieces and place it in a small mixing bowl. Use the mixer to whip together the almond paste and the remaining ⅓ cup of butter on low speed until the ingredients are blended. |
| 1 tablespoon amaretto (or milk) | |
| 1½ pints strawberries, sliced, sweetened with 1 tablespoon sugar | **8** Whip in the amaretto (or milk) and the remaining 1 to 2 tablespoons of milk until the paste mixture is of spreading consistency. |
| 8-ounce container nondairy whipped topping, thawed | **9** Place 1 cake layer on a serving dish. Spread the almond paste mixture over that layer. Top the paste with half of the whipped topping and then half of the strawberries. |
| | **10** Place the second cake layer on top of the first. Spread it with the remaining whipped topping, and arrange the remaining strawberries in an attractive pattern on top. Cover and refrigerate. |

*Per serving:* Calories: 204; Total fat: 22g; Saturated fat: 13g; Cholesterol: 107mg; Sodium: 466mg; Carbohydrates: 59g; Fiber: 3g; Sugar: 31g; Protein: 5g.

# Liqueur Cups with Mocha Raspberries

**Prep time:** 20 min • **Refrigeration time:** 1 hr • **Yield:** 16 servings

| Ingredients | Directions |
|---|---|
| 16 chocolate-covered espresso beans | **1** Insert an espresso bean in the center of each raspberry. |
| 16 fresh raspberries | **2** Melt ⅓ cup of chocolate chips with the oil in the top of a double boiler over barely simmering water (do not allow the water to boil or to touch the bottom of the top pan). |
| 1 teaspoon corn oil | |
| 1 cup semisweet chocolate chips, divided | **3** Roll the stuffed raspberries lightly in the chocolate and set them on wax paper to dry. |
| 32 large marshmallows | **4** Melt ⅓ cup of chocolate chips in a double boiler over barely simmering water (don't allow the water to boil or to touch the bottom of the top pan). Dip a new, clean, dry ½-inch pastry brush in the melted chocolate. Brush the chocolate on the bottom and insides of the baking cups, approximately ⅛-inch thick, pushing the chocolate into the ridges and smoothing as much as possible. Place the papers or foil cups into muffin pan cups. Chill until the chocolate has set. |
| ½ cup whole milk | |
| 3 tablespoons amaretto | |
| 3 tablespoons crème de cacao | |
| 8-ounce container nondairy whipped topping, thawed | |
| | **5** Carefully peel off the paper or foil; set the chocolate cups aside. |
| | **6** In a medium saucepan, combine the marshmallows, the remaining ⅓ cup of chocolate chips, and the milk. Stir constantly over low heat until the chocolate melts and the ingredients are thoroughly combined. Refrigerate the filling for a few minutes until it thickens. |
| | **7** Stir in the amaretto and crème de cacao. |
| | **8** Fold in the whipped topping. |
| | **9** Carefully spoon the mixture into the chocolate cups. Place a mocha raspberry on top of each dessert. Refrigerate until serving time. |

*Per serving: Calories: 166; Total fat: 5g; Saturated fat: 4g; Cholesterol: 1mg; Sodium: 15mg; Carbohydrates: 22g; Fiber: 1g; Sugar: 16g ; Protein: 1g.*

**Tip:** Instead of making your own chocolate cups, you can pick up a package of one of several excellent commercial gluten-free chocolate cups on the market.

# Part IV
# The Part of Tens

The 5th Wave                    By Rich Tennant

"I think my family's finally accepted my new way of cooking. I've eliminated all of the gluten, some of the fat, and most of the sarcasm."

# In this part . . .

*E*very *For Dummies* book concludes with top-ten lists, and this one is no exception. Here you can find one chapter with suggestions for gluten-free comfort foods and another with ideas for cooking gluten-free with the kids.

# Chapter 23

# Ten Easy-to-Prepare Comfort Foods

### In This Chapter

▶ Keeping it simple

▶ Warming you from the inside out

**Y**ou know what comfort foods are — they're the foods you turn to when you're stressed, sad, depressed, happy, or looking for some nostalgic association with memories of the past. But we all know what comfort food *really* means. It means carbs, and I'm not talking about the kind of carbs you get from a pile of broccoli. It means *gluten,* and you know it!

Comfort foods are foods like biscuits, breads, cinnamon rolls, donuts, bagels . . . all the stuff that's off-limits when you're gluten-free. Without those foods to turn to, you may feel stranded, deprived, and restricted, singing, "I can't get no (uh) sa-tis-FAC-tion . . ." Nope. No singing, no crying, no feeling like you can't have those old family faves. I have some ideas for satisfying those urges while staying 100 percent gluten-free. I warn you, though, they're not necessarily calorically correct, so don't come cryin' to me when your jeans don't fit anymore.

## Get Your Kicks with an Easy Mix

I know this is a cookbook. I know you, being a cookbook reader, *love* to search for hard-to-find, ridiculously expensive ingredients. I know you even don't mind measuring, and that you have the patience to let something rise. You might even know what "proofing" is.

Well, at the risk of offending those of you Real Cooks, I'm not that. Not any of it. If I want to satisfy my craving for brownies, cookies, cakes, breads, and other wumfy comfy foods, I turn to my favorite mix. Add to it a couple of eggs, a swish of oil, a glob or two of water or milk, and I stick it in the oven, patting myself on the back like I'm Danna Krocker. And you know what? No one knows the difference!

# Mom's Old-Fashioned Meatloaf

Nothing says "comfort" like Mom's meatloaf. Just take ground beef (or turkey if you're watching your weight), and add some onion, basil (or any other spices you'd like), a couple of eggs, and some gluten-free crackers or bread crumbs. It really doesn't matter how much of anything you use, so don't sweat it. Using your hands, glob it all together until it's a big ball of — well, raw meatloaf. Stuff (proper cooks might use the term *press*) it into a pan — a bread-loaf pan works well — and bake it at 325 degrees for 45 minutes to an hour. You'll know when it's done when the juices that rise to the top are no longer red — and when the crowd just can't wait any longer.

# No Woes with Nachos

Making great nachos is simple. You start by dumping a pile of gluten-free chips on a microwaveable or oven-safe plate and topping them with cheese. But from there, you really should think outside the typical-nacho-toppin's box and get creative. Add some veggies (so you can call it nutritious) — maybe sliced zucchini or yellow squash — tomatoes, jalapeños, cooked hamburger or ham slices, chunks of turkey, maybe even anchovies. Okay, I heard a collective groan of "EWWWWs" out there, but I personally love 'em, so give me a break. Leave them off yours if you want to be a party pooper. Throw the whole mess in the microwave or oven until the cheese melts, and you have yourself some nachos. Remember to top them with guacamole!

# Potato Salad with a Past

Whether it was part of the family picnics or a Saturday night staple, potato salad definitely makes it into the comfort food compartment. Start with (please tell me you can guess what I'm going to say next) potatoes. Yes! You guessed it! Potatoes! Just peel them, and then cook them for a really long time — until they're mushy-to-taste (some people like 'em chunky and crunchy). Then drain and mush 'em up. At this point, you can add pretty much anything you want and call it potato salad. Mayo, sour cream, hard-boiled eggs, onion, sweet pickles or relish (ick), salt, pepper, spices . . . you get the idea. Remember to refrigerate it if it has dairy products in it.

# Heavenly Homemade Veggie Soup (Add the Gluten-Free Pasta!)

Soup is, by definition, a potpourri of yummy stuff all melded together in a big hodge-podge of warmth and flavor. Cooking-wise, soup is my kind of recipe rebel — for the most part, no matter what you throw in there, you can't go wrong. Shopping-wise, it's easier yet: A quick stop in the meat aisle (or skip it if you're vegetarian), and another in the produce aisle, a quick grab of premade chicken or beef stock, and you're outta there. Throw everything into a slow cooker or Dutch oven, and let it cook slowly, adding spices and extra water or a little wine as you'd like. About five minutes before you want to eat, add some gluten-free pasta, if you'd like. By the time you serve it, it should be just right.

# Whip Up Some Pudding

Puddings are easy to make, using basic ingredients including milk, sugar, eggs, fruits, and spices — as well as some kind of thickener such as gluten-free flour (you may want to use rice or tapioca). Break out your most romantic spices, add a little fruit (canned blueberries are nice), a teaspoon or so of vanilla, and whip in a touch of cream. Cook the pudding slowly on the stove in a double boiler, or maybe in a water bath in the oven. Take your time, though. Puddings need to cook slowly to prevent curdling, and the family will appreciate the scents that linger longer. Make lots, however, because pudding is just as good cold as it is warm.

# Chow Down New England Style

Lots of things about clam chowder entitle it to bear the designation of a comfort food. It may bring back memories of celebrating the New Year with warm, creamy white soup topped with paprika or nutmeg. Or maybe you've visited or lived in New England, retaining nostalgic thoughts of the misty New England coastline, the seafood, frosty winters, shrimp boats, and of course, New England clam chowder!

The problem with most clam chowders is that the recipes call for flour — but just a tablespoon or so. I figure, why bother? And, more important, what's the point? If you must, use a gluten-free flour to thicken, but note that purists prefer their chowder un-thickened with plenty of crisp bacon, onion, new potatoes, and thyme — and lots of fat, fresh-from-the-ocean clams! Not being a purist *or* a Real Cook, I use canned minced clams. Serve with some crunchy gluten-free crackers or bread you've made from a recipe in this book.

# Super Simple "Mac-a-Cheese"

Few foods soothe the soul like creamy, gooey macaroni and cheese. Whipping up a gluten-free version is quick and easy. There are all types of gluten-free pastas available — some are made from corn, others from rice or brown rice, and they come in all shapes and sizes. Best of all, they taste like the real deal! They're widely available these days, and even regular grocery stores often carry them. Pick a pasta shape and taste you like, and cook it *al dente* (my Real Cook friends tell me this means "so it's not cooked all the way"). Add your favorite kind of cheese (Velveeta works well and has even less fat and calories than cheddar!), and let it melt. If you want a thinner consistency, add a little milk and butter. Then dig in and enjoy the "mac-a-cheese" satisfaction.

# Chase Away the Winter Blahs with a Big Bowl of Chili

No matter how you make chili, it always gives you that warm-you-from-the-inside comfort-food feeling. My personal favorite is black-bean chili, with or without meat. If I add meat, I usually use ground turkey. Brown the meat first (I usually sauté some veggies with the meat), and then just start adding ingredients. For this version, I use lots of black beans (hence the clever name "black bean chili"), some diced chilies, diced tomatoes, and the secrets to success: brown sugar and honey. I realize that some like it thicker than others — to thin it out you can add some chicken or beef stock, and then just let it simmer for hours. You can serve it over brown rice, or if you like Ohio-style chili, you can serve it over pasta with onions and cheese sprinkled on top.

# Cheeseburgers in Paradise

Cheeseburgers *are* paradise, no matter where you are when you eat 'em. You can try to find edible gluten-free hamburger buns, but I'll warn you that they're tough to find, and they cost a fortune. Instead, consider wrapping your burger in a crispy lettuce leaf (I like them chilled). Even most restaurants will serve them that way, but be careful that they don't just give you a burger that they've plucked the bun off of, because the burger will be gluten-ated with bun crumbs.

# Chapter 24

# Ten Ideas for Cooking Gluten-Free with the Kids

. . . . . . . . . . . . . . . . . . . . . . . . . . . . . . . . . . . . . . . . . . . . .

## In This Chapter

▶ Letting your little helpers give you a hand

▶ Sneaking in some food facts

▶ Serving meals in creative settings

. . . . . . . . . . . . . . . . . . . . . . . . . . . . . . . . . . . . . . . . . . . . .

*P*arents of young children have this June Cleaver fantasy of cooking with kids. Everyone is wearing aprons (matching and homemade, of course). The kids are standing on their stepstools (that they made with Dad in the garage that morning) and politely taking turns measuring and pouring without so much as a drop spilled on the counter. Half an hour later, a beautiful creation is passed around and hailed as holy, while the children, bursting with pride, sample their creations.

In reality, kids don't care whether the electric mixer is still on when they pull it out of the batter. Nor do they realize that holding the cracked egg over the bowl *before* breaking it open is important (but they *do* know that Mommy grumbles a lot when she cleans eggs off the kitchen floor). They're about as careful at measuring as I am (not very), and although their hand-eye coordination for video games is exceptional, they can't seem to pour an ingredient *into* a bowl. And as for politely taking turns — yeah, a mom can dream.

But ya know what? It's still fun. *Really* fun. And although little helpers are sometimes far from helpful, getting in the kitchen and cooking something is a part of life that no child should miss. Furthermore, learning to cook is educational and can encourage them to eat more nutritiously than if they become accustomed to turning to processed snack foods. So don your apron, dig up a makeshift stepstool or two, and keep the broom and mop handy. It's time to get cookin' with the kids!

# Have a Lasagna Night

Lasagna is a cinch. You can buy several varieties of gluten-free lasagna noodles in health food stores. Personally, I like the type that doesn't have to be cooked first, because — well, I've already admitted that patience isn't my greatest strength, and using noodles that don't have to be cooked first allows me to skip a step. It also prevents me from cooking them too long and ending up with mush. If you use the kind of lasagna noodles that don't have to be cooked first, be sure to make sure the dry noodles are touching sauce so they become tender while they cook. Then just layer with your favorite ingredients like you would a "regular" lasagna, bake, and voilà! It's lasagna night!

# Use Cooking to Teach Ingredient Insights

One of the best ways to know whether a prepared food is gluten-free (at a restaurant, for instance) is to know how it's usually prepared. For example, if you know that meatloaf generally has bread crumbs in it, you know that at a restaurant, social event, friend's house, or market, the meatloaf available to the general public is probably off-limits. One of the valuable lessons kids pick up when cooking with you is what ingredients generally go into what prepared foods. They also start to understand how to make choices, substitutions, and other decisions that are crucial for a gluten-free lifestyle.

# Jazz Up Meals with Colorful Vegetables

The healthiest meal is one with a rainbow of colors. Prepare a healthy supply of veggies, such as red, yellow, and green peppers, tomatoes, cucumbers, radishes, and carrots, and keep them in the refrigerator. Before serving, slice the veggies thinly — or cut them into different shapes (pointy triangles, twists, comb shapes, or whatever you can think of).

# Throw a Homemade Pizza Party

Nothing is more fun to make together (albeit messy, messy, messy) than pizza. You can make yours the way you like it, so you can turn it into a pizza party and let your guests have it their way. Use a premade gluten-free crust, or make one from the recipe in Chapter 12. Then set out a bunch of veggies, remembering to incorporate lots of color, and whatever meats the kids like (or use the leftover meatloaf from Chapter 23's recipe). Smear the crust with a little spaghetti sauce, and then let the kids add the toppings they like. Top with some grated cheese if you want, and then bake the pizzas at 325 degrees until the cheese starts to melt (about 8 to 10 minutes), and enjoy the smell as it fills the house with that pizza-to-perfection aroma.

# Try Some Herbalicious Preparations

People think children like things plain — and they do — but they also like a little excitement in their foods. As you're teaching them to cook, make sure to introduce them to herbs, which add flavor and nutrients and are *always* gluten-free. Let the kids pick out some fresh herbs from the store, or better yet, grow your own in a windowsill herb garden. Pinch off a leaf every now and then, squeeze it or rub it, and let the kids enjoy the different herbal fragrances. Let them suggest recipes that would be good with the various herbs. Here are some ideas: homemade tomato basil soup, Minty Juleps (using lemonade, Sprite, or whatever you happen to have on hand), spaghetti, salads, and omelets.

# Make It Fancy Schmancy

I know I'm all about simplicity, but everyone enjoys dressing up from time to time. And what better reason to pull out the fancy duds than for an elegant dinner that the kids plan. Don't worry, you may think they'll plan an all-dessert-day (okay, those are fun, too!), but they won't. They know what's good, and they'll probably come up with some great ideas. Use your best tableware and silverware, and make sure that good conversation is part of the meal. Maybe play some soft music in the background. Have everyone dress up! Try to have one of these elegant evenings once a month or so.

# Have Fun with Food Facts

It's never too early to teach children about good nutrition. Take time while you're cooking with your kids to talk to them about why they need to eat lots of protein (it helps their muscles grow) and explain which foods are good sources of protein. Remind them that fruits and veggies are important for lots of reasons, and have them think of healthy snacks and meals. The more they get involved with the decision-making process, the more impact it will have on their food choices in the future.

# Make Candy

You know those cute candied fruit and flowers that decorate cakes, cookies, and other treats? They're really not that hard to make! And kids love making them — just watch out for curious little fingers wanting to dip into hot syrup! Start by making sugar syrup (also called *simple syrup*) by mixing sugar and water over low heat until it turns clear — then boil it for a minute or two longer. You can make the syrup as sweet and thick as you want by adding extra sugar. I'm really not much for measuring, but if you want a starting point, try three parts water to one part sugar for thin syrup, and then keep adding sugar to make it thicker. After you have the syrup the consistency you want, dip the fruit or flowers in it. Set them on wax paper while the syrup cools and hardens.

# Add Some Fun to Breakfast

Everyone knows breakfast is the most important meal of the day, so how do you get kids to eat in the morning? It's all about the fun! Try making funny-face pancakes — just mix an egg, a little apple juice, some butter, and gluten-free baking mix (sorry, I don't measure — you *know* the consistency you're looking for!). You might want to add a little cinnamon or nutmeg for a twist. Whisk it all together, and pour the batter into a lightly oiled frying pan — make "ears" if you want — and then let the kids decorate the pancakes with powdered sugar and maple syrup. They can use fruit chunks or slices for the eyes; mouths can be made from oranges (go ahead and leave the rind on — it's edible *and* healthy!).

# Picnic in the Playroom

Picnics are a blast, but sometimes the weather just doesn't permit. That's okay. A picnic is still a picnic as long as some of the important elements are there: eating with your fingers, sitting on a blanket on the ground, and maybe even gluten-free s'mores! The important thing is to anticipate the fun of a picnic, no matter where it is. Plan special foods to eat with your fingers, like hot dogs, deviled eggs, chicken bites, and fruit chunks.

Oh, and about those s'mores. They're really easy to make gluten-free style. Just take your favorite cookie (some companies do make gluten-free "graham" crackers) and use it for the outside. Roast your marshmallows — sure, do it over the stove if you want, but be careful — then put part of a chocolate bar in the middle and squish it all together. Now *that's* a picnic!

# Appendix

# Metric Conversion Guide

· · · · · · · · · · · · · · · · · · · · · · · · · · · · · · · · · · · · · · · · · · · · · · · · · · · · · · · · · · · · · · · · · · · · · · · · ·

*N ote:* The recipes in this book weren't developed or tested using metric measurements. There may be some variation in quality when converting to metric units.

## Common Abbreviations

| Abbreviation(s) | What It Stands For |
|---|---|
| cm | Centimeter |
| C., c. | Cup |
| G, g | Gram |
| kg | Kilogram |
| L, l | Liter |
| lb. | Pound |
| mL, ml | Milliliter |
| oz. | Ounce |
| pt. | Pint |
| t., tsp. | Teaspoon |
| T., Tb., Tbsp. | Tablespoon |

## Volume

| U.S. Units | Canadian Metric | Australian Metric |
|---|---|---|
| ¼ teaspoon | 1 milliliter | 1 milliliter |
| ½ teaspoon | 2 milliliters | 2 milliliters |
| 1 teaspoon | 5 milliliters | 5 milliliters |
| 1 tablespoon | 15 milliliters | 20 milliliters |
| ¼ cup | 50 milliliters | 60 milliliters |
| ⅓ cup | 75 milliliters | 80 milliliters |

*(continued)*

## Volume *(continued)*

| U.S. Units | Canadian Metric | Australian Metric |
|---|---|---|
| ½ cup | 125 milliliters | 125 milliliters |
| ⅔ cup | 150 milliliters | 170 milliliters |
| ¾ cup | 175 milliliters | 190 milliliters |
| 1 cup | 250 milliliters | 250 milliliters |
| 1 quart | 1 liter | 1 liter |
| 1½ quarts | 1.5 liters | 1.5 liters |
| 2 quarts | 2 liters | 2 liters |
| 2½ quarts | 2.5 liters | 2.5 liters |
| 3 quarts | 3 liters | 3 liters |
| 4 quarts (1 gallon) | 4 liters | 4 liters |

## Weight

| U.S. Units | Canadian Metric | Australian Metric |
|---|---|---|
| 1 ounce | 30 grams | 30 grams |
| 2 ounces | 55 grams | 60 grams |
| 3 ounces | 85 grams | 90 grams |
| 4 ounces (¼ pound) | 115 grams | 125 grams |
| 8 ounces (½ pound) | 225 grams | 225 grams |
| 16 ounces (1 pound) | 455 grams | 500 grams (½ kilogram) |

## Length

| Inches | Centimeters |
|---|---|
| 0.5 | 1.5 |
| 1 | 2.5 |
| 2 | 5.0 |
| 3 | 7.5 |
| 4 | 10.0 |
| 5 | 12.5 |
| 6 | 15.0 |
| 7 | 17.5 |
| 8 | 20.5 |

| Inches | Centimeters |
|--------|-------------|
| 9      | 23.0        |
| 10     | 25.5        |
| 11     | 28.0        |
| 12     | 30.5        |

## Temperature (Degrees)

| Fahrenheit | Celsius |
|------------|---------|
| 32         | 0       |
| 212        | 100     |
| 250        | 120     |
| 275        | 140     |
| 300        | 150     |
| 325        | 160     |
| 350        | 180     |
| 375        | 190     |
| 400        | 200     |
| 425        | 220     |
| 450        | 230     |
| 475        | 240     |
| 500        | 260     |

# Index

## Apple & Mac

iPad 2 For Dummies,
3rd Edition
978-1-118-17679-5

iPhone 4S For Dummies,
5th Edition
978-1-118-03671-6

iPod touch For Dummies,
3rd Edition
978-1-118-12960-9

Mac OS X Lion
For Dummies
978-1-118-02205-4

## Blogging & Social Media

CityVille For Dummies
978-1-118-08337-6

Facebook For Dummies,
4th Edition
978-1-118-09562-1

Mom Blogging
For Dummies
978-1-118-03843-7

Twitter For Dummies,
2nd Edition
978-0-470-76879-2

WordPress For Dummies,
4th Edition
978-1-118-07342-1

## Business

Cash Flow For Dummies
978-1-118-01850-7

Investing For Dummies,
6th Edition
978-0-470-90545-6

Job Searching with Social
Media For Dummies
978-0-470-93072-4

QuickBooks 2012
For Dummies
978-1-118-09120-3

Resumes For Dummies,
6th Edition
978-0-470-87361-8

Starting an Etsy Business
For Dummies
978-0-470-93067-0

## Cooking & Entertaining

Cooking Basics
For Dummies, 4th Edition
978-0-470-91388-8

Wine For Dummies,
4th Edition
978-0-470-04579-4

## Diet & Nutrition

Kettlebells For Dummies
978-0-470-59929-7

Nutrition For Dummies,
5th Edition
978-0-470-93231-5

Restaurant Calorie Counter
For Dummies,
2nd Edition
978-0-470-64405-8

## Digital Photography

Digital SLR Cameras &
Photography For Dummies,
4th Edition
978-1-118-14489-3

Digital SLR Settings
& Shortcuts
For Dummies
978-0-470-91763-3

Photoshop Elements 10
For Dummies
978-1-118-10742-3

## Gardening

Gardening Basics
For Dummies
978-0-470-03749-2

Vegetable Gardening
For Dummies,
2nd Edition
978-0-470-49870-5

## Green/Sustainable

Raising Chickens
For Dummies
978-0-470-46544-8

Green Cleaning
For Dummies
978-0-470-39106-8

## Health

Diabetes For Dummies,
3rd Edition
978-0-470-27086-8

Food Allergies
For Dummies
978-0-470-09584-3

Living Gluten-Free
For Dummies,
2nd Edition
978-0-470-58589-4

## Hobbies

Beekeeping
For Dummies,
2nd Edition
978-0-470-43065-1

Chess For Dummies,
3rd Edition
978-1-118-01695-4

Drawing For Dummies,
2nd Edition
978-0-470-61842-4

eBay For Dummies,
7th Edition
978-1-118-09806-6

Knitting For Dummies,
2nd Edition
978-0-470-28747-7

## Language &
## Foreign Language

English Grammar
For Dummies,
2nd Edition
978-0-470-54664-2

French For Dummies,
2nd Edition
978-1-118-00464-7

German For Dummies,
2nd Edition
978-0-470-90101-4

Spanish Essentials
For Dummies
978-0-470-63751-7

Spanish For Dummies,
2nd Edition
978-0-470-87855-2

## Math & Science

Algebra I For Dummies,
2nd Edition
978-0-470-55964-2

Biology For Dummies,
2nd Edition
978-0-470-59875-7

Chemistry For Dummies,
2nd Edition
978-1-1180-0730-3

Geometry For Dummies,
2nd Edition
978-0-470-08946-0

Pre-Algebra Essentials
For Dummies
978-0-470-61838-7

## Microsoft Office

Excel 2010 For Dummies
978-0-470-48953-6

Office 2010 All-in-One
For Dummies
978-0-470-49748-7

Office 2011 for Mac
For Dummies
978-0-470-87869-9

Word 2010
For Dummies
978-0-470-48772-3

## Music

Guitar For Dummies,
2nd Edition
978-0-7645-9904-0

Clarinet For Dummies
978-0-470-58477-4

iPod & iTunes
For Dummies,
9th Edition
978-1-118-13060-5

## Pets

Cats For Dummies,
2nd Edition
978-0-7645-5275-5

Dogs All-in One
For Dummies
978-0470-52978-2

Saltwater Aquariums
For Dummies
978-0-470-06805-2

## Religion & Inspiration

The Bible For Dummies
978-0-7645-5296-0

Catholicism For Dummies,
2nd Edition
978-1-118-07778-8

Spirituality For Dummies,
2nd Edition
978-0-470-19142-2

## Self-Help & Relationships

Happiness For Dummies
978-0-470-28171-0

Overcoming Anxiety
For Dummies,
2nd Edition
978-0-470-57441-6

## Seniors

Crosswords For Seniors
For Dummies
978-0-470-49157-7

iPad 2 For Seniors
For Dummies, 3rd Edition
978-1-118-17678-8

Laptops & Tablets
For Seniors For Dummies,
2nd Edition
978-1-118-09596-6

## Smartphones & Tablets

BlackBerry For Dummies,
5th Edition
978-1-118-10035-6

Droid X2 For Dummies
978-1-118-14864-8

HTC ThunderBolt
For Dummies
978-1-118-07601-9

MOTOROLA XOOM
For Dummies
978-1-118-08835-7

## Sports

Basketball For Dummies,
3rd Edition
978-1-118-07374-2

Football For Dummies,
2nd Edition
978-1-118-01261-1

Golf For Dummies,
4th Edition
978-0-470-88279-5

## Test Prep

ACT For Dummies,
5th Edition
978-1-118-01259-8

ASVAB For Dummies,
3rd Edition
978-0-470-63760-9

The GRE Test For
Dummies, 7th Edition
978-0-470-00919-2

Police Officer Exam
For Dummies
978-0-470-88724-0

Series 7 Exam
For Dummies
978-0-470-09932-2

## Web Development

HTML, CSS, & XHTML
For Dummies, 7th Edition
978-0-470-91659-9

Drupal For Dummies,
2nd Edition
978-1-118-08348-2

## Windows 7

Windows 7
For Dummies
978-0-470-49743-2

Windows 7
For Dummies,
Book + DVD Bundle
978-0-470-52398-8

Windows 7 All-in-One
For Dummies
978-0-470-48763-1